The American Transcendentalists

THEIR PROSE AND POETRY

Edited by Perry Miller

Doubleday Anchor Books
Doubleday & Company, Inc.
Garden City, New York

Cover and typography by Edward Gorey

The Anchor Books edition is the first publication of
*The American Transcendentalists: Their Prose and
Poetry.*

Anchor Books edition: 1957

Library of Congress Catalog Number-57-11433

CONTENTS

CHAPTER SIX

POLITICS AND SOCIETY

CHAPTER SEVEN

FUTURE REFERENCE

FOREWORD

The "Transcendentalists" were a number of young Americans, most of them born into the Unitarianism of New England in the early nineteenth century, who in the 1830's became excited, or rather intoxicated, by the new literature of England and of the Continent (and also by a cursory introduction to that of the Orient), and who thereupon revolted against the rationalism of their fathers. Perhaps "revolted" is a bit too strong: though they said scornful things, in Emerson's phrase, about "the corpse-cold Unitarianism of Harvard College and Brattle Street," they owed much to the liberalism of the creed they out-grew. More accurately, then, they may be defined in a somewhat wider perspective as children of the Puritan past who, having been emancipated by Unitarianism from New England's original Calvinism, found a new religious expression in forms derived from romantic literature and from the philosophical idealism of Germany.

They never constituted any organized movement—as we see Emerson making clear—but there were enough of them, and they came so spontaneously and vocally to their coincident persuasions, and their activities (some of these a bit antic) seemed so to fit into a pattern, that outsiders could accuse them of being a "movement," in fact, of being a conspiracy. So, enlarging our perspective still further, we may also see in the Transcendentalists not so much a collection of exotic ideologues as the first outcry of the heart against the materialistic pressures of a business civilization. Protestant to the core, they turn their protest against what is customarily called the "Protestant ethic": they refuse to labor in a proper call-

ing, conscientiously cultivate the arts of leisure, and
strive to avoid making money.

By now almost as much has been written about the
New England Transcendentalists as they ever wrote by
themselves. They attract attention not only because they
do occupy a place in our intellectual history but even
more because they speak for an important mood in the
spiritual life of the Republic—a mood that has subsequently become, periodically, vocal. Provincial they no
doubt were, and often ludicrous in their high seriousness;
even so, they are what we have to display as an American
counterpart to the ebullient Romanticism of Europe.

Beyond doubt, an anthology of the basic texts of Trans-
cendentalism would perforce include Ralph Waldo Emer-
son's little book of 1836, *Nature*, his two seminal orations
—"The American Scholar" of 1837 and "The Divinity
School Address" of 1838—and several of his classic *Essays*
—"Self-Reliance," "The Over-Soul," "Fate," "Experience."
Also it should contain a good portion of, or all of, Henry
Thoreau's *Walden*, and probably his most formidable
declaration, that which assisted Gandhi in the fight for
Indian independence, "Civil Disobedience."

All these, however, are omitted from this collection.
In the first place, if I reprinted them, I should have little
or no space for exhibiting the wider or more ordinary
aspects of the phenomenon. In the second place, these
texts are monotonously provided in all the current
anthologies of American Literature. Thirdly, as for *Walden*, an effort to wrench portions of that intensely unified
volume out of its context is simply to desecrate it; there
is no point in anybody's reading any of it unless he
reads the whole. And finally, presuming those works to
be prerequisite to this compilation, I seek to present the
atmosphere of the Transcendental period rather than a
systematic ordering of the ideas. This endeavor is the
more legitimate because the Transcendentalists were in
fact the children of an atmosphere, in which they breathed
rather than acquired ideas, and were not at all proponents
of any systematic logic.

This volume is an offshoot of a more comprehensive anthology, *The Transcendentalists*, which I published through the Harvard University Press in 1950. Therein I traced the long argument over the historicity of the New Testament miracles, from its beginnings around 1830 to its culmination in Theodore Parker's "Transient and Permanent" in 1841. In the main, the preliminary debate is fairly technical; in any event, the development is summed up in Parker's magnificent "Discourse," which I now reprint entire.

So, this may be called an off-center collection of the material, designed to illustrate its range, to exemplify the variety, to set forth the general frame of mind and temper. I hope that the result has at least the virtue of readability. Apart from some three or four acknowledged contributions to "world literature," the ardent band left an impressive record. To read the writings of Transcendentalists with some degree of sympathy, one must in a certain measure put himself in rapport with the attitude that was fundamental to them all. Thoreau may be taken as expressing it most succinctly:

There is no ripeness which is not, so to speak, something ultimate in itself, and not merely a perfected means to a higher end. In order to be ripe it must serve a transcendent use. The ripeness of a leaf, being perfected, leaves the tree at that point and never returns to it. It has nothing to do with any other fruit which the tree may bear, and only the genius of the poet can pluck it.

My volume is, of course, no more than a poetic sampling, but if it be a fair selection of the leaves I need not concern myself about the fruits. (The arch-Transcendentalist of New York made the point even more explicit: he called his creation *Leaves of Grass*.) Thus it may, I trust, convey a sense of what was an excitement, an exhilaration, in the course of which a few bold American spirits made a gallant effort to introduce this mercantile and pragmatic nation to some of the deeper currents in the intellectual life of the West—and of the East.

THE ESSENTIAL
TRANSCENDENTALIST

HENRY DAVID THOREAU, 1817–1862

[We may as well go at once, and rudely, to the heart of the matter. For this purpose, no introducer is more qualified to serve than Henry Thoreau, especially for the rudeness. Supposedly he was inducted into the faith by his patron Emerson, and learned the doctrines either from Emerson or from the books to which Emerson led him; yet all his adult life he fought furiously, in the best Transcendental spirit, to maintain his independence, and applied himself to working away from abstract doctrine toward passionate appropriation of the concrete, the specific—the particular muskrat and the individual painted tortoise. Yet when challenged by the outside world—the conventional world of empirical and inductive science—to explain what sort of naturalist he considered himself, he exploded (in the resonant privacy of his *Journal*) with a defiant burst of what, in one form or another, was the rebellious intransigence in the heart of all participants in the "Movement."]

JOURNAL

March 5 [1853]. . . . The secretary of the Association for the Advancement of Science requests me, as he probably has thousands of others, by a printed circular letter from Washington the other day, to fill the blank against certain questions, among which the most important one was what branch of science I was especially interested in, using the term science in the most comprehensive sense possible. Now, though I could state to a select few that department of human inquiry which engages me, and should be rejoiced at an opportunity to do so, I felt that it would be to make myself the laughing-stock of the scientific community to describe or to attempt to describe to them that branch of science which specially interests me, inasmuch as they do not believe in a science which deals with the higher law. So I was obliged to speak to their condition and describe to them that poor part of me which alone they can understand. The fact is I am a mystic, a transcendentalist, and a natural philosopher to boot. Now I think of it, I should have told them at once that I was a transcendentalist. That would have been the shortest way of telling them that they would not understand my explanations.

How absurd that, though I probably stand as near to nature as any of them, and am by constitution as good an observer as most, yet a true account of my relation to nature should excite their ridicule only! If it had been the secretary of an association of which Plato or Aristotle was the president, I should not have hesitated to describe my studies at once and particularly.

CHAPTER ONE

HISTORY AND DOCTRINE

1. RALPH WALDO EMERSON, 1803-1882

[No modern historian can compose, nor should any student require, a better or more subtle account of the phenomenon that got itself called "Transcendentalism" than the lecture Emerson gave in 1880 to the Concord Lyceum—his hundredth before that body. His mind was then dissolving into benign vagueness, but the address was pieced together, with the help of a secretary and his daughter, out of older jottings (mostly from the year 1867); hence it still exudes that sense of freshness and excitement, combined with a cool, ironic appreciation of the fugitive character of the outburst, which from the beginning was Emerson's peculiar qualification for becoming and remaining its foremost spokesman.

In the portion here omitted he rather casually surveys the communistic enterprise at Brook Farm (1840-1846), which he declined to join—to the immense grief of George Ripley, its leading spirit, and of those who with Ripley felt that Transcendental premises should lead toward some such social action. Emerson's account therefore concentrates defensively upon that theme in the preaching of the band which he, by force of eloquence and example, made predominant: a full reliance upon self by the atomic and self-sufficing individual. Spatial limitations prevent a fair representation in this volume of the socialistic Transcendentalists (few of whom wrote with much distinction), but as to what the brotherhood (and sisterhood) fundamentally was, as to what ideas excited them and brought them together, Emerson's history is the most revealing of all witnesses.

William Ellery Channing (1780–1842) was the intellectual leader of those churches which by the 1820's formed the Unitarian Association; more daring and idealistic than his theological colleagues, he was revered by the young insurgents, and Emerson called him "our bishop." However, when he belatedly realized to what lengths these youths were carrying their revolt against the sensational psychology of John Locke, upon which Unitarian theology was founded—that they were proclaiming the radical notion that innate ideas "transcend" all sense experience—he drew back in horror.

Edward Everett (1794–1865) studied in Germany and brought back in 1819 a facile acquaintance with German scholarship; he quickly developed an oratorical brilliance that led him to a variegated career as statesman and diplomat. Nathaniel L. Frothingham (1793–1870), minister at the First Church of Boston, was a scholar of vast erudition who never had much sympathy for Transcendentalism. Andrews Norton (1786–1853), a scholar of still more massive erudition, as Dexter Professor of Sacred Literature in the Harvard Divinity School, constituted himself the most virulent Unitarian opponent of the Transcendentalists and in 1839 stigmatized Emerson's "Divinity School Address" and all like-minded utterances as "The Latest Form of Infidelity."

The first meeting of the Transcendental Club, described on pp. 13-14, was in 1836. It met irregularly for five or six years thereafter. The "pure idealist" at the end of the paragraph is Alcott.

To the published form of this address Emerson prefixed a gnomic verse (as he did to most of his essays) which just possibly says a bit more than he intended, though perhaps when he composed it (presumably in 1867) he really meant it as a mildly humorous yet precise characterization of the group:

> For Joy and Beauty planted it
>   With faerie gardens cheered,
> And boding Fancy haunted it
>   With men and women weird.]

HISTORIC NOTES OF LIFE AND LETTERS
IN NEW ENGLAND

The ancient manners were giving way. There grew a certain tenderness on the people, not before remarked. Children had been repressed and kept in the background; now they were considered, cosseted and pampered. I recall the remark of a witty physician who remembered the hardships of his own youth; he said, "It was a misfortune to have been born when children were nothing, and to live till men were nothing."

There are always two parties, the party of the Past and the party of the Future; the Establishment and the Movement. At times the resistance is reanimated, the schism runs under the world and appears in Literature, Philosophy, Church, State and social customs. It is not easy to date these eras of activity with any precision, but in this region one made itself remarked, say in 1820 and the twenty years following.

It seemed a war between intellect and affection; a crack in Nature, which split every church in Christendom into Papal and Protestant; Calvinism into Old and New schools; Quakerism into Old and New; brought new divisions in politics; as the new conscience touching temperance and slavery. The key to the period appeared to be that the mind had become aware of itself. Men grew reflective and intellectual. There was a new consciousness. The former generations acted under the belief that a shining social prosperity was the beatitude of man, and sacrificed uniformly the citizen to the State. The modern mind believed that the nation existed for the individual, for the guardianship and education of every man. This idea, roughly written in revolutions and national movements, in the mind of the philosopher had far more precision; the individual is the world.

This perception is a sword such as was never drawn before. It divides and detaches bone and marrow, soul and body, yea, almost the man from himself. It is the age of severance, of dissociation, of freedom, of analysis, of detachment. Every man for himself. The public speaker disclaims speaking for any other; he answers only for himself. The social sentiments are weak; the sentiment of patriotism is weak; veneration is low; the natural affections feebler than they were. People grow philosophical about native land and parents and relations. There is an universal resistance to ties and ligaments once supposed essential to civil society. The new race is stiff, heady and rebellious; they are fanatics in freedom; they hate tolls, taxes, turnpikes, banks, hierarchies, governors, yea, almost laws. They have a neck of unspeakable tenderness; it winces at a hair. They rebel against theological as against political dogmas; against mediation, or saints, or any nobility in the unseen.

The age tends to solitude. The association of the time is accidental and momentary and hypocritical, the detachment intrinsic and progressive. The association is for power, merely—for means; the end being the enlargement and independency of the individual. Anciently, society was in the course of things. There was a Sacred Band, a Theban Phalanx. There can be none now. College classes, military corps, or trades-unions may fancy themselves indissoluble for a moment, over their wine; but it is a painted hoop, and has no girth. The age of arithmetic and of criticism has set in. The structures of old faith in every department of society a few centuries have sufficed to destroy. Astrology, magic, palmistry, are long gone. The very last ghost is laid. Demonology is on its last legs. Prerogative, government, goes to pieces day by day. Europe is strewn with wrecks; a constitution once a week. In social manners and morals the revolution is just as evident. In the law courts, crimes of fraud have taken the place of crimes of force. The stockholder has stepped into the place of the warlike baron. The nobles shall not any longer, as feudal lords, have power of life and death over the churls, but now, in another shape, as capitalists, shall in all love and peace eat them up as before. Nay, government itself becomes the resort of those whom government was invented to restrain. "Are there any brigands on the road?" inquired the traveller in France. "Oh, no, set your heart at rest on that point," said the landlord; "what should these fellows keep the highway for, when they can rob just as effectually, and much more at their ease, in the bureaus of office?"

In literature the effect appeared in the decided tendency of criticism. The most remarkable literary work of the age has for its hero and subject precisely this introversion: I mean the poem of *Faust*. In philosophy, Immanuel Kant has made the best catalogue of the human faculties and the best analysis of the mind. Hegel also, especially. In science the French *savant*, exact, pitiless, with barometer, crucible, chemic test and calculus in hand, travels into all nooks and islands, to weigh, to analyze and report. And chemistry, which is the analysis of matter, has taught us that we eat gas, drink gas, tread on gas, and are gas. The same decomposition has changed the whole face of physics; the like in all arts, modes. Authority falls, in Church, College, Courts of Law, Faculties, Medicine. Experiment is credible; antiquity is grown ridiculous.

It marked itself by a certain predominance of the intellect in the balance of powers. The warm swart Earth-spirit which made the strength of past ages, mightier than it knew, with instincts instead of science, like a mother yielding food from her own breast instead of preparing it through chemic and culinary skill—warm negro ages of sentiment and vegetation—all gone; another hour had struck and other forms arose. Instead of the social existence which all shared, was now separation. Every one for himself; driven to find all his resources, hopes, rewards, society and deity within himself.

The young men were born with knives in their brain, a tendency to introversion, self-dissection, anatomizing of motives. The popular religion of our fathers had received many severe shocks from the new times; from the Arminians, which was the current name of the backsliders from Calvinism, sixty years ago; then from the English philosophic theologians, Hartley and Priestley and Belsham, the followers of Locke; and then I should say much later from the slow but extraordinary influence of Swedenborg; a man of prodigious mind, though as I think tainted with a certain suspicion of insanity, and therefore generally disowned, but exerting a singular power over an important intellectual class; then the powerful influence of the genius and character of Dr. Channing.

Germany had created criticism in vain for us until 1820, when Edward Everett returned from his five years in Europe, and brought to Cambridge his rich results, which no one was so fitted by natural grace and the splendor of his rhetoric to introduce and recommend. He made us for the first time acquainted with Wolff's theory of the Homeric writings, with the criticism of Heyne. The novelty of the learning lost nothing in the skill and genius of his relation, and the rudest undergraduate found a new morning opened to him in the lecture-room of Harvard Hall.

There was an influence on the young people from the genius of Everett which was almost comparable to that of Pericles in Athens. He had an inspiration which did not go beyond his head, but which made him the master of elegance. If any of my readers were at that period in Boston or Cambridge, they will easily remember his radiant beauty of person, of a classic style, his heavy large eye, marble lids, which gave the impression of mass which the slightness of his form needed; sculptured lips; a voice of such rich tones, such precise and perfect utterance, that, although slightly nasal, it was the most mellow and beautiful and correct of all the instruments of the time. The word that he spoke, in the manner in which he spoke it, became current and classical in New England. He had a great talent for collecting facts, and for bringing those he had to bear with ingenious felicity on the topic of the moment. Let him rise to speak on what occasion soever, a fact had always just transpired which composed, with some other fact well known to the audience, the most pregnant and happy coincidence. It was remarked that for a man who threw out so many facts he was seldom convicted of a blunder. He had a good deal of special learning, and all his learning was available for purposes of the hour. It was all new learning, that wonderfully took and stimulated the young men. It was so coldly and weightily communicated from so commanding a platform, as if in the consciousness and consideration of all history and all learning—adorned with so many simple and austere beauties of expression, and enriched with so many excellent digressions and significant quotations, that, though nothing could be conceived beforehand less attractive or indeed less fit for green boys from Connecticut, New Hampshire and Massachusetts, with their unripe Latin and Greek reading, than exegetical discourses in the style of Voss and Wolff and Ruhnken, on the Orphic and Ante-Homeric remains—yet this learning instantly took the highest place to our imagination in our unoccupied American Parnassus. All his auditors felt the extreme beauty and dignity of the manner, and even the coarsest were contented to go punctually to listen, for the manner, when they had found out that the subject-matter was not for them. In the lecture-room, he abstained from all ornament, and pleased himself with the play of detailing erudition in a style of perfect simplicity. In the pulpit (for he was then a clergyman) he made amends to himself and his auditor for the self-denial of the professor's chair, and, with an infantine simplicity still, of manner, he gave the reins to his florid, quaint and affluent fancy.

Then was exhibited all the richness of a rhetoric which we have never seen rivalled in this country. Wonderful how memorable were words made which were only pleasing pictures, and covered no new or valid thoughts. He abounded in sentences, in wit, in satire, in splendid allusion, in quotation impossible to forget, in daring imagery, in parable and even in a sort of defying experiment of his own wit and skill in giving an oracular weight to Hebrew or Rabbinical words—feats which no man could better accomplish, such was his self-command and the security of his manner. All his speech was music, and with such variety and invention that the ear was never tired. Especially beautiful were his poetic quotations. He delighted in quoting Milton, and with such sweet modulation that he seemed to give as much beauty as he borrowed; and whatever he has quoted will be remembered by any who heard him, with inseparable association with his voice and genius. He had nothing in common with vulgarity and infirmity, but, speaking, walking, sitting, was as much aloof and uncommon as a star. The smallest anecdote of his behavior or conversation was eagerly caught and repeated, and every young scholar could recite brilliant sentences from his sermons, with mimicry, good or bad, of his voice. This influence went much farther, for he who was heard with such throbbing hearts and sparkling eyes in the lighted and crowded churches, did not let go his hearers when the church was dismissed, but the bright image of that eloquent form followed the boy home to his bedchamber; and not a sentence was written in academic exercises, not a declamation attempted in the college chapel, but showed the omnipresence of his genius to youthful heads. This made every youth his defender, and boys filled their mouths with arguments to prove that the orator had a heart. This was a triumph of Rhetoric. It was not the intellectual or the moral principles which he had to teach. It was not thoughts. When Massachusetts was full of his fame it was not contended that he had thrown any truths into circulation. But his power lay in the magic of form; it was in the graces of manner; in a new perception of Grecian beauty, to which he had opened our eyes. There was that finish about this person which is about women, and which distinguishes every piece of genius from the works of talent—that these last are more or less matured in every degree of completeness according to the time bestowed on them, but works of genius in their first and slightest form are still wholes. In every public discourse there was nothing left for the indulgence of his hearer, no marks of late hours and anxious, unfinished study, but the goddess of grace had breathed on the work a last fragrancy and glitter.

By a series of lectures largely and fashionably attended for two winters in Boston he made a beginning of popular literary and miscellaneous lecturing, which in that region at least had important results. It is acquiring greater importance every day, and becoming a national institution. I am quite certain that this purely literary influence was of the first importance to the American mind.

In the pulpit Dr. Frothingham, an excellent classical and German scholar, had already made us acquainted, if prudently, with the genius of Eichhorn's theologic criticism. And Professor Norton a little later gave form and method to the like studies in the then infant Divinity School. But I think the paramount source of the religious revolution was Modern Science; beginning with Copernicus, who destroyed the pagan fictions of the Church, by showing mankind that the earth on which we live was not the centre of the Universe, around which the sun and stars revolved every day, and thus fitted to be the platform on which the Drama of the Divine Judgment was played before the assembled Angels of Heaven—"the scaffold of the divine vengeance" Saurin called it—but a little scrap of a planet, rushing round the sun in our system, which in turn was too minute to be seen at the distance of many stars which we behold. Astronomy taught us our insignificance in Nature; showed that our sacred as our profane history had been written in gross ignorance of the laws, which were far grander than we knew; and compelled a certain extension and uplifting of our views of the Deity and his Providence. This correction of our superstitions was confirmed by the new science of Geology, and the whole train of discoveries in every department. But we presently saw also that the religious nature in man was not affected by these errors in his understanding. The religious sentiment made nothing of bulk or size, or far or near; triumphed over time as well as space; and every lesson of humility, or justice, or charity, which the old ignorant saints had taught him, was still forever true.

Whether from these influences, or whether by a reaction of the general mind against the too formal science, religion and social life of the earlier period—there was, in the first quarter of our nineteenth century, a certain sharpness of criticism, an eagerness for reform, which showed itself in every quarter. It appeared in the popularity of Lavater's Physiognomy, now almost forgotten. Gall and Spurzheim's Phrenology laid a rough hand on the mysteries of animal and spiritual nature, dragging down every sacred secret to a street show. The attempt was coarse and odious to scientific men, but had a certain truth in it; it felt connection where the professors denied it, and was a leading to a truth which had not yet been announced. On the heels of this intruder came Mesmerism, which broke into the inmost shrines, attempted the explanation of miracle and prophecy, as well as of creation. What could be more revolting to the contemplative philosopher! But a certain success attended it, against all expectation. It was human, it was genial, it affirmed unity and connection between remote points, and as such was excellent criticism on the narrow and dead classification of what passed for science; and the joy with which it was greeted was an instinct of the people which no true philosopher would fail to profit by. But while society remained in doubt between the indignation of the old school and the audacity of the new, a higher note sounded. Unexpected aid from high quarters came to iconoclasts. The German poet Goethe revolted against the science of the day, against French and English science, declared war against the great name of Newton, proposed his own new and simple optics; in Botany, his simple theory of metamorphosis—the eye of a leaf is all; every part of the plant from root to fruit is only a modified leaf, the branch of a tree is nothing but a leaf whose serratures have become twigs. He extended this into anatomy and animal life, and his views were accepted. The revolt became a revolution. Schelling and Oken introduced their ideal natural philosophy, Hegel his metaphysics, and extended it to Civil History.

The result in literature and the general mind was a return to law; in science, in politics, in social life; as distinguished from the profligate manners and politics of earlier times. The age was moral. Every immorality is a departure from nature, and is punished by natural loss and deformity. The popularity of Combe's Constitution of Man; the humanity which was the aim of all the multitudinous works of Dickens; the tendency even of Punch's caricature, was all on the side of the people. There was a breath of new air, much vague expectation, a consciousness of power not yet finding its determinate aim.

I attribute much importance to two papers of Dr. Channing, one on Milton and one on Napoleon, which were the first specimens in this country of that large criticism which in England had given power and fame to the Edinburgh Review. They were widely read, and of course immediately fruitful in provoking emulation which lifted the style of Journalism. Dr. Channing, whilst he lived, was the star of the American Church, and we then thought, if we do not still think, that he left no successor in the pulpit. He could never be reported, for his eye and voice could not be printed, and his discourses lose their best in losing them. He was made for the public; his cold temperament made him the most unprofitable private companion; but all America would have been impoverished in wanting him. We could not then spare a single word he uttered in public, not so much as the reading a lesson in Scripture, or a hymn, and it is curious that his printed writings are almost a history of the times; as there was no great public interest, political, literary or even economical (for he wrote on the Tariff), on which he did not leave some printed record of his brave and thoughtful opinion. A poor little invalid all his life, he is yet one of those men who vindicate the power of the American race to produce greatness.

Dr. Channing took counsel in 1834 with George Ripley, to the point whether it were possible to bring cultivated, thoughtful people together, and make society that deserved the name. He had earlier talked with Dr. John Collins Warren on the like purpose, who admitted the wisdom of the design and undertook to aid him in making the experiment. Dr. Channing repaired to Dr. Warren's house on the appointed evening, with large thoughts which he wished to open. He found a well-chosen assembly of gentlemen variously distinguished; there was mutual greeting and introduction, and they were chatting agreeably on indifferent matters and drawing gently towards their great expectation, when a side-door opened, the whole company streamed in to an oyster supper, crowned by excellent wines; and so ended the first attempt to establish æsthetic society in Boston.

Some time afterwards Dr. Channing opened his mind to Mr. and Mrs. Ripley, and with some care they invited a limited party of ladies and gentlemen. I had the honor to be present. Though I recall the fact, I do not retain any instant consequence of this attempt, or any connection between it and the new zeal of the friends who at that time began to be drawn together by sympathy of studies and of aspiration. Margaret Fuller, George Ripley, Dr. Convers Francis, Theodore Parker, Dr. Hedge, Mr. Brownson, James Freeman Clarke, William H. Channing and many others, gradually drew together and from time to time spent an afternoon at each other's houses in a serious conversation. With them was always one well-known form, a pure idealist, not at all a man of letters, nor of any practical talent, nor a writer of books; a man quite too cold and contemplative for the alliances of friendship, with rare simplicity and grandeur of perception, who read Plato as an equal, and inspired his companions only in proportion as they were intellectual—whilst the men of talent complained of the want of point and precision in this abstract and religious thinker.

These fine conversations, of course, were incomprehensible to some in the company, and they had their revenge in their little joke. One declared that "It seemed to him like going to heaven in a swing;" another reported that, at a knotty point in the discourse, a sympathizing Englishman with squeaking voice interrupted with the question, "Mr. Alcott, a lady near me desires to inquire whether omnipotence abnegates attribute?"

I think there prevailed at that time a general belief in Boston that there was some concert of *doctrinaires* to establish certain opinions and inaugurate some movement in literature, philosophy and religion, of which design the supposed conspirators were quite innocent; for there was no concert, and only here and there two or three men or women who read and wrote, each alone, with unusual vivacity. Perhaps they only agreed in having fallen upon Coleridge and Wordsworth and Goethe, then on Carlyle, with pleasure and sympathy. Otherwise, their education and reading were not marked, but had the American superficialness, and their studies were solitary. I suppose all of them were surprised at this rumor of a school or sect, and certainly at the name of Transcendentalism, given nobody knows by whom, or when it was first applied. As these persons became in the common chances of society acquainted with each other, there resulted certainly strong friendships, which of course were exclusive in proportion to their heat: and perhaps those persons who were mutually the best friends were the most private and had no ambition of publishing their letters, diaries or conversation.

From that time meetings were held for conversation, with very little form, from house to house, of people engaged in studies, fond of books, and watchful of all the intellectual light from whatever quarter it flowed. Nothing could be less formal, yet the intelligence and character and varied ability of the company gave it some notoriety and perhaps waked curiosity as to its aims and results.

Nothing more serious came of it than the modest quarterly journal called *The Dial*, which, under the editorship of Margaret Fuller, and later of some other, enjoyed its obscurity for four years. All its papers were unpaid contributions, and it was rather a work of friendship among the narrow circle of students than the organ of any party. Perhaps its writers were its chief readers: yet it contained some noble papers by Margaret Fuller, and some numbers had an instant exhausting sale, because of papers by Theodore Parker.

Theodore Parker was our Savonarola, an excellent scholar, in frank and affectionate communication with the best minds of his day, yet the tribune of the people, and the stout Reformer to urge and defend every cause of humanity with and for the humblest of mankind. He was no artist. Highly refined persons might easily miss in him the element of beauty. What he said was mere fact, almost offended you, so bald and detached; little cared he. He stood altogether for practical truth; and so to the last. He used every day and hour of his short life, and his character appeared in the last moments with the same firm control as in the midday of strength. I habitually apply to him the words of a French philosopher who speaks of "the man of Nature who abominates the steam-engine and the factory. His vast lungs breathe independence with the air of the mountains and the woods."

The vulgar politician disposed of this circle cheaply as
"the sentimental class." State Street had an instinct that
they invalidated contracts and threatened the stability of
stocks; and it did not fancy brusque manners. Society always values, even in its teachers, inoffensive people, susceptible of conventional polish. The clergyman who would
live in the city *may* have piety, but *must* have taste, whilst
there was often coming, among these, some John the Baptist, wild from the woods, rude, hairy, careless of dress
and quite scornful of the etiquette of cities. There was a
pilgrim in those days walking in the country who stopped
at every door where he hoped to find hearing for his
doctrine, which was, Never to give or receive money. He
was a poor printer, and explained with simple warmth
the belief of himself and five or six young men with whom
he agreed in opinion, of the vast mischief of our insidious
coin. He thought every one should labor at some necessary
product, and as soon as he had made more than enough
for himself, were it corn, or paper, or cloth, or boot-jacks,
he should give of the commodity to any applicant, and in
turn go to his neighbor for any article which he had to
spare. Of course we were curious to know how he sped
in his experiments on the neighbor, and his anecdotes were
interesting, and often highly creditable. But he had the
courage which so stern a return to Arcadian manners required, and had learned to sleep, in cold nights, when
the farmer at whose door he knocked declined to give him
a bed, on a wagon covered with the buffalo-robe under
the shed—or under the stars, when the farmer denied the
shed and the buffalo-robe. I think he persisted for two years
in his brave practice, but did not enlarge his church of
believers.

These reformers were a new class. Instead of the fiery
souls of the Puritans, bent on hanging the Quaker, burning
the witch and banishing the Romanist, these were gentle
souls, with peaceful and even with genial dispositions,
casting sheep's-eyes even on Fourier and his houris. It
was a time when the air was full of reform. Robert Owen
of Lanark came hither from England in 1845, and read
lectures or held conversations wherever he found listeners;

the most amiable, sanguine and candid of men. He had not the least doubt that he had hit on a right and perfect socialism, or that all mankind would adopt it. He was then seventy years old, and being asked, "Well, Mr. Owen, who is your disciple? How many men are there possessed of your views who will remain after you are gone, to put them in practice?" "Not one," was his reply. Robert Owen knew Fourier in his old age. He said that Fourier learned of him all the truth he had; the rest of his system was imagination, and the imagination of a banker. Owen made the best impression by his rare benevolence. His love of men made us forget his "Three Errors." His charitable construction of men and their actions was invariable. He was the better Christian in his controversy with Christians, and he interpreted with great generosity the acts of the "Holy Alliance," and Prince Metternich, with whom the persevering *doctrinaire* had obtained interviews; "Ah," he said, "you may depend on it there are as tender hearts and as much good will to serve men, in palaces, as in colleges."

And truly I honor the generous ideas of the Socialists, the magnificence of their theories and the enthusiasm with which they have been urged. They appeared the inspired men of their time. Mr. Owen preached his doctrine of labor and reward, with the fidelity and devotion of a saint, to the slow ears of his generation. Fourier, almost as wonderful an example of the mathematical mind of France as La Place or Napoleon, turned a truly vast arithmetic to the question of social misery, and has put men under the obligation which a generous mind always confers, of conceiving magnificent hopes and making great demands as the right of man. He took his measure of that which all should and might enjoy, from no soup-society or charity-concert, but from the refinements of palaces, the wealth of universities and the triumphs of artists. He thought nobly. A man is entitled to pure air, and to the air of good conversation in his bringing up, and not, as we or so many of us, to the poor-smell and musty chambers, cats and fools. Fourier carried a whole French Revolution in his head, and much more. Here was arithmetic on a huge scale. His ciphering goes where ciphering never went before, namely, into stars, atmospheres and animals, and men and women, and classes of every character. It was the most entertaining of French romances, and could not but suggest vast possibilities of reform to the coldest and least sanguine. . . .

There is of course to every theory a tendency to run to an extreme, and to forget the limitations. In our free institutions, where every man is at liberty to choose his home and his trade, and all possible modes of working and gaining are open to him, fortunes are easily made by thousands, as in no other country. Then property proves too much for the man, and the men of science, art, intellect, are pretty sure to degenerate into selfish housekeepers, dependent on wine, coffee, furnace-heat, gas-light and fine furniture. Then instantly things swing the other way, and we suddenly find that civilization crowed too soon; that what we bragged as triumphs were treacheries: that we have opened the wrong door and let the enemy into the castle; that civilization was a mistake; that nothing is so vulgar as a great warehouse of rooms full of furniture and trumpery; that, in the circumstances, the best wisdom were an auction or a fire. Since the foxes and the birds have the right of it, with a warm hole to keep out the weather, and no more—a pent-house to fend the sun and rain is the house which lays no tax on the owner's time and thoughts, and which he can leave, when the sun is warm, and defy the robber. This was Thoreau's doctrine, who said that the Fourierists had a sense of duty which led them to devote themselves to their second-best. And Thoreau gave in flesh and blood and pertinacious Saxon belief the purest ethics. He was more real and practically believing in them than any of his company, and fortified you at all times with an affirmative experience which refused to be set aside. Thoreau was in his own person a practical answer, almost a refutation, to the theories of the socialists. He required no Phalanx, no Government, no society, almost no memory. He lived extempore from hour to hour, like the birds and the angels; brought every day a new proposition, as revolutionary as that of yesterday, but different: the only man of leisure in his town; and his independence made all others look like slaves. He was a good Abbot Samson, and carried a counsel in his breast. "Again and again I congratulate myself on my so-called poverty, I could not overstate this advantage." "What you call bareness and poverty, is to me simplicity. God could not be unkind to me if he should try. I love best to have each thing in its season only, and enjoy doing without it at all other times. It is the greatest of all advantages to enjoy no advantage at all. I have never got over my surprise that I should have been born into the most estimable place in all the world, and in the very nick of time too." There's an optimist for you.

I regard these philanthropists as themselves the effects of the age in which we live, and, in common with so many other good facts, the efflorescence of the period, and predicting a good fruit that ripens. They were not the creators they believed themselves, but they were unconscious prophets of a true state of society; one which the tendencies of nature lead unto, one which always establishes itself for the sane soul, though not in that manner in which they paint it; but they were describers of that which is really being done. The large cities are phalansteries; and the theorists drew all their argument from facts already taking place in our experience. The cheap way is to make every man do what he was born for. One merchant to whom I described the Fourier project, thought it must not only succeed, but that agricultural association must presently fix the price of bread, and drive single farmers into association in self-defence, as the great commercial and manufacturing companies had done. Society in England and in America is trying the experiment again in small pieces, in coöperative associations, in cheap eating-houses, as well as in the economics of club-houses and in cheap reading-rooms.

It chanced that here in one family were two brothers, one a brilliant and fertile inventor, and close by him his own brother, a man of business, who knew how to direct his faculty and make it instantly and permanently lucra-

tive. Why could not the like partnership be formed between
the inventor and the man of executive talent everywhere?
Each man of thought is surrounded by wiser men than he,
if they cannot write as well. Cannot he and they combine?
Talents supplement each other. Beaumont and Fletcher
and many French novelists have known how to utilize
such partnerships. Why not have a larger one, and with
more various members?

Housekeepers say, "There are a thousand things to
everything," and if one must study all the strokes to be
laid, all the faults to be shunned in a building or work of
art, of its keeping, its composition, its site, its color, there
would be no end. But the architect, acting under a necessity to build the house for its purpose, finds himself
helped, he knows not how, into all these merits of detail,
and steering clear, though in the dark, of those dangers
which might have shipwrecked him. . . .

I recall these few selected facts, none of them of much
independent interest, but symptomatic of the times and
country. I please myself with the thought that our American mind is not now eccentric or rude in its strength, but
is beginning to show a quiet power, drawn from wide and
abundant sources, proper to a Continent and to an educated people. If I have owed much to the special influences
I have indicated, I am not less aware of that excellent and
increasing circle of masters in arts and in song and in
science, who cheer the intellect of our cities and this
country today—whose genius is not a lucky accident, but
normal, and with broad foundation of culture, and so
inspires the hope of steady strength advancing on itself,
and a day without night.

2. CHARLES MAYO ELLIS, 1818–1878

[In the summer of 1842 an anonymous pamphlet of 104
pages, *An Essay on Transcendentalism*, was issued by a
Boston publisher. It was favorably reviewed in *The Dial*,
but hardly anywhere else even noted, and appears to

have been little considered by those we call the major figures in the movement. The most thorough of modern investigations concludes that it was almost certainly the work of Charles Mayo Ellis, who, as a student at Harvard College (class of 1839), early caught the contagion of Emerson. He became a lawyer, fought for liberal and Free Soil causes, and is the only figure attached to the group—although a minor one—who made money.

If the *Essay* was not particularly prized by Emerson or Margaret Fuller, the reason undoubtedly is that they shied away from any systematic statement of their position. For our purposes, because it does try to be logically and sequentially coherent, it can be all the more convenient. As Walter Harding remarks, while no one of the communion might accept all of Ellis' statements, no one would have rejected anything he says. Copies of the original are now exceedingly scarce, but the text is fortunately available in Mr. Harding's edition for Scholars' Facsimiles & Reprints (Gainesville, Florida, 1954). I am obliged to select what seem the more relevant chapters, but those omitted are equally instructive.]

AN ESSAY ON TRANSCENDENTALISM

Introduction

. . . It has for some time been pretty generally admitted, at least many have made the assertion and have not yet been compelled to retract it, that there is in the midst of us, beyond the reach of flesh and sense—no part of the material world—somewhat, and what the Lord only knows —a monster, horrendum, informe, ingens—seen only at rare intervals, by few people, in their accounts of which no two can agree, of which no one was ever able to give a description which should enable another to form any notion of the idea that was in his own mind—a spiritual sea-serpent, which has ventured to the top of the ocean of soul, at which many are terrified as much as if the Father of Lies had in reality appeared in his old form, whose head they must bruise; a matter of anxiety to some, of curiosity to all.

To this, as something beyond the reach of mortal ken, or at least, beyond what honest men had ever before been deemed capable of attaining to or comprehending, was given the euphonious, significant, and, as the thing was new, new name—TRANSCENDENTALISM. And as the ancients on their maps only drew the few countries they knew and set down all else as Terra Incognita, and the people there as barbarians; and as we, now-a-days, shade off about the poles, unable to say whether it is land or water, ice or fire, and enlighten the shrewd scholar by compelling him to commit the boundaries of the "unexplored regions" north by the north pole, south by Greenland, &c—so in the spiritual world they call all beyond the regions already known Transcendentalism. Every new doctrine in philosophy, every new dogma in theology, is transcendental; and so is every plan for improving man's religious institutions, or the organization of the social system. No idea can be started for a change in creed or catechism, in government or laws, in the social relations of men or their individual duties, in teaching or learning, writing or reading, criticising or creating, in art, literature, poetry or philosophy, theology or religion, but it is termed transcendental. . . .

This term is applied to many things. It might seem to mean all things to all men, or a different one to each. Talk to one of anything foreign, and he will mutter something about Transcendentalism; another thinks the Germans are given to this rather than the French; a third that all Germans even, cannot claim the name. One who has read only Locke, says it means all ideas are not innate. He who has not read at all, brings under this category all that forms no part of his week-day philosophy. It seems to bear one meaning when applied to religion; when to style, another; another, when to philosophy or art; in short there is a transcendental view of everything.

But, look a little at the matter. Man has a body, wherein he is allied to the beasts; reason which is his peculiar endowment; a soul, which connects him with Deity. As an animal, he has instincts, love for food, pleasure, which we term appetites; as rational man, love for truth, intuitions of the understanding, sympathies as a member of the human family, affections of the heart; as a child of God, religious aspirations. He is not merely an animal; nor an animal with reason. His nature is triple—animal, rational, spiritual; and it is to those systems, on whatever subject, which contemplate him as a spiritual being, that we apply the term transcendental.

That belief we term Transcendentalism which maintains that man has ideas, that come not through the five senses, or the powers of reasoning; but are either the result of direct revelation from God, his immediate inspiration, or his immanent presence in the spiritual world. . . .

It may be difficult, impossible, to prove the authority of the powers that are set over us; to vindicate the forms of government or society, or the laws by which we are controlled; to prove by abstract reasoning that *yaw* and *nein* are no better than yes and no. It is these governments, imperfect as they are, that secure to us comfort and protection; these laws which are circulating the life-blood of the community; these forms which entwine about men and keep them together, cultivate the affections, make the heart warm, kindle our holiest thoughts and waken the most delightful associations. One in a distant land, in the midst of strangers, will find the tear of joy starting at the sound of a single word in the language of his childhood. These things may be caviled at by the worst—perhaps they cannot be fairly vindicated as they are—but the best may use them to their profit. They are no more to be quarreled with than a mother's kiss, a father's smile. . . .

Principles

The history of a man is not told by the account of the particles of matter of which his body is formed. He has an existence independent on the body—on the understanding—the material world or the spiritual. No logic is required to prove this. We cannot argue "I feel," or "I think, therefore I exist." The best argument to prove this is the simple statement—I am. We know that we exist. No proof of this can be adduced which is not based on the supposition of our existence.

Any theory which seeks to show that man is a mere "conformation of material particles," or "of those immaterial ideas the whole of which form the universe," leads to the conclusion that man does not exist. Matter may be in a form called human: there may be such an association of ideas as to form what might be named man, but the existence of the soul such a theory does not recognise. But besides matter and mind there is also man. If there is not there is no immortality, no life.

It cannot be that man is merely this, endowed with certain faculties—a sort of instrument; and that the soul is merely the sound of this instrument, which may make discord or harmony, as some philosophers have said. For how has this instrument conscious life? How can it hear the sounds if the sounds make up its existence? How does it feel the pulse of life beating in its bosom? Whence has it that other part which it uses as well as the body, and feels more called on to obey, which all the logic of perfect reason could not frame from all the matter in the universe? If man is but an instrument and his soul its music, why is not his soul dead when that is dumb? Why does he not cease to be when that is broken? Why does he feel within him longings, impulses, aspirations? How is it that he not only feels that he *is*—so that he may be associated with other matter, but that he himself possesses will and power—that he is not passive but active; not only is played upon, but plays, and finds within him what he has not gained from the world, what the world cannot get from him? Whence is he? If he is but body, how has he been produced by this mysterious association? What is he? If his body be himself, how can he use it? If he is matter, how can he know of the existence of God? How can he contemplate that which is not matter, the good true, beautiful? He is not a book to be read, but he records and reads for himself.

Starting, then, with these, that man is and God is, which is involved in the first; the inquiry is, what has man? He has body, mind, *spirit*; affections, bodily, mental, *religious*; appetite, understanding, *religion*. And the latter he has and relies on as something distinct from the two former; not a combination of them. It is not because reason tells him that certain things are more for his animal comfort that he deems them right or beautiful, but because they answer the wants of the spiritual part of his nature.

Man knows of the existence of this spiritual element in his being as he knows of the existence of his mind or his body. He feels conscious of possessing it, feels it to be affected by outward objects, that some of these it loves, some it loathes. Its existence is known as that of the body, through the senses with which it is endowed.

What, then, is this part of man? Describe it. Whence, what, where? For what use? Now ask the same questions about the body. The body, you may call a structure of matter, endowed with senses by which it perceives the material world, with appetites which lead it to incorporate portions thereof with itself, and so to continue its existence. So of reason or the intellect; it is that, by whose senses, we perceive the intellectual world. This, too, has its appetites, and, making food of thought, adds to its strength and perpetuates its existence. It is the same with the religious, that which we call the highest part of our nature. This has the power of perceiving that which is independent of itself—true, good, and beautiful. For this it longs; this gives it strength and vigor. This is not doubted in every day life—all act upon it. We call him whom we find destitute of it an incomplete man, insane. Every one has the idea of God. This leads him to worship. No one can be deprived of it by education. Be where he may; do what he will, good or ill; he knows the right way. The impulses of his soul he may disregard, but he cannot deny them. To call for proof of their correctness is absurd. They are axiomatic. He knows that they are. He knows that it is by their aid alone that he perceives whatever else exists.

We have laws for the body. By exact conformity to them, by giving to each its proper food and exercise, we keep that harmony which is health. If we break these laws we incur pain, and disease ensues. The same is true of this other part of our nature. It may be strengthened by use, weakened by abuse. One part may be cultivated to an inordinate size at the expense of the rest—and the result will be deformity. But nothing can make that good which is wrong, nor that evil which is right. Nothing can deprive man of the sense of what is right. This is the law of nature—the same in all—the only foundation of practical religion, of government, laws, and the rule of right between man and man.

This, then, is the doctrine of Transcendentalism—the substantive, independent existence of the soul of man, the reality of conscience, the religious sense, the inner light, of man's religious affections, his knowledge of right and truth, his sense of duty, the *honestem* apart from the *utile*—his love for beauty and holiness, his religious aspirations—with this it starts as something not dependent on education, custom, command, or anything beyond man himself. These can only add new motives for obedience to that which he feels to be of imperative obligation; but they do not create and cannot contradict the law within him. This cannot be proved by evidence clearer than that which each man has of himself. Habit and education cannot eradicate it. Things may seem painful or inexpedient, but nothing can be just and true which this condemns. . . .

All the old systems start with the assumption of the reality of man's body and the material world, and that in the beginning man is nothing but this body. The inquiry then is, as to the ideas which are subsequently found in it, of truth, justice, beauty, God, infinity, the moral sense, his religious affections. What is their origin? How come they in the body. . . . If man does indeed find within him a page written out, his first thoughts should be whether it is in a language which he can read; what it says; whether it is the same in all other men; its relations; its use; last of all, its origin. But they are not. The first problem, nakedly stated, has always been this: Given the dead matter of the universe and the empty bodies made of it, to say how they are filled; and the answer is plain—with dead matter. Yet even this involves a new *assumption*. There must be a God, either force or Deity, to do even this. Thus this system ends in the denial of God and man.

Now this new system takes quite a different ground. In the first place, it says we have an independent existence, for we are conscious of it; we have reason, affections, religious sentiments, as well as bodies, whose existence is proved to us in the same manner as that of the bodies, through senses operated upon by that which is without them. Our sense of seeing is not created by the sun, though we are not made conscious of it till we open our eyes to the light. So with our sense of right or beauty, which we feel within us as soon as anything right or beautiful is presented to the organ which God has given us to perceive these. And as it recognises the existence of the soul as well as that of the body, and supposes the senses of the soul to be nothing introduced into the soul long after it begins to exist, but as original endowments, not effects, but conditions rather, of its existence, not thrown upon it by the world, it presents quite a different field from that of the old system. The existence of men's bodies and their senses, and the soul and its senses must both be referred to one source—God. Both are appealed to as facts in all reasonings. . . .

The results of the two systems may show their comparative merits. The old deriving all ideas from sensation, leads to atheism, to a religion which is but self-interest— an ethical code which makes right synonymous with indulgence of appetite, justice one with expediency, and reduces our love of what is good, beautiful, true and divine, to habit, association or interest. The new asserts the continual presence of God in all his works, spirit as well as matter; makes religion the natural impulse of every breast; the moral law, God's voice in every heart, independent on interest, expediency or appetite, which enables us to resist these; an universal, eternal, standard of truth, beauty, goodness, holiness, to which every man can turn and follow, if he will. . . .

Criticism

Those rules which regulate the original composition of works of imagination or art, or enable one to test their propriety, beauty or perfection, are the laws of criticism. It is the science which teaches us to estimate the creations of the mind, and pass judgment on the pictures which man paints of what passes within him. Its end is to enable us to estimate the worth of a poem, a picture, a book, or any work of art.

Most obviously it presupposes an intimate knowledge of the principles of human nature. What is it that perceives the beauty of a poem? On what does this depend? With what standard is it to be compared? Whence do we derive our knowledge of this standard? How are we to know when anything conforms to it? These and a thousand similar questions are not answered with a breath. An Indian, like an animal, might like or hate a picture merely for its color; another, more cultivated, because it caused in his mind pleasing or unpleasant associations; another because he judged it beautiful or not. Thus there would be different systems. One would take no note of what the others most esteemed. So we find several systems saying that we derive our sense of beauty from habit, association, judgment, the study of nature.

The old were mere arbitrary, conventional rules, founded in caprice. Works were judged and compared with other works. The *Iliad* or *Æneid* was the standard for a poem: the Venus de Medici a perfect form. But nothing was said to be good or perfect in itself. Every thing must stand or fall, not by its actual, but by its comparative merits. Such rules had no foundation in nature. Many of them were irreconcilable with nature and calculated only to trammel and embarrass. But now there is recognised a common, universal, natural standard, which all men possess, by which all can judge. One tries not to write like Homer or Dante, but to produce a poem beautiful in itself. Within himself he finds a standard higher than anything yet produced, an idea of what such ought to be. Thus there is one rule, uniform, not arbitrary, but natural. Perfection is but conformity with what all seek.

Formerly judgment was passed upon parts; whether they were formed according to the most approved fashion; thus the Chinese asked if the feet were small, the Indian looked for rings in the nose. Or the parts were judged in relation to the whole. The whole was never taken together, and the question put, whether it was good or beautiful in itself. It was easy to say, that this corresponded with such a model; that violated such a dictum of this or that author; that certain words were better suited to describe slow motion, others quick; that certain phrases or figures were better used in a description intended to be sublime, others in one pathetic, some in one ridiculous; these and all else in codes, of which these may serve as examples, were easy enough. And the end was attained. Of such materials a system was framed. The mistake lay in calling it the art of criticism. No doubt, it was an art to judge according to those artificial rules. But if criticism be the art of judging works of art or imagination, whether they are perfect or faulty, of pointing out their beauties or defects, there was none of it in this method. Things most dull, insipid and worthless, might be judged faultless, while things really most precious were rejected altogether. Thus the question was, whether words, sentences, ideas, acts or parts were arranged according to certain established precedents; not what emotions were excited, whether the poem kindled the fire in our breast, the song spoke the language of our hearts, the picture bore resemblance to our imaginings, and represented those glad dreams which sometimes flit through every soul—to give a form that shall wake the remembrance of which bright vision is the perfection of art. It could measure feet, scan lines, detect false rhymes, say this exceeded the length, that had fewer acts than the rules allowed, this history was faulty because it agreed not with such a model, that biography good if only a stale parody on such another. To gain favor with critics, you need only conform to the literary fashion, in bearing and dress—no matter for the man. One would stop you in the midst of a song that set the soul on fire, to see—if it corresponded with a certain canon of measure or length; instead of following out the train of thought roused by a noble sentiment, stay to remark how likely one would be to feel such under the same circumstances in actual life. As if one had nothing besides eyes and ears, as if the soul were not to be roused and the spirit kindled, as well as the reason convinced, as if one could not read an oration without stopping to see how every part compared with one of Cicero's, or one who would build a beautiful edifice must go, rule in hand, and measure the Parthenon, or one would or could read Homer with the hope of being pleased with his observance of the laws of critics, and went to see how prettily the fountains played in their marble basin, and would not bathe in the living spring to renew his own life; as well might we complain, that the mighty oak, with its iron arms, and sinews strengthened by the storms of ages, or the magnolia, pride of the earth, or the evergreen pine, in whose high tops you may hear heaven whispering, were not like the trees of Attica, or the shrubs in the gardens of Rome.

Formerly men measured but did not contemplate. They read to see how one thing compared with another, not to catch the inspiration. They virtually denied the truth of our school-room motto, "what man has done man may do," which might read better "no man has done what man may do," and proves the truth of the poet's words, "Man praises man—commemoration mad."—All were reduced to one standard, low and mean. Limits were set to progress, forms prescribed which must be conformed to. None strove for any thing new, all was made to conform with the old. The art was not to invent but imitate, to copy not to create, to receive as standards of perfection what were but poor attempts to represent it, to look on the starting point as the goal. Thus all were blind worshippers of the past; the exertions of men were limited to trials to equal what they ought to excel. All this is to be abolished, and genius left as free to obey the voice of nature as on the first day of creation. . . .

Religion

Transcendentalism is predicated on the reality of the spiritual or religious element in man; his inborn capacity to perceive truth and right, so that moral and religious truths can be proved to him with the same degree of certainty that attends mathematical demonstration; and for the same reason, because they can be shown to conform to certain fundamental truths, axioms, which all know, none can prove or deny, beyond which we cannot go. It presents no question as to the divine origin of the Sabbath or church; none in relation to the authenticity or authority of the old or new testament, their infallible or plenary inspiration. These are for critics, historians, divines, theologians. It has nothing to do with the trinity or unity, the humanity or divinity of the Saviour. In short, it relates to nothing that is in any wise connected with biblical criticism or theology. These are matters intimately connected with and often taken for religion itself; but they are distinct from it, and the most religious man may be entirely ignorant of them. He who can hear the word, believe and obey, is religious. . . .

Many confound Transcendentalism with what may be denoted rationalism. The former owns the authority of revelation because of our intuitive perception of its truth. The latter says, that the Bible is to be taken like any other book, written by and for reasonable beings, and to be rejected or received according as it approves itself to our understanding. The distinction is obvious.

That the sacred writings are to receive a rational interpretation none would deny; but few would admit that we are to exercise the same rational interpretation in relation to this which we apply to other works. All feel that this is no common book. None view it as they would another. It is an inspired book. To some, completely, infallibly so; so that to doubt a word is as bad as to deny the whole; accounts must be believed, though science, and history show they are not correct; nay, statements directly conflicting with each other must be received. Others only regard the New Testament as infallible in religious matters, and receive the Old only as the most ancient of histories, inestimable as a narrative of the olden times, and illustrative of the New, but of no intrinsic authority. But they will not attempt to account for the contradictions and inconsistencies in this. They either say they will not question; they take things as they are; there are figurative expressions; differences on minor points, proofs, rather, of the authenticity of the whole; perhaps, interpolations. One class only is consistent in its action, those who maintain the plenary and infallible inspiration of the whole, and all connected with it. But this is catholicism, most bigoted. Once leave this, and we cannot stop till we apply to this the rules of construction, which address themselves to the common understanding. It can never be understood and vindicated, till tested by the universal principles of evidence. It cannot be read as one work. The inquiries are to be made of each book, When was it written; where; by whom; for what end; what does it purport to be [?] An answer to these questions would quiet many. To these questions, different answers must be given. All, then, cannot be the word of God, written for all times and all men. If the whole is presented to one as the infallible word of God, the whole must be rejected. But all can be reconciled. All is clear enough if we say that each book is to be received and read according to what it pretends to be, and the circumstances under which it was written. Present the book to any one in this light, and he can have no ground to say it is false. But say, it is more than this, and you give reason for the rejection of all, by claiming more than you can maintain.

This is the only view in which the scriptures can safely be presented to any one. This is the only view in which apparent inconsistencies will not lead to disbelief. But under this we should be led to expect to find them, and should thereby be led to question the authenticity of the whole no more than we should doubt the early history of New England because Cotton Mather and the rest believed in witchcraft, or doubt there was such a person as

Washington, because historians differ in some circumstances and views of his character. Let the Bible be presented to ten men of mature minds, cultivated and learned, but who had never examined it, as the infallible word of God, to claim their implicit belief, and they would not finish the first chapter before they would say, "It cannot be." But give it to them as a record containing the lives of the best men, the thoughts of inspired ones, the devotion of holy ones, examples which all should imitate, the surest guide and best comforter for life, the strongest confirmation of our hopes in death, and all would read and study and not tire, and own "It is this and infinitely more."

These hints may serve to show what influence this doctrine is to have on the popular faith. Religion is to cease to be an outward form, the observance of the sabbath, attendance on church, support of the clergy, the admission of the Bible and the Saviour, the assent of the will. It is to be a personal matter of each man, which each must do for himself; not mere uprightness of conduct, but positive, actual devotion of the spirit and the heart, the strong desire, the earnest endeavor, the hearty will to do what is right and true; not the negative morality of refraining from actual sin, but the positive virtue of acting in obedience to the dictates of Christian love; not doing good because it is better for us, but pursuing virtue for virtue's sake; the religion of the spirit, not that of the body; in the beautiful language of one, whose life proves that its doctrines can be carried into the daily walks of life, that religion "whose substance is love to God, whose form is love to man, whose temple is the pure heart, whose sacrifice is a divine life."

There can be no danger from the spread of such principles; though men may mistake the means of doing so holy a work. . . .

Conclusion

Such are some of the tendencies of Transcendentalism. It extends to man in every relation. Proposes a new rule of action wherever he acts as man. Clearly the work to be done is not one of a day, nor of years or ages, but all time. There is no danger that the world shall be changed in a breath. It is not left to the hands of one or a few. It is the task of the race. Each step of humanity is one towards the goal at which it aims. He who looks forward to see what is to be done, who sees the evils that are in the world which should not be there, the false maxims and principles on which empires are based and the human race actuated, has need of courage and resolution of heart; but he who will look back on the tortuous and dangerous way the child of God has thus far travelled, and see how many that threatened his life, born of the earth, the children of superstition and sin, have fallen dead about him, will find enough to cheer him, and can never fear that the race will stop or recede.

As each man is a tree, its root of sense in the earth, its strong trunk of reason, and the holy affections its flowers, that catch the genial warmth of the sun, and the bland breath, and drink in the bright light of heaven; so it is with mankind. The ideas of the first races are all from the earth; then from those roots of sense springs the trunk of reason, and sooner or later will come the fragrant blossom that mirrors heaven, and sends new life to the roots that are toiling for it in the earth, and the fruit that bears the seed which secures its immortality.

The end proposed is almost too sublime for human conception, the perfection of humanity. The wonder is, that man should think of attaining it, with the limited means at his command, against the obstacles he has to contend with. It is always a task to pull down and build anew, to renounce an old habit, though a bad one. It gives pain to dress a wound though that is the only remedy. A system of philosophy, on which are based our governments, our laws, our religion, our social institutions, whose influence extends to man every where in public and private, if it could be demonstrated to be false as lies, would not, could not be renounced at once. All institutions, forms, doctrines, become necessary to man from use, and dear from habit and happy and holy association.

He will only see the good in these and die rather than renounce them. They are the growth of time and circumstances, and cannot be abolished at once. Though one could show every branch of our government to be bad, he must go slowly and cautiously to the work of reforming it. But the ground must be broken, the seed sown, or the harvest will be wanting. Now, this system might be engrafted on many things as they exist; but every day adds to the difficulty. "Gold in the morning, silver in the middle of the day, lead at night." There are obstacles to its progress, for there are errors which it assails. There is danger to some institutions, for it shows their falsity. There may be danger of too much zeal, which shall rid men of the old before the new is laid hold of, but it is what every mariner runs who starts upon a voyage. There may be danger that the world is not good enough, as it is said, is not yet ready for such elevated truth. Then, in God's name, let it be made better. There are means at hand for improving the condition of the mass of mankind, that the world little dreams of, of relieving their wants, lightening their burdens, cultivating their intellects, awakening their religious feelings; so that the world would wear a smile of joy at the thought of the change that might be made in its condition. To make most of these means is the office of religion. To aid this work, enforce universal obedience, to the eternal law on which it is founded, is the duty of man; this task is the end of his life.

It becomes not him, who alone is made erect, with his face turned towards the skies, to creep over the earth with his eyes fixed on the dust, the image of despair. He is the child of hope. "Let him look to Heaven, and he will not fail to find his home."

3. WILLIAM HENRY CHANNING, 1810–1884

[A nephew of the great Dr. Channing, William Henry Channing graduated from Harvard College in 1829 and from the Divinity School in 1833. In those years he was one among many of the intellectual youths who threw themselves (intellectually) at the feet of Margaret Fuller.

Later, he threw himself into Transcendental social causes, and married a girl quite other than Margaret. In 1836 he conducted a church for workers in New York City; in 1839 he joined James Freeman Clarke and Christopher Cranch in the Unitarian crusade at Cincinnati, and helped edit *The Western Messenger*. On his way back from disillusionment in the West, toward what was ultimately to be his last stand with a Unitarian Society in London, England, he was induced to coöperate (a difficult task for any Transcendentalist) with Emerson and Clarke in preparing, for publication in 1852, the *Memoirs of Margaret Fuller Ossoli* (she having drowned in 1850). These good gentlemen have exposed themselves to derisive criticism for their caution in editing Margaret's papers, but when William Channing took over his part in the assignment, at the beginning of the second volume, he felt called upon to give a brief account of what the "Movement" was all about. By 1852, Channing, along with most survivors, was a bit weary of the whole business—hence the timeworn tone he and his colleagues were able to impart to Margaret's *Memoirs*—but he was still close enough, much closer than Emerson in the *Historic Notes*, to remember what the enthusiasm of 1840 had meant to him and to Margaret.]

A PARTICIPANT'S DEFINITION

The summer of 1839 saw the full dawn of the Transcendental movement in New England. The rise of this enthusiasm was as mysterious as that of any form of revival; and only they who were of the faith could comprehend how bright was this morning-time of a new hope. Transcendentalism was an assertion of the inalienable integrity of man, of the immanence of Divinity in instinct. In part, it was a reaction against Puritan Orthodoxy; in part, an effect of renewed study of the ancients, or Oriental Pantheists, of Plato and the Alexandrians, of Plutarch's *Morals,* Seneca and Epictetus; in part, the natural product of the culture of the place and time. On the somewhat stunted stock of Unitarianism—whose characteristic dogma was trust in individual reason as correlative to Supreme Wisdom—had been grafted German Idealism, as taught by masters of most various schools—by Kant and Jacobi, Fichte and Novalis, Schelling and Hegel, Schleiermacher and De Wette, by Madame de Staël, Cousin, Coleridge, and Carlyle; and the result was a vague yet exalting conception of the godlike nature of the human spirit.

Transcendentalism, as viewed by its disciples, was a pilgrimage from the idolatrous world of creeds and rituals to the temple of the Living God in the soul. It was a putting to silence of tradition and formulas, that the Sacred Oracle might be heard through intuitions of the single-eyed and pure-hearted.

Amidst materialists, zealots, and sceptics, the Transcendentalist believed in perpetual inspiration, the miraculous power of will, and a birthright to universal good. He sought to hold communion face to face with the unnameable Spirit of his spirit, and gave himself up to the embrace of nature's beautiful joy, as a babe seeks the breast of a mother. To him the curse seemed past; and love was without fear. "All mine is thine" sounded forth to him in ceaseless benediction, from flowers and stars, through the poetry, art, heroism of all ages, in the aspirations of his own genius, and the budding promise of the time. His work was to be faithful, as all saints, sages, and lovers of man had been, to Truth, as the very Word of God. His maxims were—"Trust, dare and be; infinite good is ready for your asking; seek and find. All that your fellows can claim or need is that you should become, in fact, your highest self; fulfil, then, your ideal."

Hence, among the strong, withdrawal to private study and contemplation, that they might be "alone with the Alone"; solemn yet glad devotedness to the Divine leadings in the inmost will; calm concentration of thought to wait for and receive wisdom; dignified independence, stern yet sweet, of fashion and public opinion; honest originality of speech and conduct, exempt alike from apology or dictation, from servility or scorn. Hence, too, among the weak, whimsies, affectation, rude disregard of proprieties, slothful neglect of common duties, surrender to the claims of natural appetite, self-indulgence, self-absorption, and self-idolatry.

By their very posture of mind, as seekers of the new, the Transcendentalists were critics and "come-outers" from the old. Neither the church, the state, the college, society, nor even the reform associations, had a hold upon their hearts. The past might be well enough for those who, without make-belief, could yet put faith in common dogmas and usages; but for them the matin-bells of a new day were chiming, and the herald-trump of freedom was heard upon the mountains.

Hence, leaving ecclesiastical organizations, political parties, and familiar circles, which to them were brown with drought, they sought in covert nooks of friendship for running waters, and fruit from the tree of life. The journal, the letter, became of greater worth than the printed page; for they felt that systematic results were not yet to be looked for, and that in sallies of conjecture, glimpses and flights of ecstasy, the "Newness" lifted her veil to her votaries.

Thus, by mere attraction of affinity, grew together the brotherhood of the "Like-minded", as they were pleasantly nicknamed by outsiders, and by themselves, on the ground that no two were of the same opinion. The only password of membership to this association, which had no compact, records, or officers, was a hopeful and liberal spirit; and its chance conventions were determined merely by the desire of the caller for a "talk", or by the arrival of some guest from a distance with budget of presumptive novelties. Its "symposium" was a pic-nic, whereto each brought his gains, as he felt prompted, a bunch of wild grapes from the woods, or bread-corn from his threshing-floor. The tone of the assemblies was cordial welcome for every one's peculiarity; and scholars, farmers, mechanics, merchants, married women, and maidens, met there on a level of courteous respect. The only guest not tolerated was intolerance; though strict justice might add, that these "Illuminati" were as unconscious of their special cant as smokers are of the perfume of their weed, and that a pro-

fessed declaration of universal independence turned out
in practice to be rather oligarchic.

4. ORESTES AUGUSTUS BROWNSON, 1803–1876

[Born in Stockbridge, Vermont, Orestes Brownson was
reared in a Calvinist world, and accordingly underwent the
regular conversion at the age of nineteen, whereupon he
joined a Presbyterian church. After intense inner struggle,
he rejected Calvinism and became a Universalist preacher;
after more struggle, he rejected Universalism and went to
New York City, to associate himself with Robert Dale
Owen and Fanny Wright in an effort to organize a Work-
ingmen's Party.

The autobiography he published in 1857—*The Convert;
or, Leaves from My Experiences*—recounts these early
struggles; I open it where, recognizing his defeat both
political and spiritual in New York, Brownson has avowed
himself a Unitarian and come in 1834 to the church in
Canton, Massachusetts, just when the Transcendental enthusiasm was to tear the Unitarian community apart.

A voracious reader—second only to Theodore Parker
in his mastery of European theology and philosophy—
Brownson quickly became a vociferous spokesman for the
"newness," and performed for it prodigious services. Because after what his associates considered his betrayal of
the cause they virtually entered into a tacit conspiracy to
expunge his name from the record, it is well to let his own
frank claims for *New Views of Christianity* (1836) and
The Boston Quarterly Review (1838–1842) stand as
statements of sober historical fact.

As the event proved, Brownson, though a charter member of the Transcendental Club, was an altogether different spirit from Emerson or Parker. Where they took the
principles of the new philosophy to indicate indefinite
enlargements of individual freedom, Brownson found in
them—with a logic as clear as, if not clearer than, Emerson's—the promise of an organic authority. In 1844 he
became a convert to the Catholic Church.

With the hindsight provided by that conversion, he here reviews the tumultuous years. The foremost dissenter from Transcendentalism—the others would call him renegade— he underscores the reasoning by which he came to separate himself, at the end of a series of dissents, from that manifestation of which the very heart was intransigent dissent.

The special confidant to whom Brownson refers on p. 43 is George Ripley.]

A DISSENTING DEFINITION

I did not lose sight of the great end I proposed—the progress of man and society, and the realization of a heaven on earth. I was working in reference to it even while I was pursuing my historical and philosophical researches, and maturing my religious theories. I had been forced to resort to religious ideas and sentiments for the power to work effectually for it; and I now found that I must have a religious organization, institution, or church, in order to render these sentiments practically efficient. . . . The work of destruction, commenced by the Reformation, which had introduced an era of criticism and revolution, had, I thought, been carried far enough. All that was dissoluble had been dissolved. All that was destructible had been destroyed, and it was time to begin the work of reconstruction—a work of reconciliation and love.

Irreligious ideas and sentiments are disorganizing and destructive in their nature, and cannot be safely cherished for a single moment after the work of destruction is completed. When the work to be done is that of construction, of building up, or organizing, of founding something, we must resort to religious ideas and sentiments, for they, having love for their principle, are plastic, organic, constructive, and the only ideas and sentiments that are so. They are necessary to the new organization or institution of the race demanded; and the organization or institution, what I called the church, is necessary to the progress of man and society, or the creation of an earthly paradise. The first thing to be done is to cease our hostility to the past, discontinue the work of destruction; abandon the old war against the Papacy, which has no longer any significance, and in a spirit of universal love and conciliation, turn our attention to the work of founding a religious institution, or effecting a new church organization, adapted to our present and future wants.

This we are now, I thought, in a condition to attempt. Men are beginning to understand that Protestantism is no-churchism, is no positive religion; and while it serves the purpose of criticism and destruction, it cannot meet the wants of the soul, or erect the temple in which the human race may assemble to worship in concord and peace. Unitarianism has demolished Calvinism, made an end in all thinking minds of everything like dogmatic Protestantism, and Unitarianism itself satisfies nobody. It is negative, cold, lifeless, and all advanced minds among Unitarians are dissatisfied with it, and are craving something higher, better, more living and lifegiving. They are weary of doubt, uncertainty, disunion, individualism, and crying out from the bottom of their hearts for faith, for love, for union. They feel that life has wellnigh departed from the world; that religion is but an empty name, and morality is mere decorum or worldly prudence; that men neither worship God, nor love one another. Society as it is, is a lie, a sham, a charnel-house, a valley of dry bones. O that the Spirit of God would once more pass by, and say unto these dry bones, "Live"!

So I felt, so felt others; and whoever enjoyed the confidence of the leading Unitarian ministers in Boston and its vicinity from 1830 to 1840, well knows that they were sick at heart with what they had, and were demanding in their interior souls a religious institution of some sort, in which they could find shelter from the storms of this wintry world, and some crumbs of the bread of life to keep them from starving. Not only in Boston was this cry heard. It came to us on every wind from all quarters—from France, from Germany, from England even; and Carlyle, in his *Sartor Resartus,* seemed to lay his finger on the plague-spot of the age. Men had reached the centre of indifference; under a broiling sun in the *Rue d'Enfer,* had pronounced the everlasting "No." Were they never to be able to pronounce the everlasting "Yes"?

Among them all I was probably the most hopeful, and the most disposed to act. If I lacked faith in God, I had faith in humanity. The criticisms on all subjects sacred and profane, the bold investigations of every department of life, continued unweariedly for three hundred years, by the most intrepid, the most energetic, and the most enlightened portion of mankind, had, I thought, sufficiently developed ideas and sentiments, and obtained for us all the light needed, all the materials wanted for commencing the work of reorganization, and casting broad and deep the foundation of the Church of the Future. All that was wanting was to collect the ideas which these three hundred years of criticism and investigation had developed, and mould them into one harmonious, complete, and living system, and then to take that system as the principle and law of the new moral and religious organization. Whence that system, formed from the union of various and isolated ideas, was to derive its life, its principle of unity and vitality, so as to be living and effective, I did not at the time specially consider. I supposed ideas themselves were potent, but, hard pressed, I probably should have said, they are potent by the potency of the human mind, or the Divinity in man. . . .

Dr. Channing was not and could not be the man to found the new order, and rival or more than rival a Moses, and a greater than Moses. Among my friends and acquaintances I found none. Perhaps the thought passed through my head that I was myself the destined man; but I did not entertain it. I could not be more than John the Baptist, or the Voice of one crying in the wilderness, "Behold the Lord cometh: prepare ye to meet him." I might, perhaps, be the Precursor of the new Messias, but not the new Messias himself. My business was, not to found the new church, but to proclaim its necessity, and to prepare men's minds and hearts to welcome it. . . .

Not finding among my friends and acquaintances the "representative man," and waiting till he should reveal himself, I concluded to commence a direct preparation for his coming. One man, and one man only, shared my entire confidence, and knew my most secret thought. Him, from motives of delicacy, I do not name; but, in the formation of my mind, in systematizing my ideas, and in general development and culture, I owe more to him than to any other man among Protestants. We have since taken divergent courses, but I loved him as I have loved no other man, and shall so love and esteem him as long as I live. He encouraged me, and through him chiefly I was enabled to remove to Boston and commence operations. Dr. Channing and several of his personal friends, without knowing all my purposes, also assisted me. I was invited to Boston to preach to the laboring classes, and to do all I could to save them from the unbelief which had become quite prevalent among them. I accepted the invitation, proposing to myself to make it an opportunity to bring out my religious and socialist theories, and to call public attention to the necessity of a new religious organization of mankind. I accordingly organized, on the first Sunday in July, 1836, "The Society for Christian Union and Progress."

The name I gave to the society was indicative of the principle of the future organization, and of the end I contemplated—the union and progress of the race. I remained, with some interruption, the minister of this Society till the latter part of 1843, when I began to suspect that man is an indifferent church-builder, and that God himself had already founded a church for us, some centuries ago, quite adequate to our wants, and adapted to our nature and destiny. My Society at one time was prosperous, but in general I could not pride myself on my success; yet I saw clearly enough, that, with my own convictions, a stronger attachment to my own opinions because they were mine, and a more dogmatic temper than I possessed, I might easily succeed, not in founding a new Catholic Church indeed, but in founding a new sect, and perhaps a sect not without influence. But a new sect was not in my plan, and I took pains to prevent my movement from growing into one. What I wanted was, not sectarism, of which I felt we had quite too much, but unity and catholicity. I wished to unite men, not to divide them—to put an end to divisions, not to multiply them.

The truth is, I was not, except on a few points, settled in my own mind. I never concealed, or affected to conceal, that I regarded myself as still a learner, a seeker after truth, not as one who has found the truth, and has nothing to do but to preach it. I always told my congregation that I was looking for more light, and that I could not be sure that my convictions would be to-morrow what they are to-day. Whether I preached or wrote, I aimed simply at exciting thought and directing it to the problems to be solved, not to satisfy the mind or furnish it with dogmatic solutions of its difficulties. I was often rash in my statements, because I regarded myself not as putting forth doctrines that must be believed, but as throwing out provocatives to thought and investigation. My confidence was not in the individual mind, whether my own or another's, but in humanity, in the action and decisions of the general mind, the universal reason.

I was perfectly consistent in this; and my course, I thought then, and I think now, was the only honest course for a man who has not an infallible authority to which he can appeal, and in the name of which he is commissioned to speak. If the criterion of truth is the universal reason, or the reason of all men, not my individual reason; and if I am imperfect and yet progressive, never knowing the whole truth, yet able to know more to-morrow than I know to-day, how can I, as an honest man, regard my private opinions as dogmas, or put forth my personal convictions, as so much eternal and immutable truth? What as yet the universal reason has not passed upon, what has not as yet received the seal of approbation from universal and immutable human nature, can be regarded only as private opinion, which I have no right to ask others to believe, or to assert as indisputable. I was in fact too honest, too consistent, and too distrustful of myself to succeed.

I wrote and published, immediately after organizing my Society, a small work, entitled *New Views of Christianity*,

Society, and the Church, derived in great part from Benjamin Constant, Victor Cousin, Heinrich Heine, and the publications of the Saint-Simonians. It was designed to set forth the reasons which made a new church necessary, to assert the principles on which it must be founded or the end it must be established to effect, and to call attention to the signs of the times favorable to its speedy organization. The book made little sensation, and had few readers. It met with no success flattering to the pride or vanity of its author; yet the book is remarkable for its protest against Protestantism, and its laughable blunders as to the doctrines and tendencies of the Catholic Church, to which I was by no means hostile, but of which I was profoundly ignorant. It is no less remarkable for its acceptance and vindication, in principle, of nearly all the errors into which the human race has fallen. It is the last word of the non-Catholic world, and marks the limit beyond which it cannot advance without recoiling.

In one respect, I misjudged my countrymen: they had less understanding of their Protestantism than I gave them credit for. They were unable to recognize their own thoughts in the general and abstract form in which I stated them. The truth, I suppose, is, that Protestants, with individual exceptions, seldom reason on their Protestantism, or take the trouble to analyze it and understand what it really is. They do not reduce it to its ultimate principles, and appreciate them in their real and essential character. Perhaps they are not capable of doing it; perhaps they are too busy with the world to attempt it; perhaps, also, they have a lurking suspicion, that, should they attempt it, they would find it disappearing in the process, and themselves reduced to the necessity of choosing between Catholicity and no-religion. There is no doubt that, if they are determined to be Protestants, they are wise. Few who have thoroughly analyzed Protestantism, thoroughly mastered its distinctive principles, have been able to retain their respect for it. . . .

My views were hardly new or singular; but the manner in which they were received was instructive, and satisfied me that my Protestant countrymen, though disclaiming all authority in matters of belief, and professing to discard all authoritative tradition, were little accustomed, except in worldly affairs, to free, independent, distinct thought. For the most part, their belief, I found, was practically a prejudice. They had never thought out their doctrines, and they took them merely on trust, and that, too, without ever troubling themselves to inquire whether they accorded or not with what they held to be the principles of reason. They held all my views, though mixed up with much extraneous and contradictory matter. Yet they recoiled, or affected to recoil, with horror from my statements, and bespattered me with cant phrases and epithets, to which, I presume, not one in ten attached any definite meaning; and, of those who did attach such meaning, not one in a hundred believed it, or was not prepared in the next breath to contradict it.

I was convinced that I had gone too fast for the public, and that there remained a greater preliminary work to be done than I had supposed. To effect something in regard to this preliminary work, I established, in January, 1838, *The Boston Quarterly Review*, which I conducted almost single-handed for five years.... My *Quarterly Review* was devoted to religion, philosophy, politics, and general literature. It had no creed, no distinct doctrines to support on any subject whatever, and was intended for free and independent discussion of all questions which I might regard as worth discussing, not, however, with a view of settling them, or putting an end to any dispute. I had purposes to accomplish, but not, and I did not profess to have, a body of truth I wished to bring out and make prevail. My aim was not dogmatism, but inquiry; and my more immediate purpose was to excite thought, to quicken the mental activity of my countrymen, and force them to think freely and independently on the gravest and most delicate subjects. I aimed to startle, and made it a point to be as paradoxical and as extravagant as I could without doing violence to my own reason and conscience. Whoever reads the five volumes of that *Review*, nearly all written by myself, with the view of finding clear, distinct, and consistent doctrines on any subject, with the exception of certain political questions, will be disappointed; but whoever reads it to find provocatives to thought, stimulants to inquiry, and valuable hints on a great variety of important topics, will probably be satisfied. I did what I aimed to do, effected my purpose, and, though its circulation was limited, its influence was such as to satisfy me. The *Review* should be judged by the purpose for which it was instituted, not merely by the speculations it contains. Many of them, no doubt, are crude, rash, and thrown out with a certain recklessness which nothing, if I had aimed to dogmatize, could justify, but as designed simply to set other minds to thinking, may, perhaps, escape any great severity of censure.

None of my countrymen are less disposed to accept entire the speculations, theories, and utterances of that *Quarterly Review*, than I am, and yet I believe it deserves an honorable mention in the history of American Literature; and the opinions it enunciates on a great variety of topics are substantially such as I still hold on the same topics. On other points I should have been right if my facts had been true. It will be generally found, to speak after the manner of the logicians, that my *major* was sound, but my *minor* often needed to be denied or distinguished. There is much in these volumes, especially the later ones, to indicate that my mind did not remain stationary, that I was beginning to look in the direction of the Catholic Church, and that I had, after all, less to change on becoming a Catholic than was commonly supposed at the time. The public read me more or less, but hardly knew what to make of me. They regarded me as a bold and vigorous writer, but as eccentric, extravagant, paradoxical, constantly changing, and not to be counted on; not perceiving that I did not wish to be counted on, in their sense, as a leader whom they could safely follow, and who would save them the labor of thinking for themselves. My aim was to induce, to force, others to think for themselves, not to persuade them to permit me to do their thinking for them. This aim was just and proper in one who knew he had no authority to teach.

CHAPTER TWO

NATURALISM

1. RALPH WALDO EMERSON, 1803–1882

[The primary and most radical thrust, in terms of metaphysics, of the Transcendental religion of Nature was Emerson's volume of 1836. That book, *Nature,* arose out of what Emerson called a "Saturnalia" of faith; in the last three chapters it becomes a hymn to the mighty "Self" who may govern, actually give laws to, the objective universe. The same ecstasy informs the two seminal addresses, "The American Scholar" of 1837 and "The Divinity School Address" of 1837. Thereafter, Emerson's thinking, or rather feeling, about external reality can be described, as Stephen Whicher puts it, as an increasing "ascendency of experience over Reality." Though never surrendering his basic conviction, Emerson executes a grand retreat from natural egotism to a reconciliation of himself with objective Nature. From the demonic Protestantism of 1836 he rapidly subsides into a more acquiescent optimism, into what William James called a "soft determinism."

Hence, while on the one hand there is a propriety in reprinting Emerson's *Nature* and the two revolutionary addresses—as do other anthologies—to portray his most vital thought, this practice becomes a misrepresentation, in so far as Emerson's first trumpeting of the Transcendental ego proved to be a note he could not sustain.

Emerson delivered "The Method of Nature" before the Society of the Adelphi in Waterville College, Maine, on August 11, 1841. He composed it in July of that year while staying at a hotel on Nantasket beach; somewhat lamely he apologized to Carlyle for accepting the invitation on the plea, "I am always lured on by the hope of saying something which shall stick by the good boys." The down-easterners seem not to have been much impressed; a farmer who listened is on record as saying, "It is quite likely that the oration contained a good deal of science; but even if it did not, no one would know the fact." Conventionally printed in the first volume of the standard edition of Emerson's *Works*, "The Method of Nature" is as regularly ignored. Yet this address should be, for one who seeks to define the image that Emerson presented to younger disciples, such as Thoreau and Margaret Fuller, quite as crucial as the 1836 *Nature* or the two calls to action.

Chastened though this statement be, as contrasted with the previous arrogance, it is possibly all the more valuable to us because, while dispensing with the metaphysical framework, it makes even more explicit the Transcendental thesis that the mind of the intellectual (*i.e.*, in Emerson's terminology, the "scholar") must not and can not let itself be subjected to the predominant "material interest" of (as he calls it in a letter of that summer) this "great, intelligent, sensual, avaricious America." Indeed, as a confrontation of the issue of the mind against American materiality, this speech is as bold an utterance as Emerson was ever to achieve. Here, in essence, is the Transcendentalist's rooted belief in the glory of "Genius" (as against mere "talent"); here, as openly as Emerson ever dared to say it, is his persuasion that the old Puritan élite of predestined saints could be replaced by a more comprehensive election, into which any young American might enter by trusting his innermost imperatives.]

THE METHOD OF NATURE

Gentlemen:

Let us exchange congratulations on the enjoyments and the promises of this literary anniversary. The land we live in has no interest so dear, if it knew its want, as the fit consecration of days of reason and thought. Where there is no vision, the people perish. The scholars are the priests of that thought which establishes the foundations of the earth. No matter what is their special work or profession, they stand for the spiritual interest of the world, and it is a common calamity if they neglect their post in a country where the material interest is so predominant as it is in America. We hear something too much of the results of machinery, commerce, and the useful arts. We are a puny and a fickle folk. Avarice, hesitation, and following, are our diseases. The rapid wealth which hundreds in the community acquire in trade, or by the incessant expansions of our population and arts, enchants the eyes of all the rest; the luck of one is the hope of thousands, and the bribe acts like the neighborhood of a gold mine to impoverish the farm, the school, the church, the house, and the very body and feature of man.

I do not wish to look with sour aspect at the industrious manufacturing village, or the mart of commerce. I love the music of the water-wheel; I value the railway; I feel the pride which the sight of a ship inspires; I look on trade and every mechanical craft as education also. But let me discriminate what is precious herein. There is in each of these works an act of invention, an intellectual step, or short series of steps, taken; that act or step is the spiritual act; all the rest is mere repetition of the same a thousand times. And I will not be deceived into admiring the routine of handicrafts and mechanics, how splendid soever the result, any more than I admire the routine of the scholars or clerical class. That splendid results ensue from the labors of stupid men, is the fruit of higher laws than their will, and the routine is not to be praised for it. I would not have the laborer sacrificed to the result—I would not have the laborers sacrificed to my convenience and pride, nor to that of a great class of such as me. Let there be worse cotton and better men. The weaver should not be bereaved of his superiority to his work, and his knowledge that the product or the skill is of no value, except so far as it embodies his spiritual prerogatives. If I see nothing to admire in the unit, shall I admire a million units? Men stand in awe of the city, but do not honor any individual citizen; and are continually yielding to this dazzling result of numbers, that which they would never yield to the solitary example of any one.

Whilst the multitude of men degrade each other, and give currency to desponding doctrines, the scholar must be a bringer of hope, and must reinforce man against himself. I sometimes believe that our literary anniversaries will presently assume a greater importance, as the eyes of men open to their capabilities. Here, a new set of distinctions, a new order of ideas, prevail. Here, we set a bound to the respectability of wealth, and a bound to the pretensions of the law and the church. The bigot must cease to be a bigot to-day. Into our charmed circle, power cannot enter; and the sturdiest defender of existing institutions feels the terrific inflammability of this air which condenses heat in every corner that may restore to the elements the fabrics of ages. Nothing solid is secure; everything tilts and rocks. Even the scholar is not safe; he too is searched and revised. Is his learning dead? Is he living in his memory? The power of mind is not mortification, but life. But come forth, thou curious child! hither, thou loving, all-hoping poet! hither, thou tender, doubting heart, which hast not yet found any place in the world's market fit for thee; any wares which thou couldst buy or sell—so large is thy love and ambition —thine and not theirs is the hour. Smooth thy brow, and hope and love on, for the kind Heaven justifies thee, and the whole world feels that thou art in the right.

We ought to celebrate this hour by expressions of manly joy. Not thanks, not prayer seem quite the highest or truest name for our communication with the infinite —but glad and conspiring reception—reception that becomes giving in its turn, as the receiver is only the All-Giver in part and in infancy. I cannot—nor can any man —speak precisely of things so sublime, but it seems to me the wit of man, his strength, his grace, his tendency, his art, is the grace and the presence of God. It is beyond explanation. When all is said and done, the rapt saint is found the only logician. Not exhortation, not argument becomes our lips, but pæans of joy and praise. But not of adulation: we are too nearly related in the deep of the mind to that we honor. It is God in us which checks the language of petition by a grander thought. In the bottom of the heart it is said; "I am, and by me, O child! this fair body and world of thine stands and grows. I am; all things are mine: and all mine are thine."

The festival of the intellect and the return to its source cast a strong light on the always interesting topics of Man and Nature. We are forcibly reminded of the old want. There is no man; there hath never been. The Intellect still asks that a man may be born. The flame of life flickers feebly in human breasts. We demand of men a richness and universality we do not find. Great men do not content us. It is their solitude, not their force, that makes them conspicuous. There is somewhat indigent and tedious about them. They are poorly tied to one thought. If they are prophets they are egotists; if polite and various they are shallow. How tardily men arrive at any result! how tardily they pass from it to another! The crystal sphere of thought is as concentrical as the geological structure of the globe. As our soils and rocks lie in strata, concentric strata, so do all men's thinkings run laterally, never vertically. Here comes by a great inquisitor with auger and plumb-line, and will bore an Artesian well through our conventions and theories, and pierce to the core of things. But as soon as he probes the crust, behold gimlet, plumb-line, and philosopher take a lateral direction, in spite of all resistance, as if some strong wind took everything off its feet, and if you come month after month to see what progress our reformer has made—not an inch has he pierced—you still find him with new words in the old place, floating about in new parts of the same old vein or crust. The new book says, "I will give you the key to nature," and we expect to go like a thunderbolt to the centre. But the thunder is a surface phenomenon, makes a skin-deep cut, and so does the sage. The wedge turns out to be a rocket. Thus a man lasts but a very little while, for his monomania becomes insupportably tedious in a few months. It is so with every book and person: and yet—and yet—we do not take up a new book or meet a new man without a pulse-beat of expectation. And this invincible hope of a more adequate interpreter is the sure prediction of his advent.

In the absence of man, we turn to nature, which stands next. In the divine order, intellect is primary; nature, secondary; it is the memory of the mind. That which once existed in intellect as pure law, has now taken body as Nature. It existed already in the mind in solution; now, it has been precipitated, and the bright sediment is the world. We can never be quite strangers or inferiors in nature. It is flesh of our flesh, and bone of our bone. But we no longer hold it by the hand; we have lost our miraculous power; our arm is no more as strong as the frost, nor our will equivalent to gravity and the elective attractions. Yet we can use nature as a convenient standard, and the meter of our rise and fall. It has this advantage as a witness, it cannot be debauched. When man curses, nature still testifies to truth and love. We may therefore safely study the mind in nature, because we cannot steadily gaze on it in mind; as we explore the face of the sun in a pool, when our eyes cannot brook his direct splendors.

It seems to me therefore that it were some suitable pæan if we should piously celebrate this hour by exploring the *method of nature*. Let us see *that*, as nearly as we can, and try how far it is transferable to the literary life. Every earnest glance we give to the realities around us, with intent to learn, proceeds from a holy impulse, and is really songs of praise. What difference can it make whether it take the shape of exhortation, or of passionate exclamation, or of scientific statement? These are forms merely. Through them we express, at last, the fact that God has done thus or thus.

In treating a subject so large, in which we must necessarily appeal to the intuition, and aim much more to suggest than to describe, I know it is not easy to speak with the precision attainable on topics of less scope. I do not wish in attempting to paint a man, to describe an air-fed, unimpassioned, impossible ghost. My eyes and ears are revolted by any neglect of the physical facts, the limitations of man. And yet one who conceives the true order of nature, and beholds the visible as proceeding from the invisible, cannot state his thought without seeming to those who study the physical laws to do them some injustice. There is an intrinsic defect in the organ. Language overstates. Statements of the infinite are usually felt to be unjust to the finite, and blasphemous. Empedocles undoubtedly spoke a truth of thought, when he said, "I am God;" but the moment it was out of his mouth it became a lie to the ear; and the world revenged itself for the seeming arrogance by the good story about his shoe. How can I hope for better hap in my attempts to enunciate spiritual facts? Yet let us hope that as far as we receive the truth, so far shall we be felt by every true person to say what is just.

The method of nature: who could ever analyze it? That rushing stream will not stop to be observed. We can never surprise nature in a corner; never find the end of a thread; never tell where to set the first stone. The bird hastens to lay her egg: the egg hastens to be a bird. The wholeness we admire in the order of the world is the result of infinite distribution. Its smoothness is the smoothness of the pitch of the cataract. Its permanence is a perpetual inchoation. Every natural fact is an emanation, and that from which it emanates is an emanation also, and from every emanation is a new emanation. If anything could stand still, it would be crushed and dissipated by the torrent it resisted, and if it were a mind, would be crazed; as insane persons are those who hold fast to one thought and do not flow with the course of nature. Not the cause, but an ever novel effect, nature descends always from above. It is unbroken obedience. The beauty of these fair objects is imported into them from a metaphysical and eternal spring. In all animal and vegetable forms, the physiologist concedes that no chemistry, no mechanics, can account for the facts, but a mysterious principle of life must be assumed, which not only inhabits the organ but makes the organ.

How silent, how spacious, what room for all, yet without place to insert an atom—in graceful succession, in equal fulness, in balanced beauty, the dance of the hours goes forward still. Like an odor of incense, like a strain of music, like a sleep, it is inexact and boundless. It will not be dissected, nor unravelled, nor shown. Away profane philosopher! seekest thou in nature the cause? This refers to that, and that to the next, and the next to the third, and everything refers. Thou must ask in another mood, thou must feel it and love it, thou must behold it in a spirit as grand as that by which it exists, ere thou canst know the law. Known it will not be, but gladly beloved and enjoyed.

The simultaneous life throughout the whole body, the equal serving of innumerable ends without the least emphasis or preference to any, but the steady degradation of each to the success of all, allows the understanding no place to work. Nature can only be conceived as existing to a universal and not to a particular end; to a universe of ends, and not to one—a work of *ecstasy*, to be represented by a circular movement, as intention might be signified by a straight line of definite length. Each effect strengthens every other. There is no revolt in all the kingdoms from the commonweal; no detachment of an individual. Hence the catholic character which makes every leaf an exponent of the world. When we behold the landscape in a poetic spirit, we do not reckon individuals. Nature knows neither palm nor oak, but only vegetable life, which sprouts into forests, and festoons the globe with a garland of grasses and vines.

That no single end may be selected and nature judged thereby, appears from this, that if man himself be considered as the end, and it be assumed that the final cause of the world is to make holy or wise or beautiful men, we see that it has not succeeded. Read alternately in natural and in civil history, a treatise of astronomy, for example, with a volume of French *Mémoires pour servir*. When we have spent our wonder in computing this wasteful hospitality with which boon Nature turns off new firmaments without end into her wide common, as fast as the madrepores make coral—suns and planets hospitable to souls—and then shorten the sight to look into this court of Louis Quatorze, and see the game that is played there—duke and marshal, abbé and madame—a gambling table where each is laying traps for the other, where the end is ever by some lie or fetch to outwit your rival and ruin him with this solemn fop in wig and stars—the king —one can hardly help asking if this planet is a fair specimen of the so generous astronomy, and if so, whether the experiment have not failed, and whether it be quite worth while to make more, and glut the innocent space with so poor an article.

I think we feel not much otherwise if, instead of beholding foolish nations, we take the great and wise men, the eminent souls, and narrowly inspect their biography. None of them seen by himself, and his performance compared with his promise or idea, will justify the cost of that enormous apparatus of means by which this spotted and defective person was at last procured.

To questions of this sort, Nature replies, "I grow." All is nascent, infant. When we are dizzied with the arithmetic of the savant toiling to compute the length of her line, the return of her curve, we are steadied by the perception that a great deal is doing; that all seems just begun: remote aims are in active accomplishment. We can point nowhere to anything final; but tendency appears on all hands: planet, system, constellation, total nature is growing like a field of maize in July; is becoming somewhat else; is in rapid metamorphosis. The embryo does not more strive to be man, than yonder burr of light we call a nebula tends to be a ring, a comet, a globe, and parent of new stars. Why should not then these messieurs of Versailles strut and plot for tabourets and ribbons, for a season, without prejudice to their faculty to run on better errands by and by?

But Nature seems further to reply, "I have ventured so great a stake as my success, in no single creature. I have not yet arrived at any end. The gardener aims to produce a fine peach or pear, but my aim is the health of the whole tree—root, stem, leaf, flower, and seed—and by no means the pampering of a monstrous pericarp at the expense of all the other functions."

In short, the spirit and peculiarity of that impression nature makes on us is this, that it does not exist to any one or to any number of particular ends, but to numberless and endless benefit; that there is in it no private will, no rebel leaf or limb, but the whole is oppressed by one superincumbent tendency, obeys that redundancy or excess of life which in conscious beings we call *ecstasy*.

With this conception of the genius or method of nature, let us go back to man. It is true he pretends to give account of himself to himself, but, at last, what has he to recite but the fact that there is a Life not to be described or known otherwise than by possession? What account can he give of his essence more than *so it was to be?* The *royal* reason, the Grace of God, seems the only description of our multiform but ever identical fact. There is virtue, there is genius, there is success, or there is not. There is the incoming or the receding of God: that is all we can affirm; and we can show neither how nor why. Self-accusation, remorse, and the didactic morals of self-denial and strife with sin, is a view we are constrained by our constitution to take of the fact seen from the platform of action; but seen from the platform of intellection there is nothing for us but praise and wonder.

The termination of the world in a man appears to be the last victory of intelligence. The universal does not attract us until housed in an individual. Who heeds the waste abyss of possibility? The ocean is everywhere the same, but it has no character until seen with the shore or the ship. Who would value any number of miles of Atlantic brine bounded by lines of latitude and longitude? Confine it by granite rocks, let it wash a shore where wise men dwell, and it is filled with expression; and the point of greatest interest is where the land and water meet. So must we admire in man the form of the formless, the concentration of the vast, the house of reason, the cave of memory. See the play of thoughts! what nimble gigantic creatures are these! what saurians, what palalotheria shall be named with these agile movers? The great Pan of old, who was clothed in a leopard skin to signify the beautiful variety of things, and the firmament, his coat of stars—was but the representative of thee, O rich and various Man! thou palace of sight and sound, carrying in thy senses the morning and the night and the unfathomable galaxy; in thy brain, the geometry of the City of God; in thy heart, the bower of love and the realms of right and wrong. An individual man is a fruit which it cost all the foregoing ages to form and ripen. The history of the genesis or the old mythology repeats itself in the experience of every child. He too is a demon or god thrown into a particular chaos, where he strives ever to lead things from disorder into order. Each individual soul is such in virtue of its being a power to translate the world into some particular language of its own; if not into a picture, a statue, or a dance—why, then, into a trade, an art, a science, a mode of living, a conversation, a character, an influence. You admire pictures, but it is as impossible for you to paint a right picture as for grass to bear apples. But when the genius comes, it makes fingers: it is pliancy, and the power of transferring the affair in the street into oils and colors. Raphael must be born, and Salvator must be born.

There is no attractiveness like that of a new man. The sleepy nations are occupied with their political routine. England, France and America read Parliamentary Debates, which no high genius now enlivens; and nobody will read them who trusts his own eye: only they who are deceived by the popular repetition of distinguished names. But when Napoleon unrolls his map, the eye is commanded by original power. When Chatham leads the debate, men may well listen, because they must listen. A man, a personal ascendency, is the only great phenomenon. When Nature has work to be done, she creates a genius to do it. Follow the great man, and you shall see what the world has at heart in these ages. There is no omen like that.

But what strikes us in the fine genius is that which belongs of right to every one. A man should know himself for a necessary actor. A link was wanting between two craving parts of nature, and he was hurled into being as the bridge over that yawning need, the mediator betwixt two else unmarriageable facts. His two parents held each of them one of the wants, and the union of foreign constitutions in his enables him to do gladly and gracefully what the assembled human race could not have sufficed to do. He knows his materials; he applies himself to his work; he cannot read, or think, or look, but he unites the hitherto separated strands into a perfect cord. The thoughts he delights to utter are the reason of his incarnation. Is it for him to account himself cheap and superfluous, or to linger by the wayside for opportunities? Did he not come into being because something must be done which he and no other is and does? If only he *sees*, the world will be visible enough. He need not study where to stand, nor to put things in favorable lights; in him is the light, from him all things are illuminated to their centre. What patron shall he ask for employment and reward? Hereto was he born, to deliver the thought of his heart from the universe to the universe; to do an office which nature could not forego, nor he be discharged from rendering, and then immerge again into the holy silence and eternity out of which as a man he arose. God is rich, and many more men than one he harbors in his bosom, biding their time and the needs and the beauty of all. Is not this the theory of every man's genius or faculty? Why then goest thou as some Boswell or listening worshipper to this saint or to that? That is the only lese-majesty. Here art thou with whom so long the universe travailed in labor; darest thou think meanly of thyself whom the stalwart Fate brought forth to unite his ragged sides, to shoot the gulf, to reconcile the irreconcilable?

Whilst a necessity so great caused the man to exist, his health and erectness consist in the fidelity with which he transmits influences from the vast and universal to the point on which his genius can act. The ends are momentary; they are vents for the current of inward life which increases as it is spent. A man's wisdom is to know that all ends are momentary, that the best end must be superseded by a better. But there is a mischievous tendency in him to transfer his thought from the life to the ends, to quit his agency and rest in his acts: the tools run away with the workman, the human with the divine. I conceive a man as always spoken to from behind, and unable to turn his head and see the speaker. In all the millions who have heard the voice, none ever saw the face. As children in their play run behind each other, and seize one by the ears and make him walk before them, so is the spirit our unseen pilot. That well-known voice speaks in all languages, governs all men, and none ever caught a glimpse of its form. If the man will exactly obey it, it will adopt him, so that he shall not any longer separate it from himself in his thought; he shall seem to be it, he shall be it. If he listen with insatiable ears, richer and greater wisdom is taught him; the sound swells to a ravishing music, he is borne away as with a flood, he becomes careless of his food and of his house, he is the fool of ideas, and leads a heavenly life. But if his eye is set on the things to be done, and not on the truth that is still taught, and for the sake of which the things are to be done, then the voice grows faint, and at last is but a humming in his ears. His health and greatness consist in his being the channel through which heaven flows to earth, in short, in the fulness in which an ecstatical state takes place in him. It is pitiful to be an artist, when by forebearing to be artists we might be vessels filled with the divine overflowings, enriched by the circulations of omniscience and omnipresence. Are there not moments in the history of heaven when the human race was not counted by individuals, but was only the Influenced, was God in distribution, God rushing into multiform benefit? It is sublime to receive, sublime to love, but this lust of imparting as from *us*, this desire to be loved, the wish to be recognized as individuals—is finite, comes of a lower strain.

Shall I say then that as far as we can trace the natural history of the soul, its health consists in the fulness of its reception—call it piety, call it veneration—in fact that enthusiasm is organized therein. What is best in any work of art but that part which the work itself seems to require and do; that which the man cannot do again; that which flows from the hour and the occasion, like the eloquence of men in a tumultuous debate? It was always the theory of literature that the word of a poet was authoritative and final. He was supposed to be the mouth of a divine wisdom. We rather envied his circumstances than his talent. We too could have gladly prophesied standing in that place. We so quote our Scriptures; and the Greeks so quoted Homer, Theognis, Pindar, and the rest. If the theory has receded out of modern criticism, it is because we have not had poets. Whenever they appear, they will redeem their own credit.

This ecstatical state seems to direct a regard to the whole and not to the parts; to the cause and not to the ends; to the tendency and not to the act. It respects genius and not talent; hope, and not possession; the anticipation of all things by the intellect, and not the history itself; art, and not works of art; poetry, and not experiment; virtue, and not duties.

There is no office or function of man but is rightly discharged by this divine method, and nothing that is not noxious to him if detached from its universal relations. Is it his work in the world to study nature, or the laws of the world? Let him beware of proposing to himself any end. Is it for use? nature is debased, as if one looking at the ocean can remember only the price of fish. Or is it for pleasure? he is mocked; there is a certain infatuating air in woods and mountains which draws on the idler to want and misery. There is something social and intrusive in the nature of all things; they seek to penetrate and overpower each the nature of every other creature, and itself alone in all modes and throughout space and spirit to prevail and possess. Every star in heaven is discontented and insatiable. Gravitation and chemistry cannot content them. Ever they woo and court the eye of every beholder. Every man who comes into the world they seek to fascinate and possess, to pass into his mind, for they desire to republish themselves in a more delicate world than that they occupy. It is not enough that they are Jove, Mars, Orion, and the North Star, in the gravitating firmament; they would have such poets as Newton, Herschel and Laplace, that they may re-exist and re-appear in the finer world of rational souls, and fill that realm with their fame. So is it with all immaterial objects. These beautiful basilisks set their brute glorious eyes on the eye of every child, and, if they can, cause their nature to pass through his wondering eyes into him, and so all things are mixed.

Therefore man must be on his guard against this cup of enchantments, and must look at nature with a super-natural eye. By piety alone, by conversing with the cause of nature, is he safe and commands it. And because all knowledge is assimilation to the object of knowledge, as the power or genius of nature is ecstatic, so must its science or the description of it be. The poet must be a rhapsodist; his inspiration a sort of bright casualty; his will in it only the surrender of will to the Universal Power, which will not be seen face to face, but must be received and sympathetically known. It is remarkable that we have, out of the deeps of antiquity in the oracles ascribed to the half fabulous Zoroaster, a statement of this fact which every lover and seeker of truth will recognize. "It is not proper," said Zoroaster, "to understand the Intelligible with vehemence, but if you incline your mind, you will apprehend it: not too earnestly, but bringing a pure and inquiring eye. You will not understand it as when under-standing some particular thing, but with the flower of the mind. Things divine are not attainable by mortals who understand sensual things, but only the light-armed arrive at the summit."

And because ecstasy is the law and cause of nature, therefore you cannot interpret it in too high and deep a sense. Nature represents the best meaning of the wisest man. Does the sunset landscape seem to you the place of Friendship—those purple skies and lovely waters the amphitheatre dressed and garnished only for the exchange of thought and love of the purest souls? It is that. All other meanings which base men have put on it are conjectural and false. You cannot bathe twice in the same river, said Heraclitus; and I add, a man never sees the same object twice: with his own enlargement the object acquires new aspects.

Does not the same law hold for virtue? It is vitiated by too much will. He who aims at progress should aim at an infinite, not at a special benefit. The reforms whose fame now fills the land with Temperance, Anti-Slavery, Non-Resistance, No Government, Equal Labor, fair and generous as each appears, are poor bitter things when prosecuted for themselves as an end. To every reform, in proportion to its energy, early disgusts are incident, so that the disciple is surprised at the very hour of his first triumphs with chagrins, and sickness, and a general distrust; so that he shuns his associates, hates the enterprise which lately seemed so fair, and meditates to cast himself into the arms of that society and manner of life which he had newly abandoned with so much pride and hope. Is it that he attached the value of virtue to some particular practices, as the denial of certain appetites in certain specified indulgences, and afterward found himself still as wicked and as far from happiness in that abstinence as he had been in the abuse? But the soul can be appeased not by a deed but by a tendency. It is in a hope that she feels her wings. You shall love rectitude, and not the disuse of money or the avoidance of trade; an unimpeded mind, and not a monkish diet; sympathy and usefulness, and not hoeing or coopering. Tell me not how great your project is, the civil liberation of the world, its conversion into a Christian church, the establishment of public education, cleaner diet, a new division of labor and of land, laws of love for laws of property—I say to you plainly there is no end to which your practical faculty can aim, so sacred or so large, that, if pursued for itself, will not at last become carrion and an offence to the nostril. The imaginative faculty of the soul must be fed with objects immense and eternal. Your end should be one inapprehensible to the senses; then will it be a god always approached, never touched; always giving health. A man adorns himself with prayer and love, as an aim adorns an action. What is strong but goodness, and what is energetic but the presence of a brave man? The doctrine in vegetable physiology of the *presence,* or the general influence of any substance over and above its chemical influence, as of an alkali or a living plant, is more predicable of man. You need not speak to me, I need not go where you are, that you should exert magnetism on me. Be you only whole and sufficient, and I shall feel you in every part of my life and fortune, and I can as easily dodge the gravitation of the globe as escape your influence.

But there are other examples of this total and supreme influence, besides Nature and the conscience. "From the poisonous tree, the world," say the Brahmins, "two species of fruit are produced, sweet as the waters of life; Love or the society of beautiful souls, and Poetry, whose taste is like the immortal juice of Vishnu." What is Love, and why is it the chief good, but because it is an overpowering enthusiasm? Never self-possessed or prudent, it is all abandonment. Is it not certain admirable wisdom, preferable to all other advantages, and whereof all others are only secondaries and indemnities, because this is that in which the individual is no longer his own foolish master, but inhales an odorous and celestial air, is wrapped round with awe of the object, blending for the time that object with the real and only good, and consults every omen in nature with tremulous interest? When we speak truly—is not he only unhappy who is not in love? his fancied freedom and self-rule—is it not so much death? He who is in love is wise and is becoming wiser, sees newly every time he looks at the object beloved, drawing from it with his eyes and his mind those virtues which it possesses. Therefore if the object be not itself a living and expanding soul, he presently exhausts it. But the love remains in his mind, and the wisdom it brought him; and it craves a new and higher object. And the reason why all men honor love is because it looks up and not down; aspires and not despairs.

And what is Genius but finer love, a love impersonal, a love of the flower and perfection of things, and a desire to draw a new picture or copy of the same? It looks to the cause and life: it proceeds from within outward, whilst Talent goes from without inward. Talent finds its models, methods, and ends, in society, exists for exhibition, and goes to the soul only for power to work. Genius is its own end, and draws its means and the style of its architecture from within, going abroad only for audience and spectator, as we adapt our voice and phrase to the distance and character of the ear we speak to. All your learning of all literatures would never enable you to anticipate one of its thoughts or expressions, and yet each is natural and familiar as household words. Here about us coils forever the ancient enigma, so old and so unutterable. Behold! there is the sun, and the rain, and the rocks; the old sun, the old stones. How easy were it to describe all this fitly; yet no word can pass. Nature is a mute, and man, her articulate, speaking brother, lo! he also is a mute. Yet when Genius arrives, its speech is like a river; it has no straining to describe, more than there is straining in nature to exist. When thought is best, there is most of it. Genius sheds wisdom like perfume, and advertises us that it flows out of a deeper source than the foregoing silence, that it knows so deeply and speaks so musically, because it is itself a mutation of the thing it describes. It is sun and moon and wave and fire in music, as astronomy is thought and harmony in masses of matter.

What is all history but the work of ideas, a record of the incomputable energy which his infinite aspirations infuse into man? Has anything grand and lasting been done? Who did it? Plainly not any man, but all men: it was the prevalence and inundation of an idea. What brought the pilgrims here? One man says, civil liberty; another, the desire of founding a church; and a third discovers that the motive force was plantation and trade. But if the Puritans could rise from the dust they could not answer. It is to be seen in what they were, and not in what they designed; it was the growth and expansion of the human race, and resembled herein the sequent Revolution, which was not begun in Concord, or Lexington, or Virginia, but was the overflowing of the sense of natural right in every clear and active spirit of the period. Is a man boastful and knowing, and his own master—we turn from him without hope: but let him be filled with awe and dread before the Vast and the Divine, which uses him glad to be used, and our eye is riveted to the chain of events. What a debt is ours to that old religion which, in the childhood of most of us, still dwelt like a sabbath morning in the country of New England, teaching privation, self-denial and sorrow! A man was born not for prosperity, but to suffer for the benefit of others, like the noble rock-maple which all around our villages bleeds for the service of man. Not praise, not men's acceptance of our doing, but the spirit's holy errand through us absorbed the thought. How dignified was this! How all that is called talents and success, in our noisy capitals, becomes buzz and din before this man-worthiness! How our friendships and the complaisances we use, shame us now! Shall we not quit our companions, as if they were thieves and pot-companions, and betake ourselves to some desert cliff of Mount Katahdin, some unvisited recess in Moosehead Lake, to bewail our innocency and to recover it, and with it the power to communicate again with these sharers of a more sacred idea?

And what is to replace for us the piety of that race? We cannot have theirs; it glides away from us day by day; but we also can bask in the great morning which rises forever out of the eastern sea, and be ourselves the children of the light. I stand here to say, Let us worship the mighty and transcendent Soul. It is the office, I doubt not, of this age to annul that adulterous divorce which the superstition of many ages has effected between the intellect and holiness. The lovers of goodness have been one class, the students of wisdom another; as if either could exist in any purity without the other. Truth is always holy, holiness always wise. I will that we keep terms with sin and a sinful literature and society no longer, but live a life of discovery and performance. Accept the intellect, and it will accept us. Be the lowly ministers of that pure omniscience, and deny it not before men. It will burn up all profane literature, all base current opinions, all the false powers of the world, as in a moment of time. I draw from nature the lesson of an intimate divinity. Our health and reason as men need our respect to this fact, against the heedlessness and against the contradiction of society. The sanity of man needs the poise of this immanent force. His nobility needs the assurance of this inexhaustible reserved power. How great soever have been its bounties, they are a drop to the sea whence they flow. If you say, "The acceptance of the vision is also the act of God:"—I shall not seek to penetrate the mystery, I admit the force of what you say. If you ask, "How can any rules be given for the attainment of gifts so sublime?" I shall only remark that the solicitations of this spirit, as long as there is life, are never forborne. Tenderly, tenderly, they woo and court us from every object in nature, from every fact in life, from every thought in the mind. The one condition coupled with the gift of truth is its use. That man shall be learned who reduceth his learning to practice. Emanuel Swedenborg affirmed that it was opened to him "that the spirits who knew truth in this life, but did it not, at death shall lose their knowledge." "If knowledge," said Ali the Caliph, "calleth unto practice, well; if not, it goeth away." The only way into nature is to enact our best insight. Instantly we are higher poets, and can speak a deeper law. Do what you know, and perception is converted into character, as islands and continents were built by invisible infusories, or as these forest leaves absorb light, electricity, and volatile gases, and the gnarled oak to live a thousand years is the arrest and fixation of the most volatile and ethereal currents. The doctrine of this Supreme Presence is a cry of joy and exultation. Who shall dare think he has come late into nature, or has missed anything excellent in the past, who seeth the admirable stars of possibility, and the yet untouched continent of hope glittering with all its mountains in the vast West? I praise with wonder this great reality, which seems to drown all things in the deluge of its light. What man seeing this, can lose it from his thoughts, or entertain a meaner subject? The entrance of this into his mind seems to be the birth of man. We cannot describe the natural history of the soul, but we know that it is divine. I cannot tell if these wonderful qualities which house to-day in this mortal frame shall ever re-assemble in equal activity in a similar frame, or whether they have before had a natural history like that of this body you see before you; but this one thing I know, that these qualities did not now begin to exist, cannot be sick with my sickness, nor buried in any grave; but that they circulate through the Universe: before the world was, they were. Nothing can bar them out, or shut them in, but they penetrate the ocean and land, space and time, form an essence, and hold the key to universal nature. I draw from this faith courage and hope. All things are known to the soul. It is not to be surprised by any communication. Nothing can be greater than it. Let those fear and those fawn who will. The soul is in her native realm, and it is wider than space, older than time, wide as hope, rich as love. Pusillanimity and fear she refuses with a beautiful scorn; they are not for her who puts on her coronation robes, and goes out through universal love to universal power.

2. HENRY DAVID THOREAU, 1817–1862

[Henry Thoreau was born in Concord. Amid the literary community, he was the only "native" of the village. He grew up there, the son of a modest pencil-maker, went to Harvard College where he graduated without distinction in 1837. Thus Emerson, moving into the town as already the invested leader of the Transcendental insurgence, was in a position to encourage the young genius he found on his doorstep. Wherefore, to most contemporaries, Thoreau figured as Emerson's hired man and his literary echo; he could be accused by James Russell Lowell of stealing neighbor Emerson's apples. Wherefore, also, Henry was obliged to fight for his life against the pontifical benevolence of the Seer.

Working as pencil-maker and surveyor only to the extent necessary to keep himself clothed and fed, and that in the utmost of simplicity, Thoreau expended his large margin of ascetic leisure as "self-appointed inspector of snow storms." Endlessly trudging over all hills, meadows, swamps, within walking-distance of Concord, in every sort of weather, he fashioned his life into the supreme exemplification of Transcendental egotism.

By the most sober reckoning, Thoreau put on paper about two million words. All Transcendentalists kept accounts of their spiritual fluctuations—just as did their Puritan forbears—but none so meticulously, or with more conscious artistry, than Henry Thoreau. In his first full-fledged essay in *The Dial*, for July, 1842, he advanced the proposition—whether then he fully comprehended its drastic import may be questioned—which was thenceforth to dictate his career: "Let us not underrate the value of a fact; it will one day flower in a truth." So, he made his *Journal* first of all a voluminous record of fact; in his last years, when his energies were flagging, pages upon pages are nothing but a tedious chronicle of natural phenomena. And yet, in occasional passages, the *Journal* flowers so exquisitely as to become a refutation of its prevailing argument: the facts are there, but they blossom into generalization by a cunningly contrived persuasion. Out of unrelenting observation of nature and of himself emerge these —if I may so term them—sonatas. But the point is that they are, for all that they present themselves as spontaneous renditions of the scene, sophisticated manipulations of the landscape and the mood. In every one of these set pieces, presumably re-worked from notes taken in the field, there is an irony barely concealed (angrily blurted out in the Christmas passage of 1851): the reiterated insight that an assiduous observation of Nature throws him who would most suppress his own self back upon an even more acute sense of his own identity, of his utter uniqueness. We are bound to ask, as Thoreau was insistently asking, is *this* "the method of nature"?

The titles I have given these four selections are, of course, my own devising.]

JOURNAL

Hymn to the August Morn

August 12 [1851]. *Tuesday.* 1:30 A.M.—Full moon.

Arose and went to the river and bathed, stepping very carefully not to disturb the household, and still carefully in the street not to disturb the neighbors. I did not walk naturally and freely till I had got over the wall.

Then to Hubbard's Bridge at 2 A.M. There was a whippoor-will in the road just beyond Goodwin's, which flew up and lighted on the fence and kept alighting on the fence within a rod of me and circling round me with a slight squeak as if inquisitive about me. I do not remember what I observed or thought in coming hither.

The traveller's whole employment is to calculate what cloud will obscure the moon and what she will triumph over. In the after-midnight hours the traveller's sole companion is the moon. All his thoughts are centred in her. She is waging continual war with the clouds in his behalf. What cloud will enter the lists with her next, this employs his thoughts; and when she enters on a clear field of great extent in the heavens, and shines unobstructedly, he is glad. And when she has fought her way through all the squadrons of her foes, and rides majestic in a clear sky, he cheerfully and confidently pursues his way, and rejoices in his heart.

But if he sees that she has many new clouds to contend with, he pursues his way moodily, as one disappointed and aggrieved; he resents it as an injury to himself. It is his employment to watch the moon, the companion and guide of his journey, wading through clouds, and calculate what one is destined to shut out her cheering light. He traces her course, now almost completely obscured, through the ranks of her foes, and calculates where she will issue from them. He is disappointed and saddened when he sees that she has many clouds to contend with.

Sitting on the sleepers of Hubbard's Bridge, which is being repaired, now, 3 o'clock A.M., I hear a cock crow. How admirably adapted to the dawn is that sound! As if made by the first rays of light rending the darkness, the creaking of the sun's axle heard already over the eastern hills.

Though man's life is trivial and handselled, Nature is holy and heroic. With what infinite faith and promise and

moderation begins each new day! It is only a little after
3 o'clock, and already there is evidence of morning in the
sky.

He rejoices when the moon comes forth from the
squadrons of the clouds unscathed and there are no more
any obstructions in her path, and the cricket also seems to
express joy in his song. It does not concern men who are
asleep in their beds, but it is very important to the
traveller, whether the moon shines bright and unobstructed or is obscured by clouds. It is not easy to realize
the serene joy of all the earth when the moon commences
to shine unobstructedly, unless you have often been a
traveller by night.

The traveller also resents it if the wind rises and rustles
the leaves or ripples the water and increases the coolness
at such an hour.

A solitary horse in his pasture was scared by the sudden
sight of me, an apparition to him, standing still in the
moonlight, and moved about, inspecting with alarm, but
I spoke and he heard the sound of my voice; he was at
once reassured and expressed his pleasure by wagging
his stump of a tail, though still half a dozen rods off. How
wholesome the taste of huckleberries, when now by moonlight I feel for them amid the bushes!

And now the first signs of morning attract the traveller's
attention, and he cannot help rejoicing, and the moon
begins gradually to fade from his recollection. The wind
rises and rustles the copses. The sand is cool on the surface
but warm two or three inches beneath, and the rocks
are quite warm to the hand, so that he sits on them or
leans against them for warmth, though indeed it is not
cold elsewhere. As I walk along the side of Fair Haven
Hill, I see a ripple on the river, and now the moon has
gone behind a large and black mass of clouds, and I realize that I may not see her again in her glory this night,
that perchance ere she rises from this obscurity, the sun
will have risen, and she will appear but as a cloud herself,
and sink unnoticed into the west (being a little after full).
As yet no sounds of awakening men; only the more fre-
quent crowing of cocks, still standing on their perches

in the barns. The milkmen are the earliest risers—though I see no lanthorns carried to their barns in the distance—preparing to carry the milk of cows in their tin cans for men's breakfasts, even those who dwell in distant cities. In the twilight now, by the light of the stars alone, the moon being concealed, they are pressing the bounteous streams from full udders into their milk-pails, and the sound of the streaming milk is all that breaks the sacred stillness of the dawn; distributing their milk to such as have no cows. I perceive no mosquitoes now. Are they vespertinal, like the singing of the whip-poor-will? I see the light of the obscured moon reflected from the river brightly. With what mild emphasis Nature marks the spot—so bright and serene a sheen that does not more contrast with the night.

4 A.M.—It adds a charm, a dignity, a glory, to the earth to see the light of the moon reflected from her streams. There are but us three, the moon, the earth which wears this jewel (the moon's reflection) in her crown, and myself. Now there has come round the Cliff (on which I sit), which faces the west, all unobserved and mingled with the dusky sky of night, a lighter and more ethereal living blue, whispering of the sun still far, far away, behind the horizon. From the summit of our atmosphere, perchance, he may already be seen by soaring spirits that inhabit those thin upper regions, and they communicate the glorious intelligence to us lower ones. The real *divine*, the heavenly, blue, the Jove-containing air, it is, I see through this dusky lower stratum. The sun gilding the summits of the air. The broad artery of light flows over all the sky. Yet not without sadness and compassion I reflect that I shall not see the moon again in her glory. (Not far from four, still in the night, I heard a nighthawk squeak and *boom*, high in the air, as I sat under the Cliff. What is said about this being less of a night bird than the whip-poor-will is perhaps to be questioned. For neither do I remember to have heard the whip-poor-will *sing* at 12 o'clock, though I met one sitting and flying between two and three this morning. I believe that both may be heard at midnight, though very rarely.) Now at *very earliest* dawn

the nighthawk booms and the whip-poor-will sings. Returning down the hill by the path to where the woods [are]
cut off, I see the signs of the day, the morning red. There
is the lurid morning star, soon to be blotted out by a cloud.

There is an early redness in the east which I was not
prepared for, changing to amber or saffron, with clouds beneath in the horizon and also above this clear streak.

The birds utter a few languid and yawning notes, as if
they had not left their perches, so sensible to light to wake
so soon—a faint peeping sound from I know not what kind,
a slight, innocent, half-awake sound, like the sounds which
a quiet housewife makes in the earliest dawn. Nature
preserves her innocence like a beautiful child. I hear a
wood thrush even now, long before sunrise, as in the
heat of the day. And the pewee and the catbird and the
vireo, red-eyed? I do not hear—or do not mind, perchance
—the crickets now. Now whip-poor-wills commence to
sing in earnest, considerably *after* the wood thrush. The
wood thrush, that beautiful singer, inviting the day once
more to enter his pine woods. (So you may hear the wood
thrush and whip-poor-will at the same time.) Now go by
two whip-poor-wills, in haste seeking some coverts from
the eye of day. And the bats are flying about on the
edge of the wood, improving the last moments of their
day in catching insects. The moon appears at length, not
yet as a cloud, but with a frozen light, ominous of her
fate. The early cars sound like a wind in the woods. The
chewinks make a business now of waking each other up
with their low *yorrick* in the neighboring low copse. The
sun would have shown before but for the cloud. Now, on
his rising, not the clear sky, but the cheeks of the clouds
high and wide, are tinged with red, which, like the sky
before, turns gradually to saffron and then to the white
light of day.

Henry Thoreau's Christmas Service

December 25 [1851]. *Thursday.* Vlu spruce swamp on
Conantum to hilltop, returning across river over shrub oak
plain to Cliffs.

A wind is now blowing the light snow which fell a day or two ago into drifts, especially on the lee, now the south, side of the walls, the outlines of the drifts corresponding to the chinks in the walls and the eddies of the wind. The snow glides, unperceived for the most part, over the open fields without rising into the air (unless the ground is elevated), until it reaches an opposite wall, which it sifts through and is blown over, blowing off from it like steam when seen in the sun. As it passes through the chinks, it does not drive straight onward, but curves gracefully upwards into fantastic shapes, somewhat like the waves which curve as they break upon the shore; that is, as if the snow that passes through a chink were one connected body, detained by the friction of its lower side. It takes the form of saddles and shells and porringers. It builds up a fantastic alabaster wall behind the first—a snowy sierra. It is wonderful what sharp turrets it builds up—builds up, *i.e.* by accumulation though seemingly by attrition, though the curves upward to a point like the prows of ancient vessels look like sharp carving, or as if the material had been held before the blowpipe. So what was blown up into the air gradually sifts down into the road or field, and forms the slope of the sierra. Astonishingly sharp and thin overhanging eaves it builds, even this dry snow, where it has the least suggestion from a wall or bank—less than a mason ever springs his brick from. This is the architecture of the snow. On high hills exposed to wind and sun, it curls off like the steam from a damp roof in the morning. Such sharply defined forms it takes as if the core had been the flames of gaslights.

I go forth to see the sun set. Who knows how it will set, even half an hour beforehand? whether it will go down in clouds or a clear sky? I feel that it is late when the mountains in the north and the northwest have ceased to reflect the sun. The shadow is not partial but universal.

In a winter day the sun is almost all in all.

I witness a beauty in the form or coloring of the clouds which addresses itself to my imagination, for which you account scientifically to my understanding, but do not so account to my imagination. It is what it suggests and is the symbol of that I care for, and if, by any trick of science, you rob it of its symbolicalness, you do me no service and explain nothing. I, standing twenty miles off, see a crimson cloud in the horizon. You tell me it is a mass of vapor which absorbs all other rays and reflects the red, but that is nothing to the purpose, for this red vision excites me, stirs my blood, makes my thoughts flow, and I have new and indescribable fancies, and you have not touched the secret of that influence. If there is not something mystical in your explanation, something unexplainable to the understanding, some elements of mystery, it is quite insufficient. If there is nothing in it which speaks to my imagination, what boots it? What sort of science is that which enriches the understanding, but robs the imagination? Not merely robs Peter to pay Paul, but takes from Peter more than it ever gives to Paul? That is simply the way in which it speaks to the understanding, and that is the account which the understanding gives of it; but that is not the way it speaks to the imagination, and that is not the account which the imagination gives of it. Just as inadequate to a pure mechanic would be a poet's account of a steam-engine.

If we knew all things thus mechanically merely, should we know anything really?

Springtime Activities

April 2 [1852]. 6 A.M.—To the riverside and Merrick's pasture.

The sun is up. The water on the meadows is perfectly smooth and placid, reflecting the hills and clouds and trees. The air is full of the notes of birds—song sparrows, red-wings, robins (singing a strain), blue-birds—and I hear also a lark—as if all the earth had burst forth into song. The influence of this April morning has reached them, for they live out-of-doors all the night, and there is no danger that they will oversleep themselves such a morning. A few weeks ago, before the birds had come, there came to my mind in the night the twittering sound of birds in the early dawn of a spring morning, a semiprophecy of it, and last night I attended mentally as if I heard the spraylike dreaming sound of the midsummer frog and realized how glorious and full of revelations it was. Expectation may amount to prophecy. The clouds are *white* watery, not such as we had in the winter. I see in this fresh morning the shells left by the muskrats along the shore, and their galleries leading into the meadow, and the bright-red cranberries washed up along the shore in the old water-mark. Suddenly there is a blur on the placid surface of the waters, a rippling mistiness produced, as it were, by a slight morning breeze, and I should be sorry to show it to the stranger now. So is it with our minds.

As a fair day is promised, and the waters are falling, decide to go to the Sudbury meadows with C [hanning], 9 A.M. Started some woodcocks in a wet place in Hi Wheeler's stubble-field. Saw six spotted tortoises (*Emys guttata*), which had crawled to the shore by the side of the Hubbard Bridge causeway. Too late now for the morning influence and inspiration. The birds sing not so earnestly and joyously; there is a blurring ripple on the surface of the lake. How few valuable observations can we make in youth! What if there were united the susceptibility of youth with the discrimination of age? Once I was part and parcel of Nature; now I am observant of her.

What ails the pewee's tail? It is loosely hung, pulsating with life. What means these wag-tail birds? Cats and dogs, too, express some of their life through their tails.

The bridges are a station at this season. They are the most advantageous positions. There I would take up my stand morning and evening, looking over the water.

The Charles Miles Run full and rumbling. The water is the color of ale, here dark-red ale over the yellow sand, there yellowish frothy ale where it tumbles down. Its foam, composed of large white bubbles, makes a kind of arch over the rill, snow white and contrasting with the general color of the stream, while the latter ever runs under it carrying the lower bubbles with it and new ones ever supply their places. At least eighteen inches high, this stationary arch.

I do not remember elsewhere such highly colored water. It drains a swamp near by and is dry the greater part of the year. Course bubbles continually bursting. A striped snake by the spring, and a black one. The grass there is delightfully green while there is no fresh green anywhere else to be seen. It is the most refreshing of all colors. It is what all the meadows will soon be. The color of no flower is so grateful to the eye. Why is the dog black and the grass green? If all the banks were suddenly painted green and spotted with yellow, white, red, blue, purple, etc., we should more fully realize the miracle of the summer's coloring.

Now the snow is off, it is pleasant to visit the sandy bean-fields covered with last year's blue-curls and sorrel and the flakes of arrowhead stone. I love these sandy fields which melt the snows and yield but small crops to the farmer. Saw a striped squirrel in the wall near Lee's. Brigham, the wheelwright, building a boat. At the sight of all this water, men build boats if ever. Are those large scarred roots at the bottom of the brooks now, three inches in diameter, the roots of the pickerel-weed? What vigor! What vitality! The yellow spots of the tortoise (*Emys guttata*) on his dark shell, seen bright through clear water, remind me of flowers, the houstonias, etc., when there are no colors on the land.

Israel Rice's dog stood stock-still so long that I took him at a distance for the end of a bench. He looked much like a fox, and his fur was as soft. Rice was very ready to go with us to his boat, which we borrowed, as soon as he had driven his cow into the barn where her calf was, but she preferred to stay out in the yard this pleasant morning. He was very obliging, persisted, without regard to our suggestions that we could help ourselves, in going with us to his boat, showed us after a larger boat and made no remark on the miserableness of it. Thanks and compliments fell off him like water off a rock. If the king of the French should send him a medal, he would have to look in many dictionaries to know what the sending of a medal meant, and then he would appreciate the abstract fact merely, and it would fail of its intended effect.

Steered across for the oaks opposite the mouth of the Pantry. For a long distance, as we paddle up the river, we hear the two-stanza'd lay of the pewee on the shore—pee-wet, pee-wee, etc. Those are the two obvious facts to eye and ear, the river and the pewee. After coming in sight of Sherman's Bridge, we moored our boat by sitting on a maple twig on the east side, to take a leisurely view of the meadow. The eastern shore here is a fair specimen of New England fields and hills, sandy and barren but agreeable to my eye, covered with withered grass on their rounded slopes and crowned with low reddish bushes, shrub oaks. There is a picturesque group of eight oaks near the shore, and through a thin fringe of wood I see some boys driving home an ox-cartload of hay. I have noticed black oaks within a day or two still covered with oak-balls. In upsetting the boat, which has been newly tarred, I have got some tar on my hands, which imparts to them on the whole an agreeable fragrance. This exercise of the arms and chest after a long winter's stagnation, during which only the legs have labored, this pumping off the Lincolnshire fens, the Haarlem lakes, of wintry fumes and damps and foul blood, is perhaps the greatest value of these paddling excursions. I see, far in the south, the upright black piers of the bridge just rising above the water. They are more conspicuous than the sleepers and rails. The occasional patches of snow on the hillsides are unusually bright by contrast; they are landmarks to steer by.

It appears to me that, to one standing on the heights of philosophy, mankind and the works of man will have sunk out of sight altogether; that man is altogether too much insisted on. The poet says the proper study of mankind is man. I say, study to forget all that; take wider views of the universe. That is the egotism of the race. What is this our childish, gossiping, social literature, mainly in the hands of the publishers? When another poet says the world is too much with us, he means, of course, that man is too much with us. In the promulgated views of man, in institutions, in the common sense, there is narrowness and delusion. It is our weakness that so exaggerates the virtues of philanthropy and charity and makes it the

highest human attribute. The world will sooner or later
tire of philanthropy and all religions based on it mainly.
They cannot long sustain my spirit. In order to avoid de-
lusions, I would fain let man go by and behold a universe
in which man is but as a grain of sand. I am sure that those
of my thoughts which consist, or are contemporaneous,
with social personal connections, however humane, are not
the wisest and widest, most universal. What is the village,
city, State, nation, aye the civilized world, that it should
concern a man so much? The thought of them affects me
in my wisest hours as when I pass a woodchuck's hole. It
is a comfortable place to nestle, no doubt, and we have
friends, some sympathizing ones, it may be, and a hearth,
there; but I have only to get up at midnight, to find them
all slumbering. Look at our literature. What a poor, puny,
social thing, seeking sympathy! The author troubles himself
about his readers—would fain have one before he dies. He
stands too near his printer; he corrects the proofs. Not satisfied with defiling one another in this world, we would all
go to heaven together. To be a good man, that is, a good
neighbor in the widest sense, is but little more than to
be a good citizen. Mankind is a gigantic institution; it
is a community to which most men belong. It is a test I
would apply to my companion—can he forget man? Can
he see this world slumbering?

I do not value any view of the universe into which man
and the institutions of man enter very largely and absorb
much of the attention. Man is but the place where I stand,
and the prospect hence is infinite. It is not a chamber of
mirrors which reflect me. When I reflect, I find that there
is other than me. Man is a past phenomenon to philosophy.
The universe is larger than enough for man's abode. Some
rarely go outdoors, most are always home at night, very
few indeed have stayed out all night once in their lives,
fewer still have gone behind the world of humanity, seen
its institutions like toadstools by the wayside.

Landed on Tall's Island. It is not cold or windy enough,
perchance, for the meadow to make its most serious impression. The staddles, from which the hay has been removed,
rise a foot or two above the water. Large white gulls are

circling over the water. The shore of this meadow lake is quite wild, and in most places low and rather inaccessible to walkers. On the rocky point of this island, where the wind is felt, the waves are breaking merrily, and now for half an hour our dog has been standing in the water under the small swamp white oaks, and ceaselessly snapping at each wave as it broke, as if it were a living creature. He, regardless of cold and wet, thrusts his head into each wave to gripe it. A dog snapping at the waves as they break on a rocky shore. He then rolls himself in the leaves for a napkin. We hardly set out to return, when the water looked sober and rainy. There was more appearance of rain in the water than in the sky—April weather look. And soon we saw the dimples of drops on the surface. I forgot to mention before the cranberries seen on the bottom, as we pushed over the meadows, and the red beds of pitcher-plants.

We landed near a corn-field in the bay on the west side, below Sherman's Bridge, in order to ascend Round Hill, it still raining gently or with drops far apart. From the top we see smoke rising from the green pine hill in the southern part of Lincoln. The steam of the engine looked very white this morning against the oak-clad hillsides. The clouds, the showers, and the breaking away now in the west, all belong to the summer side of the year and remind me of long-past days. The prospect is often best from two thirds the way up a hill, where, looking directly down at the parts of the landscape—the fields and barns—nearest the base, you get the sense of height best, and see how the land slopes up to where you stand. From the top, commonly, you overlook all this, and get a sense of *distance* merely, with a break in the landscape by which the most interesting point is concealed. This hill with its adjuncts is now almost an island, surrounded by broad lakes. The south lakes reflect the most light at present, but the sober surface of the northern is yet more interesting to me.

How novel and original must be each new man's view of the universe! For though the world is so old, and so many books have been written, each object appears wholly undescribed to our experience, each field of thought wholly unexplored. The whole world is an America, a *New World*. The fathers lived in a dark age and throw no light on any of our subjects. The sun climbs to the zenith daily, high over all literature and science. Astronomy, even, concerns us worldlings only, but the sun of poetry and of each new child born into the planet has never been astronomized, nor brought nearer by a telescope. So it will be to the end of time. The end of the world is not yet. Science is young by the ruins of Luxor, unearthing the Sphinx, or Nineveh, or between the Pyramids. The parts of the meadows nearly surrounded by water form interesting peninsulas and promontories.

Return to our boat. We have to go ashore and upset it every half-hour, it leaks so fast, for the leak increases as it sinks in the water in geometrical progression. I see, among the phenomena of spring, here and there a dead sucker floating on the surface, perhaps dropped by a fish hawk or a gull, for the gulls are circling this way overhead to reconnoitre us. They will come sailing overhead to observe us. On making the eastward curve in the river, we find a strong wind against us. Pushing slowly across the meadow in front of the Pantry, the waves beat against the bows and sprinkle the water half the length of the boat. The froth is in long white streaks before the wind, as usual striping the surface.

We land in a steady rain and walk inland by R. Rice's barn, regardless of the storm, toward White Pond. Overtaken by an Irishman in search of work. Discovered some new oaks and pine groves and more New England fields. At last the drops fall wider apart, and we pause in a sandy field near the Great Road of the Corner, where it was agreeably retired and sandy, drinking up the rain. The rain was soothing, so still and sober, gently beating against and amusing our thoughts, swelling the brooks. The robin now peeps with scared note in the heavy overcast air, among the apple trees. The hour is favorable to thought. Such a day I like a sandy road, snows that melt and leave bare the corn and grain fields, with Indian relics shining on them, and prepare the ground for the farmer. Saw a cow or ox in a hollow in the woods, which had been skinned and looked red and striped, like those Italian anatomical preparations. It scared the dog. Went through a reddish andromeda swamp, where still a little icy stiffness in the crust under the woods keeps us from slumping. The rain now turns to snow with large flakes, so soft many cohere in the air as they fall. They make us white as millers and wet us through, yet it is clear gain. I hear a solitary hyla for the first time. At Hubbard's Bridge, count eight ducks going over. Had seen one with outstretched neck over the Great Meadows in Sudbury. Looking up, the flakes are black against the sky. And now the ground begins to whiten. Got home at 5:30 P.M.

How the Winter Is Justified

December 11 [1855]. P.M.—To Holden Swamp, Conantum.

For the first time I wear gloves, but I have not walked *early* this season.

I see no birds, but hear, methinks, one or two tree sparrows. No snow; scarcely any ice to be detected. It is only an aggravated November. I thread the tangle of the spruce swamp, admiring the leaflets of the swamp pyrus which had put forth again, now frost-bitten, the great yellow buds of the swamp-pink, the round red buds of the high blueberry, and the fine sharp red ones of the panicled andromeda. Slowly I worm my way amid the snarl, the thicket of black alders and blueberry, etc.: see the forms, apparently, of rabbits at the foot of maples, and catbirds' nests now exposed in the leafless thicket.

Standing there, though in this *bare* November landscape, I am reminded of the incredible phenomenon of small birds in winter. That ere long, amid the cold powdery snow, as it were a fruit of the season, will come twittering a flock of delicate crimson-tinged birds, lesser redpolls, to sport and feed on the seeds and buds now just ripe for them on the sunny side of a wood, shaking down the

powdery snow there in their cheerful social feeding, as
if it were high midsummer to them. These crimson aerial
creatures have wings which would bear them quickly to
the regions of summer, but here is all the summer they
want. What a rich contrast! tropical colors, crimson
breasts, on cold white snow! Such etherealness, such delicacy in their forms, such ripeness in their colors, in this
stern and barren season! It is as surprising as if you were
to find a brilliant crimson flower which flourished amid
snows. They greet the chopper and the hunter in their
furs. Their Maker gave them the last touch and launched
them forth the day of the Great Snow. He made this
bitter imprisoning cold before which man quails, but
He made at the same time these warm and glowing creatures to twitter and be at home in it. He said not only, Let
there be linnets in winter, but linnets of rich plumage
and pleasing twitter, bearing summer in their natures. The
snow will be three feet deep, the ice will be two feet
thick, and last night, perchance, the mercury sank to
thirty degrees below zero. All the fountains of nature
seem to be sealed up. The traveller is frozen on his way.
But under the edge of yonder birch wood will be a little
flock of crimson-breasted lesser redpolls, busily feeding
on the seeds of the birch and shaking down the powdery
snow! As if a flower were created to be now in bloom, a
peach to be now first fully ripe on its stem. I am struck by
the perfect confidence and success of nature. There is no
question about the existence of these delicate creatures,
their adaptedness to their circumstances. There is super-
added superfluous painting and adornments, a crystalline,
jewel-like health and soundness, like the colors reflected
from ice-crystals.

When some rare northern bird like the pine grosbeak is
seen thus far south in the winter, he does not suggest
poverty, but dazzles us with his beauty. There is in them
a warmth akin to the warmth that melts the icicle. Think
of these brilliant, warm-colored, and richly warbling birds,
birds of paradise, dainty-footed, downy clad, in the midst
of a New England, a Canadian winter. The woods and
fields, now somewhat solitary, being deserted by their

more tender summer residents, are now frequented by these rich but delicately tinted and hardy northern immigrants of the air. Here is no imperfection to be suggested. The winter, with its snow and ice, is not an evil to be corrected. It is as it was designed and made to be, for the artist has had leisure to add beauty to use. My acquaintances, angels from the north. I had a vision thus prospectively of these birds as I stood in the swamps. I saw this familiar—too *familiar*—fact at a different angle, and I was charmed and haunted by it. But I could only attain to be thrilled and enchanted, as by the sound of a strain of music dying away. I had seen into paradisiac regions, with their air and sky, and I was no longer wholly or merely a denizen of this vulgar earth. Yet had I hardly a foothold there. I was only sure that I was charmed, and no mistake. It is only necessary to behold thus the least fact or phenomenon, however familiar, from a point a hair's breadth aside from our habitual path or routine, to be overcome, enchanted by its beauty and significance. Only what we have touched and worn is trivial—our scurf, repetition, tradition, conformity. To perceive freshly, with fresh senses, is to be inspired. Great winter itself looked like a precious gem, reflecting rainbow colors from one angle.

My body is all sentient. As I go here or there, I am tickled by this or that I come in contact with, as if I touched the wires of a battery. I can generally recall—have fresh in my mind—several scratches last received. These I continually recall to mind, reimpress, and harp upon. The age of miracles is each moment thus returned. Now it is wild apples, now river reflections, now a flock of lesser redpolls. In winter, too, resides immortal youth and perennial summer. Its head is not silvered; its cheek is not blanched but has a ruby tinge to it.

If any part of nature excites our pity, it is for ourselves we grieve, for there is eternal health and beauty. We get only transient and partial glimpses of the beauty of the world. Standing at the right angle, we are dazzled by the colors of the rainbow in colorless ice. From the right point of view, every storm and every drop in it is a rainbow. Beauty and music are not mere traits and exceptions. They are the rule and character. It is the exception that we see and hear. Then I try to discover what it was in the vision that charmed and translated me. What if we could daguerreotype our thoughts and feelings! for I am surprised and enchanted often by some quality which I cannot detect. I have seen an attribute of another world and condition of things. It is a wonderful fact that I should be affected, and thus deeply and powerfully, more than by aught else in all my experience—that this fruit should be borne in me, sprung from a seed finer than the spores of fungi, floated from other atmospheres! finer than the dust caught in the sails of vessels a thousand miles from land! Here the invisible seeds settle, and spring, and bear flowers and fruits of immortal beauty.

3. AMOS BRONSON ALCOTT, 1799–1888

[The vagaries of Transcendentalists drew from conservatives, whether Unitarian or Orthodox, in Boston, throughout New England, and indeed in New York or South Carolina, as many hoots of derision as the revolutionary ideas elicited solemn denunciations of heresy and subversion. To the Philistines, no figure more invited ridicule than the gentle, dreamy, abstracted, utterly unworldly Bronson Alcott. Even Emerson, in his historical review, puts his tribute to the "pure idealist" (cf. p. 14) in such equivocal terms that the reader divines behind it that exasperation which Alcott generally inflicted even on those who loved him. And yet, though he took no thought for the morrow, blithely let himself be supported by the labor of his wife, and in his last years basked contentedly in the prosperity brought by his daughter's books, he all the time showed himself a shrewd judge of men, a keen analyst of politics, a competent carpenter (when he chose to be), and in general, while the most sublimely intractable, also the most cheerful and complacent being in the movement.

Alcott was born in rural poverty in Connecticut, had little or no formal schooling, and for four years tramped the muddy roads of Virginia as a Yankee pedlar, where he acquired stately manners. He came to Boston in 1828, and in 1834–37 conducted the Temple School, a radical experiment in education, what we might still call "ultra-progressive." His principle was the Transcendental one, that children are born knowing everything, and need only to have their inner thought "opened out of the soul." This enterprise came to disaster when, in his own account of his method, *Conversations on the Gospels*, he advertised that he not only dealt familiarly with any and every sacred subject but drew out of his pupils their natural and uninhibited views about procreation and birth.

Thereafter he conducted conversations, tried to set up his own Utopian community at Fruitlands, and otherwise lived on the charity of admirers until Louisa May took over.

To the first volume of *The Dial* (July, 1840) he contributed his mite in the form of fifty "Orphic Sayings." To later numbers he gave another three installments. These aroused almost universal laughter. A Boston wit called them "a train of fifteen coaches going by, with only one passenger." In fact, jokes about them became *The Dial's* one effective form of publicity. Since even to good Transcendentalists, especially to so masculine a one as Theodore Parker, "Orphic Sayings" seemed vacuous, we may content ourselves with a few examples. Of course, poor Alcott simply could not write. But that never worried him. He kept an immense *Journal*, and lived as an equal with such cosmic minds as Goethe, Coleridge, Plato and Plotinus, trusting that somehow clothing and food would be supplied him, as proved to be the case. Alcott raised a family, lectured, smiled, watched the procession, and remained always a fresh, inquisitive, untarnished intellect.]

ORPHIC SAYINGS

I

Thou art, my heart, a soul-flower, facing ever and following the motions of thy sun, opening thyself to her vivifying

ray, and pleading thy affinity with the celestial orbs.
Thou dost

> the livelong day
> Dial on time thine own eternity.

II. Enthusiasm

Believe, youth, that your heart is an oracle; trust her
instinctive auguries, obey her divine leadings; nor listen
too fondly to the uncertain echoes of your head. The
heart is the prophet of your soul, and ever fulfils her
prophecies; reason is her historian; but for the prophecy
the history would not be. Great is the heart: cherish her;
she is big with the future, she forebodes renovations. Let
the flame of enthusiasm fire alway your bosom. Enthusiasm
is the glory and hope of the world. It is the life of sanctity
and genius; it has wrought all miracles since the beginning
of time.

III. Hope

Hope deifies man; it is the apotheosis of the soul; the
prophecy and fulfilment of her destinies. The nobler her
aspirations, the sublimer her conceptions of the Godhead.
As the man, so his God: God is his idea of excellence; the
complement of his own being.

IV. Immortality

The grander my conception of being, the nobler my
future. There can be no sublimity of life without faith in
the soul's eternity. Let me live superior to sense and custom, vigilant alway, and I shall experience my divinity;
my hope will be infinite, nor shall the universe contain,
or content me. But if I creep daily from the haunts of
an ignoble past, like a beast from his burrow, neither
earth nor sky, man nor God shall appear desirable or
glorious; my life shall be loathsome to me, my future

reflect my fears. He alone, who lives nobly, oversees his own being, believes all things, and partakes of the eternity of God.

V. *Vocation*

Engage in nothing that cripples or degrades you. Your first duty is self-culture, self-exultation: you may not violate this high trust. Your self is sacred, profane it not. Forge no chains wherewith to shackle your own members. Either subordinate your vocation to your life, or quit it forever: it is not for you; it is condemnation of your own soul. Your influence on others is commensurate with the strength that you have found in yourself. First cast the demons from your own bosom, and then shall your word exorcise them from the hearts of others.

VI. *Sensualism*

He who marvels at nothing, who feels nothing to be mysterious, but must needs bare all things to sense, lacks both wisdom and piety. Miracle is the mantle in which these venerable natures wrap themselves, and he, who seeks curiously to rend this asunder, profanes their sacred countenance to enter by stealth into the Divine presence. Sanctity, like God, is ever mysterious, and all devout souls reverence her. A wonderless age is godless: an age of reverence, an age of piety and wisdom.

VII. *Spiritualism*

Piety is not scientific; yet embosoms the facts that reason develops in scientific order to the understanding. Religion, being a sentiment, is science yet in synthetic relations; truth yet undetached from love; thought not yet severed from action. For every fact that eludes the analysis of reason, conscience affirms its root in the supernatural. Every synthetic fact is supernatural and miraculous. Analysis by detecting its law resolves it into science, and renders it a fact of the understanding. Divinely seen, natural facts are symbols of spiritual laws. Miracles are of the heart; not of the head; indigenous to the soul; not freaks of nature, not growths of history. God, man, nature, are miracles.

VIII. Mysticism

Because the soul is herself mysterious, the saint is a mystic to the worldling. He lives to the soul; he partakes of her properties, he dwells in her atmosphere of light and hope. But the worldling, living to sense, is identified with the flesh; he dwells amidst the dust and vapors of his own lusts, which dim his vision, and obscure the heavens wherein the saint beholds the face of God.

IX. Aspiration

The insatiableness of her desires is an augury of the soul's eternity. Yearning for satisfaction, yet ever balked of it from temporal things, she still prosecutes her search for it, and her faith remains unshaken amidst constant disappointments. She would breathe life, organize light; her hope is eternal; a never-ending, still-beginning quest of the Godhead in her own bosom; a perpetual effort to actualize her divinity in time. Intact, aspirant, she feels the appulses of both spiritual and material things; she would appropriate the realm she inherits by virtue of her incarnation: infinite appetencies direct all her members on finite things; her vague strivings, and Cyclopean motions, confess an aim beyond the confines of transitory natures; she is quivered with heavenly desires: her quarry is above the stars: her arrows are snatched from the armory of heaven. . . .

XV. Identity and Diversity

It is the perpetual effort of conscience to divorce the soul from the dominion of sense; to nullify the dualities of the apparent, and restore the intuition of the real. The soul makes a double statement of all her facts; to conscience and sense; reason mediates between the two. Yet though double to sense, she remains single and one in herself; one in conscience, many in understanding; one in life, diverse in function and number. Sense, in its infirmity, breaks this unity to apprehend in part what it cannot grasp at once. Understanding notes diversity; conscience alone divines unity, and integrates all experience in identity of spirit. Number is predicable of body alone; not of spirit. . . .

XVII. Theocracy

In the theocracy of the soul majorities do not rule. God and the saints; against them the rabble of sinners, with clamorous voices and uplifted hand, striving to silence the oracle of the private heart. Beelzebub marshals majorities. Prophets and reformers are alway special enemies of his and his minions. Multitudes ever lie. Every age is a Judas, and betrays its Messiahs into the hands of the multitude. The voice of the private, not popular heart, is alone authentic. . . .

XXI. Originality

Most men are on the ebb; but now and then a man comes riding down sublimely in high hope from God on the flood tide of the soul, as she sets into the coasts of time, submerging old landmarks, and laying waste the labors of centuries. A new man wears channels broad and deep into the banks of the ages; he washes away the ancient boundaries, and sets afloat institutions, creeds, usages, which clog the ever-flowing Present, stranding them on the shores of the Past. Such deluge is the harbinger of a new world, a renovated age. Hope builds an ark; the dove broods over the assuaged waters; the bow of promise gilds the east; the world is again repeopled and replanted. Yet the sons of genius alone venture into the ark: while most pass rather down the sluggish stream of usage into the turbid pool of oblivion. Thitherward the retreating tide rolls, and wafted by the gales of inglorious ease, or urged by the winds of passion, they glide down the Lethean waters, and are not. Only the noble and heroic outlive in time their exit from it. . . .

XLVIII. Beauty

All departures from perfect beauty are degradations of the divine image. God is the one type, which the soul strives to incarnate in all organizations. Varieties are historical: the one form embosoms all forms; all having a common likeness at the base of difference. Human heads are images, more or less perfect, of the soul's or God's head. But the divine features do not fix in flesh; in the coarse and brittle clay. Beauty is fluent; art of highest order represents her always in flux, giving fluency and motion to bodies solid and immovable to sense. The line of beauty symbolizes motion.

L. Prometheus

Know, O man, that your soul is the Prometheus, who, receiving the divine fires, builds up this majestic statue of clay, and moulds it in the deific image, the pride of gods, the model and analogon of all forms. He chiselled that godlike brow, arched those mystic temples from whose fanes she herself looks forth, formed that miraculous globe above, and planted that sylvan grove below; graved those massive blades yoked in armed powers; carved that heaven-containing bosom, wreathed those puissant thighs, and hewed those stable columns, diffusing over all the grandeur, the grace of his own divine lineaments, and delighting in this cunning work of his hand. Mar not its beauty, spoil not its symmetry, by the deforming lines of lust and sin: dethroning the divinity incarnated therein, and transforming yourself into the satyr and the beast.

4. AMOS BRONSON ALCOTT, 1799–1888

[Since, as I suppose is evident, for the average reader a little bit of "Orphic Sayings" goes a long way (though I suggest that even among these few one can note curious twists of phrase which, despite the general ineptitude, show that Alcott did have an original mind), we may interrupt the flow, and turn to his *Journal*. Thanks to a recent selection from the ponderous tomes made by Odell Shepard (1938), students are aware that they do contain much wisdom and even some wit. For our purpose we may prefer to look at two sections, made up of several entries, which he put together for a little book in 1872, entitled *Concord Days*. Here he evaluates the two major writers in the movement, both of whom he knew as intimately as did anyone. Because the Transcendentalists, once they descended from the empyrean of ideas to this mundane sphere, were not novelists or dramatists, they were apt to say many of their best things, to declare most cogently what they were attempting, when writing about each other. In this respect, they are astonishingly similar to more cosmopolitan fellowships.]

THOREAU AND EMERSON

Outlook

One's outlook is a part of his virtue. Does it matter nothing to him what objects accost him whenever he glances from his windows, or steps out-of-doors? He who is so far weaned from the landscape, or indifferent to it, as not to derive a sweet and robust habit of character therefrom, seems out of keeping with nature and himself. I suspect something amiss in him who has no love, no enthusiasm for his surroundings, and that his friendships, if such he profess, are of a cold and isolate quality at best; one even questions, at times, whether the residents of cities, where art has thrown around them a world of its own, are compensated by all this luxury of display—to say nothing of the social artifices wont to steal into their costly compliments—for the simple surroundings of the countryman, which prompt to manliness and true gentility. A country dwelling without shrubbery, hills near or in the distance, a forest and water view, if but a rivulet, seems so far incomplete as if the occupants themselves were raw and impoverished. Wood and water god both, man loves to traverse the forests, wade the streams, and confess his kindred alliance with primeval things. He leaps not from the woods into civility at a single bound, neither comes from cities and conversations freed from the wildness of his dispositions. Something of the forester stirs within him when occasion provokes, as if men were trees transformed, and delighted to claim their affinities with their sylvan ancestry.

> Man never tires of Nature's scene,
> Himself the liveliest evergreen.

Thoreau

My friend and neighbor united these qualities of sylvan and human in a more remarkable manner than any whom it has been my happiness to know. Lover of the wild, he lived a borderer on the confines of civilization, jealous of the least encroachment upon his possessions. . . .

The most welcome of companions was this plain countryman. One seldom meets with thoughts like his, coming so scented of mountain and field breezes and rippling springs, so like a luxuriant clod from under forest leaves, moist and mossy with earth-spirits. His presence was tonic, like ice-water in dog-days to the parched citizen pent in chambers and under brazen ceilings. Welcome as the gurgle of brooks and dipping of pitchers—then drink and be cool! He seemed one with things, of Nature's essence and core, knit of strong timbers—like a wood and its inhabitants. There was in him sod and shade, wilds and waters manifold—the mould and mist of earth and sky. Self-poised and sagacious as any denizen of the elements, he had the key to every animal's brain, every plant; and were an Indian to flower forth and reveal the scents hidden in his cranium, it would not be more surprising than the speech of our Sylvanus. He belonged to the Homeric age —was older than pastures and gardens, as if he were of the race of heroes and one with the elements. He of all men seemed to be the native New-Englander, as much so as the oak, the granite ledge; our best sample of an indigenous American, untouched by the old country, unless he came down rather from Thor, the Northman, whose name he bore.

A peripatetic philosopher, and out-of-doors for the best part of his days and nights, he had manifold weather and seasons in him; the manners of an animal of probity and virtue unstained. Of all our moralists, he seemed the wholesomest, the busiest, and the best republican citizen in the world; always at home minding his own affairs. A little over-confident by genius, and stiffly individual, dropping society clean out of his theories, while standing friendly in his strict sense of friendship, there was in him an integrity and love of justice that made possible and actual the virtues of Sparta and the Stoics—all the more welcome in his time of shuffling and pusillanimity. Plutarch would have made him immortal in his pages had he lived before his day. Nor have we any so modern withal, so entirely his own and ours: too purely so to be appreciated at once. A scholar by birthright, and an author, his fame had not, at his decease, travelled far from the banks of the rivers he described in his books; but one hazards only the truth in affirming of his prose, that in substance and pith, it surpasses that of any naturalist of his time; and he is sure of large reading in the future.

There are fairer fishes in his pages than any swimming in our streams; some sleep of his on the banks of the Merrimack by moonlight that Egypt never rivalled; a morning of which Memnon might have envied the music, and a greyhound he once had, meant for Adonis; frogs, better than any of Aristophanes'; apples wilder than Adam's. His senses seemed double, giving him access to secrets not easily read by others; in sagacity resembling that of the beaver, the bee, the dog, the deer; an instinct for seeing and judging, as by some other, or seventh sense; dealing with objects as if they were shooting forth from his mind mythologically, thus completing the world all round to his senses; a creation of his at the moment.

I am sure he knew the animals one by one, as most else knowable in his town; the plants, the geography, as Adam did in his Paradise, if, indeed, he were not that ancestor himself. His works are pieces of exquisite sense, celebrations of Nature's virginity exemplified by rare learning, delicate art, replete with observations as accurate as original; contributions of the unique to the natural history of his country, and without which it were incomplete. Seldom has a head circumscribed so much of the sense and core of Cosmos as this footed intelligence.

If one would learn the wealth of wit there was in this plain man, the information, the poetry, the piety, he should have accompanied him on an afternoon walk to Walden, or elsewhere about the skirts of his village residence. Pagan as he might outwardly appear, yet he was the hearty worshipper of whatsoever is sound and wholesome in Nature—a piece of russet probity and strong sense, that Nature delighted to own and honor. His talk was suggestive, subtle, sincere, under as many masks and mimicries as the shows he might pass; as significant, substantial—Nature choosing to speak through his mouth-piece—cynically, perhaps, and searching into the marrows of men and times he spoke of, to his discomfort mostly and avoidance.

Nature, poetry, life—not politics, not strict science, not society as it is—were his preferred themes. The world was holy, the things seen symbolizing the things unseen, and thus worthy of worship, calling men out-of-doors and under the firmament for health and wholesomeness to be insinuated into their souls, not as idolators, but as idealists. His religion was of the most primitive type, inclusive of all natural creatures and things, even to "the sparrow that falls to the ground," though never by shot of his, and for whatsoever was manly in men, his worship was comparable to that of the priests and heroes of all time. I should say he inspired the sentiment of love, if, indeed, the sentiment did not seem to partake of something purer, were that possible, but nameless from its excellency. Certainly he was better poised and more nearly self-reliant than other men.

Emerson

See our Ion standing there, his audience, his manuscript before him, himself also an auditor, as he reads, of the Genius sitting behind him, and to whom he defers, eagerly catching the words—the words—as if the accents were first reaching his ears too, and entrancing alike oracle and auditor. We admire the stately sense, the splendor of diction, and are charmed as we listen. Even his hesitancy between the delivery of his periods, his perilous passages from paragraph to paragraph of manuscript, we have almost learned to like, as if he were but sorting his keys meanwhile for opening his cabinets; the spring of locks following, himself seemingly as eager as any of us to get sight of his specimens as they come forth from their proper drawers, and we wait willingly till his gem is out glittering; admire the setting, too, scarcely less than the jewel itself. The magic minstrel and speaker, whose rhetoric, voiced as by organ-stops, delivers the sentiment from his breast in cadences peculiar to himself; now hurling it forth on the ear, echoing; then, as his mood and matter invite, dying away, like

> Music of mild lutes,
> Or silver-coated flutes,
> Or the concealing winds that can convey
> Never their tone to the rude ear of day.

He works his miracles with it, as Hermes did, his voice conducting the sense alike to eye and ear by its lyrical movement and refraining melody. So his compositions affect us, not as logic linked in syllogisms, but as voluntaries rather, as preludes, in which one is not tied to any design of air, but may vary his key or note at pleasure, as if improvised without any particular scope of argument; each period, paragraph, being a perfect note in itself, however it may chance chime with its accompaniments in the piece, as a waltz of wandering stars, a dance of Hesperus with Orion. His rhetoric dazzles by its circuits, contrasts, antitheses; imagination, as in all sprightly minds, being his wand of Power. He comes along his own paths, too, and in his own fashion. What though he build his piers downwards from the firmament to the tumbling tides, and so throw his radiant span across the fissures of his argument, and himself pass over the frolic arches, Ariel-wise—is the skill less admirable, the masonry the less secure for its singularity? So his books are best read as ir-regular writings, in which the sentiment is, by his en-thusiasm, transfused throughout the piece, telling on the mind in cadences of a current undersong, giving the im-pression of a connected whole—which it seldom is—such is the rhapsodist's cunning in its structure and delivery. . . .

'Tis over thirty years since his first book was printed. Then followed volumes of essays, poems, orations, ad-dresses; and during all the intervening period, down to the present, he has read briefs of his lectures through a wide range, from Canada to the Capitol; in most of the Free States; in the large cities, East and West, before large audiences; in the smallest towns, and to the humblest companies. Such has been his appeal to the mind of his countrymen, such his acceptance by them. He has read lectures in the principal cities of England also. A poet, speaking to individuals as few others can speak, and to persons in their privileged moments, he is heard as none others are. The more personal he is, the more prevailing, if not the more popular. 'Tis everything to have a true believer in the world, dealing with men and matter as if they were divine in idea and real in fact; meeting per-sons and events at a glance directly, not at a millionth remove, and so passing fair and fresh into life and litera-ture. . . .

We read, never as if he were the dogmatist, but a fair-speaking mind, frankly declaring his convictions, and committing these to our consideration, hoping we may have thought like things ourselves; oftenest, indeed, taking this for granted as he wrote. There is nothing of the spirit of proselyting, but the delightful deference ever to our free sense and right of opinion. He might take for his motto the sentiment of Henry More, where, speaking of himself, he says: "Exquisite disquisition begets diffidence; diffidence in knowledge, humility; humility, good manners and meek conversation. For my part, I desire no man to take anything I write or speak upon trust without canvassing, and would be thought rather to propound than to assert what I have here or elsewhere written or spoken. But continually to have expressed my diffidence in the very tractates and colloquies themselves, had been languid and ridiculous."

Then he has chosen proper times and manners for saying his good things; has spoken to almost every great interest as it rose. Nor has he let the good opportunities pass unheeded, or failed to make them for himself. He has taken discretion along as his constant attendant and ally; has shown how the gentlest temper ever deals the surest blows. His method is that of the sun against his rival for the cloak, and so is free from any madness of those, who, forgetting the strength of the solar ray, go blustering against men's prejudices, as if the wearers would run at once against these winds of opposition into their arms for shelter. What higher praise can we bestow on any one than to say of him, that he harbors another's prejudices with a hospitality so cordial as to give him for the time the sympathy next best to, if, indeed, it be not edification in, charity itself? For what disturbs more, and distracts mankind, than the uncivil manners that cleave man from man? Yet, for whose amendment letters, love, Christianity, were all given! . . .

All men love the country who love mankind with a wholesome love, and have poetry and company in them. Our essayist makes good this preference. If city bred, he has been for the best part of his life a villager and countryman. Only a traveller at times professionally, he prefers home-keeping; is a student of the landscape, of mankind, of rugged strength wherever found; liking plain persons, plain ways, plain clothes; prefers earnest people; shuns egotists, publicity; likes solitude, and knows its uses. Courting society as a spectacle not less than a pleasure, he carries off the spoils. Delighting in the broadest views of men and things, he seeks all accessible displays of both for draping his thoughts and works. And how is his page produced? Is it imaginable that he conceives his piece as a whole, and then sits down to execute his task at a heat? Is not this imaginable rather, and the key to the construction of his works? Living for composition as few authors can, and holding company, studies, sleep, exercise, affairs, subservient to thought, his products are gathered as they ripen, stored in his commonplaces; their contents transcribed at intervals, and classified. It is the order of ideas, of imagination observed in the arrangement, not of logical sequence. You may begin at the last paragraph and read backwards. 'T is Iris-built. Each period is self-poised; there may be a chasm of years between the opening passage and the last written, and there is endless time in the composition. Jewels all! Separate stars. You may have them in a galaxy, if you like, or view them separate and apart. But every one finds that, if he take an essay, or verses, however the writer may have pleased himself with the cunning workmanship, 't is cloud-fashioned, and a blind pathway for any one else. Cross as you can, or not cross, it matters not, you may climb or leap, move in circles, turn somersaults;

"In sympathetic sorrow sweep the ground,"

like his swallow in "Hermione." Dissolving views, prospects, vistas opening wide and far, yet earth, sky—realities all, not illusions. Here is substance, sod, sun; much fair weather in the seer as in his leaves. The whole quaternion of the seasons, the sidereal year, has been poured into these periods. Afternoon walks furnished their perspectives, rounded and melodized them. These good things have been talked and slept over, meditated standing and sitting, read and polished in the utterance, submitted to all various tests, and, so accepted, they pass into print. Light fancies, dreams, moods, refrains, were set on foot, and sent jaunting about the fields, along wood-paths, by Walden shores, by hill and brook-sides, to come home and claim their rank and honors too in his pages. Composed of surrounding matters, populous with thoughts, brisk with images, these books are wholesome, homelike, and could have been written only in New England, and by our poet. . . .

Plutarch tells us that of old they were wont to call men Φῶτα, which imports light, not only for the vehement desire man has to know, but to communicate also. And the Platonists fancied that the gods, being above men, had something whereof man did not partake, pure intellect and knowledge, and they kept on their way quietly. The beasts, being below men, had something whereof man had less, sense and growth, so they lived quietly in their way. While man had something in him whereof neither gods nor beasts had any trace, which gave him all the trouble, and made all the confusion in the world—and that was egotism and opinion.

A finer discrimination of gifts might show that Genius ranges through this threefold dominion, partaking in turn of their essence and degrees.

Was our poet planted so fast in intellect, so firmly rooted in the mind, so dazzled with light, yet so cleft withal by the duplicity of gifts, that fated thus to traverse the mid-world of contrast and contrariety, he was ever glancing forth from his coverts at life as reflected through his dividing prism, the resident never long of the tracts he surveyed, yet their persistent Muse nevertheless? And so housed in the Mind, and sallying forth from thence in quest of his game, whether of persons or things, he was the Mercury, the merchantman of ideas to his century. Nor was he personally alone in his thinking. Beside him stood his townsman, whose sylvan intelligence, fast rooted in Nature, was yet armed with a sagacity, a subtlety and strength, that penetrated while divining the essences of

creatures and things he studied, and of which he seemed
Atlas and Head.

Forcible protestants against the materialism of their own,
as of preceding times, these masterly Idealists substantiate
beyond all question their right to the empires they sway—
the rich estates of an original Genius.

5. MARGARET FULLER, 1810–1850

[Margaret Fuller was capable, says Emerson, of announcing to her friends, in the coolest sincerity, "I know
all the people worth knowing in America, and I find no
intellect comparable to my own." She had no need to be
modest: she was indeed speaking the sober truth. But her
journals and letters show that also she was probably about
as nerve-racked, as tormented and anguished a soul as
any in her America.

The eldest daughter of a stern lawyer of Cambridge-
port, Massachusetts, Margaret was subjected by him to
a strenuous education which shattered her health but
made her a prodigy of erudition. A close friend of the
young geniuses at Harvard College and the Divinity
School who were responding to Wordsworth and Coleridge
rather than to their professors, who were heeding the
"wild bugle-call" of Carlyle and the dulcet flute of Emerson, Margaret more than kept pace with them in their
studies, and plunged deep into the supposedly mad world
of German literature. After teaching school in Providence,
she came back to Boston, in 1840–42 edited *The Dial*,
and endeavored to make a living by conducting "Conversations," mainly for ladies who likewise aspired to be
Transcendental luminaries. In the town, these were as
much laughed at as were Alcott's "Orphic Sayings," and
by all accounts were as much lacking in humor. But of
course they made up for any deficiency in that quarter
by their high, very high, seriousness. When Emerson
joined with James Freeman Clarke and William Henry
Channing to prepare Margaret's *Memoirs* in 1852, he included a stenographic transcript of one of these Conver-

sations, held on March 22, 1841, probably taken down by
Caroline Sturgis.]

A TRANSCENDENTAL CONVERSATION

March 22, 1841. The question of the day was, "What
is Life?"

"Let us define, each in turn, our idea of living." Margaret
did not believe that we had, any of us, a distinct idea
of life.

A[nna] S[haw] thought so great a question ought to
be given for a written definition. "No," said Margaret,
"that is of no use. When we go away to think of anything,
we never do think. We all talk of life. We all have some
thought now. Let us tell it. C[aroline Sturgis], what is
life?"

Caroline replied, "It is to laugh, or cry, according to
our organization."

"Good," said Margaret, "but not grave enough. Come,
what is life? I know what I think; I want you to find out
what you think."

Miss P[eabody] replied, "Life is division from one's
principle of life in order to a conscious reorganization.
We are cut up by time and circumstance, in order to
feel our reproduction of the eternal law."

Mrs. E[merson]: "We live by the will of God, and the
object of life is to submit," and went on into Calvinism.

Then came up all the antagonisms of Fate and Freedom.

Mrs. H[ooper] said, "God created us in order to have
a perfect sympathy from us as free beings."

Mrs. A[lmira] B[arlow] said she thought the object of
life was to attain absolute freedom. At this Margaret immediately and visibly kindled.

C[aroline] S[turgis] said, "God creates from the fulness of life, and cannot but create; he created us to over-
flow, without being exhausted, because what he created,
necessitated new creation. It is not to make us happy,
but creation is his happiness and ours."

Margaret was then pressed to say what she considered life to be.

Her answer was so full, clear, and concise, at once, that it cannot but be marred by being drawn through the scattering medium of my memory. But here are some fragments of her satisfying statement.

She began with God as Spirit, Life, so full as to create and love eternally, yet capable of pause. Love and creativeness are dynamic forces, out of which we, individually, as creatures, go forth bearing his image; that is, having within our being the same dynamic forces by which we also add constantly to the total sum of existence, and shaking off ignorance, and its effects, and by becoming more ourselves, *i.e.*, more divine—destroying sin in its principle, we attain to absolute freedom, we return to God, conscious like himself, and, as his friends, giving, as well as receiving, felicity forevermore. In short, we become gods, and able to give the life which we now feel ourselves able only to receive.

On Saturday morning, Mrs. L[idian] E[merson] and Mrs. E[llen] H[ooper] were present, and begged Margaret to repeat the statement concerning life, with which she closed the last conversation. Margaret said she had forgotten every word she said. She must have been inspired by a good genius, to have so satisfied everybody—but the good genius had left her. She would try, however, to say what she thought, and trusted it would resemble what she had said already. She then went into the matter, and, true enough, she did not use a single word she used before.

CHAPTER THREE

RELIGIOUS RADICALISM

THEODORE PARKER, 1810–1860

[The specific issue on which the young Transcendentalists first came into open conflict with their Unitarian elders and with the Harvard Faculty was over that of the historicity of the miracles recounted in the New Testament.

Unitarian "liberal Christianity" denied the Trinity, and along with it the entire Calvinist conception of the mediatorial sacrifice of Christ being a metaphysical prerequisite to God's forgiving of men (or of some men) for the transgression of Adam. Nevertheless, it stoutly insisted that the Messiah was a divinely commissioned emissary of Almighty God, and that his supernatural authority was attested by the miracles he performed. Andrews Norton devoted his life to a monumental *The Evidences of the Genuineness of the Four Gospels,* which today is unreadable but which then made him recognized as "the Unitarian Pope"; its thesis comes down, in short, to a blanket assertion that at Cana, on a particular day, Christ did turn the water into wine, that he did walk on the sea and did actually feed a multitude with seven loaves and a few little fishes.

As the young men studied, surreptitiously, the new theological literature of Germany, and became more and more convinced that all Nature is divine, the more they were persuaded that such concern for the literalness of the miracles was utterly pointless. Article by article, George Ripley, Frederic Henry Hedge, Orestes Brownson and others worked out their growing dissent from "liberal orthodoxy," mainly in the theological organ of the denomination, *The Christian Examiner,* until in the year 1836 Brownson's *New Views,* along with Emerson's *Nature* and Alcott's *Conversations,* brought the schism into the open.

The furor these books produced in and around Boston, and above all the angry denunciation aroused by Emerson's "Divinity School Address" of July 15, 1838, were caused not so much by their general philosophy (which to men like Norton was simply incomprehensible) as by their making clear the corollary that any distinction between Nature and the miraculous was sheer pedantry. They did not, like eighteenth-century rationalists or Deists, deny the miracles; they simply ignored them. As Emerson put their case in the crucial passage of his "Address";

"He [Christ] spoke of miracles; for he felt that man's life was a miracle, and all that man doth, and he knew that this his daily miracle shines, as the character ascends. But the Miracle, as pronounced by Christian churches, gives a false impression; it is Monster. It is not one with the blowing clover and the falling rain."

Thereupon *The Christian Examiner* was closed to Transcendentalists; Brownson founded his *Quarterly* in 1838 and in 1840 Emerson and Margaret Fuller established *The Dial.* Meanwhile, Andrews Norton launched his offensive in 1839 with *A Discourse on the Latest Form of Infidelity.* Emerson suffered deeply (he externalized his ordeal in the poem "Uriel"), while hardier souls, like Ripley and Brownson, entered the lists against the hardheaded "Pope."

They were joined in their pamphlet counter-attack by Theodore Parker, a born fighter. Emerson is entirely right in calling him the Transcendentalists' "Savonarola" (p. 15). The son of a yeoman farmer in Lexington, Massachusetts, Parker had a meagre elementary schooling, and earned his living with his hands. Admitted to Harvard, he was too poor to attend classes, but took and passed with distinction all the examinations. He did contrive to spend two years, 1834–36, in the Divinity School, by which time he was master of twenty languages and had read all the available literature in every one of them. He accepted the call from the church at West Roxbury, primarily so that he could be near the Boston libraries; his simple suburban—in fact, still rural—congregation stood by him even as he became the most outspoken and vehement champion of every extreme of liberal heresy.

By 1840 Parker was virtually ostracized by the majority of the Unitarian fellowship, who would not longer "exchange" pulpits with him. A few of the young adored him only the more passionately, and when one of these, Charles C. Shackford, was to be ordained in the South Boston Church, he asked Parker to deliver, on May 19, 1841, the sermon. Parker thus brought the debate over the historical authenticity of the miracles to a thunderous climax with the *Transient and Permanent*. The commotion he made was a hundred times greater than any caused by Alcott or Emerson. Only eight or nine of the Unitarian ministers would refuse to condemn him, and he was everywhere excoriated by respectable Boston. Parker responded, characteristically, by preaching all the more vigorously and radically, not only in Boston, but throughout the country, and by assuming the championship of every reforming cause, most particularly that of anti-slavery.

Though I printed the full text of this central discourse in my earlier *Transcendentalists*, it is not anywhere near so widely available as are the basic writings of Emerson and Thoreau; wherefore, though I omit the latter, for reasons already given, without apology I take enough pages once more to give the *Transient and Permanent* in full.]

A DISCOURSE OF THE TRANSIENT AND PERMANENT IN CHRISTIANITY

Heaven and earth shall pass away; but my words shall not pass away—Luke XXI. 33.

In this sentence we have a very clear indication that Jesus of Nazareth believed the religion he taught would be eternal, that the substance of it would last forever. Yet there are some who are affrighted by the faintest rustle which a heretic makes among the dry leaves of theology; they tremble lest Christianity itself should perish without hope. Ever and anon the cry is raised, "The philistines be upon us, and Christianity is in danger." The least doubt respecting the popular theology, or the existing machinery of the church; the least sign of distrust in the religion of the pulpit, or the religion of the street, is by some good men supposed to be at enmity with faith in Christ, and capable of shaking Christianity itself. On the other hand, a few bad men, and a few pious men, it is said, on both sides of the water, tell us the day of Christianity is past. The latter, it is alleged, would persuade us that hereafter piety must take a new form; the teachings of Jesus are to be passed by; that religion is to wing her way sublime, above the flight of Christianity, far away, toward heaven, as the fledged eaglet leaves forever the nest which sheltered his callow youth. Let us therefore devote a few moments to this subject, and consider what is *transient* in Christianity, and what is *permanent* therein. The topic seems not inappropriate to the times in which we live, or the occasion that calls us together.

Christ says his word shall never pass away. Yet, at first sight, nothing seems more fleeting than a word. It is an evanescent impulse of the most fickle element. It leaves no track where it went through the air. Yet to this, and this only, did Jesus intrust the truth wherewith he came laden to the earth—truth for the salvation of the world. He took no pains to perpetuate his thoughts; they were poured forth where occasion found him an audience—by the side of the lake, or a well; in a cottage, or the temple; in a fisher's boat, or the synagogue of the Jews. He founds no institution as a monument of his words. He appoints no order of men to preserve his bright and glad relations. He only bids his friends give freely the truth they had freely received. He did not even write his words in a book. With a noble confidence, the result of his abiding faith, he scattered them broadcast on the world, leaving the seed to its own vitality. He knew that what is of God cannot fail, for God keeps his own. He sowed his seed in the heart, and left it there, to be watered and warmed by the dew and the sun which heaven sends. He felt his words were for eternity. So he trusted them to the uncertain air; and for eighteen hundred years that faithful element has held them good—distinct as when first warm from his lips. Now they are translated into every human speech, and murmured in all earth's thousand tongues, from the pine forests of the North to the palm groves of eastern Ind. They mingle, as it were, with the roar of a populous city, and join the chime of the desert sea. Of a Sabbath morn they are repeated from church to church, from isle to isle, and land to land, till their music goes round the world. These words have become the breath of the good, the hope of the wise, the joy of the pious, and that for many millions of hearts. They are the prayers of our churches; our better devotion by fireside and fieldside; the enchantment of our hearts. It is these words that still work wonders, to which the first recorded miracles were nothing in grandeur and utility. It is these which build our temples and beautify our homes. They raise our thoughts of sublimity; they purify our ideal of purity; they hallow our prayer for truth and love. They make beauteous and divine the life which plain men lead. They give wings to our aspirations. What charmers they are! Sorrow is lulled at their bidding. They take the sting out of disease, and rob adversity of his power to disappoint. They give health and wings to the pious soul, broken-hearted and shipwrecked in his voyage through life, and encourage him to tempt the perilous way once more. They make all things ours; Christ our brother; time our servant; death our ally, and the witness of our triumph. They reveal to us the presence of God, which else we might not have seen so clearly in the first wind-flower of spring, in the falling of a sparrow, in the distress of a nation, in the sorrow or the rapture of the world. Silence the voice of Christianity, and the world is well-nigh dumb; for gone is that sweet music which kept in awe the rulers and the people, which cheers the poor widow in her lonely toil, and comes, like light through the windows of morning, to men who sit stooping and feeble, with failing eyes and a hungering heart. It is gone—all gone! only the cold, bleak world left before them.

Such is the life of these words; such the empire they have won for themselves over men's minds since they were spoken first. In the mean time, the words of great men and mighty, whose name shook whole continents, though graven in metal and stone, though stamped in institutions, and defended by whole tribes of priests and troops of followers—their words have gone to the ground, and the world gives back no echo of their voice. Meanwhile the great works, also, of old times, castle and tower, and town, their cities and their empires, have perished, and left scarce a mark on the bosom of the earth to show they once have been. The philosophy of the wise, the art of the accomplished, the song of the poet, the ritual of the priest, though honored as divine in their day, have gone down a prey to oblivion. Silence has closed over them; only their spectres now haunt the earth. A deluge of blood has swept over the nations; a night of darkness, more deep than the fabled darkness of Egypt, has lowered down upon that flood, to destroy or to hide what the deluge had spared. But through all this the words of Christianity have come down to us from the lips of that Hebrew youth, gentle and beautiful as the light of a star, not spent by their journey through time and through space. They have built up a new civilization, which the wisest Gentile never hoped for, which the most pious Hebrew never foretold. Through centuries of wasting these words have flown on, like a dove in the storm, and now wait to descend on hearts pure and earnest, as the Father's spirit, we are told, came down on his lowly Son. The old heavens and the old earth are indeed passed away, but the Word stands. Nothing shows clearer than this how fleeting is what man calls great, how lasting what God pronounces true.

Looking at the word of Jesus, at real Christianity, the pure religion he taught, nothing appears more fixed and certain. Its influence widens as light extends; it deepens as the nations grow more wise. But, looking at the history of what men call Christianity, nothing seems more uncertain and perishable. While true religion is always the same thing, in each century and every land, in each man that feels it, the Christianity of the pulpit, which is the religion taught, the Christianity of the people, which is the religion that is accepted and lived out, has never been the same thing in any two centuries or lands, except only in name. The difference between what is called Christianity by the Unitarians in our times, and that of some ages past, is greater than the difference between Mahomet and the Messiah. The difference at this day between opposing classes of Christians, the difference between the Christianity of some sects and that of Christ himself, is deeper and more vital than that between Jesus and Plato, pagan as we call him. The Christianity of the seventh century has passed away. We recognize only the ghost of superstition in its faded features, as it comes up at our call. It is one of the things which have been, and can be no more; for neither God nor the world goes back. Its terrors do not frighten, nor its hopes allure us. We rejoice that it has gone. But how do we know that our Christianity shall not share the same fate? Is there that difference between the nineteenth century and some seventeen that have gone before it since Jesus, to warrant the belief that our notion of Christianity shall last for ever? The stream of time has already beat down philosophies and theologies, temple and church, though never so old and revered. How do we know there is not a perishing element in what we call Christianity? Jesus tells us *his* word is the word of God, and so shall never pass away. But who tells us that *our* word shall never pass away? that *our notion* of his word shall stand for ever?

Let us look at this matter a little more closely. In actual Christianity—that is, in that portion of Christianity which is preached and believed—there seems to have been, ever since the time of its earthly founder, two elements, the one transient, the other permanent. The one is the thought, the folly, the uncertain wisdom, the theological notions, the impiety of man; the other, the eternal truth of God. These two bear, perhaps, the same relation to each other that the phenomena of outward nature, such as sunshine and cloud, growth, decay, and reproduction, bear to the great law of nature, which underlies and supports them all. As in that case more attention is commonly paid to the particular phenomena than to the general law, so in this case more is generally given to the transient in Christianity than to the permanent therein.

It must be confessed, though with sorrow, that transient things form a great part of what is commonly taught as religion. An undue place has often been assigned to forms and doctrines, while too little stress has been laid on the divine life of the soul, love to God, and love to man. Religious forms may be useful and beautiful. They are so, whenever they speak to the soul, and answer a want thereof. In our present state some forms are perhaps necessary. But they are only the accident of Christianity, not its substance. They are the robe, not the angel, who may take another robe quite as becoming and useful. One sect has many forms; another, none. Yet both may be equally Christian, in spite of the redundance or the deficiency. They are a part of the language in which religion speaks, and exist, with few exceptions, wherever man is found. In our calculating nation, in our rationalizing sect, we have retained but two of the rites so numerous in the early Christian Church, and even these we have attenuated to the last degree, leaving them little more than a spectre of the ancient form. Another age may continue or forsake both; may revive old forms, or invent new ones to suit the altered circumstances of the times, and yet be Christians quite as good as we, or our fathers of the dark ages. Whether the apostles designed these rites to be perpetual seems a question which belongs to scholars and antiquarians—not to us, as Christian men and women. So long as they satisfy or help the pious heart, so long they are good. Looking behind or around us, we see that the forms and rites of the Christians are quite as fluctuating as those of the heathens; from whom some of them have been, not unwisely, adopted by the earlier church.

Again, the doctrines that have been connected with Christianity, and taught in its name, are quite as changeable as the form. This also takes place unavoidably. If observations be made upon nature—which must take place so long as man has senses and understanding—there will be a philosophy of nature, and philosophical doctrines. These will differ, as the observations are just or inaccurate, and as the deductions from observed facts are true or false. Hence there will be different schools of natural philosophy, so long as men have eyes and understandings of different clearness and strength. And if men observe and reflect upon religion—which will be done so long as man is a religious and reflective being—there must also be a philosophy of religion, a theology, and theological doctrines. These will differ, as men have felt much or little of religion, as they analyze their sentiments correctly or otherwise, and as they have reasoned right or wrong. Now, the true system of nature, which exists in the outward facts, whether discovered or not, is always the same thing, though the philosophy of nature, which men invent, change every month, and be one thing at London and the opposite at Berlin. Thus there is but one system of nature as it exists in fact, though many theories of nature, which exist in our imperfect notions of that system, and by which we may approximate and at length reach it. Now, there can be but one religion which is absolutely true, existing in the facts of human nature and the ideas of infinite God. That, whether acknowledged or not, is always the same thing, and never changes. So far as a man has any real religion—either the principle or the sentiment thereof—so far he has that, by whatever name he may call it. For, strictly speaking, there is but one kind of religion, as there is but one kind of love, though the manifestations of this religion, in forms, doctrines, and life, be never so diverse. It is through these, men approximate to the true expression of this religion. Now while this religion is one and always the same thing, there may be numerous systems of theology or philosophies of religion. These, with their creeds, confessions, and collections of doctrines, deduced by reasoning upon the facts observed, may be baseless and false, either because the observation was too narrow in extent, or otherwise defective in point of accuracy, or because the reasoning was illogical, and therefore the deduction spurious. Each of these three faults is conspicuous in the systems of theology. Now, the solar system as it exists in fact is permanent, though the notions of Thales and Ptolemy, of Copernicus and Descartes, about this system, prove transient, imperfect approximations to the true expression. So the Christianity of Jesus is permanent, though what passes for Christianity with popes and catechisms, with sects and churches, in the first century or in the nineteenth century prove transient also. Now, it has sometimes happened that a man took his philosophy of nature at second-hand, and then attempted to make his observations conform to his theory, and nature ride in his panniers. Thus some philosophers refused to look at the moon through Galileo's telescope; for, according to their theory of vision, such an instrument would not aid the sight. Thus their preconceived notions stood up between them and nature. Now, it has often happened that men took their theology thus at second-hand, and distorted the history of the world and man's nature besides, to make religion conform to their notions. Their theology stood between them and God. Those obstinate philosophers have disciples in no small number.

What another has said of false systems of science will apply equally to the popular theology: "It is barren in effects, fruitful in questions, slow and languid in its improvement, exhibiting in its generality the counterfeit of perfection, but ill filled up in its details, popular in its choice, but suspected by its very promoters, and therefore bolstered up and countenanced with artifices. Even those who have been determined to try for themselves, to add their support to learning, and to enlarge its limits, have not dared entirely to desert received opinions, nor to seek the spring-head of things. But they think they have done a great thing if they intersperse and contribute something of their own; prudently considering, that by their assent they can save their modesty, and by their contributions, their liberty. Neither is there, nor ever will be, an end or limit to these things. One snatches at one thing, another is pleased with another; there is no dry nor clear sight of anything. Every one plays the philosopher out of the small treasures of his own fancy; the more sublime wits more acutely and with better success, the duller with less success, but equal obstinancy; and, by the discipline of some learned men, sciences are bounded within the limits of some certain authors which they have set down, imposing them upon old men and instilling them into young. So that now (as Tully cavilled upon Cæsar's consulship) the star Lyra riseth by an edict, and authority is taken for truth, and not truth for authority; which kind of order and discipline is very convenient for our present use, but banisheth those which are better."

Any one who traces the history of what is called Christianity, will see that nothing changes more from age to age than the doctrines taught as Christian, and insisted on as essential to Christianity and personal salvation. What is falsehood in one province passes for truth in another. The heresy of one age is the orthodox belief and "only infallible rule" of the next. Now Arius, and now Athanasius, is lord of the ascendant. Both were excommunicated in their turn, each for affirming what the other denied. Men are burned for professing what men are burned for denying. For centuries the doctrines of the Christians were no better, to say the least, than those of their contemporary pagans. The theological doctrines from our fathers seem to have come from Judaism, Heathenism, and the caprice of philosophers, far more than they have come from the principle and sentiment of Christianity. The doctrine of the Trinity, the very Achilles of theological dogmas, belongs to philosophy and not religion; its subtleties cannot even be expressed in our tongue. As old religions became superannuated, and died out, they left to the rising faith, as to a residuary legatee, their forms and their doctrines; or rather, as the giant in the fable left his poisoned garment to work the overthrow of his conqueror. Many tenets that pass current in our theology seem to be the refuse of idol temples, the off-scourings of Jewish and heathen cities, rather than the sands of virgin gold which the stream of Christianity has worn off from the rock of ages, and brought in its bosom for us. It is wood, hay, and stubble, wherewith men have built on the corner-stone Christ laid. What wonder the fabric is in peril when tried by fire? The stream of Christianity, as men receive it, has caught a stain from every soil it has filtered through, so that now it is not the pure water from the well of life which is offered to our lips, but streams troubled and polluted by man with mire and dirt. If Paul and Jesus could read our books of theological doctrines, would they accept as their teaching what men have vented in their name? Never, till the letters of Paul had faded out of his memory; never, till the words of Jesus had been torn out from the book of life. It is their notions about Christianity men have taught as the only living word of God. They have piled their own rubbish against the temple of Truth where Piety comes up to worship; what wonder the pile seems unshapely and like to fall? But these theological doctrines are fleeting as the leaves on the trees. They—

> "Are found
> Now green in youth, now withered on the ground:
> Another race the following spring supplies;
> They fall successive, and successive rise."

Like the clouds of the sky, they are here today; tomorrow, all swept off and vanished; while Christianity itself, like the heaven above, with its sun, and moon, and uncounted stars, is always over our head, though the cloud sometimes debars us of the needed light. It must of necessity be the case that our reasonings, and therefore our theological doctrines, are imperfect, and so perishing. It is only gradually that we approach to the true system of nature by observation and reasoning, and work out our philosophy and theology by the toil of the brain. But meantime, if we are faithful, the great truths of morality and religion, the deep sentiment of love to man and love to God, are perceived intuitively, and by instinct, as it were, though our theology be imperfect and miserable. The theological notions of Abraham, to take the story as it stands, were exceedingly gross, yet a greater than Abraham has told us, "Abraham desired to see my day, saw it, and was glad." Since these notions are so fleeting, why need we accept the commandment of men as the doctrine of God?

This transitoriness of doctrines appears in many instances, of which two may be selected for a more attentive consideration. First, the doctrine respecting the origin and authority of the Old and New Testament. There has been a time when men were burned for asserting doctrines of natural philosophy which rested on evidence the most incontestable, because those doctrines conflicted with sentences in the Old Testament. Every word of that Jewish record was regarded as miraculously inspired, and therefore as infallibly true. It was believed that the Christian religion itself rested thereon, and must stand or fall with the immaculate Hebrew text. He was deemed no small sinner who found mistakes in the manuscripts. On the authority of the written word man was taught to believe impossible legends, conflicting assertions; to take fiction for fact, a dream for a miraculous revelation of God, an Oriental poem for a grave history of miraculous events, a collection of amatory idyls for a serious discourse "touching the mutual love of Christ and the Church;" they have been taught to accept a picture sketched by some glowing Eastern imagination, never intended to be taken for a reality, as a proof that the infinite God spoke in human words, appeared in the shape of a cloud, a flaming bush, or a man who ate, and drank, and vanished into smoke; that he gave counsels today, and the opposite tomorrow; that he violated his own laws, was angry, and was only dissuaded by a mortal man from destroying at once a whole nation—millions of men who rebelled against their leader in a moment of anguish. Questions in philosophy, questions in the Christian religion, have been settled by an appeal to that book. The inspiration of its authors has been assumed as infallible. Every fact in the early Jewish history has been taken as a type of some analogous fact in Christian history. The most distant events, even such as are still in the arms of time, were supposed to be clearly foreseen and foretold by pious Hebrews several centuries before Christ. It has been assumed at the outset, with no shadow of evidence, that those writers held a miraculous communication with God, such as he has granted to no other man. What was originally a presumption of bigoted Jews became an article of faith, which Christians were burned for not believing. This has been for centuries the general opinion of the Christian church, both Catholic and Protestant, though the former never accepted the Bible as the *only* source of religious truth. It has been so. Still worse, it is now the general opinion of religious sects at this day. Hence the attempt, which always fails, to reconcile the philosophy of our times with the poems in Genesis writ a thousand years before Christ. Hence the attempt to conceal the contradictions in the record itself. Matters have come to such a pass that even now he is deemed an infidel, if not by implication an atheist, whose reverence for the Most High forbids him to believe that God commanded Abraham to sacrifice his son—a thought at which the flesh creeps with horror; to believe it solely on the authority of an Oriental story, written down nobody knows when or by whom, or for what purpose; which may be a poem, but cannot be the record of a fact, unless God is the author of confusion and a lie.

Now, this idolatry of the Old Testament has not always existed. Jesus says that none born of a woman is greater than John the Baptist, yet the least in the kingdom of heaven was greater than John. Paul tells us the law—the very crown of the old Hebrew revelation—is a shadow of good things which have now come; only a schoolmaster to bring us to Christ; and when faith has come, that we are no longer under the schoolmaster; that it was a law of sin and death, from which we are made free by the law of the spirit of life. Christian teachers themselves have differed so widely in their notion of the doctrines and meaning of those books that it makes one weep to think of the follies deduced therefrom. But modern criticism is fast breaking to pieces this idol which men have made out of the Scriptures. It has shown that here are the most different works thrown together; that their authors, wise as they sometimes were, pious as we feel often their spirit to have been, had only that inspiration which is common to other men equally pious and wise; that they were by no means infallible, but were mistaken in facts or in reasoning—uttered predictions which time has not fulfilled; men who in some measure partook of the darkness and limited notions of their age, and were not always above its mistakes or its corruptions.

The history of opinions on the New Testament is quite similar. It has been assumed at the outset, it would seem with no sufficient reason, without the smallest pretence on its writers' part, that all of its authors were infallibly and miraculously inspired, so that they could commit no error of doctrine or fact. Men have been bid to close their eyes at the obvious difference between Luke and John, the serious disagreement between Paul and Peter; to believe, on the smallest evidence, accounts which shock the moral sense and revolt the reason, and tend to place Jesus in the same series with Hercules, and Apollonius of Tyana; accounts which Paul in the Epistles never mentions, though he also had a vein of the miraculous running quite through him. Men have been told that all these things must be taken as part of Christianity, and if they accepted the religion, they must take all these accessories along with it; that the living spirit could not be had without the killing letter. All the books which caprice or accident had brought together between the lids of the Bible were declared to be the infallible word of God, the only certain rule of religious faith and practice. Thus the Bible was made not a single channel, but the *only* certain rule of religious faith and practice. To disbelieve any of its statements, or even the common interpretation put upon those statements by the particular age or church in which the man belonged, was held to be infidelity, if not atheism. In the name of him who forbid us to judge our brother, good men and pious men have applied these terms to others, good and pious as themselves. That state of things has been by no means passed away. Men who cry down the absurdities of paganism in the worst spirit of the French "free thinkers," call others infidels and atheist, who point out, though reverently, other absurdities which men have piled upon Christianity. So the world goes. An idolatrous regard for the imperfect scripture of God's word is the apple of Atalanta, which defeats theologians running for the hand of divine truth.

But the current notions respecting the infallible inspiration of the Bible have no foundation in the Bible itself. Which evangelist, which apostle of the New Testament, what prophet or psalmist of the Old Testament, ever claims infallible authority for himself or for others? Which of them does not in his own writings show that he was finite, and, with all his zeal and piety, possessed but a limited inspiration, the bound whereof we can sometimes discover? Did Christ ever demand that men should assent to the doctrines of the Old Testament, credit its stories, and take its poems for histories, and believe equally two accounts that contradict one another? Has he ever told you that all the truths of his religion, all the beauty of a Christian life, should be contained in the writings of those men who, even after his resurrection, expected him to be a Jewish king; of men who were sometimes at variance with one another, and misunderstood his divine teachings? Would not those modest writers themselves be confounded at the idolatry we pay them? Opinions may change on these points, as they have often changed— changed greatly and for the worse since the days of Paul. They are changing now, and we may hope for the better; for God makes man's folly as well as his wrath to praise him, and continually brings good out of evil.

Another instance of the transitoriness of doctrines taught as Christian is found in those which relate to the nature and authority of Christ. One ancient party has told us that he is the infinite God; another, that he is both God and man; a third, that he was a man, the son of Joseph and Mary, born as we are; tempted like ourselves; inspired as we may be if we will pay the price. Each of the former parties believed its doctrine on this head was infallibly true, and formed the very substance of Christianity, and was one of the essential conditions of sal-

vation, though scarce any two distinguished teachers, of
ancient or modern times, agree in their expression of this
truth.

Almost every sect that has ever been makes Christianity rest on the personal authority of Jesus, and not the
immutable truth of the doctrines themselves, or the authority of God, who sent him into the world. Yet it seems difficult to conceive any reason why moral and religious truths
should rest for their support on the personal authority of
their revealer, any more than the truths of science on that
of him who makes them known first or most clearly. It is
hard to see why the great truths of Christianity rest on
the personal authority of Jesus, more than the axioms of
geometry rest on the personal authority of Euclid or
Archimedes. The authority of Jesus, as of all teachers, one
would naturally think, must rest on the truth of his words,
and not their truth on his authority.

Opinions respecting the nature of Christ seem to be
constantly changing. In the three first centuries after
Christ, it appears, great latitude of speculation prevailed.
Some said he was God, with nothing of human nature, his
body only an illusion; others, that he was man, with
nothing of the divine nature, his miraculous birth having
no foundation in fact. In a few centuries it was decreed
by councils that he was God, thus honoring the divine
element; next, that he was man also, thus admitting the
human side. For some ages the Catholic Church seems
to have dwelt chiefly on the divine nature that was in him,
leaving the human element to mystics and other heretical
persons, whose bodies served to flesh the swords of orthodox believers. The stream of Christianity has come to us in
two channels—one within the church, the other without
the church—and it is not hazarding too much to say that
since the fourth century the true Christian life has been
out of the established church, and not in it, but rather in
the ranks of dissenters. From the Reformation till the latter
part of the last century, we are told, the Protestant Church
dwelt chiefly on the human side of Christ, and since that
time many works have been written to show how the two—
perfect Deity and perfect manhood—were united in his

character. But, all this time, scarce any two eminent teachers agree on these points, however orthodox they may be called. What a difference between the Christ of John Gerson and John Calvin, yet were both accepted teachers and pious men. What a difference between the Christ of the Unitarians and the Methodists, yet may men of both sects be true Christians and acceptable with God. What a difference between the Christ of Matthew and John, yet both were disciples, and their influence is wide as Christendom and deep as the heart of man. But on this there is not time to enlarge.

Now, it seems clear that the notions men form about the origin and nature of the Scriptures, respecting the nature and authority of Christ, have nothing to do with Christianity except as its aids or its adversaries; they are not the foundation of its truths. These are theological questions, not religious questions. Their connection with Christianity appears accidental: for if Jesus had taught at Athens, and not at Jerusalem; if he had wrought no miracle, and none but the human nature had ever been ascribed to him; if the Old Testament had forever perished at his birth—Christianity would still have been the word of God; it would have lost none of its truths. It would be just as true, just as beautiful, just as lasting, as now it is; though we should have lost so many a blessed word, and the work of Christianity itself would have been, perhaps, a long time retarded.

To judge the future by the past, the former authority of the Old Testament can never return. Its present authority cannot stand. It must be taken for what it is worth. The occasional folly and impiety of its authors must pass for no more than their value; while the religion, the wisdom, the love, which make fragrant its leaves, will still speak to the best hearts as hitherto, and in accents even more divine when reason is allowed her rights. The ancient belief in the infallible inspiration of each sentence of the New Testament is fast changing, very fast. One writer, not a sceptic, but a Christian of unquestioned piety, sweeps off the beginning of Matthew; another, of a different church and equally religious, the end of John. Numerous critics strike off several epistles. The Apocalypse itself is not spared, notwithstanding its concluding curse. Who shall tell us the work of retrenchment is to stop here; that others will not demonstrate, what some pious hearts have long felt, that errors of doctrine and errors of fact may be found in many parts of the record, here and there, from the beginning of Matthew to the end of Acts? We see how opinions have changed ever since the Apostles' time; and who shall assure us that they were not sometimes mistaken in historical, as well as doctrinal matters; did not sometimes confound the actual with the imaginary; and that the fancy of these pious writers never stood in the place of their recollection?

But what if this should take place? Is Christianity then to perish out of the heart of the nations, and vanish from the memory of the world, like the religions that were before Abraham? It must be so, if it rest on a foundation which a scoffer may shake, and a score of pious critics shake down. But this is the foundation of a theology, not of Christianity. That does not rest on the decision of Councils. It is not to stand or fall with the infallible inspiration of a few Jewish fishermen, who have writ their names in characters of light all over the world. It does not continue to stand through the forbearance of some critic, who can cut when he will the thread on which its life depends. Christianity does not rest on the infallible authority of the New Testament. It depends on this collection of books for the historical statement of its facts. In this we do not require infallible inspiration on the part of the writers, more than in the record of other historical facts. To me it seems as presumptuous, on the one hand, for the believer to claim this evidence for the truth of Christianity, as it is absurd, on the other hand, for the sceptic to demand such evidence to support these historical statements. I cannot see that it depends on the personal authority of Jesus. He was the organ through which the Infinite spoke. It is God that was manifested in the flesh by him, on whom rests the truth which Jesus brought to light, and made clear and beautiful in his life; and if Christianity be true, it seems useless to look for any other authority to uphold it, as for someone to support Almighty God. So if it could be proved—as it cannot—in opposition to the greatest amount of historical evidence ever collected on any similar point, that the Gospels were the fabrication of designing and artful men, that Jesus of Nazareth had never lived, still Christianity would stand firm, and fear no evil. None of the doctrines of that religion would fall to the ground; for, if true, they stand by themselves. But we should lose—oh, irreparable loss—the example of that character, so beautiful, so divine, that no human genius could have conceived it, as none, after all the progress and refinement of eighteen centuries, seems fully to have comprehended its lustrous life. If Christianity were true, we should still think it was so, not because its record was written by infallible pens, nor because it was lived out by an infallible teacher; but that it is true, like the axioms of geometry, because it is true, and is to be tried by the oracle God places in the breast. If it rest on the personal authority of Jesus alone, then there is no certainly of its truth if he were ever mistaken in the smallest matter—as some Christians have thought he was in predicting his second coming.

These doctrines respecting the Scriptures have often changed, and are but fleeting. Yet men lay much stress on them. Some cling to these notions as if they were Christianity itself. It is about these and similar points that theological battles are fought from age to age. Men sometimes use worst the choicest treasure which God bestows. This is especially true of the use men make of the Bible. Some men have regarded it as the heathen their idol, or the savage his fetich. They have subordinated reason, conscience, and religion to this. Thus have they lost half the treasure it bears in its bosom. No doubt the time will come when its true character shall be felt. Then it will be seen that, amid all the contradictions of the Old Testament—its legends, so beautiful as fictions, so appalling as facts; amid its predictions that have never been fulfilled; amid the puerile conceptions of God, which sometimes occur, and the cruel denunciations that disfigure both psalm and prophecy—there is a reverence for man's nature, a sublime

trust in God, and a depth of piety, rarely felt in these cold
northern hearts of ours. Then the devotion of its authors,
the loftiness of their aim, and the majesty of their life, will
appear doubly fair, and prophet and psalmist will warm
our hearts as never before. Their voice will cheer the
young, and sanctify the gray-headed; will charm us in the
toil of life, and sweeten the cup death gives us when he
comes to shake off this mantle of flesh. Then will it be seen
that the words of Jesus are the music of heaven sung in an
earthly voice, and that the echo of these words in John
and Paul owe their efficacy to their truth and their depth,
and to no accidental matter connected therewith. Then can
the Word, which was in the beginning and now is, find
access to the innermost heart of man, and speak there as
now it seldom speaks. Then shall the Bible—which is a
whole library of the deepest and most earnest thoughts and
feelings, and piety, and love, ever recorded in human
speech—be read oftener than ever before—not with superstition, but with reason, conscience, and faith, fully active.
Then shall it sustain men bowed down with many sorrows;
rebuke sin, encourage virtue, sow the world broadcast and
quick with the seed of love, that man may reap a harvest
for life everlasting.

With all the obstacles men have thrown in its path,
how much has the Bible done for mankind. No abuse has
deprived us of all its blessings. You trace its path across
the world from the day of Pentecost to this day. As a river
springs up in the heart of a sandy continent, having its
father in the skies, and its birth-place in distant unknown
mountains; as the stream rolls on, enlarging itself, making
in that arid waste a belt of verdure wherever it turns its
way; creating palm groves and fertile plains, where the
smoke of the cottager curls up at eventide, and marble
cities send the gleam of their splendor far into the sky—
such has been the course of the Bible on the earth. Despite
of idolaters bowing to the dust before it, it has made a
deeper mark on the world than the rich and beautiful
literature of all the heathen. The first book of the Old
Testament tells man he is made in the image of God; the
first of the New Testament gives us the motto, Be perfect

as your Father in heaven. Higher words were never spoken. How the truths of the Bible have blessed us! There is not a boy on all the hills of New England; not a girl born in the filthiest cellar which disgraces a capital in Europe, and cries to God against the barbarism of modern civilization; not a boy nor a girl all Christendom through, but their lot is made better by that great book.

Doubtless the time will come when men shall see Christ also as he is. Well might he still say, "Have I been so long with you, and yet hast thou not known me?" No! we have made him an idol, have bowed the knee before him, saying, "Hail, king of the Jews!" called him "Lord, Lord!" but done not the things which he said. The history of the Christian world might well be summed up in one word of the evangelist—"and there they crucified him;" for there has never been an age when man did not crucify the Son of God afresh. But if error prevail for a time and grow old in the world, truth will triumph at the last, and then we shall see the Son of God as he is. Lifted up, he shall draw all nations unto him. Then will men understand the word of Jesus, which shall not pass away. Then shall we see and love the divine life that he lived. How vast has his influence been! How his spirit wrought in the hearts of his disciples, rude, selfish, bigoted, as at first they were! How it has wrought in the world! His words judge the nations. The wisest son of man has not measured their height. They speak to what is deepest in profound men, what is holiest in good men, what is divinest in religious men. They kindle anew the flame of devotion in hearts long cold. They are spirit and life. His truth was not derived from Moses and Solomon; but the light of God shone through him, not colored, not bent aside. His life is the perpetual rebuke of all time since. It condemns ancient civilization; it condemns modern civilization. Wise men we have since had, and good men; but this Galilean youth strode before the world whole thousands of years, so much of divinity was in him. His words solve the questions of this present age. In him the Godlike and the human met and embraced, and a divine life was born. Measure him by the world's greatest sons—how poor they are! Try him

by the best of men—how little and low they appear!
Exalt him as much as we may, we shall yet perhaps come
short of the mark. But still was he not our brother; the
son of man, as we are; the son of God, like ourselves? His
excellence—was it not human excellence? His wisdom, love,
piety—sweet and celestial as they were—are they not what
we also may attain? In him, as in a mirror, we may see
the image of God, and go on from glory to glory, till we
are changed into the same image, led by the spirit which
enlightens the humble. Viewed in this way, how beautiful
is the life of Jesus! Heaven has come down to earth, or,
rather, earth has become heaven. The Son of God, come of
age, has taken possession of his birthright. The brightest
revelation is this of what is possible for all men—if not
now, at least hereafter. How pure is his spirit, and how
encouraging its words! "Lowly sufferer," he seems to say,
"see how I bore the cross. Patient laborer, be strong; see
how I toiled for the unthankful and the merciless. Mistaken
sinner, see of what thou art capable. Rise up, and be
blessed."

But if, as some early Christians began to do, you take
a heathen view, and make him a God, the Son of God in
a peculiar and exclusive sense, much of the significance
of his character is gone. His virtue has no merit, his love
no feeling, his cross no burthen, his agony no pain. His
death is an illusion, his resurrection but a show. For if
he were not a man, but a god, what are all these things?
what his words, his life, his excellence of achievement?
It is all nothing, weighed against the illimitable greatness
of Him who created the worlds and fills up all time and
space! Then his resignation is no lesson, his life no model,
his death no triumph to you or me, who are not gods, but
mortal men, that know not what a day shall bring forth,
and walk by faith "dim sounding on our perilous way."
Alas! we have despaired of man, and so cut off his brightest
hope.

In respect of doctrines as well as forms, we see all is
transitory. "Everywhere is instability and insecurity."
Opinions have changed most on points deemed most vital.
Could we bring up a Christian teacher of any age, from

the sixth to the fourteenth century, for example, though a teacher of undoubted soundness of faith, whose word filled the churches of Christendom, clergymen would scarce allow him to kneel at their altar, or sit down with them at the Lord's table. His notions of Christianity could not be expressed in our forms, nor could our notions be made intelligible to his ears. The questions of his age, those on which Christianity was thought to depend—questions which perplexed and divided the subtle doctors—are no questions to us. The quarrels which then drove wise men mad now only excite a smile or a tear, as we are disposed to laugh or weep at the frailty of man. We have other straws of our own to quarrel for. Their ancient books of devotion do not speak to us; their theology is a vain word. To look back but a short period—the theological speculations of our fathers during the last two centuries, their "practical divinity," even the sermons written by genius and piety, are, with rare exceptions, found unreadable; such a change is there in the doctrines.

Now who shall tell us that the change is to stop here; that this sect or that, or even all sects united, have exhausted the river of life, and received it all in their canonized urns, so that we need draw no more out of the eternal well, but get refreshment nearer at hand? Who shall tell us that another age will not smile at our doctrines, disputes, and unchristian quarrels about Christianity, and make wide the mouth at men who walked brave in orthodox raiment, delighting to blacken the names of heretics, and repeat again the old charge, "He hath blasphemed"? Who shall tell us they will not weep at the folly of all such as fancied truth shone only into the contracted nook of their school, or sect, or coterie? Men of other times may look down equally on the heresy-hunters, and men hunted for heresy, and wonder at both. The men of all ages before us were quite as confident as we, that their opinion was truth, that their notion was Christianity and the whole thereof. The men who lit the fires of persecution, from the first martyr to Christian bigotry down to the last murder of the innocents, had no doubt their opinion was divine. The contest about transubstantiation, and the immaculate purity of the Hebrew and Greek texts of the Scriptures, was waged with a bitterness unequalled in these days. The Protestant smiles at one, the Catholic at the other, and men of sense wonder at both. It might teach us all a lesson, at least of forbearance. No doubt an age will come in which ours shall be reckoned a period of darkness, like the sixth century—when men groped for the wall, but stumbled and fell, because they trusted a transient notion, not an eternal truth; an age when temples were full of idols, set up by human folly; an age in which Christian light had scarce begun to shine into men's hearts. But while this change goes on, while one generation of opinions passes away, and another rises up, Christianity itself, that pure religion, which exists eternal in the constitution of the soul and the mind of God, is always the same. The Word that was before Abraham, in the very beginning, will not change, for that Word is truth. From this Jesus subtracted nothing; to this he added nothing. But he came to reveal it as the secret of God, that cunning men could not understand, but which filled the souls of men meek and lowly of heart. This truth we owe to God; the revelation thereof to Jesus, our elder brother, God's chosen son.

To turn away from the disputes of the Catholics and the Protestants, of the Unitarian and the Trinitarian, of old school and new school, and come to the plain words of Jesus of Nazareth—Christianity is a simple thing, very simple. It is absolute, pure morality; absolute, pure religion—the love of man; the love of God acting without let or hindrance. The only creed it lays down is the great truth which springs up spontaneous in the holy heart—there is a God. Its watchword is, Be perfect as your Father in heaven. The only form it demands is a divine life—doing the best thing in the best way, from the highest motives; perfect obedience to the great law of God. Its sanction is the voice of God in your heart; the perpetual presence of him who made us and the stars over our head; Christ and the Father abiding within us. All this is very simple—a little child can understand it;

very beautiful—the loftiest mind can find nothing so lovely. Try it by reason, conscience, and faith—things highest in man's nature—we see no redundance, we feel no deficiency. Examine the particular duties it enjoins—humility, reverence, sobriety, gentleness, charity, forgiveness, fortitude, resignation, faith, and active love; try the whole extent of Christianity, so well summed up in the command, "Thou shalt love the Lord thy God with all thy heart, and with all thy soul, and with all thy mind; thou shalt love thy neighbor as thyself;" and is there anything therein that can perish? No, the very opponents of Christianity have rarely found fault with the teachings of Jesus. The end of Christianity seems to be to make all men one with God as Christ was one with him; to bring them to such a state of obedience and goodness that we shall think divine thoughts and feel divine sentiments, and so keep the law of God by living a life of truth and love. Its means are purity and prayer; getting strength from God, and using it for our fellow-men as well as ourselves. It allows perfect freedom. It does not demand all men to *think* alike, but to think uprightly, and get as near as possible at truth; not all men to *live* alike, but to live holy, and get as near as possible to a life perfectly divine. Christ set up no Pillars of Hercules, beyond which men must not sail the sea in quest of truth. He says, "I have many things to say unto you, but ye cannot bear them now. ... Greater works than these shall ye do." Christianity lays no rude hand on the sacred peculiarity of individual genius and character. But there is no Christian sect which does not fetter a man. It would make all men think alike, or smother their conviction in silence. Were all men Quakers or Catholics, Unitarians or Baptists, there would be much less diversity of thought, character, and life, less of truth active in the world, than now. But Christianity gives us the largest liberty of the sons of God; and were all men Christians after the fashion of Jesus, this variety would be a thousand times greater than now; for Christianity is not a system of doctrines, but rather a method of attaining oneness with God. It demands, therefore, a good life of piety within, of purity without, and gives the promise that whoso does God's will shall know of God's doctrine.

In an age of corruption, as all ages are, Jesus stood and looked up to God. There was nothing between him and the Father of all; no old world, be it of Moses or Esaias, of a living Rabbi or Sanhedrim of Rabbis; no sin or perverseness of the finite will. As the result of this virgin purity of soul and perfect obedience, the light of God shone down into the very deeps of his soul, bringing all of the Godhead which flesh can receive. He would have us do the same; worship with nothing between us and God; act, think, feel, live, in perfect obedience to him: and we never are *Christians* as he was the *Christ*, until we worship, as Jesus did, with no mediator, with nothing between us and the Father of all. He felt that God's word was in him; that he was one with God. He told what he saw—the truth; he lived what he felt—a life of love. The truth he brought to light must have been always the same before the eyes of all-seeing God, nineteen centuries before Christ, or nineteen centuries after him. A life supported by the principle and quickened by the sentiment of religion, if true to both, is always the same thing in Nazareth or New England. Now that divine man received these truths from God; was illumined more clearly by "the light that lighteneth every man;" combined or involved all the truths of religion and morality in his doctrine, and made them manifest in his life. Then his words and example passed into the world, and can no more perish than the stars be wiped out of the sky. The truths he taught; his doctrines respecting man and God; the relation between man and man, and man and God, with the duties that grow out of that relation are always the same, and can never change till man ceases to be man, and creation vanishes into nothing. No; forms and opinions change and perish, but the word of God cannot fail. The form religion takes, the doctrines wherewith she is girded, can never be the same in any two centuries or two men; for since the sum of religious doctrines is both the result and the measure of a man's total growth in wisdom, virtue, and piety, and since men will always differ in these respects, so religious *doctrines* and *forms* will always differ, always be transient, as Christianity goes forth and scatters the seed she bears in her hand. But the *Christianity holy men feel in the heart*, the Christ that is born within us, is always the same thing to each soul that feels it. This differs only in degree, and not in kind, from age to age, and man to man. There is something in Christianity which no sect, from the "Ebionites" to the "Latter-Day Saints," ever entirely overlooked. This is that common Christianity which burns in the hearts of pious men.

Real Christianity gives men new life. It is the growth and perfect action of the Holy Spirit God puts into the sons of men. It makes us outgrow any form or any system of doctrines we have devised, and approach still closer to the truth. It would lead us to take what help we can find. It would make the Bible our servant, not our master. It would teach us to profit by the wisdom and piety of David and Solomon, but not to sin their sins, nor bow to their idols. It would make us revere the holy words spoken by "godly men of old," but revere still more the word of God spoken through conscience, reason, and faith, as the holiest of all. It would not make Christ the despot of the soul, but the brother of all men. It would not tell us that even he had exhausted the fulness of God, so that he could create none greater; for with him "all things are possible," and neither Old Testament nor New Testament ever hints that creation exhausts the Creator. Still less would it tell us the wisdom, the piety, the love, the manly excellence of Jesus, was the result of miraculous agency alone, but that it was won, like the excellence of humbler men, by faithful obedience to Him who gave his Son such ample heritage. It would point to him as our brother, who went before, like the good shepherd, to charm us with the music of his words, and with the beauty of his life to tempt us up the steeps of mortal toil, within the gate of heaven. It would have us make the kingdom of God on earth, and enter more fittingly the kingdom on high. It would lead us to form Christ in the heart, on which Paul laid such stress, and work out our salvation by this. For it is not so much by the Christ who lived so blameless and beautiful eighteen centuries ago that we are saved directly, but by the Christ we form in our hearts and live out in our daily life that we save ourselves, God working with us both to will and to do.

Compare the simpleness of Christianity, as Christ sets it forth on the Mount, with what is sometimes taught and accepted in that honored name, and what a difference! One is of God, one is of man. There is something in Christianity which sects have not reached—something that will not be won, we fear, by theological battles, or the quarrels of pious men; still we may rejoice that Christ is preached in any way. The Christianity of sects, of the pulpit, of society, is ephemeral—a transitory fly. It will pass off and be forgot. Some new form will take its place, suited to the aspect of the changing times. Each will represent something of truth, but no one the whole. It seems the whole race of man is needed to do justice to the whole of truth, as "the whole church, to preach the whole gospel." Truth is intrusted for the time to a perishable ark of human contrivance. Though often shipwrecked, she always comes safe to land, and is not changed by her mishap. That pure ideal religion which Jesus saw on the mount of his vision, and lived out in the lowly life of a Galilean peasant; which transforms his cross into an emblem of all that is holiest on earth; which makes sacred the ground he trod, and is dearest to the best of men, most true to what is truest in them—cannot pass away. Let men improve never so far in civilization, or soar never so high on the wings of religion and love, they can never outgo the flight of truth and Christianity. It will always be above them. It is as if we were to fly towards a star, which becomes larger and more bright the nearer we approach, till we enter and are absorbed in its glory.

If we look carelessly on the ages that have gone by, or only on the surfaces of things as they come up before us, there is reason to fear; for we confound the truth of God with the word of man. So at a distance the cloud and the mountain seem the same. When the drift changes with the passing wind, an unpractised eye might fancy the mountain itself was gone. But the mountain stands to catch the clouds, to win the blessing they bear, and send it down to moisten the fainting violet, to form streams which gladden valley and meadow, and sweep on at last to the sea in deep channels, laden with fleets. Thus the forms of the church, the creeds of the sects, the conflicting opinions of teachers, float round the sides of the Christian mount, and swell and toss, and rise and fall, and dart their lightning, and roll their thunder, but they neither make nor mar the mount itself. Its lofty summit far transcends the tumult, knows nothing of the storm which roars below, but burns with rosy light at evening and at morn, gleams in the splendors of the mid-day sun, sees his light when the long shadows creep over plain and moorland, and all night long has its head in the heavens, and is visited by troops of stars which never set, nor veil their face to aught so pure and high.

Let then the transient pass, fleet as it will, and may God send us some new manifestation of the Christian faith, that shall stir men's hearts as they were never stirred; some new word, which shall teach us what we are, and renew us all in the image of God; some better life, that shall fulfil the Hebrew prophecy, and pour out the spirit of God on young men and maidens, and old men and children; which shall realize the word of Christ and give us the Comforter, who shall reveal all needed things! There are Simeons enough in the cottages and churches of New England, plain men and pious women, who wait for the consolation, and would die in gladness if their expiring breath could stir quicker the wings that bear him on. There are men enough, sick and "bowed down, in no wise able to lift up themselves," who would be healed could they kiss the hand of their Saviour, or touch but the hem of his garment—men who look up and are not fed, because they ask bread from heaven and water from the rock, not traditions or fancies, Jewish or heathen, or new or old; men enough who, with throbbing hearts, pray for the spirit of healing to come upon the waters, which other than angels have long kept in trouble;

men enough who have lain long time sick of theology, nothing bettered by many physicians, and are now dead, too dead to bury their dead, who would come out of their graves at the glad tidings. God send us a real religious life, which shall pluck blindness out of the heart, and make us better fathers, mothers, and children! a religious life that shall go with us where we go, and make every home the house of God, every act acceptable as a prayer. We would work for this, and pray for it, though we wept tears of blood while we prayed.

Such, then, is the transient, and such the permanent in Christianity. What is of absolute value never changes; we may cling round it and grow to it forever. No one can say his notions shall stand. But we may all say the truth, as it is in Jesus, shall never pass away. Yet there are always some, even religious men, who do not see the permanent element, so they rely on the fleeting, and, what is also an evil, condemn others for not doing the same. They mistake a defense of the truth for an attack upon the holy of holies; the removal of a theological error for the destruction of all religion. Already men of the same sect eye one another with suspicion and lowering brows that indicate a storm, and, like children who have fallen out in their play, call hard names. Now, as always, there is a collision between these two elements. The question puts itself to each man, "Will you cling to what is perishing, or embrace what is eternal?" This question each must answer for himself.

My friends, if you receive the notions about Christianity which chance to be current in your sect or church, solely because they are current, and thus accept the commandment of men instead of God's truth, there will always be enough to commend you for soundness of judgment, prudence, and good sense, enough to call you Christian for that reason. But if this is all you rely upon, alas for you! The ground will shake under your feet if you attempt to walk uprightly, and like men. You will be afraid of every new opinion, lest it shake down your church; you will fear "lest if a fox go up, he will break down your stone wall." The smallest contradiction in the New Testament or Old Testament, the least disagreement between the law and the gospel, any mistake of the apostles, will weaken your faith. It shall be with you "as when a hungry man dreameth, and behold, he eateth; but he awaketh, and his soul is empty."

If, on the other hand, you take the true word of God, and live out this, nothing shall harm you. Men may mock, but their mouthfuls of wind shall be blown back upon their own face. If the master of the house were called Beelzebub, it matters little what name is given to the household. The name Christian, given in mockery, will last till the world go down. He that loves God and man, and lives in accordance with that love, needs not fear what man can do to him. His religion comes to him in his hour of sadness, it lays its hand on him when he has fallen among thieves, and raises him up, heals and comforts him. If he is crucified, he shall rise again.

My friends, you this day receive, with the usual formalities, the man you have chosen to speak to you on the highest of all themes—what concerns your life on earth, your life in heaven. It is a work for which no talents, no prayerful diligence, no piety is too great; an office that would dignify angels, if worthily filled. If the eyes of this man be holden, that he *cannot* discern between the perishing and the true, you will hold him guiltless of all sin in this; but look for light where it can be had, for his office will then be of no use to you. But if he sees the truth, and is scared by worldly motives, and *will* not tell it, alas for him! If the watchman see the foe coming and blow not the trumpet, the blood of the innocent is on him.

Your own conduct and character, the treatment you offer this young man, will in some measure influence him. The hearer affects the speaker. There were some places where even Jesus "did not many mighty works, because of their unbelief." Worldly motives—not seeming such—sometimes deter good men from their duty. Gold and ease have, before now, enervated noble minds. Daily contact with men of low aims takes down the ideal of life, which a bright spirit casts out of itself. Terror has sometimes palsied tongues that, before, were eloquent as the voice of persuasion. But thereby truth is not holden. She speaks in a thousand tongues, and with a pen of iron graves her sentence on the rock forever. You may prevent the freedom of speech in this pulpit if you will. You may hire you servants to preach as you bid; to spare your vices, and flatter your follies; to prophesy smooth things, and say, It is peace, when there is no peace. Yet in so doing you weaken and enthrall yourselves. And alas for that man who consents to think one thing in his closet and preach another in his pulpit! God shall judge him in his mercy, not man in his wrath. But over his study and over his pulpit might be writ, EMPTINESS; on his canonical robes, on his forehead and right hand, DECEIT! DECEIT!

But, on the other hand, you may encourage your brother to tell you the truth. Your affection will then be precious to him, your prayers of great price. Every evidence of your sympathy will go to baptize him anew to holiness and truth. You will then have his best words, his brightest thoughts, and his most hearty prayers. He may grow old in your service, blessing and blest. He will have—

> "The sweetest, best of consolation,
>   The thought, that he has given,
>   To serve the cause of Heaven,
>
> The freshness of his early inspiration."

Choose as you will choose; but weal or woe depends upon your choice.

CHAPTER FOUR

THE LITERARY ASPIRATION

1. THE DIAL, 1840-1844

[The New England Society wherein the Transcendentalists came of age, in the 1830's, was already embarked upon an industrial revolution which was rapidly transforming the rural region into an economy of factories and investment, which was demoting its remaining country population to the status of vestigial survivals from a vanished order. (Hence, in part, the ferocity of Thoreau's dedication to the Concord swamps.) Even so, the public life of New England professed to be still concentrated upon religion. Two or three of those who eventually played a part in the Transcendental drama—Alcott, Sylvester Judd, Brownson—came into it from orthodox Calvinist backgrounds, but most of the actors were children of Unitarianism, and the others went through a preparatory Unitarian phase.

This liberal theology served, ironically, in their development, as it definitely did not in the lives of their fathers (except perhaps for Channing), as a liberation from all theological concern. While it is entirely fair to say that in their new-found pursuits, they generally re-enacted the spiritual patterns of Puritan behavior, still we must recognize that most of them aspired to escape from the clutch of the old preoccupation, to expend themselves not in the vindication of any doctrine whatsoever, but in the creation of an American literature.

By force of circumstances, much of their initial energy had to be devoted to ridding themselves of the incubus of the miracles. Since Theodore Parker remained in the pulpit—albeit, in the pulpit of his own creating, without any association with any denomination—he continued to address himself to the theological as well as the sociological problems; the incurably theologically minded Brownson could fight with others and with himself only within the area of doctrine, until at last he accepted the miracles entirely and found, in 1844, his surcease in the Catholic Church.

But Emerson quietly though emphatically withdrew from all churches by resigning his pulpit at the Second Church in 1832 (though occasionally thereafter he did preach in such churches as would invite him). Margaret Fuller and Bronson Alcott simply left organized Christianity to one side, while Thoreau, serving notice on the selectmen of Concord that he resigned from all societies he had never joined, viciously attacked the churches and devoted himself to rendering pure nature into pure prose.

Under such leadership, the like-minded got themselves sufficiently, though with difficulty, together in 1840 to issue, in July, the first number of their quarterly, *The Dial*. Margaret Fuller served as editor for two years, and Emerson finished out the job for two more. The magazine never made any money, and never attained more than three hundred subscribers. (Copies of the original now fetch fantastic prices in the rare-book market.) Judged by modern standards of journalism, it was an abysmal failure; judged by other standards, it was a first and memorably gallant effort of the mind in America.

Evidently, Margaret prepared a draft of the introductory manifesto; Emerson seems to have rewritten it so extensively that it must be considered primarily his. However, it is not printed in the standard editions of his work. The principal point, I imagine, is the graciousness of the tone, all the most striking in the terms of 1840, when the controversy had become so acrimonious. Furthermore, on the second level, it displays Emerson's cool realization that not too much in the way of creativity could yet be expected from this provincial, mercantile New England—or as yet from America.]

THE EDITORS TO THE READER

We invite the attention of our countrymen to a new design. Probably not quite unexpected or unannounced will our Journal appear, though small pains have been taken to secure its welcome. Those, who have immediately acted in editing the present Number, cannot accuse themselves of any unbecoming forwardness in their undertaking, but rather of a backwardness, when they remember how often in many private circles the work was projected, how eagerly desired, and only postponed because no individual volunteered to combine and concentrate the freewill offerings of many coöperators. With some reluctance the present conductors of this work have yielded themselves to the wishes of their friends, finding something sacred and not to be withstood in the importunity which urged the production of a Journal in a new spirit.

As they have not proposed themselves to the work, neither can they lay any the least claim to an option or determination of the spirit in which it is conceived, or to what is peculiar in the design. In that respect, they have obeyed, though with great joy, the strong current of thought and feeling, which, for a few years past, has led many sincere persons in New England to make new demands on literature, and to reprobate that rigor of our conventions of religions and education which is turning us to stone, which renounces hope, which looks only backward, which asks only such a future as the past, which suspects improvement, and holds nothing so much in horror as new views and the dreams of youth.

With these terrors the conductors of the present Journal have nothing to do—not even so much as a word of reproach to waste. They know that there is a portion of the youth and of the adult population of this country, who have not shared them; who have in secret or in public paid their vows to truth and freedom; who love reality too well to care for names, and who live by a Faith too earnest and profound to suffer them to doubt the eternity of its object, or to shake themselves free from its authority.

Under the fictions and customs which occupied others, these have explored the Necessary, the Plain, the True, the Human—and so gained a vantage ground, which commands the history of the past and the present.

No one can converse much with different classes of society in New England, without remarking the progress of a revolution. Those who share in it have no external organization, no badge, no creed, no name. They do not vote, or print, or even meet together. They do not know each other's faces or names. They are united only in a common love of truth, and love of its work. They are of all conditions and constitutions. Of these acolytes, if some are happily born and well-bred, many are no doubt ill dressed, ill placed, ill made—with as many scars of hereditary vice as other men. Without pomp, without trumpet, in lonely and obscure places, in solitude, in servitude, in compunctions and privations, trudging beside the team in the dusty road, or drudging a hierling in other men's corn-fields, schoolmasters, who teach a few children rudiments for a pittance, ministers of small parishes of the obscurer sects, lone women in dependent condition, matrons and young maidens, rich and poor, beautiful and hard-favored, without concert of proclamation of any kind, they have silently given in their several adherence to a new hope, and in all companies do signify a greater trust in the nature and resources of man, than the laws or the popular opinions will well allow.

This spirit of the time is felt by every individual with some difference—to each one casting its light upon the objects nearest to his temper and habits of thought—to one, coming in the shape of special reforms in the state; to another, in modifications of the various callings of men, and the customs of business; to a third, opening a new scope for literature and art; to a fourth, in philosophical insight; to a fifth, in the vast solitudes of prayer. It is in every form a protest against usage, and a search for principles. In all its movements, it is peaceable, and in the very lowest marked with a triumphant success. Of course, it rouses the opposition of all which it judges and condemns, but it is too confident in its tone to comprehend an objection, and so builds no outworks for possible defence against contingent enemies. It has the step of Fate, and goes on existing like an oak or a river, because it must.

In literature, this influence appears not yet in new books so much as in the higher tone of criticism. The antidote to all narrowness is the comparison of the record with nature, which at once shames the record and stimulates to new attempts. Whilst we look at this, we wonder how any book has been thought worthy to be preserved. There is somewhat in all life untranslatable into language. He who keeps his eye on that will write better than others, and think less of his writing, and of all writing. Every thought has a certain imprisoning as well as uplifting quality, and, in proportion to its energy on the will, refuses to become an object of intellectual contemplation. Thus what is great usually slips through our fingers, and it seems wonderful how a lifelike word ever comes to be written. If our Journal share the impulses of the time, it cannot now prescribe its own course. It cannot foretell in orderly propositions what it shall attempt. All criticism should be poetic; unpredictable; superseding, as every new thought does, all foregone thoughts, and making a new light on the whole world. Its brow is not wrinkled with circumspection, but serene, cheerful, adoring. It has all things to say, and on less than all the world for its final audience.

Our plan embraces much more than criticism; were it not so, our criticism would be naught. Everything noble is directed on life, and this is. We do not wish to say pretty or curious things, or to reiterate a few propositions in varied forms, but, if we can, to give expression to that spirit which lifts men to a higher platform, restores to them the religious sentiment, brings them worthy aims and pure pleasures, purges the inward eye, makes life less desultory, and, through raising man to the level of nature, takes away its melancholy from the landscape, and reconciles the practical with the speculative powers.

But perhaps we are telling our little story too gravely. There are always great arguments at hand for a true action, even for the writing of a few pages. There is nothing but seems near it and prompts it—the sphere in the ecliptic, the sap in the apple tree—every fact, every appearance seem to persuade to it.

Our means correspond with the ends we have indicated. As we wish not to multiply books, but to report life, our resources are therefore not so much the pens of practised writers, as the discourse of the living, and the portfolios which friendship has opened to us. From the beautiful recesses of private thought; from the experience and hope of spirits which are withdrawing from all old forms, and seeking in all that is new somewhat to meet their inappeasable longings; from the secret confession of genius afraid to trust itself to aught but sympathy; from the conversation of fervid and mystical pietists; from tearstained diaries of sorrow and passion; from the manuscripts of young poets; and from the records of youthful taste commenting on old works of art; we hope to draw thoughts and feelings, which being alive can impart life.

And so with diligent hands and good intent we set down our *Dial* on the earth. We wish it may resemble that instrument in its celebrated happiness, that of measuring no hours but those of sunshine. Let it be one cheerful rational voice amidst the din of mourners and polemics. Or to abide by our chosen image, let it be such a *Dial*, not as the dead face of a clock, hardly even such as the Gnomon in a garden, but rather such a *Dial* as is the Garden itself, in whose leaves and flowers and fruits the suddenly awakened sleeper is instantly apprised not what part of dead time, but what state of life and growth is now arrived and arriving.

2. HENRY DAVID THOREAU, 1817-1862

[In the last six or seven years of his life, driven by economic necessity but also by an irrepressible desire to communicate with his fellow-travellers, Henry Thoreau attempted to give lectures in several of neighboring Lyceums. As far as we can gather, the result was not successful, either in terms of remuneration or of communication.

To compose these "lectures," Henry drew upon his *Journal*, especially on his most fecund years, about 1850 to 1855. He tried to make of these compilations moderately coherent discourses, following the method of Emerson, as we have heard Alcott describe it (pp. 97-98). Often the announced topic—in this case "Walking"—serves only as a starting point for later digressions. This compiled essay was printed in *The Atlantic Monthly* for June, 1862, a little month after his death, just past the age of forty-four, on the previous May 6.

Upon the announced theme, the speech has many amusing and rich observations, but we have already accompanied Thoreau on several of his typical walks. In this confined space, let us listen to the major digression, the most energetic statement on record of the Transcendental program in literature. Thus conceived by the most rigorous of its exponents, it was tragically given to the world only after both he and the movement had expired.]

WALKING

I wish to speak a word for Nature, for absolute freedom and wildness, as contrasted with a freedom and culture merely civil—to regard man as an inhabitant, or a part and parcel of Nature, rather than a member of society. I wish to make an extreme statement, if so I may make an emphatic one, for there are enough champions of civilization: the minister and the school-committee, and every one of you will take care of that. . . .

What is it that makes it so hard sometimes to determine whither we will walk? I believe that there is subtle magnetism in Nature, which, if we unconsciously yield to it, will direct us aright. It is not indifferent to us which way we walk. There is a right way; but we are very liable from heedlessness and stupidity to take the wrong one. We would fain take that walk, never yet taken by us through this actual world, which is perfectly symbolical of the path which we love to travel in the interior and ideal world; and sometimes, no doubt, we find it difficult to choose our direction, because it does not yet exist distinctly in our idea.

When I go out of the house for a walk, uncertain as yet whither I will bend my steps, and submit myself to my instinct to decide for me, I find, strange and whimsical as it may seem, that I finally and inevitably settle southwest, toward some particular wood or meadow or deserted pasture or hill in that direction. My needle is slow to settle—varies a few degrees, and does not always point due southwest, it is true, and it has good authority for this variation, but it always settles between west and south-southwest. The future lies that way to me, and the earth seems more unexhausted and richer on that side. The outline which would bound my walks would be, not a circle, but a parabola, or rather like one of those cometary orbits which have been thought to be non-returning curves, in this case opening westward, in which my house occupies the place of the sun. I turn round and round irresolute sometimes for a quarter of an hour, until I decide, for a thousandth time, that I will walk into the southwest or west. Eastward I go only by force; but westward I go free. Thither no business leads me. It is hard for me to believe that I shall find fair landscapes or sufficient wildness and freedom behind the eastern horizon. I am not excited by the prospect of a walk thither; but I believe that the forest which I see in the western horizon stretches uninterruptedly toward the setting sun, and there are no towns nor cities in it of enough consequence to disturb me. Let me live where I will, on this side is the city, on that the wilderness, and ever I am leaving the city more and more, and withdrawing into the wilderness. I should not lay so much stress on this fact, if I did not believe that something like this is the prevailing tendency of my countrymen. I must walk toward Oregon, and not toward Europe. And that way the nation is moving, and I may say that mankind progresses from east to west. Within a few years we have witnessed the phenomenon of a southeastward migration, in the settlement of Australia; but this affects us as a retrograde movement, and, judging from the moral and physical character of the first generation of Australians, has not yet proved a successful experiment. The eastern Tartars think that there is nothing west beyond Thibet. "The world ends there," say they: beyond there is nothing but a shoreless sea." It is unmitigated East where they live.

We go eastward to realize history and study the works of art and literature, retracing the steps of the race; we go westward as into the future, with a spirit of enterprise and adventure. The Atlantic is a Lethean stream, in our passage over which we have had an opportunity to forget the Old World and its institutions. If we do not succeed this time, there is perhaps one more chance for the race left before it arrives on the banks of the Styx; and that is the Lethe of the Pacific, which is three times as wide. . . .Some months ago I went to see a panorama of the Rhine. It was like a dream of the Middle Ages. I floated down its historic stream in something more than imagination, under bridges built by the Romans, and repaired by later heroes, past cities and castles whose very names were music to my eyes, and each of which was the subject of a legend. . . .

Soon after, I went to see a panorama of the Mississippi, and as I worked my way up the river in the light of to-day, and saw the steam-boats wooding up, counted the rising cities, gazed on the fresh ruins of Nauvoo, beheld the Indians moving west across the stream, and, as before I had looked up the Moselle now looked up the Ohio and the Missouri, and heard the legends of Dubuque and of Wenona's Cliff—still thinking more of the future than of the past or present—I saw that this was a Rhine stream of a different kind; that the foundations of castles were yet to be laid, and the famous bridges were yet to be thrown over the river; and I felt that this was the heroic age itself, though we know it not, for the hero is commonly the simplest and obscurest of men.

The West of which I speak is but another name for the

Wild; and what I have been preparing to say is, that in Wilderness is the preservation of the World. Every tree sends its fibres forth in search of the Wild. The cities import it at any price. Men plow and sail for it. From the forest and wilderness come the tonics and barks which brace mankind. Our ancestors were savages. The story of Romulus and Remus being suckled by a wolf is not a meaningless fable. The founders of every state which has risen to eminence have drawn their nourishment and vigor from a similar wild source. It was because the children of the Empire were not suckled by the wolf that they were conquered and displaced by the children of the northern forests who were.

I believe in the forest, and in the meadow, and in the night in which the corn grows. We require an infusion of hemlock spruce or arbor-vitae in our tea. There is a difference between eating and drinking for strength and from mere gluttony. The Hottentots eagerly devour the marrow of the koodoo and other antelopes raw, as a matter of course. Some of our northern Indians eat raw the marrow of the Arctic reindeer, as well as various other parts, including the summits of the antlers, as long as they are soft. And herein, perchance, they have stolen a march on the cooks of Paris. They get what usually goes to feed the fire. This is probably better than stall-fed beef and slaughter-house pork to make a man of. Give me a wildness whose glance no civilization can endure—as if we live on the marrow of koodoos devoured raw. . . .

In literature it is only the wild that attracts us. Dullness is but another name for tameness. It is the uncivilized free and wild thinking in *Hamlet* and the *Iliad,* in all the scriptures and mythologies, not learned in the schools, that delights us. As the wild duck is more swift and beautiful than the tame, so is the wild—the mallard—thought, which 'mid falling dews wings its way above the fens. A truly good book is something as natural, and as unexpectedly and unaccountably fair and perfect, as a wild-flower discovered on the prairies of the West or in the jungles of the East. Genius is a light which makes the darkness visible, like the lightning's flash, which perchance shatters the temple of knowledge itself—and not a taper lighted at the hearth-stone of the race, which pales before the light of common day.

English literature, from the days of the minstrels to the Lake Poets—Chaucer and Spenser and Milton, and even Shakespeare, included—breathes no quite fresh and, in this sense, wild strain. It is essentially tame and civilized literature, reflecting Greece and Rome. Her wilderness is a greenwood, her wild man a Robin Hood. There is plenty of genial love of Nature, but not so much of Nature herself. Her chronicles inform us when her wild animals, but not when the wild man in her, became extinct.

The science of Humboldt is one thing, poetry is another thing. The poet to-day, nothwithstanding all the discoveries of science, and the accumulated learning of mankind, enjoys no advantage over Homer.

Where is the literature which gives expression to Nature? He would be a poet who could impress the winds and streams into his service, to speak for him; who nailed words to their primitive senses, as farmers drive down stakes in the spring, which the frost has heaved; who derived his words as often as he used them—transplanted them to his page with earth adhering to their roots; whose words were so true and fresh and natural that they would appear to expand like the buds at the approach of spring, though they lay half smothered between two musty leaves in a library—aye, to bloom and bear fruit there, after their kind, annually, for the faithful reader, in sympathy with surrounding Nature.

I do not know of any poetry to quote which adequately expresses this yearning for the Wild. Approached from this side, the best poetry is tame. I do not know where to find in any literature, ancient or modern, any account which contents me of that Nature with which even I am acquainted. You will perceive that I demand something which no Augustan nor Elizabethan age, which no *culture*, in short, can give. Mythology comes nearer to it than anything. How much more fertile a Nature, at least, has

Grecian mythology its root in than English literature! Mythology is the crop which the Old World bore before its soil was exhausted, before the fancy and imagination were affected with blight; and which it still bears, wherever its pristine vigor is unabated. All other literatures endure only as the elms which overshadow our houses; but this is like the great dragon-tree of the Western Isles, as old as mankind, and, whether that does or not, will endure as long; for the decay of other literatures makes the soil in which it thrives.

The West is preparing to add its fables to those of the East. The valleys of the Ganges, the Nile, and the Rhine having yielded their crop, it remains to be seen what the valleys of the Amazon, the Plate, the Orinoco, the St. Lawrence, and the Mississippi will produce. Perchance, when, in the course of ages, American liberty has become a fiction of the past—as it is to some extent a fiction of the present—the poets of the world will be inspired by American mythology.

3. MARGARET FULLER, 1810-1850

[Alas! as Emerson's foreword to *The Dial* fearfully anticipated, the first requirement in that literary America was not so much a way to achieve "wildness" as a lesson in discrimination. The fraternity had first to establish "the higher tone of criticism." The young geniuses of 1840 were disgusted with what they saw of book-reviewing, let alone anything approaching mature criticism, in the country. (They were never to show the slightest appreciation of the lonely labor of Edgar Allan Poe.) Not many pages out of the four volumes of *The Dial* are memorable for original creation; but as an endeavor to set up catholic standards of "poetic" criticism, the magazine remains a landmark in our intellectual history.

Yet, that success, if success it may be termed, was wrought at the cost of deeply disturbing feelings of guilt. After all, is not criticism an inferior form of literature, surely as compared with living and throbbing poetry? In the number for April, 1841, Margaret Fuller tried to argue the problem out with herself, and so let the fellowship listen to a dialogue which each, along with her, was strenuously conducting in his own self.]

A DIALOGUE

POET. Approach me not, man of cold steadfast eye and compressed lips. At thy coming nature shrouds herself in dull mist; fain would she hide her sighs and smiles, her buds and fruits even in a veil of snow. For thy unkindly breath, as it pierces her mystery, destroys its creative power. The birds draw back into their nests, the sunset hues into their clouds, when you are seen in the distance with your tablets all ready to write them into prose.

CRITIC. O my brother, my benefactor, do not thus repel me. Interpret me rather to our common mother; let her not avert her eyes from a younger child. I know I can never be dear to her as thou art, yet I am her child, nor would the fated revolutions of existence be fulfilled without my aid.

POET. How meanest thou? What have thy measurements, thy artificial divisions and classifications to do with the natural revolutions? In all real growths there is a "give and take" of unerring accuracy; in all the acts of thy life there is a falsity, for all are negative. Why do you not receive and produce in your kind, like the sunbeam and the rose? Then new life would be brought out, were it but the life of a weed, to bear witness to the healthful beatings of the divine heart. But this perpetual analysis, comparison, and classification never add one atom to the sum of existence.

CRITIC. I understand you.

POET. Yes, that is always the way. You understand me, who never have the arrogance to pretend that I understand myself.

CRITIC. Why should you—that is my province. I am the rock which gives you back the echo. I am the tuning-key, which harmonizes your instrument, the regulator to your watch. Who would speak, if no ear heard? nay, if no mind knew what the ear heard?

POET. I do not wish to be heard in thought but in love, to be recognised in judgment but in life. I would pour forth my melodies to the rejoicing winds. I would scatter my seed to the tender earth. I do not wish to hear in prose the meaning of my melody. I do not wish to see my seed neatly put away beneath a paper label. Answer in new paeons to the soul of our souls. Wake me to sweeter childhood by a fresher growth. At present you are but an excrescence produced by my life; depart, self-conscious Egotist, I know you not.

CRITIC. Dost thou so adore Nature, and yet deny me? Is not Art the child of Nature, Civilization of Man? As Religion into Philosophy, Poetry into Criticism, Life into Science, Love into Law, so did thy lyric in natural order transmute itself into my review.

POET. Review! Science! the very etymology speaks. What is gained by looking again at what has already been seen? What by giving a technical classification to what is already assimilated with the mental life?

CRITIC. What is gained by living at all?

POET. Beauty loving itself—Happiness!

CRITIC. Does not this involve consciousness?

POET. Yes! consciousness of Truth manifested in the individual form.

CRITIC. Since consciousness is tolerated, how will you limit it?

POET. By the instincts of my nature, which rejects yours as arrogant and superfluous.

CRITIC. And the dictate of my nature compels me to the processes which you despise, as essential to my peace. My brother (for I will not be rejected) I claim my place in the order of nature. The word descended and became flesh for two purposes, to organize itself, and to take cognizance of its organization. When the first Poet worked alone, he paused between the cantos to proclaim, "It is very good." Dividing himself among men, he made some to create and others to proclaim the merits of what is created.

POET. Well! if you were content with saying, "it is very good"; but you are always crying, "it is very bad," or ignorantly prescribing how it might be better. What do you know of it? Whatever is good could not be otherwise than it is. Why will you not take what suits you, and leave the rest? True communion of thought is worship, not criticism. Spirit will not flow through the sluices nor endure the locks of canals.

CRITIC. There is perpetual need of protestantism in every church. If the church be catholic, yet the priest is not infallible. Like yourself, I sigh for a perfectly natural state, in which the only criticism shall be tacit rejection, even as Venus glides not into the orbit of Jupiter, nor do the fishes seek to dwell in fire. But as you soar towards this as a Maker, so do I toil towards the same aim as a Seeker. Your pinions will not upbear you towards it in steady flight. I must often stop to cut away the brambles from my path. The law of my being is on me, and the ideal standard seeking to be realized in my mind bids me demand perfection from all I see. To say how far each object answers this demand is my criticism.

POET. If one object does not satisfy you, pass on to another, and say nothing.

CRITIC. It is not so that it would be well with me. I must penetrate the secret of my wishes, verify the justice of my reasonings. I must examine, compare, sift, and winnow; what can bear this ordeal remains to me as pure gold. I cannot pass on till I know what I feel and why. An object that defies my utmost rigor of scrutiny is a new step on the stair I am making to the Olympian tables.

POET. I think you will not know the gods when you get there, if I may judge from the cold presumption I feel in your version of the great facts of literature.

CRITIC. Statement of a part always looks like ignorance, when compared with the whole, yet may promise the whole. Consider that a part implies the whole, as the ever-lasting No the everlasting Yes, and permit to exist the shadow of your light, the register of your inspiration.

As he spake the word he paused, for with it his companion vanished, and floating on the cloud left a starry banner with the inscription "AFFLATUR NUMINE." The Critic unfolded one on whose flag-staff he had been leaning. Its heavy folds of pearly gray satin slowly unfolding, gave to view the word NOTITIA, and *Causarum* would have followed, when a sudden breeze from the west caught it, those heavy folds fell back round the poor man, and stifled him probably—at least he has never since been heard of.

4. MARGARET FULLER 1810-1850

[If then, for better or worse, *The Dial* was bound to be mainly a vehicle of criticism, it would assuredly have to confront the most challenging figure of the age. In the issue for July, 1841, Margaret Fuller pitted herself against colossal Goethe.

We have seen how Emerson, looking back in the perspective of time upon the period, stressed the fundamental importance of Goethe, the central position of *Faust,* the stimulation of Goethe's scientific speculations (pp. 7, 12). Emerson's *Journal* is full of his long struggle with Goethe, the fascination of whom he could not resist, the revolutionary modernity of whose thought he fully appreciated, but the coldness of whose Olympian egotism dismayed him and the laxness of whose morals repeatedly scandalized him. In most American journalism of the time Goethe was steadlly denounced as an immoralist beyond even Byron, and a corrupter of youth—"a writer," said *The Knickerbocker Magazine* in 1839, "who never hesitates to paint the grossest depravity, and even depicts it with a sort of zest; whose sensual scenes and sentiments debauch the understanding, inflame the sleeping passions, and prepare the reader to give way as soon as a tempter appears." At times, Emerson is almost as censorious—"the Puritan in me," he writes to Carlyle, "accepts no apology for bad morals in such as *he*"—yet when a minister at the Harvard Phi Beta Kappa celebration of 1844 denounced Goethe's morals in similar terms, Emerson jeered that he and his kind wanted Goethe to be a New England Calvinist, showed their ignorance that the entire movement which created these "Unitarian dissenters" in America "began in the mind of this great man he traduces." Emerson brought together and held in momentary equilibrium his conflicting feelings about Goethe in the final essay of *Representative Men* (1850), wherein Goethe figures, along with Napoleon, as spokesman for "the impatience and reaction of nature against the *morgue* of convention."

The younger Transcendentalists worshipped Goethe with a passion so idolatrous that Emerson sometimes had to break out in irritation that they would listen to no criticism against him from any quarter, though he would say that Margaret's piece was her best writing. She was steeped in Goethe's works, dreamed in her many moments of acute depression that if only she could tell him the state of her mind "he would support and guide me!" She gathered materials for writing a biography, and publicly avowed that she would treat *all* its aspects, and she did translate Eckermann's *Conversations*.

Goethe was simply irresistible to the Transcendentalists because more than any other modern figure he embodied their loftiest notions of "Genius." From one point of view, the movement may well be defined, in all its otherwise disparate manifestations, as an effort to accommodate the Transcending "self" on its highest plane—that is as Genius—to the full expanse of divine and moral nature. Goethe was *the* Genius who, showing himself fully at home in nature, still maintained his separate individuality and made himself equally at home in the artificial court of Weimar. Margaret's can hardly be called a critical estimate; it is rather a succession of fluctuations between the two poles of adoration and repulsion. Thus it comes palpitating from the heart of the cult.]

GOETHE

Nemo contra Deum nisi Deus ipse.
Wer Grosses will muss sich zusammen raffen;
In der Beschränkung zeigt sich erst der Meister,
Under der Gesetz nur kann uns Freiheit geben *

The first of these mottoes is that prefixed by Goethe to
the last books of *Dichtung und Wahrheit.* These books
record the hour of turning tide in his life, the time when
he was called on for a choice at the "Parting of the Ways."
From these months which gave the sun of his youth, the
crisis of his manhood, date the birth of *Egmont* and of
Faust too, though the latter was not published so early
They saw the rise and decline of his love for Lili, apparently the truest love he ever knew. That he was not himself dissatisfied with the results to which the decisions of
this era led him we may infer from his choice of a motto
and from the calm beauty with which he has invested the
record.

The Parting of the Ways! The way he took led to court-
favor, wealth, celebrity, and an independence of celebrity
It led to large performance and a wonderful economical
management of intellect. It led Faust, the Seeker, from
the heights of his own mind to the trodden ways of the
world. There indeed he did not lose sight of the mountains, but he never breathed their keen air again.

After this period we find in him rather a wide and deep
wisdom than the inspiration of Genius. His faith, that all
must issue well, wants the sweetness of piety, and the
God he manifests to us is one of law or necessity rather
than of intelligent love. As this God makes because he
must, so Goethe, his instrument, observes and recreates
because he must, observing with minutest fidelity the outward exposition of Nature; never blinded by a sham or

---

* "He who would do great things must quickly draw together
his forces. The master can only show himself such through
limitation, and the law alone can give us freedom." [M.F.
note]

detained by a fear, he yet makes us feel that he wants insight to her sacred secret. The calmest of writers does not give us repose because it is too difficult to find his centre. Those flame-like natures which he undervalues give us more peace and hope through their restless aspirations than he with his hearth-enclosed fires of steady fulfillment. For true as it is that God is everywhere, we must not only see him but see him acknowledged. Through the consciousness of man "shall not Nature interpret God?" We wander in diversity and, with each new turning of the path, long anew to be referred to the One.

Of Goethe, as of other natures where the intellect is too much developed in proportion to the moral nature, it is difficult to speak without seeming narrow, blind, and impertinent. For such men *see* all that others *live*, and if you feel a want of a faculty in them, it is hard to say they have it not, lest next moment they puzzle you by giving some indication of it. Yet they are not, nay, *know* not; they only discern. The difference is that between sight and life, prescience and being, wisdom and love. Thus with Goethe. Naturally of a deep mind and shallow heart, he felt the sway of the affections enough to appreciate their workings in other men, but never enough to receive their inmost regenerating influence.

How this might have been had he ever once abandoned himself entirely to a sentiment, it is impossible to say. But the education of his youth seconded rather than balanced his natural tendency. His father was a gentlemanly martinet: dull, sour, well-informed, and of great ambition as to externals. His influence on the son was wholly artificial. He was always turning his powerful mind from side to side in search of information, for the attainment of what are called accomplishments. The mother was a delightful person in her way: open, genial, playful, full of lively talent, but without earnestness of soul. She was one of those charming but not noble persons who take the day and the man as they find them, seeing the best that is there already, but never making the better grow in its stead. His sister, though of graver kind, was social and intellectual, not religious or tender. The mortifying repulse of his early love checked the few pale buds of faith and tenderness that his heart put forth. His friends were friends of the intellect merely; altogether he seemed led by destiny to the place he was to fill.

Pardon him, World, that he was too worldly. Do not wonder, Heart, that he was so heartless. Believe, Soul, that one so true as far as he went must yet be initiated into the deeper mysteries of Soul. Perhaps even now he sees that we must accept limitations only to transcend them; work in processes only to detect the organizing power which supersedes them; and that Sphinxes of fifty-five volumes might well be cast into the abyss before the single word that solves them all.

Now when I think of Goethe, I seem to see his soul all the variegated plumes of knowledge, artistic form, *und so weiter*, burnt from it by the fires of divine love, wingless, motionless, unable to hide from itself in any subterfuge of labor, saying again and again the simple word which he would never distinctly say on earth—God beyond Nature—Faith beyond Sight—the Seeker nobler than the *Meister*.

For this mastery that Goethe prizes seems to consist rather in the skillful use of means than in the clear manifestation of ends. His Master indeed makes acknowledgment of a divine order, but the temporal uses are always uppermost in the mind of the reader....

Apart from this want felt in his works, there is a littleness in his aspect as a character. Why waste his time in Weimar court entertainments? His duties as minister were not unworthy of him, though it would have been perhaps finer if he had not spent so large a portion of that prime of intelllectual life, from five and twenty to forty, upon them.

But granted that the exercise these gave his faculties, the various lore they brought, and the good they did to the community, made them worth his doing—why that perpetual dangling after the royal family? Why all that verse-making for the albums of serene highnesses, and those pretty poetical entertainments for the young princesses, and that cold setting himself apart from his true peers, the real sovereigns of Weimar—Herder, Wieland, and the others? The excuse must be found in circumstances of his time and temperament, which made the character of man of the world and man of affairs more attractive to him than the children of nature can conceive it to be in the eyes of one who is capable of being a consecrated bard.

The man of genius feels that literature has become too much a craft by itself. No man should live by or for his pen. Writing is worthless except as the record of life; and no great man ever was satisfied thus to express all his being. His book should be only an indication of himself. The obelisk should point to a scene of conquest. In the present state of division of labor, the literary man finds himself condemned to be nothing else. Does he write a good book? it is not received as evidence of his ability to live and act, but rather the reverse. Men do not offer him the care of embassies, as an earlier age did to Petrarca; they would be surprised if he left his study to go forth to battle like Cervantes. We have the swordsman, and states-man, and penman, but it is not considered that the same mind which can rule the destiny of a poem, may as well that of an army or an empire. Yet surely it should be so. The scientific man may need seclusion from the common affairs of life, for he has his materials before him; but the man of letters must seek them in life, and he who cannot act will but imperfectly appreciate action.

The literary man is impatient at being set apart. He feels that monks and troubadours, though in a similar position, were brought into more healthy connection with man and nature, than he who is supposed to look at them merely to write them down. So he rebels; and Sir Walter Scott is prouder of being a good sheriff and farmer, than of his reputation as the Great Unknown. Byron piques himself on his skill in shooting and swimming. Sir H. Davy and Schlegel would be admired as dandies, and Goethe, who had received an order from a publisher "for a dozen more dramas in the same style as *Götz von Berlichingen*," and though (in sadder sooth) he had already *Faust* in his head asking to be written out, thought it no degradation to become premier in the little Duchy of Weimar.

"Straws show which way the wind blows," and a comment may be drawn from the popular novels, where the literary man is obliged to wash off the ink in a violet bath, attest his courage in the duel, and hide his idealism beneath the vulgar nonchalance and coxcombry of the man of fashion.

If this tendency of his time had some influence in making Goethe find pleasure in tangible power and decided relations with society, there were other causes which worked deeper. The growth of genius in its relations to men around must always be attended with daily pain. The enchanted eye turns from the far-off star it has detected to the short-sighted bystander, and the seer is mocked for pretending to see what others cannot. The large and generalizing mind infers the whole from a single circumstance, and is reproved by all around for its presumptuous judgment. Its Ithuriel temper pierces shams, creeds, covenants, and chases the phantoms which others embrace, till the lovers of the false Florimels hurl the true knight to the ground. Little men are indignant that Hercules, yet an infant, declares he has strangled the serpent; they demand a proof; they send him out into scenes of labor to bring thence the voucher that his father is a god. What the ancients meant to express by Apollo's continual disappointment in his loves is felt daily in the youth of genius. The sympathy he seeks flies his touch, the objects of his affection sneer at his sublime credulity, his self-reliance is arrogance, his farsightedness infatuation, and his ready detection of fallacy fickleness and inconsistency. Such is the youth of genius, before the soul has given that sign of itself which an unbelieving generation cannot controvert. Even then he is little benefited by the transformation of the mockers into worshippers. For the soul seeks not adorers but peers; not blind worship but intelligent sympathy. The best consolation even then is that which Goethe puts into the mouth of Tasso: "To me gave a God to tell what I suffer." In *Tasso* Goethe has described the position of the poetical mind in its prose relations with equal depth and fullness. We see what he felt must be the result of entire abandonment to the highest nature. We see why he valued himself on being able to understand the Alphonsos, and meet as an equal the Antonios of every-day life.

But, you say, there is no likeness between Goethe and Tasso. Never believe it; such pictures are not painted from observation merely. That deep coloring which fillls them with light and life is given by dipping the brush in one's own life-blood. Goethe had not from nature that character of self-reliance and self-control in which he so long appeared to the world. It was wholly acquired, and so highly valued because he was conscious of the opposite tendency. He was by nature as impetuous though not as tender as Tasso, and the disadvantage at which this constantly placed him was keenly felt by a mind made to appreciate the subtlest harmonies in all relations. Therefore was it that when he at last cast anchor, he was so reluctant again to trust himself to wave and breeze.

I have before spoken of the antagonistic influences under which he was educated. He was driven from the severity of study into the world and then again drawn back many times in the course of his crowded youth. Both the world and the study he used with unceasing ardor, but not with the sweetness of a peaceful hope. Most of the traits which are considered to mark his character at a later period were wanting to him in youth. He was very social, and continually perturbed by his social sympathies. He was deficient both in outward self-possession and mental self-trust. "I was always," he says, "either *too volatile or too infatuated,* so that those who looked kindly on me did by no means always honor me with their esteem." He wrote much and with great freedom. The pen came naturally to his hand, but he had no confidence in the merit of what he wrote, and much inferior persons to Merck and Herder might have induced him to throw aside as worthless what it had given him sincere pleasure to compose. It was hard for him to isolate himself, to console himself, and though his mind was always busy with important thoughts, they did not free him from the pressure of other minds. His youth was as sympathetic and impetuous as any on record.

The effect of all this outward pressure on the poet is recorded in *Werther*—a production that he afterward undervalued, and to which he even felt positive aversion. It was natural that this should be. In the calm air of the cultivated plain he attained, the remembrance of the miasma of sentimentality was odious to him. Yet sentimentality is but sentiment diseased, which to be cured must be patiently observed by the wise physician; so are the morbid desire and despair of Werther, the sickness of a soul aspiring to a purer, freer state, but mistaking the way.

The best or the worst occasion in man's life is precisely that misused in Werther, when he longs for more love, more freedom, and a larger development of genius than the limitations of this terrene sphere permit. Sad is it indeed if persisting to grasp too much at once, he lose all as Werther did. He must accept limitation, must consent to do his work in time, must let his affections be baffled by the barriers of convention. Tantalus-like, he makes this world a Tartarus, or, like Hercules, rises in fires to heaven, according as he knows how to interpret his lot. But he must only use, not adopt it. The boundaries of the man must never be confounded with the destiny of the soul. If he does not decline his destiny as Werther did, it is his honor to have felt its unfitness for his eternal scope. He was born for wings; he is held to walk in leading-strings; nothing lower than faith must make him resigned, and only in hope should he find content—a hope not of some slight improvement in his own condition or that of other men, but a hope justified by the divine justice, which is bound in due time to satisfy every want of his nature.

Schiller's great command is, "Keep true to the dream of thy youth." The great problem is how to make the dream real, through the exercise of the waking will.

This was not exactly the problem Goethe tried to solve. To *do* somewhat, became too important, as is indicated both by the second motto of this essay, and by his maxim,

"It is not the knowledge of what *might be,* but what *is,* that forms us."

Werther, like his early essays now republished from the *Frankfort Journal,* is characterized by a fervid eloquence of Italian glow, which betrays a part of his character almost lost sight of in the quiet transparency of his later productions, and may give us some idea of the mental conflicts through which he passed to manhood.

The acting out the mystery into life, the calmness of survey, and the passionateness of feeling, above all the ironical baffling at the end, and want of point to a tale got up with such an eye to effect as he goes along, mark well the man that was to be. Even so did he demand in *Werther;* even so resolutely open the door in the First Part of *Faust;* even so seem to play with himself and his contemporaries in the Second Part of *Faust* and *Wilhelm Meister.*

Yet was he deeply earnest in his play, not for men, but for himself. To himself as a part of Nature it was important to grow, to lift his head to the light. In Nature he had all confidence; for man, as a part of Nature, infinite hope; but in him as an individual will, seemingly, not much trust at the earliest age.

The history of his intimacies marks his course; they were entered into with passionate eagerness, but always ended in an observation of the intellect, and he left them on his road, as the snake leaves his skin. The first man he met of sufficient force to command a large share of his attention was Herder, and the benefit of this intercourse was critical, not genial. Of the good Lavater he soon perceived the weakness. Merck, again, commanded his respect; but the force of Merck also was cold.

But in the Grand Duke of Weimar he seems to have met a character strong enough to exercise a decisive influence upon his own. Goethe was not so politic and worldly that a little man could ever have become his Maecenas. In the Duchess Amelia and her son he found that practical sagacity, large knowledge of things as they are, active force, and genial feeling, which he had never before seen combined. . . .

The Duke seems to have been one of those characters which are best known by the impression their personal presence makes on us, resembling an elemental and pervasive force, rather than wearing the features of an individuality. Goethe describes him as *"Dämonische,"* that is, gifted wih an instinctive, spontaneous force, which at once, without calculation or foresight, chooses the right means to an end. As these beings do not calculate, so is their influence incalculable. Their repose has as much influence over other beings as their action, even as the thunder cloud, lying black and distant in the summer sky, is not less imposing than when it bursts forth its quick lightnings. Such men were Mirabeau and Swift. They had also distinct talents, but their influence was from a perception in the minds of men of this spontaneous energy in their natures. Sometimes, though rarely, we see such a man in an obscure position; circumstances have not led him to a large sphere; he may not have expressed in words a single thought worth recording; but by his eye and voice he rules all around him.

He stands upon his feet with a firmness and calm security which make other men seem to halt or totter in their gait. In his deep eye is seen an infinite comprehension, an infinite reserve of power. No accent of his sonorous voice is lost on any ear within hearing; and, when he speaks, men hate or fear perhaps the disturbing power they feel, but never dream of disobeying. But hear Goethe himself:

"The boy believed in nature, in the animate and inanimate, the intelligent and unconscious, to discover somewhat which manifested itself only through contradiction, and therefore could not be comprehended by any conception, much less defined by a word. It was not divine, for it seemed without reason; not human, because without understanding; not devilish, because it worked to good; not angelic, because it often betrayed a petulant love of mischief. It was like chance in that it proved no sequence; it suggested the thought of Providence, because it indicated connection. To this all our limitations seem penetrable; it seemed to play at will with all the elements of our being; it compressed time and dilated space. Only in the impossible did it seem to delight, and to cast the possible aside with disdain.

"This existence which seemed to mingle with others, sometimes to separate, sometimes to unite, I called the *Dämonische*, after the example of the ancients, and others who have observed somewhat similar."—*Dichtung und Wahrheit*.

"The *Dämonische* is that which cannot be explained by reason or understanding; it lies not in my nature, but I am subject to it.

"Napoleon was a being of this class, and in so high a degree that scarce anyone is to be compared with him. Also our late Grand Duke was such a nature, full of unlimited power of action and unrest, so that his own dominion was too little for him, and the greatest would have been too little. Demoniac beings of this sort the Greeks reckoned among their demigods."—*Eckermann's Conversations with Goethe*.

This great force of will, this instinctive directness of action, gave the Duke an immediate ascendancy over Goethe which no other person had ever possessed. It was by no means mere sycophancy that made him give up the next ten years, in the prime of his manhood, to accompanying the Grand Duke in his revels, or aiding him in his schemes of practical utility, or to contriving elegant amusements for the ladies of the court. It was a real admiration for the character of the genial man of the world and its environment.

Whoever is turned from his natural path may, if he will, gain in largeness and depth what he loses in simple beauty; and so it was with Goethe, Faust became a wiser if not a nobler being. Werther, who must die because life was not wide enough and rich enough in love for him, ends as the Meister of the *Wanderjahre*, well content to be one never inadequate to the occasion, "help-full, comfort-full."

A great change was during these years perceptible to his friends in the character of Goethe. From being always "either too volatile or infatuated," he retreated into a self-collected state which seemed at first even icy to those around him. No longer he darted about him the lightnings of his genius, but sat Jove-like and calm, with the thunderbolts grasped in his hand and the eagle gathered to his feet. His freakish wit was subdued into a calm and even cold irony; his multiplied relations no longer permitted him to abandon himself to any; the minister and courtier could not expatiate in the free regions of invention and bring upon paper the signs of his higher life, without subjecting himself to an artificial process of isolation. Obliged to economy of time and means, he made of his intimates not objects of devout tenderness, of disinterested care, but the crammers and feeders of his intellect. The world was to him an arena or a studio, but not a temple.

"Ye cannot serve God and Mammon."

Had Goethe entered upon practical life from the dictate of his spirit, which bade him not be a mere author but a living, loving man, then had all been well. But he must also be a man of the world, and nothing can be more unfavorable to true manhood than this ambition. The citizen, the hero, the general, the poet, all these are in true relations; but what is called being a man of the world is to truckle to it, not truly to serve it.

Thus fettered in false relations, detained from retirement upon the center of his being, yet so relieved from the early pressure of his great thoughts as to pity more pious souls for being restless seekers, no wonder that he wrote:

"Es ist dafür gesorgt dass die Bäume nicht in den Himmel wachsen."

("Care is taken that the trees grow not up into the heavens.") Aye, Goethe, but in proportion to their force of aspiration is their height.

Yet never let him be confounded with those who sell all their birthright. He became blind to the more generous virtues, the nobler impulses, but ever in self-respect was busy to develop his nature. He was kind, industrious, wise, gentlemanly if not manly. If his genius lost sight of the highest aim, he is the best instructor in the use of means; ceasing to be a prophet, poet, he was still a poetic artist. From this time forward he seems a listener to

Nature, but not himself the highest product of Nature—
a priest to the soul of Nature. His works grow out of life,
but are not instinct with the peculiar human resolve, as are
Shakespeare's or Dante's.

Faust contains the great idea of his life, as indeed
there is but one great poetic idea possible to man—the
progress of a soul through the various forms of existence.

All his other works, whatever their miraculous beauty of
execution, are mere chapters to this poem, illustrative of
particular points. *Faust*, had it been completed in the spirit
in which it was begun, would have been the *Divina Com-
media* of its age.

But nothing can better show the difference of result
between a stern and earnest life, and one of partial accom-
modation, than a comparison between the *Paradiso* and
that of the Second Part of *Faust*. In both a soul, gradually
educated and led back to God, is received at last not
through merit, but grace. But O the difference between
the grandly humble reliance of old Catholicism, and the
loophole redemption of modern sagacity! Dante was a
man, of vehement passions, many prejudices, bitter as
much as sweet. His knowledge was scanty, his sphere of
observation narrow, the objects of his active life petty,
compared with those of Goethe. But, constantly retiring
to his deepest self, clearsighted to the limitations of man,
but no less so to the illimitable energy of the soul, the
sharpest details in his work convey a largest sense, as his
strongest and steadiest flights only direct the eye to heavens
yet beyond.

Yet perhaps he had not so hard a battle to wage, as this
other great poet. The fiercest passions are not so dangerous foes to the soul as the cold scepticism of the understanding. The Jewish demon assailed the man of Uz with
physical ills, the Lucifer of the middle ages tempted his
passions; but the Mephistopheles of the eighteenth century bade the finite strive to compass the infinite, and the
intellect attempt to solve all the problems of the soul.

This path Faust had taken: it is that of modern necro-
mancy. Not willing to grow into God by steady worship
of a life, men would enforce his presence by a spell; not

willing to learn his existence by the slow processes of
their own, they strive to bind it in a word that they may
wear it about the neck as a talisman.

Faust, bent upon reaching the centre of the universe
through the intellect alone, naturally, after a length of
trial which has prevented the harmonious unfolding of his
nature, falls into despair. He has striven for one object, and
that object eludes him. Returning upon himself, he finds
large tracts of his nature lying waste and cheerless. He is
too noble for apathy, too wise for vulgar content with the
animal enjoyments of life. Yet the thirst he has been so
many years increasing is not to be borne. Give me, he
cries, but a drop of water to cool my burning tongue! Yet
in casting himself with a wild recklessness upon the impulses of his nature yet untried, there is a disbelief that
anything short of the All can satisfy the immortal spirit.
His first attempt was noble though mistaken, and under the
saving influence of it he makes the compact whose condition cheats the fiend at last.

> *Kannst du mich schmeichelnd je belügen*
> *Dass ich mir selbst gefallen mag,*
> *Kannst du mich mit Genuss betrügen:*
> *Das sey für mich der letzte Tag.*
>
> *Werd ich zum Augenblicke sagen:*
> *Verweile doch! du bist so schön!*
> *Dann magst du mich in Fesseln schlagen,*
> *Dann will ich gern zu Grunde gehen.*
>
> (Canst thou by falsehood or by flattery
> Make me one moment with myself at peace,
> Cheat me into tranquillity? Come then
> And welcome, life's last day.
> Make me but to the moment say,
> O fly not yet, thou art so fair,
> Then let me perish, etc.)

But this condition is never fulfilled. Faust cannot be
content with sensuality, with the charlatanry of ambition,
nor with riches. His heart never becomes callous, nor his

moral and intellectual perceptions obtuse. He is saved at last.

With the progress of an individual soul is shadowed forth that of the soul of the age; beginning in intellectual scepticism; sinking into license; cheating itself with dreams of perfect bliss, to be at once attained by means no surer than a spurious paper currency; longing itself back from conflict between the spirit and the flesh, induced by Christianity, to the Greek era with its harmonious development of body and mind; striving to reëmbody the loved phantom of classical beauty in the heroism of the middle age; flying from the Byron despair of those who die because they cannot soar without wings, to schemes however narrow, of practical utility—redeemed at last through mercy alone.

The Second Part of *Faust* is full of meaning, resplendent with beauty; but it is rather an appendix to the First Part than a fulfilment of its promise. The world, remembering the powerful stamp of individual feeling, universal indeed in its application, but individual in its life, which had conquered all its scruples in the First Part, was vexed to find, instead of the man Faust, the spirit of the age—discontented with the shadowy manifestations of truths it longed to embrace, and, above all, disappointed that the author no longer met us face to face, or riveted the ear by his deep tones of grief and resolve.

When the world shall have got rid of the still overpowering influence of the First Part, it will be seen that the fundamental idea is never lost sight of in the Second. The change is that Goethe, though the same thinker, is no longer the same person. . . .

But those who demand from him a life-long continuance of the early ardor of *Faust*, who wish to see, throughout his works not only such manifold beauty and subtle wisdom, but the clear assurance of divinity, the pure white light of Macaria, wish that he had not so variously unfolded his nature, and concentred it more. They would see him slaying the serpent with the divine wrath of Apollo, rather than taming it to his service, like Æsculapius. They wish that he had never gone to Weimar, had never become a universal connoisseur and dilettante in science, and courtier as "graceful as a born nobleman," but had endured the burden of life with the suffering crowd, and deepened his nature in loneliness and privation, till Faust had conquered, rather than cheated the devil, and the music of heavenly faith superseded the grave and mild eloquence of human wisdom.

The expansive genius which moved so gracefully in its self-imposed fetters, is constantly surprising us by its content with a choice low, in so far as it was not the highest of which the mind was capable. The secret may be found in the second motto of this slight essay. . . .

But there is a higher spiritual law always ready to supersede the temporal laws at the call of the human soul. The soul that is too content with usual limitations will never call forth this unusual manifestation.

If there be a tide in the affairs of men which must be taken at the right moment to lead on to fortune, it is the same with inward as with outward life. He who in the crisis hour of youth has stopped short of himself, is not likely to find again what he has missed in one life, for there are a great number of blanks to a prize in each lottery.

But the pang we feel that "those who are so much are not more," seems to promise new spheres, new ages, new crises to enable these beings to complete their circle.

Perhaps Goethe is even now sensible that he should not have stopped at Weimar as his home, but made it one station on the way to Paradise; not stopped at humanity, but regarded it as symbolical of the divine, and given to others to feel more distinctly the centre of the universe, as well as the harmony in its parts. It is great to be an Artist, a Master, greater still to be a Seeker till the Man has found all himself.

What Goethe meant by self-collection was a collection of means for work, rather than to divine the deepest truths of being. Thus are these truths always indicated, never declared; and the religious hope awakened by his subtle discernment of the workings of nature never gratified, except through the intellect.

He whose prayer is only work will not leave his treasure in the secret shrine.

One is ashamed when finding any fault with one like Goethe, who is so great. It seems the only criticism should be to do all he omitted to do, and that none who cannot is entitled to say a word. Let that one speak who was all Goethe was not—noble, true, virtuous, but neither wise nor subtle in his generation, a divine ministrant, a baffled man, ruled and imposed on by the pygmies whom he spurned, a heroic artist, a democrat to the tune of Burns:

> The rank is but the guinea's stamp;
> The man's the gowd for a' that.

Hear Beethoven speak of Goethe on an occasion which brought out the two characters in strong contrast:

"Kings and princes can indeed make professors and privy councilors, and hang upon them titles; but great men they cannot make; souls that rise above the mud of the world, these they must let be made by other means than theirs, and should therefore show them respect. When two such as I and Goethe come together, then must great lords observe what is esteemed great by one of us. Coming home yesterday we met the whole imperial family. We saw them coming, and Goethe left me and insisted on standing to one side; let me say what I would, I could not make him come on one step. I pressed my hat upon my head, buttoned my surtout, and passed on through the thickest crowd. Princes and parasites made way; the Archduke Rudolph took off his hat; the Empress greeted me first. Their highnesses KNOW ME. I was well amused to see the crowd pass by Goethe. At the side stood he, hat in hand, low bowed in reverence till all had gone by. Then I scolded him well; I gave no pardon, but reproached him with all his sins, most of all those towards you, dearest Bettina; we had just been talking of you."

If Beethoven appears in this scene somewhat arrogant and bearish, yet how noble his extreme compared with the opposite! Goethe's friendship with the Grand Duke we respect, for Karl August was a strong man. But we regret to see at the command of any and all members of the ducal family and their connections, who had nothing but rank to recommend them, his time and thoughts, of which he was so chary to private friends. Beethoven could not endure to teach the Archduke Rudolph, who had the soul duty to revere his genius, because he felt it to be *Hofdienst*, court service. He received with perfect non-chalance the homage of the sovereigns of Europe. Only the Empress of Russia and the Archduke Karl, whom he esteemed as individuals, had power to gratify him by their attentions. Compare with Goethe's obsequious pleasure at being able gracefully to compliment such high personages, Beethoven's conduct with regard to the famous *Heroic Symphony*. This was composed at the suggestion of Berna-dotte while Napoleon was still in his first glory. He was then the hero of Beethoven's imagination, who hoped from him the liberation of Europe. With delight the great artist expressed in his eternal harmonies the progress of the hero's soul. The symphony was finished, and even dedicated to Bonaparte, when the news came of his declaring himself Emperor of the French. The first act of the indignant artist was to tear off his dedication and trample it under foot; nor could he endure again even the mention of Napoleon until the time of his fall.

Admit that Goethe had a natural taste for the trappings of rank and wealth, from which the musician was quite free, yet we cannot doubt that both saw through these externals to man as a nature; there can be no doubt on whose side was the simple greatness, the noble truth. We pardon thee, Goethe—but thee, Beethoven, we revere, for thou hast maintained the worship of the Manly, the Permanent, the True!

5. RALPH WALDO EMERSON, 1803–1882

[While Emerson and his associates hoped they might do something toward creating an American Literature, and that they might lend at least encouragement to the other arts, they were too much the children of a Puritan culture to be comfortable with a conception of their mission as merely literary or artistic. Unitarianism had done away with, for them, all vestiges of Calvinism as a system of belief, but it now seemed to starve their spiritual life. The new ideas they received from Wordsworth, Coleridge, Carlyle and the Germans were religious, metaphysical and ethical, and only incidentally literary. While the Transcendentalists tried not to waste precious energies haggling over the sterile issue of the miracles, still in the situation of the time they were obliged to make their assertion a new form of Puritanism rather than simply a literary fashion.

Hence, whenever Emerson did address himself to a theme in what we might call aesthetics, he could not forget that while in his pantheon of "representative" men there was a place for Goethe the writer and for Shakespeare the poet, they could be there only alongside Montaigne the skeptic, Swedenborg the mystic, and Plato the philosopher. Various of his essays endeavor to set forth the peculiar synthesis of the several points of view which would have to be contained in any American aesthetic of Transcendentalism; most successful, or at any rate most widely read, was "The Poet" from *Essays, Second Series* (1844). Since, however, that is reprinted in hundreds of collections and so is widely known, I select this later and (to my view) more central statement from *The Conduct of Life* (1860).

"Seyd" in the motto (who sometimes is spelled "Saadi") here figures as one of Emerson's names for the ideal poet.]

BEAUTY

Was never form and never face
So sweet to SEYD as only grace
Which did not slumber like a stone
But hovered gleaming and was gone.
Beauty chased he everywhere,

In flame, in storm, in clouds of air.
He smote the lake to feed his eye
    With the beryl beam of the broken wave.
He flung in pebbles well to hear
    The moment's music which they gave.
Oft pealed for him a lofty tone
From nodding pole and belting zone.
He heard a voice none else could hear
From centred and from errant sphere.
The quaking earth did quake in rhyme,
Seas ebbed and flowed in epic chime.
In dens of passion, and pits of woe,
He saw strong Eros struggling through,
To sun the dark and solve the curse,
And beam to the bounds of the universe.
While thus to love he gave his days
In loyal worship, scorning praise,
How spread their lures for him, in vain,
Thieving ambition and paltering Gain!
He thought it happier to be dead,
To die for Beauty, than live for bread.

The spiral tendency of vegetation infects education also. Our books approach very slowly the things we most wish to know. What a parade we make of our science, and how far off and at arm's length it is from its objects! Our botany is all names, not powers: poets and romancers talk of herbs of grace and healing, but what does the botanist know of the virtues of his weeds? The geologist lays bare the strata and can tell them all on his fingers; but does he know what effect passes into the man who builds his house in them? what effect on the race that inhabits a granite shelf? what on the inhabitants of marl and of alluvium?

We should go to the ornithologist with a new feeling if he could teach us what the social birds say when they sit in the autumn council, talking together in the trees. The want of sympathy makes his record a dull dictionary. His result is a dead bird. The bird is not in its ounces and inches, but in its relations to Nature; and the skin or skeleton you show me is no more a heron, than a heap of ashes or a bottle of gases into which his body has been reduced, is Dante or Washington. The naturalist is led *from* the road by the whole distance of his fancied advance. The boy had juster views when he gazed at the shells on the beach or the flowers in the meadow, unable to call them by their names, than the man in the pride of his nomenclature. Astrology interested us, for it tied man to the system. Instead of an isolated beggar, the farthest star felt him and he felt the star. However rash and however falsified by pretenders and traders in it, the hint was true and divine, the soul's avowal of its large relations, and that climate, century, remote natures as well as near, are part of its biography. Chemistry takes to pieces, but it does not construct. Alchemy, which sought to transmute one element into another, to prolong life, to arm with power—that was in the right direction. All our science lacks a human side. The tenant is more than the house. Bugs and stamens and spores, on which we lavish so many years, are not finalities; and man, when his powers unfold in order, will take Nature along with him, and emit light into all her recesses. The human heart concerns us more than the poring into microscopes, and is larger than can be measured by the pompous figures of an astronomer.

We are just so frivolous and skeptical. Men hold themselves cheap and vile; and yet a man is a fagot of thunderbolts. All the elements pour through his system; he is the flood of the flood and fire of the fire; he feels the antipodes and the pole as drops of his blood; they are the extension of his personality. His duties are measured by that instrument he is; and a right and perfect man would be felt to the centre of the Copernican system. 'T is curious that we only believe as deep as we live. We do not think heroes can exert any more awful power than that surface-play which amuses us. A deep man believes in miracles, waits for them, believes in magic, believes that the orator will decompose his adversary; believes that the evil eye can wither, that the heart's blessing can heal; that love can exalt talent; can overcome all odds. From a great heart secret magnetisms flow incessantly to draw great events. But we prize very humble utilities, a prudent husband, a good son, a voter, a citizen, and deprecate any romance of character; and perhaps reckon only his money value, his intellect, his affection—as a sort of bill of exchange easily convertible into fine chambers, pictures, music, and wine.

The motive of science was the extension of man, on all sides, into Nature, till his hands should touch the stars, his eyes see through the earth, his ears understand the language of beast and bird, and the sense of the wind; and, through his sympathy, heaven and earth should talk with him. But that is not our science. These geologies, chemistries, astronomies, seem to make wise, but they leave us where they found us. The invention is of use to the inventor, of questionable help to any other. The formulas of science are like the papers in your pocket-book, of no value to any but the owner. Science in England, in America, is jealous of theory, hates the name of love and moral purpose. There's a revenge for this inhumanity. What manner of man does science make? The boy is not attracted. He says, I do not wish to be such a kind of man as my professor is. The collector has dried all the plants in his herbal, but he has lost weight and humor. He has got all snakes and lizards in his phials, but science has done for him also, and has put the man into a bottle. Our reliance on the physician is a kind of despair of ourselves. The clergy have bronchitis, which does not seem a certificate of spiritual health. Macready thought it came of the *falsetto* of their voicing. An Indian prince, Tisso, one day riding in the forest, saw a herd of elk sporting. "See how happy," he said, "these browsing elks are! Why should not priests, lodged and fed comfortably in the temples, also amuse themselves?" Returning home, he imparted this reflection to the king. The king, on the next day, conferred the sovereignty on him, saying, "Prince, administer this empire for seven days; at the termination of that period I shall put thee to death." At the end of the seventh day the king inquired, "From what cause hast thou become so emaciated?" He answered, "From the horror of death." The monarch rejoined, "Live, my child, and be wise. Thou hast ceased to take recreation, saying to thyself, In seven days I shall be put to death. These priests in the temple incessantly meditate on death; how can they enter into healthful diversions?" But the men of science or the doctors or the clergy are not victims of their pursuits more than others. The miller, the lawyer, and the merchant, dedicate themselves to their own details, and do not come out men of more force. Have they divination, grand aims, hospitality of soul, and the equality to any event which we demand in man, or only the reactions of the mill, of the wares, of the chicane?

No object really interests us but man, and in man only his superiorities; and though we are aware of a perfect law in Nature, it has fascination for us only through its relation to him, or as it is rooted in the mind. At the birth of Winckelmann, more than a hundred years ago, side by side with this arid, departmental, *post mortem* science, rose an enthusiasm in the study of Beauty; and perhaps some sparks from it may yet light a conflagration in the other. Knowledge of men, knowledge of manners, the power of form, and our sensibility to personal influence never go out of fashion. These are facts of a science which we study without book, whose teachers and subjects are always near us.

So inveterate is our habit of criticism that much of our knowledge in this direction belongs to the chapter of pathology. The crowd in the street oftener furnishes degradations than angels or redeemers, but they all prove the transparency. Every spirit makes its house, and can give a shrewd guess from the house to the inhabitant. But not less does Nature furnish us with every sign of grace and goodness. The delicious faces of children, the beauty of school-girls, "the sweet seriousness of sixteen," the lofty air of well-born, well-bred boys, the passionate histories in the looks and manners of youth and early manhood and the varied power in all that well-known company that escort us through life—we know how these forms thrill, paralyze, provoke, inspire, and enlarge us.

Beauty is the form under which the intellect prefers to study the world. All privilege is that of beauty; for there are many beauties; as, of general nature, of the human face and form, of manners, of brain or method, moral beauty or beauty of the soul.

The ancients believed that a genius or demon took possession at birth of each mortal, to guide him; that these genii were sometimes seen as a flame of fire partly immersed in the bodies which they governed; on an evil man, resting on his head; in a good man, mixed with his substance. They thought the same genius, at the death of its ward, entered a new-born child, and they pretended to guess the pilot by the sailing of the ship. We recognize obscurely the same fact, though we give it our own names. We say that every man is entitled to be valued by his best moment. We measure our friends so. We know they have intervals of folly, whereof we take no heed, but wait the reappearings of the genius, which are sure and beautiful. On the other side, everybody knows people who appear beridden, and who, with all degrees of ability, never impress us with the air of free agency. They know it too, and peep with their eyes to see if you detect their sad plight. We fancy, could we pronounce the solving word and disenchant them, the cloud would roll up, the little rider would be discovered and unseated, and they would regain their freedom. The remedy seems never to be far off, since the first step into thought lifts this mountain of necessity. Thought is the pent air-ball which can rive the planet, and the beauty which certain objects have for him is the friendly fire which expands the thought and acquaints the prisoner that liberty and power await him.

The question of Beauty takes us out of surfaces to thinking of the foundations of things. Goethe said, "The beautiful is a manifestation of secret laws of Nature which, but for this appearance, had been forever concealed from us." And the working of this deep instinct makes all the excitement—much of it superficial and absurd enough—about works of art, which leads armies of vain travellers every year to Italy, Greece, and Egypt. Every man values every acquisition he makes in the science of beauty, above his possessions. The most useful man in the most useful world, so long as only commodity was served, would remain unsatisfied. But as fast as he sees beauty, life acquires a very high value.

I am warned by the ill fate of many philosophers not to attempt a definition of Beauty. I will rather enumerate a few of its qualities. We ascribe beauty to that which is simple; which has no superfluous parts; which exactly answers its end; which stands related to all things; which is the mean of many extremes. It is the most enduring quality and the most ascending quality. We say love is blind, and the figure of Cupid is drawn with a bandage round his eyes. Blind: yes, because he does not see what he does not like; but the sharpest-sighted hunter in the universe is Love, for finding what he seeks, and only that; and the mythologists tell us that Vulcan was painted lame and Cupid blind, to call attention to the fact that one was all limbs, and the other all eyes. In the true mythology Love is an immortal child, and Beauty leads him as a guide: nor can we express a deeper sense than when we say, Beauty is the pilot of the young soul.

Beyond their sensuous delight, the forms and colors of Nature have a new charm for us in our perception that not one ornament was added for ornament, but each is a sign of some better health or more excellent action. Elegance of form in bird or beast, or in the human figure, marks some excellence of structure: or, beauty is only an invitation from what belongs to us. 'Tis a law of botany that in plants the same virtues follow the same forms. It is a rule of largest application, true in a plant, true in a loaf of bread, that in the construction of any fabric or organism any real increase of fitness to its end is an increase of beauty.

The lesson taught by the study of Greek and of Gothic art, of antique and of Pre-Raphaelite painting, was worth all the research—namely, that all beauty must be organic; that outside embellishment is deformity. It is the soundness of the bones that ultimates itself in a peach-bloom complexion; health of constitution that makes the sparkle and the power of the eye. 'Tis the adjustment of the size and of the joining of the sockets of the skeleton that gives grace of outline and the finer grace of movement. The cat and the deer cannot move or sit inelegantly. The dancing-master can never teach a badly built man to walk well. The tint of the flower proceeds from its root, and the lustres of the sea-shell begin with its existence. Hence our taste in building rejects paint, and all shifts, and shows the original grain of the wood: refuses pilasters and columns that support nothing, and allows the real supporters of the house honestly to show themselves. Every necessary or organic action pleases the beholder. A man leading a horse to water, a farmer sowing seed, the labors of haymakers in the field, the carpenter building a ship, the smith at his forge, or whatever useful labor, is becoming to the wise eye. But if it is done to be seen, it is mean. How beautiful are ships on the sea! but ships in the theatre—or ships kept for picturesque effect on Virginia Water by George IV, and men hired to stand in fitting costumes at a penny an hour! What a difference in effect between a battalion of troops marching to action, and one of our independent companies on a holiday! In the midst of a military show and a festal procession gay with banners, I saw a boy seize an old tin pan that lay rusting under a wall, and poising it on the top of a stick, he set it turning and made it describe the most elegant imaginable curves, and drew away attention from the decorated procession by this startling beauty.

Another text from the mythologists. The Greeks fabled that Venus was born of the foam of the sea. Nothing interests us which is stark or bounded, but only what streams with life, what is in act or endeavor to reach somewhat beyond. The pleasure a palace or a temple gives the eye is, that an order and method has been communicated to stones, so that they speak and geometrize, become tender or sublime with expression. Beauty is the moment of transition, as if the form were just ready to flow into other forms. Any fixedness, heaping, or concentration on one feature—a long nose, a sharp chin, a hump-back—is the reverse of the flowing, and therefore deformed. Beautiful as is the symmetry of any form, if the form can move we seek a more excellent symmetry. The interruption of equilibrium stimulates the eye to desire the restoration of symmetry, and to watch the steps through which it is attained. This is the charm of running water, sea-waves, the flight of birds and the locomotion of animals. This is the theory of dancing, to recover continually in changes the lost equilibrium, not by abrupt and angular but by gradual and curving movements. I have been told by persons of experience in matters of taste that the fashions follow a law of gradation, and are never arbitrary. The new mode is always only a step onward in the same direction as the last mode, and a cultivated eye is prepared for and predicts the new fashion. This fact suggests the reason of all mistakes and offence in our own modes. It is necessary in music, when you strike a discord, to let down the ear by an intermediate note or two to the accord again; and many a good experiment, born of good sense and destined to succeed, fails only because it is offensively sudden. I suppose the Parisian milliner who dresses the world from her imperious boudoir will know how to reconcile the Bloomer costume to the eye of mankind, and make it triumphant over Punch himself, by interposing the just gradations. I need not say how wide the same law ranges, and how much it can be hoped to effect. All that is a little harshly claimed by progressive parties may easily come to be conceded without question, if this rule be observed. Thus the circumstances may easily be imagined in which woman may speak, vote, argue causes, legislate, and drive a coach, and all the most naturally in the world, if only it come by degrees. To this streaming or flowing belongs the beauty that all circular movement has; as the circulation of waters, the circulation of the blood, the periodical motion of planets, the annual wave of vegetation, the action and reaction of Nature; and if we follow it out, this demand in our thought for an everonward action is the argument for the immortality.

One more text from the mythologists is to the same purpose—*Beauty rides on a lion*. Beauty rests on necessities. The line of beauty is the result of perfect economy. The cell of the bee is built at that angle which gives the most strength with the least wax; the bone or the quill of the bird gives the most alar strength with the least weight.

"It is the purgation of superfluities," said Michael Angelo. There is not a particle to spare in natural structures. There is a compelling reason in the uses of the plant for every novelty of color or form; and our art saves material by more skilful arrangement, and reaches beauty by taking every superfluous ounce that can be spared from a wall, and keeping all its strength in the poetry of columns. In rhetoric, this art of omission is a chief secret of power, and, in general, it is proof of high culture to say the greatest matters in the simplest way.

Veracity first of all, and forever. *Rien de beau que le vrai.* In all design, art lies in making your object prominent, but there is a prior art in choosing objects that are prominent. The fine arts have nothing casual, but spring from the instincts of the nations that created them.

Beauty is the quality which makes to endure. In a house that I know, I have noticed a block of spermaceti lying about closets and mantel-pieces, for twenty years together, simply because the tallow-man gave it the form of a rabbit; and I suppose it may continue to be lugged about unchanged for a century. Let an artist scrawl a few lines or figures on the back of a letter, and that scrap of paper is rescued from danger, is put in portfolio, is framed and glazed, and, in proportion to the beauty of the lines drawn, will be kept for centuries. Burns writes a copy of verses and sends them to a newspaper, and the human race take charge of them that they shall not perish.

As the flute is heard farther than the cart, see how surely a beautiful form strikes the fancy of men, and is copied and reproduced without end. How many copies are there of the Belvedere Apollo, the Venus, the Psyche, the Warwick Vase, the Parthenon and the Temple of Vesta? These are objects of tenderness to all. In our cities an ugly building is soon removed and is never repeated, but any beautiful building is copied and improved upon, so that all masons and carpenters work to repeat and preserve the agreeable forms, whilst the ugly ones die out.

The felicities of design in art or in works of Nature are shadows or forerunners of that beauty which reaches its perfection in the human form. All men are its lovers.

Wherever it goes it creates joy and hilarity, and everything is permitted to it. It reaches its height in woman. "To Eve," say the Mahometans, "God gave two thirds of all beauty." A beautiful woman is a practical poet, taming her savage mate, planting tenderness, hope, and eloquence in all whom she approaches. Some favors of condition must go with it, since a certain serenity is essential, but we love its reproofs and superiorities. Nature wishes that woman should attract man, yet she often cunningly moulds into her face a little sarcasm, which seems to say, 'Yes, I am willing to attract, but to attract a little better kind of man than any I yet behold.' French *mémoires* of the sixteenth century celebrate the name of Pauline de Viguier, a virtuous and accomplished maiden who so fired the enthusiasm of her contemporaries by her enchanting form, that the citizens of her native city of Toulouse obtained the aid of the civil authorities to compel her to appear publicly on the balcony at least twice a week, and as often as she showed herself, the crowd was dangerous to life. Not less in England in the last century was the fame of the Gunnings, of whom Elizabeth married the Duke of Hamilton, and Maria, the Earl of Coventry. Walpole says, "The concourse was so great, when the Duchess of Hamilton was presented at court, on Friday, that even the noble crowd in the drawing-room clambered on chairs and tables to look at her. There are mobs at their doors to see them get into their chairs, and people go early to get places at the theatres, when it is known they will be there." "Such crowds," he adds elsewhere, "flock to see the Duchess of Hamilton, that seven hundred people sat up all night, in and about an inn in Yorkshire, to see her get into her post-chaise next morning."

But why need we console ourselves with the fames of Helen and Argos, or Corinna, or Pauline of Toulouse, or the Duchess of Hamilton? We all know this magic very well, or can divine it. It does not hurt weak eyes to look into beautiful eyes never so long. Women stand related to beautiful Nature around us, and the enamored youth mixes their form with moon and stars, with woods and waters, and the pomp of summer. They heal us of awkwardness by their words and looks. We observe their intellectual influence on the most serious student. They refine and clear his mind; teach him to put a pleasing method into what is dry and difficult. We talk to them and wish to be listened to; we fear to fatigue them, and acquire a facility of expression which passes from conversation into habit of style.

That Beauty is the normal state is shown by the perpetual effort of Nature to attain it. Mirabeau had an ugly face on a handsome ground; and we see faces every day which have a good type but have been marred in the casting; a proof that we are all entitled to beauty, should have been beautiful if our ancestors had kept the laws—as every lily and every rose is well. But our bodies do not fit us, but caricature and satirize us. Thus, short legs which constrain us to short mincing steps are a kind of personal insult and contumely to the owner; and long stilts again put him at perpetual disadvantage, and force him to stoop to the general level of mankind. Martial ridicules a gentleman of his day whose countenance resembled the face of a swimmer seen under water. Saadi describes a schoolmaster "so ugly and crabbed that a sight of him would derange the ecstasies of the orthodox." Faces are rarely true to any ideal type, but are a record in sculpture of a thousand anecdotes of whim and folly. Portrait-painters say that most faces and forms are irregular and unsymmetrical; have one eye blue and one gray; the nose not straight, and one shoulder higher than another; the hair unequally distributed, etc. The man is physically as well as metaphysically a thing of shreds and patches, borrowed unequally from good and bad ancestors, and a misfit from the start.

A beautiful person among the Greeks was thought to betray by this sign some secret favor of the immortal gods; and we can pardon pride, when a woman possesses such a figure that wherever she stands or moves or leaves a shadow on the wall, or sits for a portrait to the artist, she confers a favor on the world. And yet—it is not beauty that inspires the deepest passion. Beauty without grace is the hook without the bait. Beauty, without expression, tires. Abbé Ménage said of the President Le Bailleul that "he was fit for nothing but to sit for his portrait." A Greek epigram intimates that the force of love is not shown by the courting of beauty, but when the like desire is inflamed for one who is ill-favored. And petulant old gentlemen, who have chanced to suffer some intolerable weariness from pretty people, or who have seen cut flowers to some profusion, or who see, after a world of pains have been successfully taken for the costume, how the least mistake in sentiment takes all the beauty out of your clothes—affirm that the secret of ugliness consists not in irregularity, but in being uninteresting.

We love any forms, however ugly, from which great qualities shine. If command, eloquence, art or invention exist in the most deformed person, all the accidents that usually displease, please, and raise esteem and wonder higher. The great orator was an emaciated, insignificant person, but he was all brain. Cardinal De Retz says of De Bouillon, "With the physiognomy of an ox, he had the perspicacity of an eagle." It was said of Hooke, the friend of Newton, "He is the most, and promises the least, of any man in England." "Since I am so ugly," said Du Guesclin, "it behooves that I be bold." Sir Philip Sidney, the darling of mankind, Ben Jonson tells us, "was no pleasant man in countenance, his face being spoiled with pimples, and of high blood, and long." Those who have ruled human destinies like planets for thousands of years, were not handsome men. If a man can raise a small city to be a great kingdom, can make bread cheap, can irrigate deserts, can join oceans by canals, can subdue steam, can organize victory, can lead the opinions of mankind, can enlarge knowledge—'t is no matter whether his nose is parallel to his spine, as it ought to be, or whether he has a nose at all; whether his legs are straight, or whether his legs are amputated: his deformities will come to be reckoned ornamental and advantageous on the whole. This is the triumph of expression, degrading beauty, charming us with a power so fine and friendly and intoxicating that it makes admired persons insipid, and the thought of passing our lives with them insupportable. There are faces so fluid with expression, so flushed and rippled by the play of thought that we can hardly find what the mere features really are. When the delicious beauty of lineaments loses its power, it is because a more delicious beauty has appeared; that an interior and durable form has been disclosed. Still, Beauty rides on her lion, as before. Still, "it was for beauty that the world was made." The lives of the Italian artists, who established a despotism of genius amidst the dukes and kings and mobs of their stormy epoch, prove how loyal men in all times are to a finer brain, a finer method than their own. If a man can cut such a head on his stone gate-post as shall draw and keep a crowd about it all day, by its beauty, good nature, and inscrutable meaning—if a man can build a plain cottage with such symmetry as to make all the fine palaces look cheap and vulgar; can take such advantages of Nature that all her powers serve him; making use of geometry, instead of expense; tapping a mountain for his water-jet; causing the sun and moon to seem only the decorations of his estate—this is still the legitimate dominion of beauty.

The radiance of the human form, though sometimes astonishing, is only a burst of beauty for a few years or a few months at the perfection of youth, and in most, rapidly declines. But we remain lovers of it, only transferring our interest to interior excellence. And it is not only admirable in singular and salient talents, but also in the world of manners.

But the sovereign attribute remains to be noted. Things are pretty, graceful, rich, elegant, handsome, but, until they speak to the imagination, not yet beautiful. This is the reason why beauty is still escaping out of all analysis. It it not yet possessed, it cannot be handled. Proclus says, "It swims on the light of forms." It is properly not in the form, but in the mind. It instantly deserts possession, and flies to an object in the horizon. If I could put my hand on the North Star, would it be as beautiful? The sea is lovely, but when we bathe in it the beauty forsakes all the near water. For the imagination and senses cannot be gratified at the same time. Wordsworth rightly speaks of "a light that never was on sea or land," meaning that it was supplied by the observer; and the Welsh bard warns his countrywomen, that

—"Half of their charms with Cadwallon shall die."

The new virtue which constitutes a thing beautiful is a certain cosmical quality, or a power to suggest relation to the whole world, and so lift the object out of a pitiful individuality. Every natural feature—sea, sky, rainbow, flowers, musical tone—has in it somewhat which is not private but universal, speaks of that central benefit which is the soul of Nature, and thereby is beautiful. And in chosen men and women I find somewhat in form, speech, and manners, which is not of their person and family, but of a humane, catholic, and spiritual character, and we love them as the sky. They have a largeness of suggestion, and their face and manners carry a certain grandeur, like time and justice.

The feat of the imagination is in showing the convertibility of every thing into every other thing. Facts which had never before left their stark common sense, suddenly figure as Eleusinian mysteries. My boots and chair and candlestick are fairies in disguise, meteors and constellations. All the facts in Nature are nouns of the intellect, and make the grammar of the eternal language. Every word has a double, treble, or centuple use and meaning. What! has my stove and pepper-pot a false bottom? I cry you mercy, good shoe-box! I did not know you were a jewel-case. Chaff and dust begin to sparkle, and are clothed about with immortality. And there is a joy in perceiving the representative or symbolic character of a fact, which no bare fact or event can ever give. There are no days in life so memorable as those which vibrated to some stroke of the imagination.

The poets are quite right in decking their mistresses with the spoils of the landscape, flower-gardens, gems, rainbows, flushes of morning and stars of night, since all beauty points at identity; and whatsoever thing does not express to me the sea and sky, day and night, is somewhat forbidden and wrong. Into every beautiful object there enters somewhat immeasurable and divine, and just as much into form bounded by outlines, like mountains on the horizon, as into tones of music or depths of space. Polarized light showed the secret architecture of bodies; and when the *second-sight* of the mind is opened, now one color or form or gesture and now another has a pungency, as if a more interior ray had been emitted, disclosing its deep holdings in the frame of things.

The laws of this translation we do not know, or why one feature or gesture enchants, why one word or syllable intoxicates; but the fact is familiar that the fine touch of the eye, or a grace of manners, or a phrase of poetry, plants wings at our shoulders; as if the Divinity, in his approaches, lifts away mountains of obstruction, and deigns to draw a truer line, which the mind knows and owns. This is that haughty force of beauty, *"vis superba formae,"* which the poets praise—under calm and precise outline the immeasurable and divine; Beauty hiding all wisdom and power in its calm sky.

All high beauty has a moral element in it, and I find the antique sculpture as ethical as Marcus Antoninus; and the beauty ever in proportion to the depth of thought. Gross and obscure natures, however decorated, seem impure shambles; but character gives splendor to youth and awe to wrinkled skin and gray hairs. An adorer of truth we cannot choose but obey, and the woman who has shared with us the moral sentiment—her locks must appear to us sublime. Thus there is a climbing scale of culture, from the first agreeable sensation which a sparkling gem or a scarlet stain affords the eye, up through fair outlines and details of the landscape, features of the human face and form, signs and tokens of thought and character in manners, up to the ineffable mysteries of the intellect. Wherever we begin, thither our steps tend: an ascent from the joy of a horse in his trappings, up to the perception of Newton that the globe on which we ride is only a larger apple falling from a larger tree; up to the perception of Plato that globe and universe are rude and early expressions of an all-dissolving Unity—the first stair on the scale to the temple of the Mind.

6. MARGARET FULLER, 1810–1850

[In the autumn of 1844, just after the death of *The Dial*, Margaret Fuller exercised her Transcendental freedom by an act so daring, not to say treasonable, that it took the breath away from even her most emancipated associates: she moved from Boston to New York. Still more astounding, she became a professional newspaper writer, doing book reviews and occasional pieces for Horace Greeley's *Tribune*. Though several American women had already begun to write for money, and one or two had become publishers of women's magazines and gift-books, Margaret is the first who can be said to have become a member of the working press.

Emerson looked with cold disapproval on this, as he regarded it, vulgarization of her lofty mission; he was glad in 1846 when she gave up such employment and went to Europe, from which she sent to Greeley's paper accounts of her travels and encounters that now can be seen to constitute an epoch in foreign reporting. In 1847 she reached Rome, and found that city indeed the goal of her passionate pilgrimage.

"Had I only come ten years earlier!" she wrote out of anguish: "Now my life must be a failure, so much strength has been wasted on abstractions, which only came because I grew not in the right soil." Emerson, Clarke and Channing let this letter stand in their edition of her *Memoirs*, though they can hardly have failed to note that it was an indictment of themselves.

They had in effect to confess, by their reticences, that they were incapable of comprehending the sequel. She married a minor member of the impecunious Italian nobility, Angelo Ossoli, who seems to have been gracious and brave, was several years her junior, and clearly no intellectual at all. They had a child, born in September, 1848. She played a heroic part as nurse in the hospitals during the siege of Rome; with the suppression of Mazzini's Republic, she decided to bring her husband and baby with her to America, in the desperate hope that she could make a living for them. She wrote her mother her forebodings of disaster: "My life proceeds as regularly as the fates of a Greek tragedy, and I can but accept the pages as they turn." While her friends were asking themselves in perturbation how they could cope with this apparition, the ship was wrecked off Fire Island on July 19, 1850, and all three perished.

While in New York, 1844 to 1846, Margaret quickly became an ally of the metropolitan school of nationalists, the group priding themselves in the name "Young America." Transcendentalists looked down their noses at these Gothamites as so lacking in intellect and spirit as not fit to be linked with them in the holy cause of realizing the American Genius (the New Yorkers in turn were contemptuous of Transcendental paganism and of their cloudy "metaphysics"), while non-transcendental gentlemen in Boston, like Dr. Oliver Wendell Holmes, regarded them as a collection of boors. Nevertheless, Margaret reached across the gulf of sectional prejudice, and turned the New Yorker's hostility into admiration.

The leader of Young America was Evert Augustus Duyckinck, then an editor for the firm of Wiley and Putnam. He persuaded this highly commercial outfit, against their better judgment, to undertake a "Library of American Books," thus bullying them into printing, if not exactly patronizing, native talent. Duyckinck arranged with Margaret, before her departure, to issue a collection of her writings, entitled, *Papers on Literature and Art*. It appeared, in two volumes, late in 1846.

It reprinted most of her pieces from *The Dial*, but more notably salvaged the substance of her *Tribune* journalism. The section called "American Literature" is a composite of several notices in the newspaper, to which she hastily strove to give some semblance of coherent form. If the result betrays more than a bit of her usual impetuousness, or of the general Transcendental inconsecutiveness, still it stands as one of the boldest and most courageous utterances of the era.

Evert Duyckinck was also the editor, in this same year

1846, of Herman Melville's first book, *Typee,* of which Margaret wrote a moderately favorably review. (*Typee* had also been issued in the "American" series.) Considering the closeness of Melville's relation at this time to Duyckinck, we may suppose that Melville would have read Margaret's effusion. Whether he did or not, she spoke for (and predicted) the dedication which both he and Whitman were, in their different but equally disastrous ways (disastrous, that is, in so far as commanding any contemporaneous audience is concerned), to carry forward.]

AMERICAN LITERATURE; ITS POSITION IN THE PRESENT TIME, AND PROSPECTS FOR THE FUTURE

Some thinkers may object to this essay, that we are about to write of that which has, as yet, no existence.

For it does not follow because many books are written by persons born in America that there exists an American literature. Books which imitate or represent the thoughts and life of Europe do not constitute an American literature. Before such can exist, an original idea must animate this nation and fresh currents of life must call into life fresh thoughts along its shores.

We have no sympathy with national vanity. We are not anxious to prove that there is as yet much American literature. Of those who think and write among us in the methods and of the thoughts of Europe, we are not impatient; if their minds are still best adapted to such food and such action. If their books express life of mind and character in graceful forms, they are good and we like them. We consider them as colonists and useful schoolmasters to our people in a transition state; which lasts rather longer than is occupied in passing, bodily, the ocean which separates the new from the old world.

We have been accused of an undue attachment to foreign continental literature, and, it is true, that in childhood, we had well nigh "forgotten our English," while constantly reading in other languages. Still, what we loved in the literature of continental Europe was the range and force of ideal manifestations in forms of national and individual greatness. A model was before us in the great Latins of simple masculine minds seizing upon life with unbroken power. The stamp both of nationality and individuality was very strong upon them; their lives and thoughts stood out in clear and bold relief. The English character has the iron force of the Latins, but not the frankness and expansion. Like their fruits, they need a summer sky to give them more sweetness and a richer flavor. This does not apply to Shakespeare, who has all the fine side of English genius, with the rich colouring, and more fluent life, of the Catholic countries. Other poets, of England also, are expansive more or less, and soar freely to seek the blue sky, but take it as a whole, there is in English literature, as in English character, a reminiscence of walls and ceilings, a tendency to the arbitrary and conventional that repels a mind trained in admiration of the antique spirit. It is only in later days that we are learning to prize the peculiar greatness which a thousand times outweighs this fault, and which has enabled English genius to go forth from its insular position and conquer such vast dominion in the realms both of matter and of mind.

Yet there is, often, between child and parent, a reaction from excessive influence having been exerted, and such an one we have experienced, in behalf of our country, against England. We use her language, and receive, in torrents, the influence of her thought, yet it is, in many respects, uncongenial and injurious to our constitution. What suits Great Britain, with her insular position and consequent need to concentrate and intensify her life, her limited monarchy, and spirit of trade, does not suit a mixed race, continually enriched with new blood from other stocks the most unlike that of our first descent, with ample field and verge enough to range in and leave every impulse free, and abundant opportunity to develop a genius, wide and full as our rivers, flowery, luxuriant and impassioned as our vast prairies, rooted in strength as the rocks on which the Puritan fathers landed.

That such a genius is to rise and work in this hemisphere we are confident; equally so that scarce the first faint streaks of that day's dawn are yet visible. It is sad for those that foresee, to know they may not live to share its glories, yet it is sweet, too, to know that every act and word, uttered in the light of that foresight, may tend to hasten or ennoble its fulfilment.

That day will not rise till the fusion of races among us is more complete. It will not rise till this nation shall attain sufficient moral and intellectual dignity to prize moral and intellectual, no less highly than political, freedom, not till, the physical resources of the country being explored, all its regions studded with towns, broken by the plow, netted together by railways and telegraph lines, talent shall be left at leisure to turn its energies upon the higher department of man's existence. Nor then shall it be seen till from the leisurely and yearning soul of that riper time national ideas shall take birth, ideas craving to be clothed in a thousand fresh and original forms.

Without such ideas all attempts to construct a national literature must end in abortions like the monster of Frankenstein, things with forms, and the instincts of forms, but soulless, and therefore revolting. We cannot have expression till there is something to be expressed.

The symptoms of such a birth may be seen in a longing felt here and there for sustenance of such ideas. At present, it shows itself, where felt, in sympathy with the prevalent tone of society, by attempts at external action, such as are classed under the head of social reform. But it needs to go deeper, before we can have poets, needs to penetrate beneath the springs of action, to stir and remake the soil as by the action of fire.

Another symptom is the need felt by individuals of being even sternly sincere. This is the one great means by which alone progress can be essentially furthered. Truth is the nursing mother of genius. No man can be absolutely true to himself, eschewing cant, compromise, servile imitation, and complaisance, without becoming original, for there is in every creature a fountain of life which, if not choked back by stones and other dead rubbish, will create a fresh atmosphere, and bring to life fresh beauty. And it is the same with the nation as with the individual man.

The best work we do for the future is by such truth. By use of that, in whatever way, we harrow the soil and lay it open to the sun and air. The winds from all quarters of the globe bring seed enough, and there is nothing wanting but preparation of the soil, and freedom in the atmosphere, for ripening of a new and golden harvest.

We are sad that we cannot be present at the gathering in of this harvest. And yet we are joyous, too, when we think that though our name may not be writ on the pillar of our country's fame, we can really do far more towards rearing it, than those who come at a later period and to a seemingly fairer task. *Now*, the humblest effort, made in a noble spirit, and with religious hope, cannot fail to be even infinitely useful. Whether we introduce some noble model from another time and clime, to encourage aspiration in our own, or cheer into blossom the simplest wood-flower that ever rose from the earth, moved by the genuine impulse to grow, independent of the lures of money or celebrity; whether we speak boldly when fear or doubt keep others silent, or refuse to swell the popular cry upon an unworthy occasion, the spirit of truth, purely worshipped, shall turn our acts and forbearances alike to profit, informing them with oracles which the latest time shall bless.

Under present circumstances the amount of talent and labour given to writing ought to surprise us. Literature is in this dim and struggling state, and its pecuniary results exceedingly pitiful. From many well known causes it is impossible for ninety-nine out of the hundred, who wish to use the pen, to ransom, by its use, the time they need. This state of things will have to be changed in some way. No man of genius writes for money; but it is essential to the free use of his powers, that he should be able to disembarrass his life from care and perplexity. This is very difficult here; and the state of things gets worse and worse, as less and less is offered in pecuniary meed for works demanding great devotion of time and labour (to say nothing of the ether engaged) and the publisher, obliged to regard the transaction as a matter of business, demands of the author to give him only what will find an immediate market, for he cannot afford to take any thing else. This will not do! When an immortal poet was secure only of a few copyists to circulate his works, there were princes and nobles to patronize literature and the arts. Here is only the public, and the public must learn how to cherish the nobler and rarer plants, and to plant the aloe, able to wait a hundred years for its bloom, or its garden will contain, presently, nothing but potatoes and pot-herbs. We shall have, in the course of the next two or three years, a convention of authors to inquire into the causes of this state of things and propose measures for its remedy. Some have already been thought of that look promising, but we shall not announce them till the time be ripe; that date is not distant, for the difficulties increase from day to day, in consequence of the system of cheap publication, on a great scale. . . .

Meanwhile, the most important part of our literature, while the work of diffusion is still going on, lies in the journals, which monthly, weekly, daily, send their messages to every corner of this great land, and form, at present, the only efficient instrument for the general education of the people.

Among these, the Magazines take the lowest rank. Their object is principally to cater for the amusement of vacant hours, and, as there is not a great deal of wit or light talent in this country, they do not even this to much advantage. More wit, grace, and elegant trifling, embellish the annals of literature in one day of France than in a year of America.

The Reviews are more able. If they cannot compare, on equal terms, with those of France, England, and Germany, where, if genius be rare, at least a vast amount of talent and culture are brought to bear upon all the departments of knowledge, they are yet very creditable to a new country, where so large a portion of manly ability must be bent on making laws, making speeches, making rail-roads and canals. They are, however, much injured by a partisan spirit, and the fear of censure from their own public. This last is always slow death to a journal; its natural and only safe position is *to lead*; if, instead, it bows to the will of the multitude, it will find the ostracism of democracy far more dangerous than the worst censure of a tyranny could be. It is not half so dangerous to a man to be immured in a dungeon alone with God and his own clear conscience, as to walk the streets fearing the scrutiny of a thousand eyes, ready to veil, with anxious care, whatever may not suit the many-headed monster in its momentary mood. Gentleness is dignified, but caution is debasing; only a noble fearlessness can give wings to the mind, with which to soar beyond the common ken, and learn what may be of use to the crowd below. Writers have nothing to do but to love truth fervently, seek justice according to their ability, and then express what is in the mind; they have nothing to do with consequences, God will take care of those. The want of such noble courage, such faith in the power of truth and good desire, paralyze mind greatly in this country. Publishers are afraid; authors are afraid; and if a worthy resistance is not made by religious souls, there is danger that all the light will soon be put under bushels, lest some wind should waft from it a spark that may kindle dangerous fire.

CHAPTER FIVE

THE POETIC ENDEAVOR

1. RALPH WALDO EMERSON, 1803–1882

[Committed before the fact, by the very way in which they appropriated their fundamental ideas from European sources, to making a case for themselves in religion, ethics, and sociology, the Transcendentalists somehow assumed from the beginning that even so their primary function was the creation of an American poetry. Here again, they conceived of a literary aim as being something more than mere literature. To them, poetry was *the* divinely appointed medium (from what little they knew of music, they could see that Beethoven might also have his claims, and possibly sculpture and painting, but even so, poetry was the supreme form) of the new, and yet eternal, philosophy. They revolted against the prosaic didacticism they associated with the name of Alexander Pope, but they were convinced that their poetic expression, if it were to achieve the desired "sublime" and to eschew the commonplace, should convey, even in its most transient lyric moments, a message from the realms of Transcendental verity.

All of them theorized about this difficult assignment, so extensively that we may be astonished that they ever left off talking about poetry in order to try composing some. Possibly the answer is obvious; they were all so entranced with great poets and great mystics that few of them dared venture to make themselves either poets or mystics. So they theorized.

However, the most gifted of them as creators, Emerson, was also the most articulate formulator of the doctrine. The patient reader may collect—as in fact patient scholars have done—the corpus of his preachment out of the *Essays* and out of the passing astutenesses of the *Journal*.

In 1870, alarmed by the news that an English publisher intended to pirate some of his uncollected pieces, Emerson was persuaded, much against his faltering will, to put together a last volume. He drew upon portions of early lectures and upon notes from the *Journal*, and in 1872 was able to set up a longish dissertation which he called "Poetry and Imagination." The effort was already too much for his failing powers, and he got help from his secretary; even so, the result is by no means an enfeebled expression of his senility, but an adroit reversion to his most vigorous years. It was printed as the first item in *Letters and Social Aims* in 1876; though it appears thus late, and in this form does not resound with the clarion call of *Nature* or the early *Essays*, nevertheless there is no more precise summation of the poetic program to which the group as a whole had dedicated themselves in the 1830's.

The whole of "Poetry and Imagination" is too discursive to be given here, but these extracts provide the crux of the position—the Transcendental doctrine of the "symbol" and the basic distinction (derived by them from Coleridge) between the Fancy and the Imagination. Still more, we can see here, late in the nineteenth century, how gallantly the Transcendental mentality, striving all of the time not to yield to a glib hostility to science, was obliged from the outset to contend against the easy victory which the natural and applied sciences were winning over the intellect of the period.]

POETRY AND IMAGINATION

Introductory

THE perception of matters is made the common sense, and for cause. This was the cradle, this the go-cart, of the human child. We must learn the homely laws of fire and water; we must feed, wash, plant, build. These are ends of necessity, and first in the order of nature. Poverty, frost, famine, disease, debt, are the beadles and guardsmen that hold us to common-sense. The intellect, yielded up to itself, cannot supersede this tyrannic necessity. The restraining grace of common-sense is the mark of all the valid minds of Æsop, Aristotle, Alfred, Luther, Shakspeare, Cervantes, Franklin, Napoleon. The common-sense which does not meddle with the absolute, but takes things at their word—things as they appear—believes in the existence of matter, not because we can touch it or conceive of it, but because it agrees with ourselves, and the universe does not jest with us, but is in earnest, is the house of health and life. In spite of all the joys of poets and the joys of saints, the most imaginative and abstracted person never makes with impunity the least mistake in this particular—never tries to kindle his oven with water, nor carries a torch into a powder-mill, nor seizes his wild charger by the tail. We should not pardon the blunder in another, nor endure it in ourselves.

But whilst we deal with this as finality, early hints are given that we are not to stay here; that we must be making ready to go—a warning that this magnificent hotel and conveniency we call Nature is not final. First innuendoes, then broad hints, then smart taps are given, suggesting that nothing stands still in nature but death; that the creation is on wheels, in transit, always passing into something else, streaming into something higher; that matter is not what it appears—that chemistry can blow it all into gas. Faraday, the most exact of natural philosophers, taught that when we should arrive at the monads, or primordial elements (the supposed little cubes or prisms of which all matter was built up), we should not find cubes, or prisms, or atoms, at all, but spherules of force. It was whispered that the globes of the universe were precipitates of something more subtle; nay, somewhat was murmured in our ear that dwindled astronomy into a toy—that too was no finality; only provisional, a makeshift; that under chemistry was power and purpose: power and purpose ride on matter to the last atom. It was steeped in thought, did everywhere express thought; that, as great conquerors have burned their ships when once they were landed on the wished-for shore, so the noble house of Nature we inhabit has temporary uses, and we can afford to leave it one day. The ends of all are moral, and therefore the beginnings are such. Thin or solid, everything is in flight. I believe this conviction makes the charm of chemistry—that we have the same avoirdupois matter in an alembic, without a vestige of the old form; and in animal transformation not less, as in grub and fly, in egg and bird, in embryo and man; everything undressing and stealing away from its old into new form, and nothing fast but those invisible cords which we call laws, on which all is strung. Then we see that things wear different names and faces, but belong to one family; that the secret cords or laws show their well-known virtue through every variety, be it animal, or plant, or planet, and the interest is gradually transferred from the forms to the lurking method.

This hint, however conveyed, upsets our politics, trade, customs, marriages, nay, the common-sense side of religion and literature, which are all founded on low nature—on the clearest and most economical mode of administering the material world, considered as final. The admission, never so covertly, that this is a makeshift, sets the dullest brain in ferment: our little sir, from his first tottering steps, as soon as he can crow, does not like to be practised upon, suspects that some one is "doing" him, and at this alarm everything is compromised; gunpowder is laid under every man's breakfast-table.

But whilst the man is startled by this closer inspection of the laws of matter, his attention is called to the independent action of the mind; its strange suggestions and laws; a certain tyranny which springs up in his own thoughts, which have an order, method, and beliefs of their own, very different from the order which this common-sense uses.

Suppose there were in the ocean certain strong currents which drove a ship, caught in them, with a force that no skill of sailing with the best wind, and no strength of oars, or sails, or stream, could make any head against, any more than against the current of Niagara. Such cur-

rents, so tyrannical, exist in thoughts, those finest and subtilest of all waters, that as soon as once thought begins,
it refuses to remember whose brain it belongs to; what
country, tradition, or religion; and goes whirling off—swim
we merrily—in a direction self-chosen, by law of thought
and not by law of kitchen clock or county committee. It
has its own polarity. One of these vortices or self-direc-
tions of thought is the impulse to search resemblance,
affinity, identity, in all its objects, and hence our science,
from its rudest to its most refined theories.

The electric word pronounced by John Hunter a hundred years ago, *arrested and progressive development*, in-
dicating the way upward from the invisible protoplasm
to the highest organisms, gave the poetic key to Natural
Science, of which the theories of Geoffroy St. Hilaire, of
Oken, of Goethe, of Agassiz and Owen and Darwin in
zoölogy and botany, are the fruits—a hint whose power is
not yet exhausted, showing unity and perfect order in
physics.

The hardest chemist, the severest analyzer, scornful of
all but dryest fact, is forced to keep the poetic curve of
nature, and his result is like a myth of Theocritus. All
multiplicity rushes to be resolved into unity. Anatomy,
osteology, exhibit arrested or progressive ascent in each
kind; the lower pointing to the higher forms, the higher to
the highest, from the fluid in an elastic sack, from radiate,
mollusk, articulate, vertebrate, up to man; as if the whole
animal world were only a Hunterian museum to exhibit the
genesis of mankind.

Identity of law, perfect order in physics, perfect parallelism between the laws of Nature and the laws of thought
exist. In botany we have the like, the poetic perception of
metamorphosis—that the same vegetable point or eye which
is the unit of the plant can be transformed at pleasure into
every part, as bract, leaf, petal, stamen, pistil, or seed.

In geology, what a useful hint was given to the early
inquirers on seeing in the possession of Professor Play-
fair a bough of a fossil tree which was perfect wood at one
end and perfect mineral coal at the other. Natural objects,
if individually described and out of connection, are not yet

known, since they are really parts of a symmetrical universe, like words of a sentence; and if their true order is found, the poet can read their divine significance orderly as in a Bible. Each animal or vegetable form remembers the next inferior and predicts the next higher.

There is one animal, one plant, one matter, and one force. The laws of light and of heat translate each other— so do the laws of sound and of color; and so galvanism, electricity, and magnetism are varied forms of the selfsame energy. While the student ponders this immense unity, he observes that all things in Nature, the animals, the mountain, the river, the seasons, wood, iron, stone, vapor, have a mysterious relation to his thoughts and his life; their growths, decays, quality and use so curiously resemble himself, in parts and in wholes, that he is compelled to speak by means of them. His words and his thoughts are framed by their help. Every noun is an image. Nature gives him, sometimes in a flattered likeness, sometimes in caricature, a copy of every humor and shade in his character and mind. The world is an immense picture-book of every passage in human life. Every object he beholds is the mask of a man.

> "The privates of man's heart
> They speken and sound in his ear
> As tho' they loud winds were;"

for the universe is full of their echoes.

Every correspondence we observe in mind and matter suggests a substance older and deeper than either of these old nobilities. We see the law gleaming through, like the sense of a half-translated ode of Hafiz. The poet who plays with it with most boldness best justifies himself; is most profound and devout. Passion adds eyes; is a magnifying-glass. Sonnets of lovers are mad enough, but are valuable to the philosopher, as are prayers of saints, for their potent symbolism.

Science was false by being unpoetical. It assumed to explain a reptile or mollusk, and isolated it—which is hunting for life in graveyards. Reptile or mollusk or man or angel only exists in system, in relation. The metaphysician, the poet, only sees each animal form as an inevitable step in the path of creating mind. The Indian, the hunter, the boy with his pets, have sweeter knowledge of these than the savant. We use semblances of logic until experience puts us in possession of real logic. The poet knows the missing link by the joy it gives. The poet gives us the eminent experiences only—a god stepping from peak to peak, not planting his foot but on a mountain.

Science does not know its debt to imagination. Goethe did not believe that a great naturalist could exist without this faculty. He was himself conscious of its help, which made him a prophet among the doctors. From this vision he gave brave hints to the zoölogist, the botanist and the optician.

Poetry

The primary use of a fact is low; the secondary use, as it is a figure or illustration of my thought, is the real worth. First the fact; second its impression, or what I think of it. Hence Nature was called "a kind of adulterated reason." Seas, forests, metals, diamonds and fossils interest the eye, but t' is only with some preparatory or predicting charm. Their value to the intellect appears only when I hear their meaning made plain in the spiritual truth they cover. The mind, penetrated with its sentiment or its thought, projects it outward on whatever it beholds. The lover sees reminders of his mistress in every beautiful object; the saint, an argument for devotion in every natural process; and the facility with which Nature lends itself to the thoughts of man, the aptness with which a river, a flower, a bird, fire, day or night, can express his fortunes, is as if the world were only a disguised man, and, with a change of form, rendered to him all his experience. We cannot utter a sentence in sprightly conversation without a similitude. Note our incessant use of the word *like*— like fire, like a rook, like thunder, like a bee, "like a year without a spring." Conversation is not permitted without tropes; nothing but great weight in things can afford a quite literal speech. It is ever enlivened by inversion and trope. God himself does not speak prose, but communicates with us by hints, omens, inference, and dark resemblances in objects lying all around us.

Nothing so marks a man as imaginative expressions. A figurative statement arrests attention, and is remembered and repeated. How often has a phrase of this kind made a reputation. Pythagoras's Golden Sayings were such, and Socrates's, and Mirabeau's, and Burke's, and Bonaparte's. Genius thus makes the transfer from one part of Nature to a remote part, and betrays the rhymes and echoes that pole makes with pole. Imaginative minds cling to their images, and do not wish them rashly rendered into prose reality, as children resent your showing them that their doll Cinderella is nothing but pine wood and rags; and my young scholar does not wish to know what the leopard, the wolf, or Lucia, signify in Dante's Inferno, but prefers to keep their veils on. Mark the delight of an audience in an image. When some familiar truth or fact appears in a new dress, mounted as on a fine horse, equipped with a grand pair of ballooning wings, we cannot enough testify our surprise and pleasure. It is like the new virtue shown in some unprized old property, as when a boy finds that his pocket-knife will attract steel filings and take up a needle; or when the old horse-block in the yard is found to be a Torso Hercules of the Phidian age. Vivacity of expression may indicate this high gift, even when the thought is of no great scope, as when Michel Angelo, praising the *terra cottas*, said, "If this earth were to become marble, woe to the antiques!" A happy symbol is a sort of evidence that your thought is just. I had rather have a good symbol of my thought, or a good analogy, than the suffrage of Kant or Plato. If you agree with me, or if Locke or Montesquieu agree, I may yet be wrong; but if the elm-tree thinks the same thing, if running water, if burning coal, if crystals, if alkalies, in their several fashions say what I say, it must be true. Thus a good symbol is the best argument, and is a missionary to persuade thousands. The Vedas, the Edda, the Koran, are each remembered by their happiest figure. There is no more welcome gift to men than a new symbol. That satiates, transports, converts them. They assimilate themselves to it, deal with it in all ways, and it will last a hundred years. Then comes a new genius, and brings another. Thus the Greek mythology called the sea "the tear of Saturn." The return of the soul to God was described as "a flask of water broken in the sea." Saint John gave us the Christian figure of "souls washed in the blood of Christ." The aged Michel Angelo indicates his perpetual study as in boyhood—"I carry my satchel still." Machiavel described the papacy as "a stone inserted in the body of Italy to keep the wound open." To the Parliament debating how to tax America, Burke exclaimed, "Shear the wolf." Our Kentuckian orator said of his dissent from his companion, "I showed him the back of my hand." And our proverb of the courteous soldier reads: "An iron hand in a velvet glove."

This belief that the higher use of the material world is to furnish us types or pictures to express the thoughts of the mind, is carried to its logical extreme by the Hindoos, who, following Buddha, have made it the central doctrine of their religion that what we call Nature, the external world, has no real existence—is only phenomenal. Youth, age, property, conditions, events, persons—self, even—are successive *maias* (deceptions) through which Vishnu mocks and instructs the soul. I think Hindoo books the best gymnastics for the mind, as showing treatment. All European libraries might almost be read without the swing of this gigantic arm being suspected. But these Orientals deal with worlds and pebbles freely.

For the value of a trope is that the hearer is one: and indeed Nature itself is a vast trope, and all particular natures are tropes. As the bird alights on the bough, then plunges into the air again, so the thoughts of God pause but for a moment in any form. All thinking is analogizing, and it is the use of life to learn metonymy. The endless passing of one element into new forms, the incessant metamorphosis, explains the rank which the imagination holds in our catalogue of mental powers. The imagination is the leader of these forms. The poet accounts all productions and changes of Nature as the nouns of language, uses them representatively, too well pleased with their ulterior to value much their primary meaning. Every new object so seen gives a shock of agreeable surprise. The impressions on the imagination make the great days of life: the book, the landscape or the personality which did not stay on the surface of the eye or ear but penetrated to the inward sense, agitates us, and is not forgotten. Walking, working, or talking, the sole question is how many strokes vibrate on this mystic string—how many diameters are drawn quite through from matter to spirit; for whenever you enunciate a natural law you discover that you have enunciated a law of the mind. Chemistry, geology, hydraulics, are secondary science. The atomic theory is only an interior process *produced,* as geometers say, or the effect of a foregone metaphysical theory. Swedenborg saw gravity to be only an external of the irresistible attractions of affection and faith. Mountains and oceans we think we understand—yes, so long as they are contented to be such, and are safe with the geologist—but when they are melted in Promethean alembics and come out men, and then, melted again, come out words, without any abatement, but with an exaltation of power!

In poetry we say we require the miracle. The bee flies among the flowers, and gets mint and marjoram, and generates a new product, which is not mint and marjoram, but honey; the chemist mixes hydrogen and oxygen to yield a new product, which is not these, but water; and the poet listens to conversation and beholds all objects in nature, to give back, not them, but a new and transcendent whole.

Poetry is the perpetual endeavor to express the spirit of the thing, to pass the brute body and search the life and reason which causes it to exist—to see that the object is always flowing away, whilst the spirit or necessity which causes it subsists. Its essential mark is that it betrays in every word instant activity of mind, shown in new uses of every fact and image, in preternatural quickness or perception of relations. All its words are poems. It is a presence of mind that gives a miraculous command of all means of uttering the thought and feeling of the moment. The poet squanders on the hour an amount of life that would more than furnish the seventy years of the man that stands next him.

The term "genius," when used with emphasis, implies imagination; use of symbols, figurative speech. A deep insight will always, like Nature, ultimate its thought in a thing. As soon as a man masters a principle and sees his facts in relation to it, fields, waters, skies, offer to clothe his thoughts in images. Then all men understand him; Parthian, Mede, Chinese, Spaniard and Indian hear their own tongue. For he can now find symbols of universal significance, which are readily rendered into any dialect; as a painter, a sculptor, a musician, can in their several ways express the same sentiment of anger, or love, or religion.

The thoughts are few; the forms many; the large vocabulary or many-colored coat of the indigent unity. The *savans* are chatty and vain, but hold them hard to principle and definition, and they become mute and near-sighted. What is motion? what is beauty? what is matter? what is life? what is force? Push them hard and they will not be loquacious. They will come to Plato, Proclus, and Swedenborg. The invisible and imponderable is the sole fact. "Why changes not the violet earth into musk?" What is the term of the everflowing metamorphosis? I do not know what are the stoppages, but I see that a devouring unity changes all into that which changes not.

The act of imagination is ever attended by pure delight. It infuses a certain volatility and intoxication into all nature. It has a flute which sets the atoms of our frame in a dance. Our indeterminate size is a delicious secret which it reveals to us. The mountains begin to dislimn, and float in the air. In the presence and conversation of a true poet, teeming with images to express his enlarging thought, his person, his form, grows larger to our fascinated eyes. And thus begins that deification which all nations have made of their heroes in every kind—saints, poets, lawgivers, and warriors.

Imagination

Whilst common sense looks at things or visible Nature as real and final facts, poetry, or the imagination which dictates it, is a second sight, looking through these, and using them as types or words for thoughts which they signify. Or is this belief a metaphysical whim of modern times, and quite too refined? On the contrary, it is as old as the human mind. Our best definition of poetry is one of the oldest sentences, and claims to come down to us from the Chaldæn Zoroaster, who wrote it thus: "Poets are standing transporters, whose employment consists in speaking to the Father and to matter; in producing apparent imitations of unapparent natures, and inscribing things unapparent in the apparent fabrication of the world;" in other words, the world exists for thought: it is to make appear things which hide: mountains, crystals, plants, animals, are seen; that which makes them is not seen: these, then, are "apparent copies of unapparent natures." Bacon expressed the same sense in his definition, "Poetry accommodates the shows of things to the desires of the mind;" and Swedenborg, when he said, "There is nothing existing in human thought, even though relating to the most mysterious tenet of faith, but has combined with it a natural and sensuous image." And again: "Names, countries, nations, and the like are not at all known to those who are in heaven; they have no idea of such things, but of the realities signified thereby." A symbol always stimulates the intellect; therefore is poetry ever the best reading. The very design of imagination is to domesticate us in another, in a celestial, nature.

This power is in the image because this power is in nature. It so affects, because it so is. All that is wondrous in Swedenborg is not his invention, but his extraordinary perception—that he was necessitated so to see. The world realizes the mind. Better than images is seen through them. The selection of the image is no more arbitrary than the power and significance of the image. The selection must follow fate. Poetry, if perfected, is the only verity; is the speech of man after the real, and not after the apparent.

Or shall we say that the imagination exists by sharing the ethereal currents? The poet contemplates the central identity, sees it undulate and roll this way and that, with divine flowings, through remotest things; and, following it, can detect essential resemblances in natures never before compared. He can class them so audaciously because he is sensible of the sweep of the celestial stream, from which nothing is exempt. His own body is a fleeing apparition —his personality as fugitive as the trope he employs. In certain hours we can almost pass our hand through our own body. I think the use or value of poetry to be the suggestion it affords of the flux or fugaciousness of the poet. The mind delights in measuring itself thus with matter, with history, and flouting both. A thought, any thought, pressed, followed, opened, dwarfs matter, custom, and all but itself. But this second sight does not necessarily impair the primary or common sense. Pindar, and Dante, yes, and the gray and timeworn sentences of Zoroaster, may all be parsed, though we do not parse them. The poet has a logic, thought it be subtile. He observes higher laws than he transgresses. "Poetry must first be good sense, though it is something better."

This union of first and second sight reads Nature to the end of delight and of moral use. Men are imaginative, but not overpowered by it to the extent of confounding its suggestions with external facts. We live in both spheres, and must not mix them. Genius certifies its entire possession of its thought, by translating it into a fact which perfectly represents it, and is hereby education. Charles James Fox thought "Poetry the great refreshment of the human mind—the only thing, after all; that men first found out they had minds, by making and tasting poetry."

Man runs about restless and in pain when his condition or the objects about him do not fully match his thought. He wishes to be rich, to be old, to be young, that things may obey him. In the ocean, in fire, in the sky, in the forest, he finds facts adequate and as large as he. As his thoughts are deeper than he can fathom, so also are these.

It is easier to read Sanscrit, to decipher the arrowhead character, then to interpret these familiar sights. It is even much to name them. Thus Thomson's "Seasons" and the best parts of many old and many new poets are simply enumerations by a person who felt the beauty of the common sights and sounds, without any attempt to draw a moral or affix a meaning.

The poet discovers that what men value as substances have a higher value as symbols; that Nature is the immense shadow of man. A man's action is only a picture-book of his creed. He does after what he believes. Your condition, your employment, is the fable of *you*. The world is thoroughly anthropomorphized, as if it had passed through the body and mind of man, and taken his mould and form. Indeed, good poetry is always personification, and heightens every species of force in Nature by giving it a human volition. We are advertised that there is nothing to which man is not related; that every thing is convertible into every other. The staff in his hand is the *radius vector* of the sun. The chemistry of this is the chemistry of that. Whatever one act we do, whatever one thing we learn, we are doing and learning all things—marching in the direction of universal power. Every healthy mind is a true Alexander or Sesostris, building a universal monarchy.

The senses imprison us, and we help them with metres as limitary—with a pair of scales and a foot-rule and a clock. How long it took to find out what a day was, or what this sun, that makes days! It cost thousands of years only to make the motion of the earth suspected. Slowly, by comparing thousands of observations, there dawned on some mind a theory of the sun—and we found the astronomical fact. But the astronomy is in the mind: the senses affirm that the earth stands still and the sun moves. The senses collect the surface facts of matter. The intellect acts on these brute reports, and obtains from them results which are the essence or intellectual form of the experiences. It compares, distributes, generalizes and uplifts them into its own sphere. It knows that these transfigured results are not the brute experiences, just as souls in heaven are not the red bodies they once animated. Many transfigurations have befallen them. The atoms of the body were once nebulæ, then rock, then loam, then corn, then chyme, then chyle, then blood; and now the beholding and co-energizing mind sees the same refining and ascent to the third, the seventh, or the tenth power of the daily accidents which the senses report, and which make the raw material of knowledge. It was sensation; when memory came, it was experience; when mind acted, it was knowledge; when mind acted on it as knowledge, it was thought.

This metonymy, or seeing the same sense in things so diverse, gives a pure pleasure. Every one of a million times we find a charm in the metamorphosis. It makes us dance and sing. All men are so far poets. When people tell me they do not relish poetry, and bring me Shelley, or Aikin's Poets, or I know not what volumes of rhymed English, to show that it has no charm, I am quite of their mind. But this dislike of the books only proves their liking of poetry. For they relish Æsop cannot forget him, or not use him; bring them Homer's Iliad, and they like that; or the Cid, and that rings well; read to them from Chaucer, and they reckon him an honest fellow. Lear and Macbeth and Richard III. they know pretty well without guide. Give them Robin Hood's ballads or Griselda, or Sir Andrew Barton, or Sir Patrick Spens, or Chevy Chase, or Tam O'Shanter, and they like these well enough. They like to see statues; they like to name the stars; they like to talk and hear of Jove, Apollo, Minerva, Venus and the Nine. See how tenacious we are of the old names. They like poetry without knowing it as such. They like to go to the theatre and be made to weep; to Faneuil Hall, and be taught by Otis, Webster, or Kossuth, or Phillips, what great hearts they have, what tears, what new possible enlargements of their narrow horizons. They like to see sunsets on the hills or on a lake shore. Now a cow does not gaze at the rainbow, or show or affect any interest in the landscape, or a peacock, or the song of thrushes.

Nature is the true idealist. When she serves us best, when, on rare days, she speaks to the imagination, we feel that the huge heaven and earth are but a web drawn around us, that the light, skies, and mountains are but the painted vicissitudes of the soul. Who has heard our hymn in the churches without accepting the truth—

> "As o'er our heads the seasons roll,
> And soothe with *change of bliss* the soul"?

Of course, when we describe man as poet, and credit him with the triumphs of the art, we speak of the potential or ideal man—not found now in any one person. You must go through a city or a nation, and find one faculty here, one there, to build the true poet withal. Yet all men know the portrait when it is drawn, and it is part of religion to believe its possible incarnation.

He is the healthy, the wise, the fundamental, the manly man, seer of the secret; against all the appearance he sees and reports the truth, namely that the soul generates matter. And poetry is the only verity—the expression of a sound mind speaking after the ideal, and not after the apparent. As a power it is the perception of the symbolic character of things, and the treating them as representative: as a talent it is a magnetic tenaciousness of an image, and by the treatment demonstrating that this pigment of thought is as palpable and objective to the poet as is the ground on which he stands, or the walls of houses about him. And this power appears in Dante and Shakspeare. In some individuals this insight or second sight has an extraordinary reach which compels our wonder, as in Behmen, Swedenborg, and William Blake the painter.

William Blake, whose abnormal genius, Wordsworth said, interested him more than the conversation of Scott or of Byron, writes thus: "He who does not imagine in stronger and better lineaments and in stronger and better light than his perishing mortal eye can see, does not imagine at all. The painter of this work asserts that all his imaginations appear to him infinitely more perfect and more minutely organized than anything seen by his mortal eye. . . . I assert for myself that I do not behold the outward creation, and that to me it would be a hinderance, and not action. I question not my corporeal eye any more than I would question a window concerning a sight. I look through it, and not with it."

It is a problem of metaphysics to define the province of Fancy and Imagination. The words are often used, and the things confounded. Imagination respects the cause. It is the vision of an inspired soul reading arguments and affirmations in all Nature of that which it is driven to say. But as soon as this soul is released a little from its passion, and at leisure plays with the resemblances and types, for amusement, and not for its moral end, we call its action Fancy. Lear, mad with his affliction, thinks every man who suffers must have the like cause with his own. "What, have his daughters brought him to this pass?" But when, his attention being diverted, his mind rests from this thought, he becomes fanciful with Tom, playing with the superficial resemblances of objects. Bunyan, in pain for his soul, wrote Pilgrim's Progress; Quarles, after he was quite cool, wrote Emblems.

Imagination is central; fancy, superficial. Fancy relates to surface, in which a great part of life lies. The lover is rightly said to fancy the hair, eyes, complexion of the maid. Fancy is a wilful, imagination a spontaneous act; fancy, a play as with dolls and puppets which we choose to call men and women; imagination, a perception and affirming of a real relation between a thought and some material fact. Fancy amuses; imagination expands and exalts us. Imagination uses an organic classification. Fancy joins by accidental resemblance, surprises and amuses the idle, but is silent in the presence of great passion and action. Fancy aggregates; imagination animates. Fancy is related to color; imagination, to form. Fancy paints; imagination sculptures.

Veracity

I do not wish, therefore, to find that my poet is not partaker of the feast he spreads, or that he would kindle or amuse me with that which does not kindle or amuse him. He must believe in his poetry. Homer, Milton, Hafiz, Herbert, Swedenborg, Wordsworth, are heartily enamoured of their sweet thoughts. Moreover, they know that this correspondence of things to thoughts is far deeper than they can penetrate—defying adequate expression; that it is elemental, or in the core of things. Veracity therefore is that which we require in poets— that they shall say how it was with them, and not what might be said. And the fault of our popular poetry is that it is not sincere.

"What news?" asks man of man everywhere. The only teller of news is the poet. When he sings, the world listens with the assurance that now a secret of God is to be spoken. The right poetic mood is or makes a more complete sensibility, piercing the outward fact to the meaning of the fact; shows a sharper insight: and the perception creates the strong expression of it, as the man who sees his way walks in it.

It is a rule in eloquence, that the moment the orator loses command of his audience, the audience commands him. So in poetry, the master rushes to deliver his thought, and the words and images fly to him to express it; whilst colder moods are forced to respect the ways of saying it, and insinuate, or, as it were, muffle the fact to suit the poverty or caprice of their expression, so that they only hint the matter, or allude to it, being unable to fuse and mould their words and images to fluid obedience. See how Shakspeare grapples at once with the main problem of the tragedy, as in Lear and Macbeth, and the opening of the Merchant of Venice.

All writings must be in a degree exoteric, written to a human *should* or *would*, instead of to the fatal *is:* this holds even of the bravest and sincerest writers. Every writer is a skater, and must go partly where he would, and partly where the skates carry him; or a sailor, who can only land where sails can be blown. And yet it is to be added that high poetry exceeds the fact, or Nature itself, just as skates allow the good skater far more grace than his best walking would show, or sails more than riding. The poet writes from a real experience, the amateur feigns one. Of course one draws the bow with his fingers and the other with the strength of his body; one speaks with his lips and the other with a chest voice. Talent amuses, but if your verse has not a necessary and autobiographic basis, though under whatever gay poetic veils, it shall not waste my time.

For poetry is faith. To the poet the world is virgin soil; all is practicable; the men are ready for virtue; it is always time to do right. He is a true re-commencer, or Adam in the garden again. He affirms the applicability of the ideal law to this moment and the present knot of affairs. Parties, lawyers and men of the world will invariably dispute such an application, as romantic and dangerous: they admit the general truth, but they and their affair always constitute a case in bar of the statute. Free-trade, they concede, is very well as a principle, but it is never quite the time for its adoption without prejudicing actual interests. Chastity, they admit, is very well—but then think of Mirabeau's passion and temperament! Eternal laws are very well, which admit no violation—but so extreme were the times and manners of mankind, that you must admit miracles, for the times constituted a case. Of course, we know what you say, that legends are found in all tribes—but this legend is different. And so throughout; the poet affirms the laws, prose busies itself with exceptions—with the local and individual.

I require that the poem should impress me so that after I have shut the book it shall recall me to itself, or that passages should. And inestimable is the criticism of memory as a corrective to first impressions. We are dazzled at first by new words and brilliancy of color, which occupy the fancy and deceive the judgment. But all this is easily forgotten. Later, the thought, the happy image which expressed it and which was a true experience of the poet, recurs to mind, and sends me back in search of the book. And I wish that the poet should foresee this habit of readers, and omit all but the important passages. Shakspeare is made up of important passages, like Damascus steel made up of old nails. Homer has his own—

"One omen is best, to fight for one's country;"
and again—

"They heal their griefs, for curable are the hearts of the
noble."

Write, that I may know you. Style betrays you, as your
eyes do. We detect at once by it whether the writer has
a firm grasp on his fact or thought—exists at the moment
for that alone, or whether he has one eye apologizing,
deprecatory, turned on his reader. In proportion always
to his possession of his thought is his defiance of his readers.
There is no choice of words for him who clearly sees the
truth. That provides him with the best word.

Great design belongs to a poem, and is better than any
skill of execution—but how rare! I find it in the poems of
Wordsworth—Laodamia, and the Ode to Dion, and the
plan of The Recluse. We want design, and do not forgive
the bards if they have only the art of enamelling. We want
an architect, and they bring us an upholsterer.

If your subject do not appear to you the flower of the
world at this moment, you have not rightly chosen it. No
matter what it is, grand or gay, national or private, if it
has a natural prominence to you, work away until you
come to the heart of it: then it will, though it were a
sparrow or a spider-web, as fully represent the central law
and draw all tragic or joyful illustration, as if it were the
book of Genesis or the book of Doom. The subject—we
must so often say it—is indifferent. Any word, every word
in language, every circumstance, becomes poetic in the
hands of a higher thought.

The test or measure of poetic genius is the power to
read the poetry of affairs—to fuse the circumstance of
to-day; not to use Scott's antique superstitions, or Shakspeare's, but to convert those of the nineteenth century
and of the existing nations into universal symbols. 'T is
easy to repaint the mythology of the Greeks, or of the
Catholic Church, the feudal castle, the crusade, the martyr-
doms of mediæval Europe; but to point out where the
same creative force is now working in our own houses and
public assemblies; to convert the vivid energies acting at

this hour in New York and Chicago and San Francisco, into universal symbols, requires a subtile and commanding thought. 'T is boyish in Swedenborg to cumber himself with the dead scurf of Hebrew antiquity, as if the Divine creative energy had fainted in his own century. American life storms about us daily, and is slow to find a tongue. This contemporary insight is transubstantiation, the conversion of daily bread into the holiest symbols; and every man would be a poet if his intellectual digestion were perfect. The test of the poet is the power to take the passing day, with its news, its cares, its fears, as he shares them, and hold it up to a divine reason, till he sees it to have a purpose and beauty, and to be related to astronomy and history and the eternal order of the world. Then the dry twig blossoms in his hand. He is calmed and elevated.

The use of "occasional poems" is to give leave to originality. Every one delights in the felicity frequently shown in our drawing-rooms. In a game-party or picnic poem each writer is released from the solemn rhythmic traditions which alarm and suffocate his fancy, and the result is that one of the partners offers a poem in a new style that hints at a new literature. Yet the writer holds it cheap, and could do the like all day. On the stage, the farce is commonly far better given than the tragedy, as the stock actors understand the farce, and do not understand the tragedy. The writer in the parlor has more presence of mind, more wit and fancy, more play of thought, on the incidents that occur at table or about the house, than in the politics of Germany or Rome. Many of the fine poems of Herrick, Jonson, and their contemporaries had this casual origin.

I know there is entertainment and room for talent in the artist's selection of ancient or remote subjects; as when the poet goes to India, or to Rome, or Persia, for his fable. But I believe nobody knows better than he that herein he consults his ease rather than his strength or his desire. He is very well convinced that the great moments of life are those in which his own house, his own body, the tritest and nearest ways and words and things have been illuminated into prophets and teachers. What else is it to be a poet? What are his garland and singing-robes? What but a sensibility so keen that the scent of an elder-blow, or the timber-yard and corporation-works of a nest of pismires is event enough for him—all emblems and personal appeals to him. His wreath and robe is to do what he enjoys; emancipation from other men's questions, and glad study of his own; escape from the gossip and routine of society, and the allowed right and practice of making better. He does not give his hand, but in sign of giving his heart; he is not affable with all, but silent, uncommitted or in love, as his heart leads him. There is no subject that does not belong to him—politics, economy, manufacturers and stock-brokerage, as much as sunsets and souls; only, these things, placed in their true order, are poetry; displaced, or put in kitchen order, they are unpoetic. Malthus is the right organ of the English proprietors; but we shall never understand political economy until Burns or Béranger or some poet shall teach it in songs, and he will not teach Malthusianism.

Poetry is the *gai science*. The trait and test of the poet is that he builds, adds and affirms. The critic destroys: the poet says nothing but what helps somebody; let others be distracted with cares, he is exempt. All their pleasures are tinged with pain. All his pains are edged with pleasure. The gladness he imparts he shares. As one of the old Minnesingers sung—

> "Oft have I heard, and now believe it true,
> Whom man delights in, God delights in too."

Poetry is the consolation of mortal men. They live cabined, cribbed, confined in a narrow and trivial lot—in wants, pains, anxieties and superstitions, in profligate politics, in personal animosities, in mean employments—and victims of these; and the nobler powers untried, unknown. A poet comes who lifts the veil; gives them glimpses of the laws of the universe; shows them the circumstance as illusion; shows that nature is only a language to express the laws, which are grand and beautiful—and lets them, by his songs, into some of the realities. Socrates, the Indian teachers of the Maia, the Bibles of the nations,

Shakspeare, Milton, Hafiz, Ossian, the Welsh Bards—these all deal with nature and history as means and symbols, and not as ends. With such guides they begin to see that what they had called pictures are realities, and the mean life is pictures. And this is achieved by words; for it is a few oracles spoken by perceiving men that are the texts on which religions and states are founded. And this perception has at once its moral sequence. Ben Jonson said, "The principal end of poetry is to inform men in the just reason of living."

2. RALPH WALDO EMERSON, 1803–1882

[Emerson is the only one among the Transcendental versifiers whose works have a position in the world's literature. In general his contemporaries thought his poetry inferior to his prose; they were often apologetic about it, explaining that poor Mr. Emerson lacked "ear." Margaret Fuller put her loyalty to the test by saying of his verse in *The New York Tribune* that it took high rank for subtle beauty of thought and expression; however, she was candidly obliged to add, his poems are mostly philosophical, which is not the truest kind of poetry; they interest the mind, but fail to wake echoes in the heart, and "the imagery wears a symbolical air." In less respectful quarters the criticism was more bluntly put: Emerson could not keep metre. In these estimations Emerson was compared, to his disadvantage, with his melodious contemporaries, Longfellow, Lowell, Holmes.

At the present writing, when, I take it, the stock of these three is fairly low, the rhymes of Emerson stand out as prognostications of a revolution, if not indeed the first victories of modernism. He may have failed to make clear to his age just what he was attempting, and may not have been too conscious of his design; even so, take such a line as this from "Hamatreya" and compare it with anything of Longfellow's:

"Háy, córn, roóts, hémp, fláx, ápplĕs, wóol, ănd wóod."
The steady, heavy beat of these monosyllables would seem

even to his admirers a barbarism; to us, it is the commencement of an age of vital experiment, a daring departure from the jingle of convention.

Were I adequately to represent Emerson the poet in these pages I should, once more, have to reproduce all the items appearing in every routine anthology. But since copies of his poetry are universally available, I call attention here to only the few which succinctly bespeak the "Transcendental" mentality.

"The Apology," being an early exercise (probably about 1834), is not a memorable utterance, but it proclaims that truculence (which in his personal relations Emerson tempered by graciousness of manner), that scorn of the polite and genteel, which critics of the movement found sheer boorishness but which to some of us remains the most engaging trait of New England Transcendentalism.

"Uriel" is (arrogantly) Emerson's borrowing of Milton's Archangel of Sun to allegorize the ordeal to which he was subjected by those he horrified with "The Divinity School Address" of July 15, 1838. Externally, Emerson maintained his classic poise, but, as Stephen Whicher's fine analysis demonstrates, within he was profoundly troubled. So, in this poem, he calls up "Uriel" to combat the Unitarians. To our eyes, however, this piece speaks of a wider theme: considering that not only was Emerson excoriated because of "The Divinity School Address" but also Alcott was denounced for his School, Parker for his "Transient and Permanent," Margaret Fuller for her feminism, and Thoreau for his village nonconformity, we may then take this poem, in its context, as in effect an apology for subversion.

"Destiny" was first printed with the title "Fate" in *The Dial* for October, 1841. The issue of determinism versus free-will was still oppressive in New England, even to Transcendentalists, because in their effort to escape the frying pan of Calvinism they plunged into the fire of metaphysical idealism. Emerson would struggle with the worrisome problem all his conscious life, and achieve momentary solutions in such essays as "Experience" and "Fate." Revealing is the way in which even this short meditation obliquely confesses that the theological conception of fate as divine decree was crumbling only because the more cogent conception was becoming fate as a decree of natural environment. In either cosmology, the sign of election turns out to be "success." Wherefore, in the last couplet, Emerson once more asserts that success for the Transcendentalists will look to most citizens like recalcitrance.

"Each and All," as we know from a *Journal* entry of May 16, 1834, recounts an actual experience. Perhaps this poem illustrates most neatly that injunction which Thoreau formulated as never underestimating the value of a fact, for someday it might flower into a "truth."

The piece to which, following precedent, I have given the title of "The Eternal Pan" is the concluding passage in the second part of "Woodnotes." This strophe appeared first in *The Dial* for October, 1841, and was somewhat revised for the *Poems* of 1847. It may well stand here as one of the best expressions of the Transcendental conception of the relation of Self to Nature.

"Hamatreya" is a good illustration, on the elementary level, of how Yankee Uriels went about appropriating the wisdom of the Orient. Emerson's poem is a free rendering of a passage in the *Vishnu Purana* which he copied into his *Journal* in 1845. Emerson domesticated this exotic in Massachusetts by substituting the names of the founding fathers of Concord (the first "inland" settlement of the Puritans, in 1637) for the glittering parade of Hindu sovereigns, upon whom the Hindu Earth was bestowing an ambiguous benediction while reciting to the listening "Maitreya."

Hence, with "Brahma" we reach the inescapable selection from Emerson's mature poetic achievement. This is a relatively late creation (it was published in the *Atlantic* of November, 1857), and its charm, as with the "Historic Notes," is that of summation rather than of freshness. He was experimenting with this poem early in the 1840's. In the final form, I think it fair to say, Emerson's debt to the Orient is much less than the title suggests: this is not a rendition of anything in the *Bhagavad-Gita*; it is New England's old Puritanism decked out in Oriental imagery.]

POEMS

The Apology

Think me not unkind and rude
    That I walk alone in grove and glen;
I go to the god of the wood
    To fetch his word to men.

Tax not my sloth that I
    Fold my arms beside the brook;
Each cloud that floated in the sky
    Writes a letter in my book.

Chide me not, laborious band,
    For the idle flowers I brought;
Every aster in my hand
    Goes home loaded with a thought.

There was never mystery
    But 'tis figured in the flowers;
Was never secret history
    But birds tell it in the bowers.

One harvest from thy field
    Homeward brought the oxen strong;
A second crop thine acres yield,
    Which I gather in a song.

Uriel

It fell in the ancient periods
    Which the brooding soul surveys,
Or ever the wild Time coined itself
    Into calendar months and days.

This was the lapse of Uriel,
Which in Paradise befell.

Once, among the Pleiads walking,
Seyd overheard the young gods talking;
And the treason, too long pent,
To his ears was evident.
The young deities discussed
Laws of form, and metre just,
Orb, quintessence, and sunbeams,
What subsisteth, and what seems.
One, with low tones that decide,
And doubt and reverend use defied,
With a look that solved the sphere,
And stirred the devils everywhere,
Gave his sentiment divine
Against the being of a line.
'Line in nature is not found;
Unit and universe are round;
In vain produced, all rays return;
Evil will bless, and ice will burn.'
As Uriel spoke with piercing eye,
A shudder ran around the sky;
The stern old war-gods shook their heads,
The seraphs frowned from myrtle-beds;
Seemed to the holy festival
The rash word boded ill to all;
The balance-beam of Fate was bent;
The bounds of good and ill were rent;
Strong Hades could not keep his own,
But all slid to confusion.

A sad self-knowledge, withering, fell
On the beauty of Uriel;
In heaven once eminent, the god
Withdrew, that hour, into his cloud;
Whether doomed to long gyration
In the sea of generation,
Or by knowledge grown too bright
To hit the nerve of feebler sight.
Straightway, a forgetting wind
Stole over the celestial kind,
And their lips the secret kept,

If in ashes the fire-seed slept.
But now and then, truth-speaking things
Shamed the angels' veiling wings;
And, shrilling from the solar course,
Or from fruit of chemic force,
Procession of a soul in matter,
Or the speeding change of water,
Or out of the good of evil born,
Came Uriel's voice of cherub scorn,
And a blush tinged the upper sky,
And the gods shook, they knew not why.

Destiny

That you are fair or wise is vain,
Or strong, or rich, or generous;
You must add the untaught strain
That sheds beauty on the rose.
There's a melody born of melody,
Which melts the world into a sea.
Toil could never compass it;
Art its height could never hit;
It came never out of wit;
But a music music-born
Well may Jove and Juno scorn.
Thy beauty, if it lack the fire
Which drives me mad with sweet
        desire,
What boots it? What the soldier's mail,
Unless he conquer and prevail?
What all the goods thy pride which lift,
If thou pine for another's gift?
Alas! that one is born in blight,
Victim of perpetual slight:
When thou lookest on his face,
Thy heart saith, 'Brother, go thy ways!
None shall ask thee what thou doest,
Or care a rush for what thou knowest,
Or listen when thou repliest,

Or remember where thou liest,
Or how thy supper is sodden;'
And another is born
To make the sun forgotten.
Surely he carries a talisman
Under his tongue;
Broad his shoulders are and strong;
And his eye is scornful,
Threatening and young.
I hold it of little matter
Whether your jewel be of pure water,
A rose diamond or a white,
But whether it dazzle me with light.
I care not how you are dressed,
In coarsest weeds or in the best;
Nor whether your name is base or brave:
Nor for the fashion of your behavior;
But whether you charm me,
Bid my bread feed and my fire warm me
And dress up Nature in your favor.
One thing is forever good;
That one thing is Success—
Dear to the Eumenides,
And to all the heavenly brood.
Who bides at home, nor looks abroad,
Carries the eagles, and masters the sword.

Each and All

Little thinks, in the field, yon red-cloaked clown
Of thee from the hill-top looking down;
The heifer that lows in the upland farm,
Far-heard, lows not thine ear to charm;
The sexton, tolling his bell at noon,
Deems not that great Napoleon
Stops his horse, and lists with delight,
Whilst his files sweep round yon Alpine height;
Nor knowest thou what argument
Thy life to thy neighbor's creed has lent.

All are needed by each one;
Nothing is fair or good alone.
I thought the sparrow's note from heaven,
Singing at dawn on the alder bough;
I brought him home, in his nest, at even;
He sings the song, but it cheers not now,
For I did not bring home the river and sky—
He sang to my ear—they sang to my eye.
The delicate shells lay on the shore;
The bubbles of the latest wave
Fresh pearls to their enamel gave,
And the bellowing of the savage sea
Greeted their safe escape to me.
I wiped away the weeds and foam,
I fetched my sea-born treasures home;
But the poor, unsightly, noisome things
Had left their beauty on the shore
With the sun and the sand and the wild uproar.
The lover watched his graceful maid,
As 'mid the virgin train she strayed,
Nor knew her beauty's best attire
Was woven still by the snow-white choir.
At last she came to his hermitage,
Like the bird from the woodlands to the cage—
The gay enchantment was undone,
A gentle wife, but fairy none.
Then I said, 'I covet truth;
Beauty is unripe childhood's cheat;
I leave it behind with the games of youth'—
As I spoke, beneath my feet
The ground-pine curled its pretty wreath,
Running over the club-moss burrs;
I inhaled the violet's breath;
Around me stood the oaks and firs;
Pine-cones and acorns lay on the ground;
Over me soared the eternal sky,
Full of light and of deity;
Again I saw, again I heard,
The rolling river, the morning bird—

Beauty through my senses stole;
I yielded myself to the perfect whole.

The Eternal Pan

All the forms are fugitive,
But the substances survive.
Ever fresh the broad creation,
A divine improvisation,
From the heart of God proceeds,
A single will, a million deeds.
Once slept the world an egg of stone,
And pulse, and sound, and light was none;
And God said, "Throb!" and there was motion
And the vast mass became vast ocean.
Onward and on, the eternal Pan,
Who layeth the world's incessant plan,
Halteth never in one shape,
But forever doth escape,
Like wave or flame, into new forms
Of gem, and air, or plants, and worms.
I, that to-day am a pine,
Yesterday was a bundle of grass.
He is free and libertine,
Pouring of his power the wine
To every age, to every race;
Unto every race and age
He emptieth the beverage;
Unto each, and unto all,
Maker and original.
The world is the ring of his spells,
And the play of his miracles.
As he giveth to all to drink,
Thus or thus they are and think.
With one drop sheds form and feature;
With the next a special nature;
The third adds heat's indulgent spark;
The fourth gives light which eats the dark;

Into the fifth himself he flings,
And conscious Law is King of kings.
As the bee through the garden ranges,
From world to world the godhead changes;
As the sheep go feeding in the waste,
From form to form He maketh haste;
This vault which glows immense with light
Is the inn where he lodges for a night.
What recks such Traveller if the bowers
Which bloom and fade like meadow flowers
A bunch of fragrant lilies be,
Or the stars of eternity?
Alike to him the better, the worse—
The glowing angel, the outcast corse.
Thou metest him by centuries,
And lo! he passes like the breeze;
Thou seek'st in globe and galaxy,
He hides in pure transparency;
Thou askest in fountains and in fires,
He is the essence that inquires.
He is the axis of the star;
He is the sparkle of the spar;
He is the heart of every creature;
He is the meaning of each feature;
And his mind is the sky,
Than all it holds more deep, more high.

Hamatreya

Bulkeley, Hunt, Willard, Hosmer, Meriam, Flint,
Possessed the land which rendered to their toil
Hay, corn, roots, hemp, flax, apples, wool, and wood.
Each of these landlords walked amidst his farm,
Saying, ' 'Tis mine, my children's and my name's.
How sweet the west wind sounds in my own trees!
How graceful climb those shadows on my hill!
I fancy these pure waters and the flags
Know me, as does my dog: we sympathize;
And, I affirm, my actions smack of the soil.'

Where are these men? Asleep beneath their grounds:
And strangers, fond as they, their furrows plough.
Earth laughs in flowers, to see her boastful boys
Earth-proud, proud of the earth which is not theirs;
Who steer the plough, but cannot steer their feet
Clear of the grave.
They added ridge to valley, brook to pond,
And sighed for all that bounded their domain;
'This suits me for a pasture; that's my park;
We must have clay, lime, gravel, granite-ledge,
And misty lowland, where to go for peat.
The land is well—lies fairly to the south.
'Tis good, when you have crossed the sea and back,
To find the sitfast acres where you left them.'
Ah! the hot owner sees not Death, who adds
Him to his land, a lump of mould the more.
Hear what the Earth says—

Earth-Song

'Mine and yours;
Mine, not yours.
Earth endures;
Stars abide—
Shine down in the old sea;
Old are the shores;
But where are old men?
I who have seen much,
Such have I never seen.

'The lawyer's deed
Ran sure,
In tail,
To them and to their heirs
Who shall succeed,
Without fail,
Forevermore.

'Here is the land
Shaggy with wood,
With its old valley,
Mound and flood.
But the heritors?—
Fled like the flood's foam.
The lawyer, and the laws,
And the kingdom,
Clean swept herefrom.

'They called me theirs,
Who so controlled me;
Yet every one
Wished to stay, and is gone,
How am I theirs,
If they cannot hold me,
But I hold them?'

When I heard the Earth-song
I was no longer brave;
My avarice cooled
Like lust in the chill of the grave.

Brahma

If the red slayer think he slays,
    Or if the slain think he is slain,
They know not well the subtle ways
    I keep, and pass, and turn again.

Far or forgot to me is near;
    Shadow and sunlight are the same;
The vanished gods to me appear;
    And one to me are shame and fame.

They reckon ill who leave me out;
    When me they fly, I am the wings;
I am the doubter and the doubt,
    And I the hymn the Brahmin sings.

The strong gods pine for my abode,
   And pine in vain the sacred Seven;
But thou, meek lover of the good!
   Find me, and turn thy back on heaven.

3. HENRY DAVID THOREAU, 1817–1862

[A look at a manuscript collection of Thoreau's poetry first excited Emerson's interest in the Concord Genius. For a time, the prophet hailed them as infallible evidences of Genius: "the purest strain, and loftiest," he wrote to Carlyle, "that has yet pealed from this unpoetic American forest." So he urged Margaret Fuller, who was not quite so impressed, to make room for them in *The Dial*, and after he took over the burden of editing, continued to print his protegé's verse. As far as we can make out, somewhere in 1844 Emerson decided that Thoreau's poetry did not live up to expectations. Apparently he told the younger man his opinion, and Thoreau destroyed his remaining manuscripts. This act Henry repented; his resentment entered into that bill of ingratitude he finally treasured up against the man who had been so rash as to patronize him.

Thus what survives of Thoreau's poetry comes from his youthful years—that is, before he was twenty-seven or twenty-eight—when he was still musing upon the generalizations of Transcendentalism and had barely begun his journey toward that fanatical devotion to the specific which makes the last portion of his *Journal* a welter of detail. Whether these verses are or are not of much literary value, they are eloquent, often poignant, records of a young Transcendentalist's initiation.

I arrange these selections in the order of their appearance in print, and in general have followed the form of *The Dial*, except when it seems clear that Thoreau revised those he used in *A Week on the Concord and Merrimack Rivers* (1849). The last three were not published before that volume. "Inspiration" is a composite of bits scattered through the book, and was put into its present pattern by Thoreau's friend, F. B. Sanborn; hence it should not be read as a finished piece but simply for its content. My treatment of the texts has been guided by Carl Bode's *Collected Poems of Henry Thoreau,* to which all students are greatly in debt.]

POEMS

Sympathy

Lately, alas, I knew a gentle boy,
Whose features all were cast in Virtue's mould,
As one she had designed for Beauty's toy,
But after manned him for her own stronghold.

On every side he open was as day,
That you might see no lack of strength within,
For walls and ports do only serve alway
For a pretense to feebleness and sin.

Say not that Cæsar was victorious,
With toil and strife who stormed the House of Fame:
In other sense this youth was glorious,
Himself a kingdom wherso'er he came.

No strength went out to get him victory,
When all was income of its own accord;
For where he went none other was to see,
But all were parcel of their noble lord.

He forayed like the subtle haze of summer,
That stilly shows fresh landscapes to our eyes,
And revolutions works without a murmur,
Or rustling of a leaf beneath the skies.

So was I taken unawares by this,
I quite forgot my homage to confess;
Yet now am forced to know, though hard it is,
I might have loved him had I loved him less.

Each moment, as we nearer drew to each,
A stern respect withheld us farther yet,
So that we seemed beyond each other's reach,
And less acquainted than when first we met.

We two were one while we did sympathize,
So could we not the simplest bargain drive;
And what avails it now that we are wise,
If absence doth this doubleness contrive?

Eternity may not the chance repeat,
But I must tread by single way alone,
In sad remembrance that we once did meet,
And know that bliss irrevocably gone.

The spheres henceforth my elegy shall sing,
For elegy has other subject none;
Each strain of music in my ears shall ring
Knell of departure from that other one.

Make haste and celebrate my tragedy;
With fitting strain resound ye woods and fields;
Sorrow is dearer in such case to me
Than all the joys other occasion yields.

Is't then too late the damage to repair?
Distance, forsooth, from my weak grasp hath reft
The empty husk, and clutched the useless tare,
But in my hands the wheat and kernel left.

But if I love that virtue which he is,
Though it be scented in the morning air,
Still shall we be truest acquaintances,
Nor mortals know a sympathy more rare.

Sic Vita

I am a parcel of vain strivings tied
    By a chance bond together,

Dangling this way and that, their links
　　Were made so loose and wide,
　　　　Methinks,
　　For milder weather.

A bunch of violets without their roots,
　　And sorrel intermixed,
Encircled by a wisp of straw
　　Once coiled about their shoots,
　　　　The law
　　By which I'm fixed.

A nosegay which Time clutched from out
　　Those fair Elysian fields,
With weeds and broken stems, in haste,
　　Doth make the rabble rout
　　　　That waste
　　The day he yields.

And here I bloom for a short hour unseen,
　　Drinking my juices up,
With no root in the land
　　To keep my branches green,
　　　　But stand
　　In a bare cup.

Some tender buds were left upon my stem
　　In mimicry of life,
But ah! the children will not know
　　Till time has withered them,
　　　　The woe
　　With which they're rife.

But now I see I was not plucked for naught,
　　And after in life's vase
Of glass set while I might survive,
　　But by a kind hand brought
　　　　Alive
　　To a strange place.

That stock thus thinned will soon redeem its hours,
    And by another year,
Such as God knows, with freer air,
    More fruits and fair flowers
        Will bear,
    While I droop here.

Friendship

"Friends, Romans, Countrymen, and Lovers."

    Let such pure hate still underprop
    Our love, that we may be
    Each other's conscience,
    And have our sympathy
    Mainly from thence.

    We'll one another treat like gods,
    And all the faith we have
    In virtue and in truth, bestow
    On either, and suspicion leave
    To gods below.

    Two solitary stars—
    Unmeasured systems far
    Between us roll;
    But by our conscious light we are
    Determined to one pole.

    What need confound the sphere?—
    Love can afford to wait;
    For it no hour's too late
    That witnesseth one duty's end,
    Or to another doth beginning lend.

    It will subserve no use,
    More than the tints of flowers;
    Only the independent guest
    Frequents its bowers,
    Inherits its bequest.

No speech, though kind, has it;
But kinder silence doles
Unto its mates;
By night consoles,
By day congratulates.

What saith the tongue to tongue?
What heareth ear of ear?
By the decrees of fate
From year to year,
Does it communicate.

Pathless the gulf of feeling yawns;
No trivial bridge of words,
Or arch of boldest span,
Can leap the moat that girds
The sincere man.

No show of bolts and bars
Can keep the foeman out,
Or 'scape his secret mine,
Who entered with the doubt
That drew the line.

No warder at the gate
Can let the friendly in;
But, like the sun, o'er all
He will the castle win,
And shine along the wall.

There's nothing in the world I know
That can escape from love,
For every depth it goes below,
And every height above.
It waits, as waits the sky,
Until the clouds go by,
Yet shines serenely on
With an eternal day,
Alike when they are gone,
And when they stay.

Implacable is Love—
Foes may be bought or teased
From their hostile intent,
But he goes unappeased
Who is on kindness bent.

Prayer

Great God, I ask thee for no meaner pelf
Than that I may not disappoint myself,
That in my action I may soar as high
As I can now discern with this clear eye.

And next in value, which thy kindness lends,
That I may greatly disappoint my friends,
Howe'er they think or hope that it may be,
They may not dream how thou'st distinguished me.

That my weak hand may equal my firm faith,
And my life practise more than my tongue saith;
That my low conduct may not show,
Nor my relenting lines,
That I thy purpose did not know,
Or overrated thy designs.

Independence

My life more civil is and free
Than any civil polity.

Ye princes keep your realms
And circumscribed power,
Not wide as are my dreams,
Nor rich as is this hour.

What can he give which I have not?
What can ye take which I have got?
Can ye defend the dangerless?
Can ye inherit nakedness?

To all true wants time's ear is deaf,
Penurious states lend no relief
Out of their pelf—
But a free soul—thank God—
Can help itself.

Be sure your fate
Doth keep apart its state—
Not linked with any band—
Even the nobles of the land

In tented fields with cloth of gold—
No place doth hold
But is more chivalrous than they are.
And sigheth for a nobler war.
A finer strain its trumpet rings—
A brighter gleam its armor flings.

The life that I aspire to live
No man proposeth me—
No trade upon the street
Wears its emblazonry.

The Inward Morning

Packed in my mind lie all the clothes
  Which outward nature wears,
And in its fashion's hourly change
  It all things else repairs.

In vain I look for change abroad,
  And can no difference find,
Till some new ray of peace uncalled
  Illumes my inmost mind.

What is it gilds the trees and clouds,
  And paints the heavens so gay,
But yonder fast-abiding light
  With its unchanging ray?

Lo, when the sun streams through the wood,
  Upon a winter's morn,
Where'er his silent beams intrude
  The murky night is gone.

How could the patient pine have known
  The morning breeze would come,
Or humble flowers anticipate
  The insect's noonday hum—

Till the new light with morning cheer
  From far streamed through the aisles,
And nimbly told the forest trees
  For many stretching miles?

I've heard within my inmost soul
  Such cheerful morning news,
In the horizon of my mind
  Have seen such orient hues,

As in the twilight of the dawn,
  When the first birds awake,
Are heard within some silent wood,
  Where they the small twigs break,

Or in the eastern skies are seen,
  Before the sun appears,
The harbingers of summer heats
  Which from afar he bears.

My Love Must Be as Free

My love must be as free
  As is the eagle's wing,
Hovering o'er land and sea
  And everything.

I must not dim my eye
  In thy saloon,
I must not leave my sky
  And nightly moon.

Be not the fowler's net
    Which stays my flight,
And craftily is set
    T'allure the sight.

But be the favoring gale
    That bears me on,
And still doth fill my sail
    When thou art gone.

I cannot leave my sky
    For thy caprice,
True love would soar as high
    As heaven is.

The eagle would not brook
    Her mate thus won,
Who trained his eye to look
    Beneath the sun.

The Poet's Delay

In vain I see the morning rise,
    In vain observe the western blaze,
Who idly look to other skies,
    Expecting life by other ways.

Amidst such boundless wealth without,
    I only still am poor within,
The birds have sung their summer out,
    But still my spring does not begin.

Shall I then wait the autumn wind,
    Compelled to seek a milder day,
And leave no curious nest behind,
    No woods still echoing to my lay?

Rumors from an Aeolian Harp

There is a vale which none hath seen,
Where foot of man has never been,
Such as here lives with toil and strife
An anxious and a sinful life.

There every virtue has its birth,
Ere it descends upon the earth,
And thither every deed returns,
Which in the generous bosom burns.

There love is warm, and youth is young,
And poetry is yet unsung,
For Virtue still adventures there,
And freely breathes her native air.

And ever, if you hearken well,
You still may hear its vesper bell,
And tread of high-souled men go by,
Their thoughts conversing with the sky.

The Summer Rain

My books I'd fain cast off, I cannot read,
  'Twixt every page my thoughts go stray at large
Down in the meadow, where is richer feed,
  And will not mind to hit their proper targe.

Plutarch was good, and so was Homer too,
  Our Shakespeare's life were rich to live again,
What Plutarch read, that was not good nor true,
  Nor Shakespeare's books, unless his books were men.

Here while I lie beneath this walnut bough,
  What care I for the Greeks or for Troy town,
If juster battles are enacted now
  Between the ants upon this hummock's crown?

Bid Homer wait till I the issue learn,
    If red or black the gods will favor most,
Or yonder Ajax will the phalanx turn,
    Struggling to heave some rock against the host.

Tell Shakespeare to attend some leisure hour,
    For now I've business with this drop of dew,
And see you not, the clouds prepare a shower—
    I'll meet him shortly when the sky is blue.

This bed of herd's-grass and wild oats was spread
    Last year with nicer skill than monarchs use.
A clover tuft is pillow for my head,
    And violets quite overtop my shoes.

And now the cordial clouds have shut all in,
    And gently swells the wind to say all's well;
The scattered drops are falling fast and thin,
    Some in the pool, some in the flower-bell.

I am well drenched upon my bed of oats;
    But see that globe come rolling down its stem,
Now like a lonely planet there it floats,
    And now it sinks into my garment's hem.

Drip drip the trees for all the country round,
    And richness rare distills from every bough;
The wind alone it is makes every sound,
    Shaking down crystals on the leaves below.

For shame the sun will never show himself,
    Who could not with his beams e'er melt me so;
My dripping locks—they would become an elf,
    Who in a beaded coat does gayly go.

Smoke

Light-wingèd Smoke, Icarian bird,
    Melting thy pinions in thy upward flight,
Lark without song, and messenger of dawn,

Circling above the hamlets as thy nest;
Or else, departing dream, and shadowy form
Of midnight vision, gathering up thy skirts;
By night star-veiling, and by day
Darkening the light and blotting out the sun;
Go thou my incense upward from this hearth,
And ask the gods to pardon this clear flame.

Haze

Woof of the sun, ethereal gauze,
Woven of Nature's richest stuffs,
Visible heat, air-water, and dry sea,
Last conquest of the eye;
Toil of the day displayed, sun-dust,
Aerial surf upon the shores of earth,
Ethereal estuary, frith of light,
Breakers of air, billows of heat,
Fine summer spray on inland seas;
Bird of the sun, transparent-winged,
Owlet of noon, soft-pinioned,
From heath or stubble rising without song;
Establish thy serenity o'er the fields.

Smoke in Winter

The sluggish smoke curls up from some deep dell,
The stiffened air exploring in the dawn,
And making slow acquaintance with the day;
Delaying now upon its heavenward course,
In wreathèd loiterings dallying with itself,
With as uncertain purpose and slow deed,
As its half-wakened master by the hearth,
Whose mind still slumbering and sluggish thoughts
Have not yet swept into the onward current
Of the new day—and now it streams afar,
The while the chopper goes with step direct,
And mind intent to swing the early axe.

First in the dusky dawn he sends abroad
His early scout, his emmissary, smoke,
The earliest, latest pilgrim from the roof,
To feel the frosty air, inform the day;
And while he crouches still beside the hearth,
Nor musters courage to unbar the door,
It has gone down the glen with the light wind,
And o'er the plain unfurled its venturous wreath,
Draped the treetops, loitered upon the hill,
And warmed the pinions of the early bird;
And now, perchance, high in the crispy air,
Has caught sight of the day o'er the earth's edge,
And greets its master's eye at his low door,
As some refulgent cloud in the upper sky.

The Respectable Folks

The respectable folks—
Where dwell they?
They whisper in the oaks,
And they sigh in the hay;
Summer and winter, night and day,
Out on the meadow, there dwell they.
They never die,
Nor snivel, nor cry,
Nor ask our pity
With a wet eye.
A sound estate they ever mend,
To every asker readily lend;
To the ocean wealth,
To the meadow health,
To Time his length,
To the rocks strength,
To the stars light,
To the weary night,
To the busy day,
To the idle play;
And so their good cheer never ends,
For all are their debtors, and all their friends.

Conscience

Conscience is instinct bred in the house,
Feeling and Thinking propagate the sin
By an unnatural breeding in and in.
I say, Turn it out doors,
Into the moors.
I love a life whose plot is simple,
And does not thicken with every pimple,
A soul so sound no sickly conscience binds it,
That makes the universe no worse than't finds it.
I love an earnest soul,
Whose mighty joy and sorrow
Are not drowned in a bowl,
And brought to life to-morrow;
That lives one tragedy,
And not seventy;
A conscience worth keeping,
Laughing not weeping;
A conscience wise and steady,
And for ever ready;
Not changing with events,
Dealing in compliments;
A conscience exercised about
Large things, where one *may* doubt.
I love a soul not all of wood,
Predestinated to be good,
But true to the backbone
Unto itself alone,
And false to none;
Born to its own affairs,
Its own joys and own cares;
By whom the work which God begun
Is finished, and not undone;
Taken up where he left off,
Whether to worship or to scoff;
If not good, why then evil,
If not good god, good devil.
Goodness—you hypocrite, come out of that,

Live your life, do your work, then take your hat.
I have no patience towards
Such conscientious cowards.
Give me simple laboring folk,
Who love their work,
Whose virtue is a song
To cheer God along.

Inspiration

Whate'er we leave to God, God does,
    And blesses us;
The work we choose should be our own,
    God leaves alone.

If with light head erect I sing,
    Though all the Muses lend their force,
From my poor love of anything,
    The verse is weak and shallow as its source.

But if with bended neck I grope
    Listening behind me for my wit,
With faith superior to hope,
    More anxious to keep back than forward it;

Making my soul accomplice there
    Unto the flame my heart hath lit,
Then will the verse forever wear—
    Time cannot bend the line which God hath writ.

Always the general show of things
    Floats in review before my mind,
And such true love and reverence brings,
    That sometimes I forget that I am blind.

But now there comes unsought, unseen,
    Some clear divine electuary,
And I, who had but sensual been,
    Grow sensible, and as God is, am wary.

I hearing get, who had but ears,
   And sight, who had but eyes before,
I moments live, who lived but years,
   And truth discern, who knew but learning's lore.

I hear beyond the range of sound,
   I see beyond the range of sight,
New earths and skies and seas around,
   And in my day the sun doth pale his light.

A clear and ancient harmony
   Pierces my soul through all its din,
As through its utmost melody—
   Farther behind than they, farther within.

More swift its bolt than lightning is,
   Its voice than thunder is more loud,
It doth expand my privacies
   To all, and leave me single in the crowd.

It speaks with such authority,
   With so serene and lofty tone,
That idle Time runs gadding by,
   And leaves me with Eternity alone.

Now chiefly is my natal hour,
   And only now my prime of life;
Of manhood's strength it is the flower,
   'Tis peace's end and war's beginning strife.

It comes in summer's broadest noon,
   By a grey wall or some chance place,
Unseasoning Time, insulting June,
   And vexing day with its presuming face.

Such fragrance round my couch it makes,
   More rich than are Arabian drugs,
That my soul scents its life and wakes
   The body up beneath its perfumed rugs.

Such is the Muse, the heavenly maid,
    The star that guides our mortal course,
Which shows where life's true kernel's laid,
    Its wheat's fine flour, and its undying force.

She with one breath attunes the spheres,
    And also my poor human heart,
With one impulse propels the years
    Around, and gives my throbbing pulse its start.

I will not doubt for evermore,
    Nor falter from a steadfast faith,
For though the system be turned o'er,
    God takes not back the word which once He saith.

I will not doubt the love untold
    Which not my worth nor want has bought,
Which wooed my young, and wooes me old,
    And to this evening hath me brought.

My memory I'll educate
    To know the one historic truth,
Remembering to the latest date
    The only true and sole immortal youth.

Be but thy inspiration given,
    No matter through what danger sought,
I'll fathom hell or climb to heaven,
    And yet esteem that cheap which love has bought.

Fame cannot tempt the bard
    Who's famous with his God,
Nor laurel him reward
    Who has his Maker's nod.

4. WILLIAM ELLERY CHANNING, 1818–1901

[A nephew of the mighty Dr. Channing, for whom he
was named, this William Ellery entered Harvard in 1834
but rebelled against compulsory chapel and so left the

College to shift for itself while he devoted himself to poetry. He spent a year on the prairies of Illinois; in 1842 he married a demure sister of Margaret Fuller. They settled in Concord, avowedly to be near Mr. Emerson, but Channing's principal occupation soon turned out to be walking companion for Henry Thoreau—not, as Henry had been at some pains to make clear, a paying proposition.

As they both entertained the most exalted of Transcendental ideals about "friendship," their union was enlivened by accusations, one against the other, of falling short of perfection. In one of these moods Thoreau said that Channing's literary style might be described as the "sublimo-slipshod."

More to the point, perhaps, is a passage in the *Journal* that depicts Channing as trying to emulate Henry in taking notes on a walk, then giving up the competition by announcing, "I am universal; I have nothing to do with the particular and definite." Henry concluded that Channing wanted something for which he was not willing to pay the price: "He will only learn slowly by failure." Even more than Bronson Alcott, Channing became the movement's most spectacular and sustained failure. How much he learned by it is difficult to say.

Emerson introduced him to the world as a young Genius by focusing upon him an article in *The Dial* for October, 1840, entitled "The New Poetry." Edgar Allan Poe made enormous fun of Channing's effusions; even so, the Transcendental epigonists stood for the remainder of the century behind Sanborn's opinion that "A Poet's Hope" could not be matched "for wild and sustained imagination and a magical harmony of verse in its best stanzas." Be that as it may, we can safely perceive in the poem another assertion of the egotistical dissent from American utilitarianism which, as must be evident by now, was a main element in the Transcendental complex. To paraphrase him, not unjustly, Channing freed himself from the demons of dull care and want, and so did defy the external; if in the operation he lamentably failed to rule the whole, it can at least be said on his behalf that for a long time he did not die.

Separated from his family, Channing lingered on in Concord with no visible means of support, a pensioner in the house of Sanborn, the last dried leaf on the Transcendental tree. However, he had sired Edward Channing, who became the distinguished historian of America, through all of whose work runs a violent detestation of the futilities (as they had been embodied for him) of Transcendentalism.

"The Earth Spirit," "Una" (privately dedicated to Elizabeth Hoar), and "Hymn of the Earth" first appeared in *The Dial,* but I have followed the text of *Poems,* 1843 and 1847. "A Poet's Hope" was dashed off as an improvisation upon a challenge from the beautiful Mrs. Samuel G. Ward.

In presenting so large a representation from Channing my concern is not to rescue a poetic reputation but to illustrate the mentality here displayed by its most whimsical disciple. It is worth noting that in the 1847 volume Channing printed a long and turgid poem entitled "The Island Nukuheva," a versified rendition of *Typee* as related by "the bold, adventurous Melville," which dwells with sensuous pleasure upon the charms of naked Fayaway. Wherefore, it is fitting that Channing, the "restless mind," should be left to address his "Companion" voyagers over the Transcendental seas with a lament that neither he nor they had finally solved that epistemological doubt about the reality of natural appearances which Emerson in the *Nature* of 1836 termed a "noble" one, but which, Emerson insisted, could, in America if not elsewhere, be transcended.]

POEMS

The Earth Spirit

Then spoke the Spirit of the Earth,
    Her gentle voice like a soft water's song—
None from my loins have ever birth,
    But what to joy and love belong;
I faithful am, and give to thee
Blessings great, and give them free.

I have woven shrouds of air
   In a loom of hurrying light,
For the trees which blossoms bear,
   And gilded them with sheets of bright;
I fall upon the grass like love's first kiss,
I make the golden flies and their fine bliss.
   I paint the hedge-rows in the lane,
And clover white and red the pathways bear,
   I laugh aloud in sudden gusts of rain,
To see the ocean lash himself in air;
I throw smooth shells and weeds along the beach,
And pour the curling waves far o'er the glassy reach;
Swing birds' nests in the elms, and shake cool moss
Along the aged beams and hide their loss.
The very broad rough stones I gladden too;
   Some willing seeds I drop along their sides,
Nourish the generous plant with freshening dew,
   Till there, where all was waste, true joy abides.
The peaks of aged mountains, with my care
   Smile in the red of glowing morn elate;
I bind the caverns of the sea with hair,
   Glossy, and long, and rich as king's estate;
I polish the green ice, and gleam the wall
With the white frost, and leaf the brown trees tall.

* * * * * * *

'T was so—t'was thine. Earth! thou wast true:
   I kneel, thy grateful child, I kneel,
Thy full forgiveness for my sins I sue,
   My mother! learn thy child can think and feel.
Mother dear! wilt pardon one
   Who loved not the generous sun,
Nor thy seasons loved to hear
Singing to the busy year—
Thee neglected—shut his heart
In thy being had no part?

Mother dear! I list thy song
In the autumn eve along;

Now thy chill airs round the day
And leave me my time to pray.
Mother dear! The day must come,
When I, thy child, shall make my home,
My long, last home amid the grass,
Over which thy warm hands pass.
Ah me! do let me lie
Gently on thy breast to die;
I know my prayers will reach thy ear,
   Thou art with me while I ask,
Nor a child refuse to hear,
   Who would learn his little task.
Let me take my part with thee
   In the gray clouds, or thy light,
Laugh with thee upon the sea,
   Or idle on the land by night.
In the trees I will with thee,
In the flowers, like any bee.

I feel it shall be so. We are not born
   To sink our finer feelings in the dust;
And better to the grave with feelings torn,
   So in our step strides truth and honest trust
In the great love of things, than to be slaves
   To forms, whose ringing sides each stroke we give
Stamps with a hollower want. Yes, to our graves
   Hurry, before we in the heavens' look live,
Strangers to our best thoughts, and fearing men,
And fearing death, and to be born again.

Una

We are centered deeper far
Than the eye of any star,
Nor can rays of long sunlight
Thread a pace of our delight.
In thy form I see the day
Burning, of a kingdom higher,

In thy silver net-work play
Thoughts that to the Gods aspire;
In thy cheek I see the flame
Of the studious taper burn,
And thy Grecian eye might tame
Nature's ashes in antique urn;
Yet with this lofty element
Flows a pure stream of gentle kindness,
And thou to life thy strength hast lent,
And borne profoundest tenderness
In thy Promethean fearless arm,
With mercy's love that would all angels charm.

So trembling meek, so proudly strong,
Thou dost to higher worlds belong,
Than where I sing this empty song:
Yet I, a thing of mortal kind,
Can kneel before thy pathless mind,
And see in thee what my mates say
Sank o'er Judea's hills one crimson day.
Yet flames on high the keen Greek fire,
And later ages rarefies,
And even on my tuneless lyre
A faint, wan beam of radiance dies.
And might I say what I have thought
Of thee, and those I love to-day,
Then had the world an echo caught
Of that intense, impassioned lay,
Which sung in those thy being sings,
And from the deepest ages rings.

Hymn of the Earth

My highway is unfeatured air,
My consorts are the sleepless Stars,
And men, my giant arms upbear,
My arms unstained and free from scars.

I rest forever on my way,
Rolling around the happy Sun.
My children love the sunny day,
But noon and night to me are one.

My heart has pulses like their own,
I am their Mother, and my veins
Though built of the enduring stone,
Thrill as do theirs with godlike pains.

The forests and the mountains high,
The foaming ocean and the springs,
The plains—O pleasant Company,
My voice through all your anthem rings.

Ye are so cheerful in your minds,
Content to smile, content to share,
My being in your Chorus finds
The echo of the spheral air.

No leaf may fall, no pebble roll,
No drop of water lose the road,
The issues of the general Soul
Are mirrored in its round abode.

Nature

I love the universe—I love the joy
Of every living thing. Be mine the sure
Felicity, which ever shall endure;
While passion whirls the madmen, as they toy,
To hate, I would my simple being warm
In the calm pouring sun; and in that pure
And motionless silence, ever would employ
My best true powers, without a thought's annoy.
See and be glad! O high imperial race,
Dwarfing the common attitude of strength,
Learn that ye stand on an unshaken base;
Your powers will carry you to any length.

Up! earnestly feel the gentle sunset beams;
Be glad in woods, o'er sands; by marsh, or streams.

Content

Within the unpainted cottage dwell
   The spirits of serene content,
As clear as from its moss-grown well
   Rises the crystal element.

Above, the elm, whose trunk is scarred
   With many a dint of stormy weather,
Rises, a sumptuous screen, debarred
   Of nothing that links life together.

Our common life may gratify
   More feelings than the rarest art,
For nothing can aspire so high
   As beatings of the human heart.

O! value then thy daily cheer,
   Poor pensioner on nature's store,
And clasp the least, and hold most dear
   What seemeth small, and add the more.

A Poet's Hope

Flying—flying beyond all lower regions,
Beyond the light called day, and night's repose,
Where the untrammelled soul, on her wind-pinions
Fearlessly sweeping, defies my earthly woes—
There—there, upon that infinitest sea,
Lady, thy hope—so fair a hope, summons me.

Fall off, ye garments of my misty weather,
Drop from my eyes, ye scales of time's applying;
Am I not godlike? meet not here together
A past and future infinite, defying,
The cold, still, callous moment of to-day?
Am I not master of the calm alway?

Would I could summon from the deep, deep mine,
Glutted with shapely jewels, glittering bright,
One echo of that splendor, call it thine,
And weave it in the strands of living light;
For it is in me, and the sea smiles fair,
And thitherward I rage, on whirling air.

Unloose me, demons of dull care and want,
I will not stand your slave, I am your king;
Think not within your meshes vile I pant
For the wild liberty of an unclipt wing;
My empire is myself, and I defy
The external; yes! I rule the whole, or die.

All music that the fullest breeze can play
In its melodious whisperings in the wood,
All modulations which entrance the day
And deify a sunlight solitude;
All anthems that the waves sing to the ocean
Are mine for song, and yield to my devotion.

And mine the soft glaze of a loving eye,
And mine the pure shapes of the human form,
And mine the bitterest sorrow's witchery,
And spells enough to make a snow-king warm;
For an undying hope thou breathest me—
Hope which can ride the tossing, foaming sea.

Lady, there is a hope that all men have,
Some mercy for their faults, a grassy place
To rest in, and a flower-strown, gentle grave;
Another hope which purifies our race,
That when that fearful bourne forever past,
They may find rest—and rest *so* long to last.

I seek it not, I ask not rest for ever,
My path is onward to the farthest shores—
Upbear me in your arms, unceasing river,
That from the soul's clear fountain swiftly pours,
Motionless not, until the end is won,
Which now I feel hath scarcely felt the sun.

To feel, to know, to soar unlimited,
Mid throngs of light-winged angels sweeping far,
And pore upon the realms unvisited,
That tesselate the unseen unthought star,
To be the thing that now I feebly dream
Flashing within my faintest, deepest gleam.

Ah! caverns of my soul! how thick your shade,
Where flows that life by which I faintly see—
Wave your bright torches, for I need your aid,
Golden-eyed demons of my ancestry!
Your son though blinded hath a light within,
A heavenly fire which ye from suns did win.

And, lady, in thy hope my life will rise
Like the air-voyager, till I upbear
These heavy curtains of my filmy eyes,
Into a lighter, more celestial air;
A mortal's hope shall bear me safely on,
Till I the higher region shall have won.

O Time! O death! I clasp you in my arms,
For I can soothe an infinite cold sorrow,
And gaze contented on your icy charms,
And that wild snow-pile, which we call to-morrow;
Sweep on, O soft, and azure-lidded sky,
Earth's waters to your gentle gaze reply.

I am not earth-born, though I here delay;
Hope's child, I summon infiniter powers,
And laugh to see the mild and sunny day
Smile on the shrunk and thin autumnal hours;
I laugh, for hope hath happy place with me,
If my bark sinks, 'tis to another sea.

The Restless Mind

By the bleak wild hill,
Or the deep lake still,
In the silent grain
On the upland plain,
I would that the unsparing Storm might rage,
And blot with gloom the fair day's sunny page.

The lightning's gleam
Should gentle seem,
The thunder's blow
Both soft and low,
For now the world hath fill of summer weather,
Ye shining days why throng you thus together.

I am possest
With strange Unrest,
My feelings jar.
My heart is war,
A spirit dances in my dreams to-day.
I am too cold, for its strange, sunny play.

Then hurry down
With angry frown,
Thou sudden storm
Come fierce and warm,
And splinter trees and whistle o'er the moor,
For in thy Bravery I can life endure.

To My Companions

Ye heavy-hearted Mariners
    Who sail this shore—
Ye patient! ye who labor
    Sitting at the sweeping oar,
And see afar the flashing sea-gulls play
On the free waters, and the glad, bright Day
    Twine with his hand the spray—
From out your dreariness
From your heart-weariness,
I speak; for I am yours,
On these gray shores.

In vain—I know not, Mariners,
    What cliffs these are
That high uplift their smooth, dark fronts
    And sadly 'round us bar;

I do imagine that the free clouds play
Above those eminent heights; that somewhere Day
    Rides his triumphant way
  Over our stern oblivion;
  And hath his pure dominion.
  But see no path thereout
  To free from doubt.

5. AMOS BRONSON ALCOTT, 1799–1888

[If ever a gentle soul was deceived about his talent for
writing poetry, it was Alcott. Still, all Transcendentalists
felt called upon to prove themselves as poets, and Alcott's
"orphic" utterances could be printed as easily in the form
of verse as of prose.]

POEMS

Man

He omnipresent is,
All round himself he lies,
Osiris spread abroad,
Upstaring in all eyes:
Nature has globèd thought,
Without him she were not,
Cosmos from Chaos were not spoken,
And God bereft of visible token.

Approaching God

When thou approachest to the One,
Self from thyself thou first must free,
Thy cloak duplicity cast clean aside,
And in thy Being's being be.

Matter

Out of the chaos dawns in sight
The globe's full form in orbèd light;
Beam kindles beam, kind mirrors kind,
Nature's the eyeball of the Mind;
The fleeting pageant tells for nought
Till shaped in Mind's creative thought.

6. MARGARET FULLER, 1810–1850

[Margaret Fuller had almost as little aptitude for poetic composition as Alcott; but she was *the* Genius of all the geniuses, and so often lisped in numbers. Into these experiments, as into everything she wrote, she poured her store of nervous and undisciplined energy. The experience related in "Encouragement" is palpably the death of her father. "Dryad Song" gives voice to that lust for Bacchic ecstasy which so strangely possessed these children of New England Puritanism.]

POEMS

Encouragement

"I will not leave you comfortless"

O Friend divine, this promise dear
Falls sweetly on the weary ear!
Often, in hours of sickening pain,
It soothes me to thy rest again.

Might I a true disciple be,
Following thy footsteps faithfully,
Then should I still the succor prove
Of him who gave his life for love.

When this fond heart would vainly beat
For bliss that ne'er on earth we meet,
For perfect sympathy of soul,
For those such heavy laws control;

When, roused from passion's ecstasy,
I see the dreams that filled it fly,
Amid my bitter tears and sighs
Those gentle words before me rise.

With aching brows and feverish brain
The founts of intellect I drain,
And con with over-anxious thought
What poets sung and heroes wrought.

Enchanted with their deeds and lays,
I with like gems would deck my days;
No fires creative in me burn,
And, humbled, I to Thee return;

When blackest clouds around me rolled
Of skepticism drear and cold,
When love, and hope, and joy, and pride,
Forsook a spirit deeply tried;

My reason wavered in that hour,
Prayer, too impatient, lost its power;
From thy benignity a ray
I caught, and found the perfect day.

A head revered in dust was laid;
For the first time I watched my dead;
The widow's sobs were checked in vain,
And childhood's fears pour down like rain.

In awe I gazed on that dear face,
In sorrow years gone by retrace,
When, nearest duties most forgot,
I might have blessed, and did it not!

Ignorant, his wisdom I reproved,
Heedless, passed by what most he loved,
Knew not a life like his to prize,
Of ceaseless toil and sacrifice.

No tears can now that hushed heart move,
No cares display a daughter's love,
The fair occasion lost, no more
Can thoughts more just to thee restore.

What can I do? And how atone
For all I've done, and left undone?
Tearful I search the parting words
Which the belovèd John records.

"Not comfortless!" I dry my eyes,
My duties clear before me rise—
Before thou think'st of taste or pride,
See home affections satisfied!

Be not with generous thoughts content,
But on well-doing constant bent:
When self seems dear, self-seeking fair,
Remember this sad hour in prayer!

Though all thou wishest fly thy touch,
Much can one do who loveth much.
More of thy spirit, Jesus, give,
Not comfortless, though sad, to live.

And yet not sad, if I can know
To copy him who here below
Sought but to do his Father's will,
Though from such sweet composure still

My heart be far. Wilt thou not aid
One whose best hopes on thee are stayed?
Breathe into me thy perfect love,
And guide me to thy rest above!

Dryad Song

I am immortal! I know it! I feel it!
  Hope floods my heart with delight!
Running on air, mad with life, dizzy, reeling,
Upward I mount—faith is sight, life is feeling,
  Hope is the day-star of might!

It was thy kiss, Love, that made me immortal—
  " 'Kiss,' Love? Our lips have not met!"
Ah, but I felt thy soul through night's portal
Swoon on my lips at night's sweet silent portal,
  Wild and as sweet as regret.

Come, let us mount on the wings of the morning,
  Flying for joy of the flight,
Wild with all longing, now soaring, now staying,
Mingling like day and dawn, swinging and swaying,
  Hung like a cloud in the light:
I am immortal! I feel it! I feel it!
  Love bears me up, love is might!

Chance cannot touch me! Time cannot hush me!
  Fear, Hope, and Longing, at strife,
Sink as I rise, on, on, upward forever,
Gathering strength, gaining breath—naught can sever
  Me from the Spirit of Life!

7. CHRISTOPHER PEARSE CRANCH, 1813–1892

[Christopher Cranch was born in what is now Alexandria, Virginia, but of a Massachusetts family, and so came to the Harvard Divinity School in 1831. He followed James Freeman Clarke and William Henry Channing to Cincinnati in 1835; for a few years he manfully strove to preach the Transcendental version of Unitarianism in the West, and helped to edit *The Western Messenger*, but he was not the stuff of which pioneers are made. He had a sense of humor and did a little volume of caricatures upon the "new philosophy" which poked mild fun at some of its more sententious attitudes. He spent seventeen years in Europe, returned to Cambridge in 1873, to live out his days as a charming eccentric who dabbled in painting and music as well as poetry. In contrast to Emerson and Ripley, who gave up the pulpit under high moral convictions, or to Parker, who stayed there under militant devotion, Cranch climbed down in order to become Transcendentalism's foremost dilettante.

He contributed to *The Dial* some of its best verse; the occasional pieces of his later years are less inspired, though in 1877 he published "The Pines and the Sea": he was still insisting upon the Emersonian proposition that what one perceives in Nature is what one projects into it from the self. But there is a melancholy in this late reflection which suggests that by this time the Transcendental insight had become something of a burden.]

POEMS

Gnosis

Thought is deeper than all speech,
    Feeling deeper than all thought:
Souls to souls can never teach
    What unto themselves was taught.

We are spirits clad in veils:
    Man by man was never seen:
All our deep communing fails
    To remove the shadowy screen.

Heart to heart was never known:
    Mind with mind did never meet:
We are columns left alone,
    Of a temple once complete.

Like the stars that gem the sky,
  Far apart, though seeming near,
In our light we scattered lie;
  All is thus but starlight here.

What is social company
  But a babbling summer stream?
What our wise philosophy
  But the glancing of a dream?

Only when the Sun of Love
  Melts the scattered stars of thought;
Only when we live above
  What the dim-eyed world hath taught,

Only when our souls are fed
  By the Fount which gave them birth,
And by inspiration led,
  Which they never drew from earth,

We, like parted drops of rain,
  Swelling till they meet and run,
Shall be all absorbed again,
  Melting, flowing into one.

Correspondences

All things in Nature are beautiful types to the soul that
    will read them;
  Nothing exists upon earth, but for unspeakable ends.
Every object that speaks to the senses was meant for
    the spirit:
  Nature is but a scroll—God's hand-writing thereon.
Ages ago, when man was pure, ere the flood overwhelmed
    him,
  While in the image of God every soul yet lived,
Everything stood as a letter or word of a language familiar,
  Telling of truths which *now* only the angels can read.

Lost to man was the key of those sacred hieroglyphics—
  Stolen away by sin—till with Jesus restored.
Now with infinite pains we here and there spell out a
    letter;
  Now and then will the sense feebly shine through the
    dark.
When we perceive the light which breaks through the
    visible symbol,
  What exultation is ours! *we* the discovery have made!
Yet is the meaning the same as when Adam lived sinless
    in Eden,
  Only long-hidden it slept and now again is restored.
Man unconsciously uses figures of speech every moment,
  Little dreaming the cause why to such terms he is
    prone—
Little dreaming that everything has its own correspondence
  Folded within it of old, as in the body the soul.
Gleams of the mystery fall on us still, though much is
    forgotten,
  And through our commonest speech illumines the path
    of our thoughts.
Thus does the lordly sun shine out a type of the Godhead;
  Wisdom and Love the beams that stream on a darkened
    world.
Thus do the sparkling waters flow, giving joy to the desert,
  And the great Fountain of Life opens itself to the thirst.
Thus does the word of God distil like the rain and the
    dew-drops,
  Thus does the warm wind breathe like to the Spirit of
    God,
And the green grass and the flowers are signs of the
    regeneration.

O thou Spirit of Truth; visit our minds once more!
Give us to read, in letters of light, the language celestial,
  Written all over the earth—written all over the sky:
Thus may we bring our hearts at length to know our
    Creator,
  Seeing in all things around types of the Infinite Mind.

The Ocean

"In a season of calm weather
Though inland far we be,
Our souls have sight of that immortal sea
That brought us hither,
Can in a moment travel thither,
And see the children sport upon the shore,
And hear the mighty waters rolling evermore"—
Wordsworth

———

Tell me, brother, what are we?
Spirits bathing in the sea
   Of Deity!
Half afloat, and half on land,
Wishing much to leave the strand,
Standing, gazing with devotion,
Yet afraid to trust the ocean—
   Such are we.

Wanting love and holiness,
To enjoy the wave's caress;
Wanting faith and heavenly hope,
Buoyantly to bear us up;
Yet impatient in our dwelling,
When we hear the ocean swelling,
And in every wave that rolls
We behold the happy souls
Peacefully, triumphantly
Swimming on the smiling sea,
Then we linger round the shore,
Lovers of the earth no more.

Once—'t was in our infancy,
We were drifted by this sea
To the coast of human birth,
To this body and this earth:
Gentle were the hands that bore

Our young spirits to the shore;
Gentle lips that bade us look
Outward from our cradle-nook
To the spirit-bearing ocean
With such wonder and devotion,
As, each stilly sabbath day,
We were led a little way,
Where we saw the waters swell
Far away from inland dell,
And received with grave delight
Symbols of the Infinite—
Then our home was near the sea;
"Heaven was round our infancy"—
Night and day we heard the waves
Murmuring by us to their caves—
Floated in unconscious life
With no later doubts at strife,
Trustful of the Upholding Power,
Who sustained us hour by hour.
Now we've wandered from the shore,
Dwellers by the sea no more;
Yet at times there comes a tone
Telling of the visions flown,
Sounding from the distant sea
Where we left our purity:
Distant glimpses of the surge
Lure us down to ocean's verge;
There we stand with vague distress,
Yearning for the measureless,
By half-wakened instincts driven,
Half loving earth, half loving heaven,
Fearing to put off and swim,
Yet impelled to turn to Him,
In whose life we live and move,
And whose very name is Love.

Grant me, courage, Holy One,
To become indeed thy son,
And in thee, thou Parent-Sea,
Live and love eternally.

I in Thee, and Thou In Me

I am but clay in thy hands, but thou art the all-loving
    artist;
    Passive I lie in thy sight, yet in my selfhood I strive
So to embody the life and love thou ever impartest
    That in my sphere of the finite I may be truly alive.

Knowing thou needest this form, as I thy divine inspiration,
    Knowing thou shapest the clay with a vision and purpose
    divine,
So would I answer each touch of thy hand in its loving
    creation,
    That in my conscious life thy power and beauty may
    shine.

Reflecting the noble intent thou hast in forming thy
    creatures;
    Waking from sense into life of the soul, and the image
    of thee;
Working with thee in thy work to model humanity's
    features
    Into the likeness of God, myself from myself I would
    free.

One with all human existence, no one above or below me;
    Lit by thy wisdom and love, as roses are steeped in
    the morn;
Growing from clay to statue, from statue to flesh, till
    thou know me
    Wrought into manhood celestial, and in thine image
    reborn.

So in thy love will I trust, bringing me sooner or later
    Past the dark screen that divides these shows of the
    finite from thee.
Thine, thine only, this warm dear life, O loving Creator!
    Thine the invisible future, born of the present, must be.

Human Helpers

Praise, praise ye the prophets, the sages
Who lived and who died for the ages;
The grand and magnificent dreamers;
The heroes, and mighty redeemers;
The martyrs, reformers, and leaders;
The voices of mystical Vedas;
The bibles of races long shrouded
Who left us their wisdom unclouded;
The truth that is old as their mountains,
But fresh as the rills from their fountains.

And praise ye the poets whose pages
Give solace and joy to the ages;
Who have seen in their marvelous trances
Of thought and of rhythmical fancies,
The manhood of Man in all errors;
The triumph of hope over terrors;
The great human heart ever pleading
Its kindred divine, though misleading,
Fate held it aloof from the heaven
That to spirits untempted was given.

The creeds of the past that have bound us,
With visions of terror around us
Like dungeons of stone that have crumbled,
Beneath us lie shattered and humbled.
The tyranny mitred and crested,
Flattered and crowned and detested;
The blindness that trod upon Science
    The bigotry Ignorance cherished;
The armed and the sainted alliance
    Of conscience and hate—they have perished,
Have melted like mists in the splendor
    Of life and of beauty supernal—
Of love ever watchful and tender,
    Of love ever one and eternal.

So Far, So Near

Thou, so far, we grope to grasp thee—
Thou, so near, we cannot clasp thee—
Thou, so wise, our prayers grow heedless—
Thou, so loving, they are needless!
In each human soul thou shinest;
Human-best is thy divinest.
In each deed of love thou warmest;
Evil into good transformest.
Soul of all, and moving centre
Of each moment's life we enter.
Breath of breathing—light of gladness—
Infinite antidote of sadness—
All-preserving ether flowing
Through the worlds, yet past our knowing
Never past our trust and loving,
Nor from thine our life removing.
Still creating, still inspiring,
Never of thy creatures tiring.
Artist of thy solar spaces,
And thy humble human faces;
Mighty glooms and splendors voicing;
In thy plastic work rejoicing;
Through benignant law connecting
Best with best—and all perfecting,
Though all human races claim thee,
Thought and language fail to name thee,
Mortal lips be dumb before thee,
Silence only can adore thee!

The Pines and the Sea

Beyond the low marsh-meadows and the beach,
Seen through the hoary trunks of windy pines,
The long blue level of the ocean shines.
The distant surf, with hoarse, complaining speech,

Out from its sandy barrier seems to reach;
And while the sun behind the woods declines,
The moaning sea with sighing boughs combines,
And waves and pines make answer, each to each.
O melancholy soul, whom far and near,
In life, faith, hope, the same sad undertone
Pursues from thought to thought! thou needs must hear
An old refrain, too much, too long thine own:
'Tis thy mortality infects thine ear;
The mournful strain was in thyself alone.

8. FREDERIC HENRY HEDGE, 1805–1890

[Frederic Hedge should have made a great name for himself in American intellectual history; his life conveys the impression of an unrealized talent. Starting with the inestimable privilege of studying in Germany, he had the best knowledge of any in the group of German literature and theology. In the 1830's he published in Unitarian periodicals studies that were of immense influence in shaping the new philosophy. After 1835, when he accepted a call to the church of Bangor, Maine, his returns to Boston became occasions for assembling the Transcendental society, so that these sessions were called "the Hedge Club." In 1848 he edited *The Prose Writers of Germany*, which is a workmanlike job, though by then "the German disease" was no longer so virulent in this country. In 1872 he became Professor of German Literature in Harvard University.

This collection is obliged to pass over Hedge's rôle in the formative period, and so to present his single most effective statement. A scholar and historian, Hedge made no pretense to being a poet; but one morning, after being kept awake all night while riding the mail coach, he wrote down these lines. They were published in *The Dial* for January, 1841, and were highly prized by all the fellowship.]

QUESTIONINGS

Hath this world, without me wrought,
Other substance than my thought?
Lives it by my sense alone,
Or by essence of its own?
Will its life, with mine begun,
Cease to be when that is done,
Or another consciousness
With the self-same forms impress?

Doth yon fireball, poised in air,
Hang by my permission there?
Are the clouds that wander by,
But the offspring of mine eye,
Born with every glance I cast,
Perishing when that is past?
And those thousand, thousand eyes,
Scattered through the twinkling skies,
Do they draw their life from mine,
Or, of their own beauty shine?

Now I close my eyes, my ears,
And creation disappears;
Yet if I but speak the word,
All creation is restored.
Or—more wonderful—within,
New creations do begin;
Hues more bright and forms more rare,
Than reality doth wear,
Flash across my inward sense,
Born of the mind's omnipotence.

Soul! that all informest, say!
Shall these glories pass away?
Will those planets cease to blaze,
When these eyes no longer gaze?

And the life of things be o'er
When these pulses beat no more?

Thought! that in me works and lives—
Life to all things living gives—
Art thou not thyself, perchance,
But the universe in trance?
A reflection inly flung
By that world thou fanciedst sprung
From thyself—thyself a dream—
Of the world's thinking thou the theme.

Be it thus, or be thy birth
From a source above the earth—
Be thou matter, be thou mind,
In thee alone myself I find,
And through thee alone, for me,
Hath this world reality.
Therefore, in thee will I live,
To thee all myself will give,
Losing still, that I may find,
This bounded self in boundless Mind.

9. ELLEN STURGIS HOOPER, 1812–1848

[The elder of the Sturgis sisters, Ellen married a distinguished physician; her death at the age of thirty-six enshrined her in the memories of her associates as a Transcendental angel. Margaret Fuller wrote from Rome in 1849, after having encountered many great personages, "I have seen in Europe no woman more gifted by nature than she." Ellen's verses in *The Dial*, and those long treasured in manuscript by her admirers, constitute another of New England's objections to the materialistic temper of the age and of the nation. In her gentle, feminine way, Ellen Hooper takes her stand beside Henry Thoreau. And in paying her woman's tribute to the preëminence of Emerson, she frankly allows herself to recognize those limitations which his "dry lighted" temperament imposed upon his leadership.]

POEMS

Beauty and Duty

I slept, and dreamed that life was Beauty;
I woke, and found that life was Duty.
Was thy dream then a shadowy lie?
Toil on, sad heart, courageously,
And thou shalt find thy dream to be
A noonday light and truth to thee.

The Straight Road

Beauty may be the path to highest good,
And some successfully have it pursued.
Thou, who wouldst follow, be well warned to see
That way prove not a curved road to thee.
The straightest path perhaps which may be sought,
Lies through the great highway men call "I ought."

The Heart's Cure

"Heart, heart, lie still!
Life is fleeting fast,
Strife will soon be past."
    "I cannot lie still
    Beat strong I will."

"Heart, heart, lie still!
Joy's but joy, and pain's but pain,
Either, little loss or gain."
    "I cannot lie still,
    Beat strong I will."

"Heart, heart, lie still!
Heaven is over all,
Rules this earthly hall,"
    "I cannot lie still,
    Beat strong I will."

"Heart, heart, lie still!
Heaven's sweet grace alone
Can keep in peace its own."
"Let that me fill,
And I am still."

The Goal

I sprang on life's free course, I tasked myself,
　And questioned what and how I meant to be;
And leaving far behind me power and pelf,
　I fixed a goal—nor farther could I see.

For this I toiled, for this I ran and bled,
　And proudly thought upon my laurels there.
Lo, here I stand! all childlike to be led.
　My goal, self-fixed, has vanished into air.
I run, I toil, but see not all my way;
Ever more pure it shines into a perfect day.

To R. W. E.

Dry lighted soul, the ray that shines in thee,
　Shot without reflex from primeval sun,
We twine the laurel for the victories
　Which thou on thought's broad, bloodless field has won.

Thou art the mountain where we climb to see
　The land our feet have trod this many a year.
Thou art the deep and crystal winter sky,
　Where noiseless, one by one, bright stars appear.

It may be Bacchus, at thy birth, forgot
　That drop from out the purple grape to press
Which is his gift to man, and so thy blood
　Doth miss the heat which ofttimes breeds excess.

But, all more surely do we turn to thee
   When the day's heat and blinding dust are o'er,
And cool our souls in thy refreshing air,
   And find the peace which we had lost before.

10. CAROLINE STURGIS TAPPAN, 1818–1888

[The younger of the Sturgis sisters, Caroline managed
to be both the intimate friend of Margaret Fuller and the
special confidante of Emerson (all of them subscribing to
the same exalted conception of "Friendship"), as well as
a serious correspondent of the elder Henry James. The
novelist Henry James knew her as she graced the Newport
scene in 1861, after many happy years in Europe: she
was fascinating to him as a lovely survivor "of that young
band of the ardent and uplifted" which, as James made out,
had found "its prime inspirer in Emerson and become
more familiarly, if a shade less authentically, vocal in
Margaret Fuller." Young James was struck with how easily
Caroline could display "a delicate and casual irreverence,"
how unafraid she was of anything to which she had been
vicariously exposed. There is possibly no higher or more
accurate tribute to the fine courage with which Transcendentalism fired its adherents.

Caroline Tappan was never afraid either of Margaret
Fuller or Emerson. She sailed superbly through their
little tempests, and in passing, graceful creature that she
was, let fall her simplifications of the ardent and uplifted
creed.]

POEMS

Lyric

The stars coldly glimmer—
   And I am alone.
The pale moon grows dimmer,
   And now it has gone.
Loud shrieks the owl, night presses round,
The little flowers lie low on the ground
   And sadly moan.

Why is the earth so sad?
  Why doth she weep?
Methinks she would be glad
  Calmly to sleep.
But the dews are falling, heavy and fast,
Sadly sighs the cold night-blast,
  Loud roars the deep.

I press my hands upon my heart—
  'Tis very cold!
And swiftly through the forest dart
  With footsteps bold.
What shall I seek? Where shall I go?
Earth and ocean shudder with woe!
  Their tale is untold!

Life

Greatly to Be
Is enough for me,
Is enough for thee.

Why for work art thou striving,
Why seek'st thou for aught?
To the soul that is living
All things shall be brought.

What thou art thou wilt do,
And thy work will be true.

But how can I Be
Without labor or love?
Life comes not to me
As to calm gods above.

Not only above
May spirit be found,
The sunshine of love
Streams all around.

The sun does not say,
"I will not shine
Unless every ray
Falls on planets divine."

He shines upon dust,
Upon things mean and low,
His own inward thought
Maketh him glow.

Art and Artist

With dauntless eye the lofty one
  Moves on through life;
Majestic as the mighty sun
  He knows no strife.

He sees the thought flow to the form,
  And rise like bubble bright;
A moment of beauty—and it is gone.
  Dissolved in light.

Lines

You go to the woods—what there have you seen?
Quivering leaves glossy and green;
Lights and shadows dance to and fro,
Beautiful flowers in the soft moss grow.
Is the secret of these things known to you?
Can you tell what gives the flower its hue?
Why the oak spreads out its limbs so wide?
And the graceful grape-vine grows by its side?
Why clouds full of sunshine are piled on high?
What sends the wind to sweep through the sky?
No! the secret of Nature I do not know—
A poor groping child, through her marvels I go!

The Hero

Thou has learned the woes of all the world!
  From thine own longings and lone tears,
And now thy broad sails are unfurled,
  And all men hail thee with loud cheers.

The flowing sunlight is thy home,
  And billows of the sea are thine,
To all the nations shalt thou roam,
  Through every heart thy love shall shine.

The subtlest thought that finds its goal
  Far, far beyond the horizon's verge,
Oh, shoot it forth on arrows bold,
  The thoughts of men, on, on, to urge.

Toil not to free the slave from chains,
  Think not to give the laborer rest;
Unless rich beauty fills the plains,
  The free man wanders still unblest.

All men can dig, and hew rude stone,
  But thou must carve the frieze above;
And columned high, through thee alone,
  Shall rise our frescoed homes of love.

11. JONES VERY, 1813–1880

[The son of a Salem sea captain, who early accompanied his father on long voyages, Jones Very graduated from Harvard College in 1836, and was promptly appointed tutor in Greek even while entering the Divinity School. Shortly thereafter he began to receive communications directly from the Holy Ghost and to have visions. For a time in 1838 he had to be shut up in the McLean Asylum. Emerson was firmly persuaded of his Genius, and in 1839 secured the publication of Very's *Essays and Poems*.

Very was a trial to his friends, and an oddity among the Transcendentalists, because his passion was poured into older forms of traditional Christianity. His essays, which I am obliged here to omit, were as sophisticated literary theorizing as any in the movement produced; while his poetic ability may not be of major stature, assuredly his creations are authentic. He lived the last forty years of his life in Salem, in rigorous seclusion, though there seem to have been occasional flashes of the enthusiasm which in the 1830's had driven him literally insane.]

POEMS

The New Birth

'Tis a new life—thoughts move not as they did
With slow uncertain steps across my mind,
In thronging haste fast pressing on they bid
The portals open to the viewless wind
That comes not save when in the dust is laid
The crown of pride that gilds each mortal brow,
And from before man's vision melting fade
The heavens and earth—their walls are falling now—
Fast crowding on, each thought asks utterance strong;
Storm-lifted waves swift rushing to the shore,
On from the sea they send their shouts along,
Back through the cave-worn rocks their thunders roar;
And I a child of God by Christ made free
Start from death's slumbers to Eternity.

Love

I asked of Time to tell me where was Love;
He pointed to her foot-steps on the snow,
Where first the angel lighted from above,
And bid me note the way and onward go;
Through populous streets of cities spreading wide,

By lonely cottage rising on the moor,
Where bursts from sundered cliff the struggling tide,
To where it hails the sea with answering roar,
She led me on; o'er mountain's frozen head,
Where mile on mile still stretches on the plain,
Then homeward whither first my feet she led,
I traced her path along the snow again;
But there the sun had melted from the earth
The prints where first she trod, a child of mortal birth.

The Presence

I sit within my room, and joy to find
That Thou who always lov'st, art with me here,
That I am never left by Thee behind,
But by thyself Thou keep'st me ever near;
The fire burns brighter when with Thee I look,
And seems a kinder servant sent to me;
With gladder heart I read thy holy book,
Because thou art the eyes by which I see;
This aged chair, that table, watch and door
Around in ready service ever wait;
Nor can I ask of Thee a menial more
To fill the measure of my large estate,
For Thou thyself, with all a father's care,
Where'er I turn, art ever with me there.

The Dead

I see them, crowd on crowd they walk the earth,
Dry leafless trees no autumn wind laid bare;
And in their nakedness find cause for mirth,
And all unclad would winter's rudeness dare;
No sap doth through their clattering branches flow,
Whence springing leaves and blossoms bright appear;
Their hearts the living God have ceased to know,
Who gives the springtime to th' expectant year.
They mimic life, as if from him to steal

His glow of health to paint the livid cheek;
They borrow words for thoughts they cannot feel,
That with a seeming heart their tongue may speak;
And in their show of life more dead they live
Than those that to the earth with many tears they give.

Nature

The bubbling brook doth leap when I come by,
Because my feet find measure with its call,
The birds know when the friend they love is nigh,
For I am known to them both great and small;
The flower that on the lovely hill-side grows
Expects me there when Spring its bloom has given;
And many a tree and bush my wanderings know,
And e'en the clouds and silent stars of heaven;
For he who with his Maker walks aright,
Shall be their lord as Adam was before;
His ear shall catch each sound with new delight,
Each object wear the dress that then it wore;
And he, as when erect in soul he stood
Hear from his Father's lips that all is good.

The War

I saw a war, yet none the trumpets blew,
Nor in their hands the steel-wrought weapons bare;
And in that conflict armed there fought but few,
And none that in the world's loud tumults share.
They fought against their wills—the stubborn foe
That mail-clad warriors left unfought within,
And wordy champions left unslain below—
The ravening wolf though drest in fleecy skin—
They fought for peace—not that the world can give,
Whose tongue proclaims the war its hands have
    ceased,
And bids us as each other's neighbor live,

Ere haughty Self within us has deceased;
They fought for Him whose kingdom must increase
Good will to men, on earth forever peace.

Beauty

I gazed upon thy face—and beating life
Once stilled its sleepless pulses in my breast,
And every thought whose being was a strife
Each in its silent chamber sank to rest;
I was not, save it were a thought of thee;
The world was but a spot where thou had'st trod;
From every star they glance seemed fixed on me;
Almost I loved thee better than my God.
And still I gaze—but 'tis a holier thought
Than that which in my spirit lived before,
Each star a purer ray of love has caught,
Earth wears a lovelier robe than then it wore,
And every lamp that burns around thy shrine
Is fed with fire whose fountain is Divine.

The Barberry-Bush

The bush that has most briers and bitter fruit
Waits till the frost has turned its green leaves red,
Its sweetened berries will thy palate suit,
And thou mayst find e'en there a homely bread;
Upon the hills of Salem scattered wide,
Their yellow blossoms gain the eye in Spring;
And straggling e'en upon the turnpike's side,
Their ripened branches to your hand they bring,
I've plucked them oft in boyhood's early hour,
That then I gave such name, and thought it true;
But now I know that other fruit as sour,
Grows on what now thou callest *Me* and *You*;
Yet wilt thou wait the autumn that I see,
Will sweeter taste than these red berries be.

The Fox and the Bird

The bird that has no nest,
　　The Fox that has no hole;
He's wiser than the rest,
　　Her eggs are never stole.

She builds where none can see,
　　He hides where none can find;
The bird can rest where'er she be,
　　He freely moves as wind.

Thou has not found her little young,
　　E'en though thou'st sought them long;
Thou from thine earliest day they've sung,
　　Thou has not heard their song.

Thou has not found that Fox's brood,
　　That nestle under ground;
Though through all time his burrow's stood,
　　His whelps thou'st never found.

The Prayer

Wilt Thou not visit me?
The plant beside me feels Thy gentle dew;
　　And every blade of grass I see,
From Thy deep earth its quickening moisture drew.

Wilt Thou not visit me?
Thy morning calls on me with cheering tone;
　　And every hill and tree
Lends but one voice, the voice of Thee alone.

Come, for I need Thy love,
More than the flower the dew, or grass the rain;
　　Come, gently as Thy holy dove;
And let me in thy sight rejoice to live again.

I will not hide from them,
When Thy storms come, though fierce may be their wrath;
    But bow with leafy stem,
And strengthened follow on Thy chosen path.

    Yes, Thou wilt visit me,
Nor plant nor tree Thine eye delights so well,
    As when from sin set free
My spirit loves with Thine in peace to dwell.

Health of Body Dependent on the Soul

    Not from the earth, or skies,
        Or seasons as they roll,
    Come health and vigor to the frame,
        But from the living soul.

    Is this alive to God,
        And not the slave to sin?
    Then will the body, too, receive
        Health from the soul within.

    But if disease has touched
        The spirit's inmost part,
    In vain we seek from outward things
        To heal the deadly smart.

    The mind, the heart unchanged,
        Which clouded e'en our home,
    Will make the outward world the same
        Where'er our feet may roam.

    The fairest scenes on earth,
        The mildest, purest sky,
    Will bring no vigor to the step,
        No lustre to the eye.

    For He who formed our frame
        Made man a perfect whole,
    And made the body's health depend
        Upon the living soul.

The Light from Within

I saw on earth another light
  Than that which lit my eye
Come forth as from my soul within,
  And from a higher sky.

Its beams shone still unclouded on,
  When in the farthest west
The sun I once had known had sunk
  Forever to his rest.

And on I walked, though dark the night,
  Nor rose his orb by day;
As one who by a surer guide
  Was pointed out the way.

'Twas brighter far than noonday's beam;
  It shone from God within,
And lit, as by a lamp from heaven,
  The world's dark track of sin.

CHAPTER SIX

POLITICS AND SOCIETY

1. RALPH WALDO EMERSON, 1803–1882

[No sooner did the new philosophy discover in the romantic concept of Nature the basis for its synthesis, and on that basis erect the figure of the "self-reliant" individual, than it found itself tormented not only by the problem of the self's relation to the totality of the natural universe but still more pressingly by that of the relation of this triumphant individual to the society of his fellow men.

In America, this social problem was, paradoxically, all the more annoying because the organized power of the community, in that era, purported to be the least intrusive of any on earth. It was democratic, and in the 1830's the regime of Andrew Jackson had vociferously dedicated it to providing opportunities for the "common" man. There was, at least in theory, no legally recognized "aristocracy" to close any career to any talent. By all considerations, historical or relative, the insurgent youth of New England, it might seem, should have been at home in their towns. Why then were they so uncomfortable?

Adequately to answer this question—if indeed it ever can be answered—would require a large volume. The basic data is, I believe, contained in these four selections, though I assure the student that each of the authors wrote voluminously on the topic, that these arbitrary choices by no means represent the whole of their thinking. (Also, I have not space for any of Theodore Parker's grandiloquent denunciations of the evils concealed behind the facade of this officially optimistic civilization.)

For Emerson, the debate between "society and solitude"

went on inside his mind for all his life. In the course of heeding it, in his *Journal* or in such essays as that called "Politics," he said many pungent things; I must content myself with the lecture he first delivered in London, on his second visit to England, in 1848. The form in which it was finally printed, in *Lectures and Biographical Sketches* of 1883, incorporates several revisions (we know that he frequently repeated it in Boston and elsewhere), and is here addressed to American rather than to English listeners. If only for that reason, the address may figure as Emerson's most mature, though most inconclusive, discussion of the confrontation of Self and society, Genius and the democracy.

To the distress of his friends—those who developed Transcendental premises into an extreme anarchy of individualism, or those who proceeded from the same assumption toward socialism or authoritarianism—Emerson guarded his "armed neutrality." As he elsewhere said—and this may indeed summarize his ambiguous position—"The relation of men of thought to society is always the same; they refuse that necessity of mediocre men, to take sides."

The identification of spine with lightning-rod is borrowed from Thoreau. The "naturalist" who unified the grumpy democracy of Concord was Louis Agassiz.]

ARISTOCRACY

There is an attractive topic, which never goes out of vogue and is impertinent in no community—the permanent traits of the Aristocracy. It is an interest of the human race, and, as I look at it, inevitable, sacred and to be found in every country and in every company of men. My concern with it is that concern which all well-disposed persons will feel, that there should be model men—true instead of spurious pictures of excellence, and, if possible, living standards.

I observed that the word *gentleman* is gladly heard in all companies; that the cogent motive with the best young men who are revolving plans and forming resolutions for the future, is the spirit of honor, the wish to be gentlemen. They do not yet covet political power, nor any exuberance of wealth, wealth that costs too much; nor do they wish to be saints; for fear of partialism; but the middle term, the reconciling element, the success of the manly character, they find in the idea of gentleman. It is not to be a man of rank, but a man of honor, accomplished in all arts and generosities, which seems to them the right mark and the true chief of our modern society. A reference to society is part of the idea of culture; science of a gentleman; art of a gentleman; poetry in a gentleman: intellectually held, that is, for their own sake, for what they are; for their universal beauty and worth—not for economy, which degrades them, but not over-intellectually, that is, not to ecstasy, entrancing the man, but redounding to his beauty and glory.

In the sketches which I have to offer I shall not be surprised if my readers should fancy that I am giving them, under a gayer title, a chapter on Education. It will not pain me if I am found now and then to rove from the accepted and historic, to a theoretic peerage; or if it should turn out, what is true, that I am describing a real aristocracy, a chapter of Templars who sit indifferently in all climates and under the shadow of all institutions, but so few, so heedless of badges, so rarely convened, so little in sympathy with the predominant politics of nations, that their names and doings are not recorded in any Book of Peerage, or any Court Journal, or even Daily Newspaper of the world.

I find the caste in the man. The Golden Book of Venice, the scale of European chivalry, the Barons of England, the hierarchy of India with its impassable degrees, is each a transcript of the decigrade or centigraded Man. A many-chambered Aristocracy lies already organized in his moods and faculties. Room is found for all the departments of the state in the moods and faculties of each human spirit, with separate function and difference of dignity.

The terrible aristocracy that is in Nature. Real people dwelling with the real, face to face, undaunted: then, far down, people of taste, people dwelling in a relation, or rumor, or influence of good and fair, entertained by it, superficially touched, yet charmed by these shadows—and, far below these, gross and thoughtless, the animal man, billows of chaos, down to the dancing and menial organizations.

I observe the inextinguishable prejudice men have in favor of a hereditary transmission of qualities. It is in vain to remind them that Nature appears capricious. Some qualities she carefully fixes and transmits, but some, and those the finer, she exhales with the breath of the individual, as too costly to perpetuate. But I notice also that they may become fixed and permanent in any stock, by painting and repainting them on every individual, until at last Nature adopts them and bakes them into her porcelain.

At all events I take this inextinguishable persuasion in men's minds as a hint from the outward universe to man to inlay as many virtues and superiorities as he can into this swift fresco of the day, which is hardening to an immortal picture.

If one thinks of the interest which all men have in beauty of character and manners; that it is of the last importance to the imagination and affection, inspiring as it does that loyalty and worship so essential to the finish of character—certainly, if culture, if laws, if primogeniture, if heraldry, if money could secure such a result as superior and finished men, it would be the interest of all mankind to see that the steps were taken, the pains incurred. No taxation, no concession, no conferring of privileges never so exalted would be a price too large.

The old French Revolution attracted to its first movement all the liberality, virtue, hope and poetry in Europe. By the abolition of kingship and aristocracy, tyranny, inequality and poverty would end. Alas! no; tyranny, inequality, poverty, stood as fast and fierce as ever. We likewise put faith in Democracy; in the Republican principle carried out to the extremes of practice in universal suffrage, in the will of majorities. The young adventurer finds that the relations of society, the position of classes, irk and sting him, and he lends himself to each malignant party that assails what is eminent. He will one day know that this is not removable, but a distinction in the nature of things; that neither the caucus, nor the newspaper, nor the Congress, nor the mob, nor the guillotine, nor fire, nor all together, can avail to outlaw, cut out, burn or destroy the offence of superiority in persons. The manners, the pretension, which annoy me so much, are not superficial, but built on a real distinction in the nature of my companion. The superiority in him is inferiority in me, and if this particular companion were wiped by a sponge out of Nature, my inferiority would still be made evident to me by other persons everywhere and every day.

No, not the hardest utilitarian will question the value of an aristocracy if he love himself. For every man confesses that the highest good which the universe proposes to him is the highest society. If a few grand natures should come to us and weave duties and offices between us and them, it would make our bread ambrosial.

I affirm that inequalities exist, not in costume, but in the powers of expression and action; a primitive aristocracy; and that we, certainly, have not come here to describe well-dressed vulgarity. I cannot tell how English titles are bestowed, whether on pure blood, or on the largest holder in the three-per-cents. The English government and people, or the French government, may easily make mistakes; but Nature makes none. Every mark and scutcheon of hers indicates constitutional qualities. In science, in trade, in social discourse, as in the state, it is the same thing. Forever and ever it takes a pound to lift a pound.

It is plain that all the deference of modern society to this idea of the Gentleman, and all the whimsical tyranny of Fashion which has continued to engraft itself on this reverence, is a secret homage to reality and love which ought to reside in every man. This is the steel that is hid under gauze and lace, under flowers and spangles. And it is plain that instead of this idolatry, a worship; instead of this impure, a pure reverence for character, a new respect for the sacredness of the individual man, is that antidote which must correct in our country the disgraceful deference to public opinion, and the insane subordination of the end to the means. From the folly of too much association we must come back to the repose of self-reverence and trust.

The game of the world is a perpetual trial of strength between man and events. The common man is the victim of events. Whatever happens is too much for him, he is drawn this way and that way, and his whole life is a hurry. The superior man is at home in his own mind. We like cool people, who neither hope nor fear too much, but seem to have many strings to their bow, and can survive the blow well enough if stocks should rise or fall, if parties should be broken up, if their money or their family should be dispersed; who can stand a slander very well; indeed on whom events make little or no impression, and who can face death with firmness. In short, we dislike every mark of a superficial life and action, and prize whatever mark of a central life.

What is the meaning of this invincible respect for war, here in the triumphs of our commercial civilization, that we can never quite smother the trumpet and the drum? How is it that the sword runs away with all the fame from the spade and the wheel? How sturdy seem to us in the history, those Merovingians, Guelphs, Dorias, Sforzas, Burgundies and Guesclins of the old warlike ages! We can hardly believe they were all such speedy shadows as we; that an ague or fever, a drop of water or a crystal of ice ended them. We give soldiers the same advantage today. From the most accumulated culture we are always running back to the sound of any drum and fife. And in any trade, or in law-courts, in orchard and farm, and even in saloons, they only prosper or they prosper best who have a military mind, who engineer in sword and cannon style, with energy and sharpness. Why, but because courage never loses its high price? Why, but because we wish to see those to whom existence is most adorned and attractive, foremost to peril it for their object, and ready to answer for their actions with their life.

The existence of an upper class is not injurious, as long as it is dependent on merit. For so long it is provocation to the bold and generous. These distinctions exist, and they are deep, not to be talked or voted away. If the differences are organic, so are the merits, that is to say the power and excellence we describe are real. Aristocracy is the class eminent by personal qualities, and to them belongs without assertion a proper influence. Men of aim must lead the aimless; men of invention the uninventive. I wish catholic men, who by their science and skill are at home in every latitude and longitude, who carry the world in their thoughts; men of universal politics, who are interested in things in proportion to their truth and magnitude; who know the beauty of animals and the laws of their nature, whom the mystery of botany allures, and the mineral laws; who see general effects and are not too learned to love the Imagination, the power and the spirits of Solitude—men who see the dance in men's lives as well as in a ball-room, and can feel and convey the sense which is only collectively or totally expressed by a population; men who are charmed by the beautiful Nemesis as well as by the dire Nemesis, and dare trust their inspiration for their welcome; who would find their fellows in persons of real elevation of whatever kind of speculative or practical ability. We are fallen on times so acquiescent and traditionary that we are in danger of forgetting so simple a fact as that the basis of all aristocracy must be truth—the doing what elsewhere is pretended to be done. One would gladly see all our institutions rightly aristocratic in this wise.

I enumerate the claims by which men enter the superior class.

1. A commanding talent. In every company one finds the best man; and if there be any question, it is decided the instant they enter into any practical enterprise. If the finders of glass, gunpowder, printing, electricity—if the healer of small-pox, the contriver of the safety-lamp, of the aqueduct, of the bridge, of the tunnel; if the finders of parallax, of new planets, of steam power for boat and carriage, the finder of sulphuric ether and the electric telegraph—if these men should keep their secrets, or only communicate them to each other, must not the whole race

of mankind serve them as gods? It only needs to look at the social aspect of England and America and France, to see the rank which original practical talent commands.

Every survey of the dignified classes, in ancient or modern history, imprints universal lessons, and establishes a nobility of a prouder creation. And the conclusion which Roman Senators, Indian Brahmins, Persian Magians, European Nobles and great Americans inculcate—that which they preach out of their material wealth and glitter, out of their old war and modern land-owning, even out of sensuality and sneers, is, that the radical and essential distinctions of every aristocracy are moral. Do not hearken to the men, but to the Destiny in the institutions. An aristocracy is composed of simple and sincere men for whom Nature and ethics are strong enough, who say what they mean and go straight to their objects. It is essentially real.

The multiplication of monarchs known by telegraph and daily news from all countries to the daily papers, and the effect of freer institutions in England and America, has robbed the title of king of all its romance, as that of our commercial consuls as compared with the ancient Roman. We shall come to add "Kings" in the "Contents" of the Directory, as we do "Physicians," "Brokers," etc. In simple communities, in the heroic ages, a man was chosen for his knack; got his name, rank and living for that; and the best of the best was the aristocrat or king. In the Norse Edda it appears as the curious but excellent policy of contending tribes, when tired of war, to exchange hostages, and in reality each to adopt from the other a first-rate man, who thus acquired a new country; was at once made a chief. And no wrong was so keenly resented as any fraud in this transaction. In the heroic ages, as we call them, the hero uniformly has some real talent. Ulysses in Homer is represented as a very skilful carpenter. He builds the boat with which he leaves Calypso's isle, and in his own palace carves a bedstead out of the trunk of a tree and inlays it with gold and ivory. Epeus builds the wooden horse. The English nation down to a late age inherited the reality of the Northern stock. In 1373, in writs of summons of members of Parliament, the sheriff of every county is to cause "two dubbed knights, or the most worthy esquires, the most expert in feats of arms, and no others; and of every city, two citizens, and of every borough, two burgesses, such as have greatest skill in shipping and merchandising, to be returned."

The ancients were fond of ascribing to their nobles gigantic proportions and strength. The hero must have the force of ten men. The chief is taller by a head than any of his tribe. Douglas can throw the bar a greater cast. Richard can sever the iron bolt with his sword. The horn of Roland, in the romance, is heard sixty miles. The Cid has a prevailing health that will let him nurse the leper, and share his bed without harm. And since the body is the pipe through which we tap all the succors and virtues of the material world, it is certain that a sound body must be at the root of any excellence in manners and actions; a strong and supple frame which yields a stock of strength and spirits for all the needs of the day, and generates the habit of relying on a supply of power for all extraordinary exertions. When Nature goes to create a national man, she put a symmetry between the physical and intellectual powers. She moulds a large brain, and joins to it a great trunk to supply it; as if a fine alembic were fed with liquor for its distillations from broad full vats in the vaults of the laboratory.

Certainly, the origin of most of the perversities and absurdities that disgust us is, primarily, the want of health. Genius is health and Beauty is health and Virtue is health. The petty arts which we blame in the half-great seem as odious to them also—the resources of weakness and despair. And the manners betray the like puny constitution. Temperament is fortune, and we must say it so often. In a thousand cups of life, only one is the right mixture— a fine adjustment to the existing elements. When that befalls, when the well-mixed man is born, with eyes not too dull nor too good, with fire enough and earth enough, capable of impressions from all things, and not too susceptible—then no gift need be bestowed on him, he brings with him fortune, followers, love, power.

"I think he'll be to Rome
As is the osprey to the fish, who takes it
By sovereignty of nature."

Not the phrenologist but the philosopher may well say, Let me see his brain, and I will tell you if he shall be poet, king, founder of cities, rich, magnetic, of a secure hand, of a scientific memory, a right classifier; or whether he shall be a bungler, driveller, unlucky, heavy and tedious.

It were to dispute against the sun, to deny this difference of brain. I see well enough that when I bring one man into an estate, he sees vague capabilities, what others might, could, would or should do with it. If I bring another, he sees what *he* should do with it. He appreciates the water-privilege, land fit for orchard, tillage, pasturage, wood-lot, cranberry-meadow; but just as easily he forsees all the means, all the steps of the process, and could lay his hand as readily on one as on another point in that series which opens the capability to the last point. The poet sees wishfully enough the result; the well-built head supplies all the steps, one as perfect as the other, in the series. Seeing this working head in him, it becomes to me as certain that he will have the direction of estates, as that there are estates. If we see tools in a magazine, as a file, an anchor, a plough, a pump, a paint-brush, a cider-press, a diving-bell, we can predict well enough their destination; and the man's associations, fortunes, love, hatred, residence, rank, the books he will buy, the roads he will traverse are predetermined in his organism. Men will need him, and he is rich and eminent by nature. That man cannot be too late or too early. Let him not hurry or hesitate. Though millions are already arrived, his seat is reserved. Though millions attend, they only multiply his friends and agents. It never troubles the Senator what multitudes crack the benches and bend the galleries to hear. He who understands the art of war, reckons the hostile battalions and cities, opportunities and spoils.

An aristocracy could not exist unless it were organic. Men are born to command, and—it is even so—"come into the world booted and spurred to ride." The blood royal never pays, we say. It obtains service, gifts, supplies, furtherance of all kinds from the love and joy of those who feel themselves honored by the service they render.

Dull people think it Fortune that makes one rich and another poor. Is it? Yes, but the fortune was earlier than they think, namely, in the balance or adjustment between devotion to what is agreeable to-day and the forecast of what will be valuable to-morrow.

Certainly I am not going to argue the merits of gradation in the universe; the existing order of more or less. Neither do I wish to go into a vindication of the justice that disposes the variety of lot. I know how steep the contrast of condition looks; such excess here and such destitution there; like entire chance, like the freaks of the wind, heaping the snow-drift in gorges, stripping the plain; such despotism of wealth and comfort in banquet-halls, whilst death is in the pots of the wretched—that it behooves a good man to walk with tenderness and heed amidst so much suffering. I only point in passing to the order of the universe, which makes a rotation—not like the coarse policy of the Greeks, ten generals, each commanding one day and then giving place to the next, or like our democratic politics, my turn now, your turn next—but the constitution of things has distributed a new quality or talent to each mind, and the revolution of things is always bringing the need, now of this, now of that, and is sure to bring home the opportunity to every one.

The only relief that I know against the invidiousness of superior position is, that you exert your faculty; for whilst each does that, he excludes hard thoughts from the spectator. All right activity is amiable. I never feel that any man occupies my place, but that the reason why I do not have what I wish, is, that I want the faculty which entitles. All spiritual or real power makes its own place.

We pass for what we are, and we prosper or fail by what we are. There are men who may dare much and will be justified in their daring. But it is because they know they are in their place. As long as I am in my place, I am safe. "The best lightning-rod for your protection is your own spine." Let a man's social aims be proportioned to his means and power. I do not pity the misery of a man underplaced: that will right itself presently: but I pity the man overplaced. A certain quantity of power belongs to a certain quantity of faculty. Whoever wants more power than is the legitimate attraction of his faculty, is a politician, and must pay for that excess; must truckle for it. This is the whole game of society and the politics of the world. Being will always seem well—but whether possibly I cannot contrive to seem, without the trouble of being? Every Frenchman would have a career. We English are not any better with our love of making a figure. "I told the Duke of Newcastle," says Bubb Dodington in his Memoirs, "that it must end one way or another, it must not remain as it was; for I was determined to make some sort of a figure in life; I earnestly wished it might be under his protection, but if that could not be, I must make some figure; what it would be I could not determine yet; I must look round me a little and consult my friends, but some figure I was resolved to make."

It will be agreed everywhere that society must have the benefit of the best leaders. How to obtain them? Birth has been tried and failed. Caste in India has no good result. Ennobling of one family is good for one generation; not sure beyond. Slavery had mischief enough to answer for, but it had this good in it—the pricing of men. In the South a slave was bluntly but accurately valued at five hundred to a thousand dollars, if a good field-hand; if a mechanic, as carpenter or smith, twelve hundred or two thousand. In Rome or Greece what sums would not be paid for a superior slave, a confidential secretary and manager, an educated slave; a man of genius, a Moses educated in Egypt? I don't know how much Epictetus was sold for, or Æsop, or Toussaint l'Ouverture, and perhaps it was not a good market-day. Time was, in England, when the state stipulated beforehand what price should be paid for each citizen's life, if he was killed. Now, if it were possible, I should like to see that appraisal applied to every man, and every man made acquainted with the true number and weight of every adult citizen, and that he be placed where he belongs, with so much power confided to him as he could carry and use.

In the absence of such anthropometer I have a perfect confidence in the natural laws. I think that the community —every community, if obstructing laws and usages are removed—will be the best measure and the justest judge of the citizen, or will in the long run give the fairest verdict and reward; better than any royal patronage; better than any premium on race; better than any statute elevating families to hereditary distinction, or any class to sacerdotal education and power. The verdict of battles will best prove the general; the town-meeting, the Congress, will not fail to find out legislative talent. The prerogatives of a right physician are determined, not by his diplomas, but by the health he restores to body and mind; the powers of a geometer by solving his problem; of a priest by the act of inspiring us with a sentiment which disperses the grief from which we suffered. When the lawyer tries his case in court he himself is also on trial and his own merits appear as well as his client's. When old writers are consulted by young writers who have written their first book, they say, Publish it by all means; so only can you certainly know its quality.

But we venture to put any man in any place. It is curious how negligent the public is of the essential qualifications of its representatives. They ask if a man is a Republican, a Democrat? Yes. Is he a man of talent? Yes. Is he honest and not looking for an office or any manner of bribe? He is honest. Well then choose him by acclamation. And they go home and tell their wives with great satisfaction what a good thing they have done. But they forgot to ask the fourth question, not less important than either of the others, and without which the others do not avail. Has he a will? Can he carry his points against opposition? Probably not. It is not sufficient that your work follows your genius, or is organic, to give you the magnetic power over men. More than taste and talent must go to the Will. That must also be a gift of Nature. It is in some; it is not in others. But I should say, if it is not in you, you had better not put yourself in places where not to have it is to be a public enemy.

The expectation and claims of mankind indicate the duties of this class. Some service they must pay. We do not expect them to be saints, and it is very pleasing to see the instinct of mankind on this matter—how much they will forgive to such as pay substantial service and work energetically after their kind; but they do not extend the same indulgence to those who claim and enjoy the same prerogative but render no returns. The day is darkened when the golden river runs down into mud; when genius grows idle and wanton and reckless of its fine duties of being Saint, Prophet, Inspirer to its humble fellows, balks their respect and confounds their understanding by silly extravagances. To a right aristocracy, to Hercules, to Theseus, Odin, the Cid, Napoleon; to Sir Robert Walpole, to Fox, Chatham, Mirabeau, Jefferson, O'Connell—to the men, that is, who are incomparably superior to the populace in ways agreeable to the populace, showing them the way they should go, doing for them what they wish done and cannot do—of course everything will be permitted and pardoned—gaming, drinking, fighting, luxury. These are the heads of party, who can do no wrong —everything short of infamous crime will pass. But if those who merely sit in their places and are not, like them, able; if the dressed and perfumed gentleman, who serves the people in no wise and adorns them not, is not even *not afraid of them,* if such an one go about to set ill examples and corrupt them, who shall blame them if they burn his barns, insult his children, assault his person, and express their unequivocal indignation and contempt? He eats their bread, he does not scorn to live by their labor, and after breakfast he cannot remember that there are human beings. To live without duties is obscene.

2. Genius, what is so called in strictness—the power to affect the Imagination, as possessed by the orator, the poet, the novelist or the artist—has a royal right in all possessions and privileges, being itself representative and accepted by all men as their delegate. It has indeed the best right, because it raises men above themselves, intoxi-

cates them with beauty. They are honored by rendering it honor, and the reason of this allowance is that Genius unlocks for all men the chains of use, temperament and drudgery, and gives them a sense of delicious liberty and power.

The first example that occurs is an extraordinary gift of eloquence. A man who has that possession of his means and that magnetism that he can at all times carry the convictions of a public assembly, we must respect, and he is thereby ennobled. He has the freedom of the city. He is entitled to neglect trifles. Like a great general, or a great poet, or a millionaire, he may wear his coat out at elbows, and his hat on his feet, if he will. He has established relation, representativeness. The best feat of genius is to bring all the varieties of talent and culture into its audience; the mediocre and the dull are reached as well as the intelligent. I have seen it conspicuously shown in a village. Here are classes which day by day have no intercourse, nothing beyond perhaps a surly nod in passing. But I have seen a man of teeming brain come among these men, so full of his facts, so unable to suppress them, that he has poured out a river of knowledge to all comers, and drawing all these men round him, all sorts of men, interested the whole village, good and bad, bright and stupid, in his facts; the iron boundary lines had all faded away; the stupid had discovered that they were not stupid; the coldest had found themselves drawn to their neighbors by interest in the same things. This was a naturalist

The more familiar examples of this power certainly are those who establish a wider dominion over men's minds than any speech can; who think, and paint, and laugh, and weep, in their eloquent closets, and then convert the world into a huge whispering-gallery, to report the tale to all men, and win smiles and tears from many generations. The eminent examples are Shakspeare, Cervantes, Bunyan, Burns, Scott, and now we must add Dickens. In the fine arts, I find none in the present age who have any popular power, who have achieved any nobility by ennobling the people.

3. Elevation of sentiment, refining and inspiring the

manners, must really take the place of every distinction
whether of material power or of intellectual gifts. The
manners of course must have that depth and firmness of
tone to attest their centrality in the nature of the man.
I mean the things themselves shall be judges, and determine. In the presence of this nobility even genius must
stand aside. For the two poles of nature are Beauty and
Meanness, and noble sentiment is the highest form of
Beauty. He is beautiful in face, in port, in manners, who is
absorbed in objects which he truly believes to be superior
to himself. Is there any parchment or any cosmetic or any
blood that can obtain homage like that security of air pre-
supposing so undoubtingly the sympathy of men in his
designs? What is it that makes the true knight? Loyalty
to his thought. That makes the beautiful scorn, the elegant
simplicity, the directness, the commanding port which all
men admire and which men not noble affect. For the
thought has no debts, no hunger, no lusts, no low obliga-
tions or relations, no intrigue or business, no murder, no
envy, no crime, but large leisures and an inviting future.

The service we receive from the great is a mutual deference. If you deal with the vulgar, life is reduced to
beggary indeed. The astronomers are very eager to know
whether the moon has an atmosphere; I am only concerned
that every man have one. I observe, however, that it takes
two to make an atmosphere. I am acquainted with persons
who go attended with this ambient cloud. It is sufficient
that they come. It is not important what they say. The sun
and the evening sky are not calmer. They seem to have
arrived at the fact, to have got rid of the show, and to be
serene. Their manners and behavior in the house and in
the field are those of men at rest: what have they to
conceal? what have they to exhibit? Others I meet, who
have no deference, and who denude and strip one of all
attributes but material values. As much health and muscle
as you have, as much land, as much house-room and
dinner, avails. Of course a man is a poor bag of bones.
There is no gracious interval, not an inch allowed. Bone
rubs against bone. Life is thus a Beggar's Bush. I know
nothing which induces so base and forlorn a feeling as

when we are treated for our utilities, as economists do, starving the imagination and the sentiment. In this impoverishing animation, I seem to meet a Hunger, a wolf. Rather let us be alone whilst we live, than encounter these lean kine. Man should emancipate man. He does so, not by jamming him, but by distancing him. The nearer my friend, the more spacious is our realm, the more diameter our spheres have. It is a measure of culture, the number of things taken for granted. When a man begins to speak, the churl will take him up by disputing his first words, so he cannot come at his scope. The wise man takes all for granted until he sees the parallelism of that which puzzled him with his own view.

I will not protract this discourse by describing the duties of the brave and generous. And yet I will venture to name one, and the same is almost the sole condition on which knighthood is to be won; this, namely, loyalty to your own order. The true aristocrat is he who is at the head of his own order, and disloyalty is to mistake other chivalries for his own. Let him not divide his homage, but stand for that which he was born and set to maintain. It was objected to Gustavus that he did not better distinguish between the duties of a carabine and a general, but exposed himself to all dangers and was too prodigal of a blood so precious. For a soul on which elevated duties are laid will so realize its special and lofty duties as not to be in danger of assuming through a low generosity those which do not belong to it.

There are all degrees of nobility, but amid the levity and giddiness of people one looks round, as for a tower of strength, on some self-dependent mind, who does not go abroad for an estimate, and has long ago made up its conclusion that it is impossible to fail. The great Indian sages had a lesson for the Brahmin, which every day returns to mind, "All that depends on another gives pain; all that depends on himself gives pleasure; in these few words is the definition of pleasure and pain." The noble mind is here to teach us that failure is a part of success. Prosperity and pound-cake are for very young gentlemen, whom such things content; but a hero's, a man's success is made up of failures, because he experiments and ventures every day, and "the more falls he gets, moves faster on"; defeated all the time and yet to victory born. I have heard that in horsemanship he is not the good rider who never was thrown, but rather that a man never will be a good rider until he is thrown; then he will not be haunted any longer by the terror that he shall tumble, and will ride—that is his business—to *ride*, whether with falls or whether with none, to ride unto the place whither he is bound. And I know no such unquestionable badge and ensign of a sovereign mind, as that tenacity of purpose which, through all change of companions, of parties, of fortunes—changes never, bates no jot of heart or hope, but wearies out opposition, and arrives at its port. In his consciousness of deserving success, the caliph Ali constantly neglected the ordinary means of attaining it, and to the grand interests, a superficial success is of no account. It prospers as well in mistake as in luck, in obstruction and nonsense, as well as among the angels; it reckons fortunes mere paint; difficulty is its delight: perplexity is its noonday: minds that make their way without winds and against tides. But these are rare and difficult examples, we can only indicate them to show how high is the range of the realm of Honor.

I know the feeling of the most ingenious and excellent youth in America; I hear the complaint of the aspirant that we have no prizes offered to the ambition of virtuous young men; that there is no Theban Band; no stern exclusive Legion of Honor, to be entered only by long and real service and patient climbing up all the steps. We have a rich men's aristocracy, plenty of bribes for those who like them; but a grand style of culture, which, without injury, an ardent youth can propose to himself as a Pharos through long dark years, does not exist, and there is no substitute. The youth, having got through the first thickets that oppose his entrance into life, having got into decent society, is left to himself, and falls abroad with too much freedom. But in the hours of insight we rally against this skepticism. We then see that if the ignorant are around us, the great are much more near;

that there is an order of men, never quite absent, who enroll no names in their archives but of such as are capable of truth. They are gathered in no one chamber; no chamber would hold them; but, out of the vast duration of man's race, they tower like mountains, and are present to every mind in proportion to its likeness to theirs. The solitariest man who shares their spirit walks environed by them; they talk to him, they comfort him, and happy is he who prefers these associates to profane companions. They also take shape in men, in women. There is no heroic trait, no sentiment or thought that will not sometime embody itself in the form of a friend. That highest good of rational existence is always coming to such as reject mean alliances.

One trait more we must celebrate, the self-reliance which is the patent of royal natures. It is so prized a jewel that it is sure to be tested. The rules and discipline are ordered for that. The Golden Table never lacks members; all its seats are kept full; but with this strange provision, that the members are carefully withdrawn into deep niches, so that no one of them can see any other of them, and each believes himself alone. In the presence of the Chapter it is easy for each member to carry himself royally and well; but in the absence of his colleagues and in the presence of mean people he is tempted to accept the low customs of towns. The honor of a member consists in an indifference to the persons and practices about him, and in the pursuing undisturbed the career of a Brother, as if always in their presence, and as if no other existed. Give up, once for all, the hope of approbation from the people in the street, if you are pursuing great ends. How can they guess your designs?

All reference to models, all comparison with neighboring abilities and reputations, is the road to mediocrity. The generous soul, on arriving in a new port, makes instant preparation for a new voyage. By experiment, by original studies, by secret obedience, he has made a place for himself in the world; stands there a real, substantial, unprecedented person, and when the great come by, as always there are angels walking in the earth, they know him at sight. Effectual service in his own legitimate fashion distiguishes the true man. For he is to know that the distinction of a royal nature is a great heart; that not Louis Quatorze, not Chesterfield, nor Byron, nor Bonaparte is the model of the Century, but, wherever found, the old renown attaches to the virtues of simple faith and stanch endurance and clear perception and plain speech, and that there is a master grace and dignity communicated by exalted sentiments to a human form, to which utility and even genius must do homage. And it is the sign and badge of this nobility, the drawing his counsel from his own breast. For to every gentleman grave and dangerous duties are proposed. Justice always wants champions. The world waits for him as its defender, for he will find in the well-dressed crowd, yes, in the civility of whole nations, vulgarity of sentiment. In the best parlors of modern society he will find the laughing devil, the civil sneer; in English palaces the London twist, derision, coldness, contempt of the masses, contempt of Ireland, dislike of the Chartist. The English House of Commons is the proudest assembly of gentlemen in the world, yet the genius of the House of Commons, its legitimate expression, is a sneer. In America he shall find deprecation of purism on all questions touching the morals of trade and of social customs, and the narrowest contraction of ethics to the one duty of paying money. Pay that, and you may play the tyrant at discretion and never look back to the fatal question—where had you the money that you paid?

I know the difficulties in the way of a man of honor, The man of honor is a man of taste and humanity. By tendency, like all magnanimous men, he is a democrat. But the revolution comes, and does he join the standard of Chartist and outlaw? No, for these have been dragged in their ignorance by furious chiefs to the Red Revolution; they are full of murder, and the student recoils—and joins the rich. If he cannot vote with the poor, he should stay by himself. Let him accept the position of armed neutrality, abhorring the crimes of the Chartist, abhorring the selfishness of the rich, and say, "The time will come when these poor *enfans perdus* of revolution will have instructed their party, if only by their fate, and wiser counsels will prevail; the music and the dance of liberty will come up to bright and holy ground and will take me in also. Then I shall not have forfeited my right to speak and act for mankind." Meantime shame to the fop of learning and philosophy who suffers a vulgarity of speech and habit to blind him to the grosser vulgarity of pitiless selfishness, and to hide from him the current of Tendency; who abandons his right position of being priest and poet of these impious and unpoetic doers of God's work. You must, for wisdom, for sanity, have some access to the mind and heart of the common humanity. The exclusive excludes himself. No great man has existed who did not rely on the sense and heart of mankind as represented by the good sense of the people, as correcting the modes and over-refinements and class prejudices of the lettered men of the world.

There are certain conditions in the highest degree favorable to the tranquillity of spirit and to that magnanimity we so prize. And mainly the habit of considering large interests, and things in masses, and not too much in detail. The habit of directing large affairs generates a nobility of thought in every mind of average ability. For affairs themselves show the way in which they should be handled; and a good head soon grows wise, and does not govern too much.

Now I believe in the closest affinity between moral and material power. Virtue and genius are always on the direct way to the control of the society in which they are found. It is the interest of society that good men should govern, and there is always a tendency so to place them. But, for the day that now is, a man of generous spirit will not need to administer public offices or to direct large interests of trade, or war, or politics, or manufacture, but he will use a high prudence in the conduct of life to guard himself from being dissipated on many things. There is no need that he should count the pounds of property or the numbers of agents whom his influence touches; it suffices that his aims are high, that the interest of intellectual and moral beings is paramount with him, that he comes into what is called fine society from higher ground, and he has an elevation of habit which ministers of empires will be forced to see and to remember.

I do not know whether that word Gentleman, although it signifies a leading idea in recent civilization, is a sufficiently broad generalization to convey the deep and grave fact of self-reliance. To many the word expresses only the outsides of cultivated men—only graceful manners, and independence in trifles; but the fountains of that thought are in the deeps of man, a beauty which reaches through and through, from the manners to the soul; an honor which is only a name for sanctity, a self-trust which is a trust in God himself. Call it man of honor, or call it Man, the American who would serve his country must learn the beauty and honor of perseverance, he must reinforce himself by the power of character, and revisit the margin of that well from which his fathers drew waters of life and enthusiasm, the fountain I mean of the moral sentiments, the parent fountain from which this goodly Universe flows as a wave.

2. HENRY DAVID THOREAU, 1817–1862

[Obviously, the one of all the Transcendental society who carried Emerson's injunctions about "self-reliance" to such extremes of individualism that he can hardly be accounted a member of even that society, let alone of any more formal organization, is Henry Thoreau. He frequently announced his resignation from all societies he never joined, in the *Week*, in *Walden*, and most explicitly with "Resistance to Civil Government" (in Elizabeth Peabody's anthology of *Æsthetic Papers*, Boston, 1849). This last essay, frequently republished as "Civil Disobedience," is his classic statement, and at this point should be consulted. For reasons aforesaid, I refuse to excerpt from the unified *Walden*, and even (except for the few verses) from the discursive *Week*; and then, since "Civil Disobedience" appears by now in almost all anthologies, I elect to call attention to the less known but equally viable "Life Without Principle." This, the late product of the most principled of the Transcendentally unprincipled, appeared in *The Atlantic Monthly* for October, 1863. Like *Walking* of the previous June, it is a mosaic out of his *Journal*, mostly from the years 1850 to 1855. How much of the finishing form is his and how much is his editor's we do not know; however, since the compilation does come from the recesses of his intense and private thinking, the result must be read as the essence of Henry Thoreau.

Topical references are to the times of the *Journal* entries, not to the year of posthumous publication. When he was writing, the gold rush to California was still in progress. Many of the rushers took the route through the "Isthmus of Darien" (*i.e* Panama), and there perished of terrible fevers. "Burker's Guide" is an invention of Thoreau's: a "burker" in contemporaneous slang was one who murdered his victims in order to steal the bodies for dissection. Dr. Kane is the American Arctic explorer (1820–1857), who led two expeditions in a vain effort to find his predecessor, the English Sir John Franklin (1786–1847) who perished on his last venture into Labrador. Louis Kossuth (1802–1894) is the Hungarian patriot whose visit to America in 1851 produced a storm of patriotic fervor and of hostile criticism. "The Spirit of Lodin" refers to a debate in James Macpherson's Ossianic poem *Carricthura* (1761). William Lewis Herndon was a Virginian who, as an American naval officer, explored the Amazon and wrote approvingly of Brazilian slavery.

When Thoreau's piece was published, the joke about "the poor President" was taken to mean Abraham Lincoln; in the *Journal*, the original passage clearly has in mind Hawthorne's friend, President Franklin Pierce. The wrecked ship, whose futile cargo Thoreau found on the shore, is the *Elizabeth*, on which Margaret Fuller was lost.

LIFE WITHOUT PRINCIPLE

At a lyceum, not long since, I felt that the lecturer had

chosen a theme too foreign to himself, and so failed to interest me as much as he might have done. He described things not in or near to his heart, but toward his extremities and superficies. There was, in this sense, no truly central or centralizing thought in the lecture. I would have had him deal with his privatest experience, as the poet does. The greatest compliment that was ever paid me was when one asked me what I *thought*, and attended to my answer. I am surprised, as well as delighted, when this happens, it is such a rare use he would make of me, as if he were acquainted with the tool. Commonly, if men want anything of me, it is only to know how many acres I make of their land—since I am a surveyor—or, at most, what trivial news I have burdened myself with. They never will go to law for my meat; they prefer the shell. A man once came a considerable distance to ask me to lecture on Slavery; but on conversing with him, I found that he and his clique expected seven eighths of the lecture to be theirs, and only one eighth mine; so I declined. I take it for granted, when I am invited to lecture anywhere—for I have had a little experience in that business—that there is a desire to hear what I *think* on some subject, though I may be the greatest fool in the country—and not that I should say pleasant things merely, or such as the audience will assent to; and I resolve, accordingly, that I will give them a strong dose of myself. They have sent for me, and engaged to pay for me, and I am determined that they shall have me, though I bore them beyond all precedent.

So now I would say something similar to you, my readers. Since *you* are my readers, and I have not been much of a traveler, I will not talk about people a thousand miles off, but come as near home as I can. As the time is short, I will leave out all the flattery, and retain all the criticism.

Let us consider the way in which we spend our lives.

This world is a place of business. What an infinite bustle! I am awaked almost every night by the panting of the locomotive. It interrupts my dreams. There is no sabbath. It would be glorious to see mankind at leisure for once.

It is nothing but work, work, work. I cannot easily buy a blank-book to write thoughts in; they are commonly ruled for dollars and cents. An Irishman, seeing me make a minute in the fields, took it for granted that I was calculating my wages. If a man was tossed out of a window when an infant, and so made a cripple for life, or scared out of his wits by the Indians, it is regretted chiefly because he was thus incapacitated for—business! I think that there is nothing, not even crime, more opposed to poetry, to philosophy, ay, to life itself, than this incessant business.

There is a coarse and boisterous money-making fellow in the outskirts of our town, who is going to build a bank-wall under the hill along the edge of his meadow. The powers have put this into his head to keep him out of mischief, and he wishes me to spend three weeks digging there with him. The result will be that he will perhaps get some more money to hoard, and leave for his heirs to spend foolishly. If I do this, most will commend me as an industrious and hard-working man; but if I choose to devote myself to certain labors which yield more real profit, though but little money, they may be inclined to look on me as an idler. Nevertheless, as I do not need the police of meaningless labor to regulate me, and do not see anything absolutely praiseworthy in this fellow's undertaking any more than in many an enterprise of our own or foreign governments, however amusing it may be to him or them, I prefer to finish my education at a different school.

If a man walk in the woods for love of them half of each day, he is in danger of being regarded as a loafer; but if he spends his whole day as a speculator, shearing off those woods and making earth bald before her time, he is esteemed an industrious and enterprising citizen. As if a town had no interest in its forests but to cut them down!

Most men would feel insulted if it were proposed to employ them in throwing stones over a wall, and then in throwing them back, merely that they might earn their wages. But many are no more worthily employed now.

For instance: just after sunrise, one summer morning, I noticed one of my neighbors walking beside his team, which was slowly drawing a heavy hewn stone swung under the axle, surrounded by an atmosphere of industry—his day's work begun—his brow commenced to sweat—a reproach to all sluggards and idlers—pausing abreast the shoulders of his oxen, and half turning round with a flourish of his merciful whip, while they gained their length on him. And I thought: Such is the labor which the American Congress exists to protect—honest, manly toil—honest as the day is long—that makes his bread taste sweet, and keeps society sweet—which all men respect and have consecrated; one of the sacred band, doing the needful but irksome drudgery. Indeed, I felt a slight reproach, because I observed this from a window, and was not abroad and stirring about a similar business. The day went by, and at evening I passed the yard of another neighbor, who keeps many servants, and spends much money foolishly, while he adds nothing to the common stock, and there I saw the stone of the morning lying beside a whimsical structure intended to adorn this Lord Timothy Dexter's premises, and the dignity forthwith departed from the teamster's labor, in my eyes. In my opinion, the sun was made to light worthier toil than this. I may add that his employer has since run off, in debt to a good part of the town, and, after passing through Chancery, has settled somewhere else, there to become once more a patron of the arts.

The ways by which you may get money almost without exception lead downward. To have done anything by which you earned money *merely* is to have been truly idle or worse. If the laborer gets no more than the wages which his employer pays him, he is cheated, he cheats himself. If you would get money as a writer or lecturer, you must be popular, which is to go down perpendicularly. Those services which the community will most readily pay for, it is most disagreeable to render. You are paid for being something less than a man. The state does not commonly reward a genius any more wisely. Even the poet laureate would rather not have to celebrate the accidents of royalty.

He must be bribed with a pipe of wine; and perhaps another poet is called away from his muse to gauge that very pipe. As for my own business, even that kind of surveying which I could do with most satisfaction, my employers do not want. They would prefer that I should do my work coarsely and not too well, ay, not well enough. When I observe that there are different ways of surveying, my employer commonly asks which will give him the most land, not which is most correct. I once invented a rule for measuring cord-wood, and tried to introduce it in Boston; but the measurer there told me that sellers did not wish to have their wood measured correctly—that he was already too accurate for them, and therefore they commonly got their wood measured in Charlestown before crossing the bridge.

The aim of the laborer should be, not to get his living, to get "a good job," but to perform well a certain work; and, even in a pecuniary sense, it would be economy for a town to pay its laborers so well that they would not feel that they were working for low ends, as for a livelihood merely, but for scientific, or even moral ends. Do not hire a man who does your work for money, but him who does it for love of it.

It is remarkable that there are few men so well employed, so much to their minds, but that a little money or fame would commonly buy them off from their present pursuit. I see advertisements for *active* young men, as if activity were the whole of a young man's capital. Yet I have been surprised when one has with confidence proposed to me, a grown man, to embark in some enterprise of his, as if I had absolutely nothing to do, my life having been a complete failure hitherto. What a doubtful compliment this to pay to me! As if he had met me half-way across the ocean beating up against the wind, but bound nowhere, and proposed to me to go along with him! If I did, what do you think the underwriters would say? No, no! I am not without employment at this stage of the voyage. To tell the truth, I saw an advertisement for able-bodied seamen, when I was a boy, sauntering in my native port, and as soon as I came of age I embarked.

The community has no bribe that will tempt a wise man. You may raise enough money to tunnel a mountain, but you cannot raise money enough to hire a man who is minding *his own* business. An efficient and valuable man does what he can, whether the community pay him for it or not. The inefficient offer their inefficiency to the highest bidder, and are forever expecting to be put into office. One would suppose that they were rarely disappointed.

Perhaps I am more than usually jealous with respect to my freedom. I feel that my connection with and obligation to society are still very slight and transient. Those slight labors which afford me a livelihood, and by which it is allowed that I am to some extent serviceable to my contemporaries, are as yet commonly a pleasure to me, and I am not often reminded that they are a necessity. So far I am successful. But I foresee that if my wants should be much increased, the labor required to supply them would become a drudgery. If I should sell both my forenoons and afternoons to society, as most appear to do, I am sure that for me there would be nothing left worth living for. I trust that I shall never thus sell my birthright for a mess of pottage. I wish to suggest that a man may be very industrious, and yet not spend his time well. There is no more fatal blunderer than he who consumes the greater part of his life getting his living. All great enterprises are self-supporting. The poet, for instance, must sustain his body by his poetry, as a steam planing-mill feeds its boilers with the shavings it makes. You must get your living by loving. But as it is said of the merchants that ninety-seven in a hundred fail, so the life of men generally, tried by this standard, is a failure, and bankruptcy may be surely prophesied.

Merely to come into the world the heir of a fortune is not to be born, but to be still-born, rather. To be supported by the charity of friends, or a government pension—provided you continue to breathe—by whatever fine synonyms you describe these relations, is to go into the almshouse. On Sundays the poor debtor goes to church to take an account of stock, and find, of course, that his outgoes have been greater than his income. In the Catholic Church, especially, they go into chancery, make a clean confession, give up all, and think to start again. Thus men will lie on their backs, talking about the fall of man, and never make an effort to get up.

As for the comparative demand which men make on life, it is an important difference between two, that the one is satisfied with a level success, that his marks can all be hit by point-blank shots, but the other, however low and unsuccessful his life may be, constantly elevates his aim, though at a very slight angle to the horizon. I should much rather be the last man—though, as the Orientals say, "Greatness doth not approach him who is forever looking down; and all those who are looking high are growing poor."

It is remarkable that there is little or nothing to be remembered written on the subject of getting a living; how to make getting a living not merely honest and honorable, but altogether inviting and glorious; for if *getting* a living is not so, then living is not. One would think, from looking at literature, that this question had never disturbed a solitary individual's musings. Is it that men are too much disgusted with their experience to speak of it? The lesson of value which money teaches, which the Author of the Universe has taken so much pains to teach us, we are inclined to skip altogether. As for the means of living, it is wonderful how indifferent men of all classes are about it, even reformers, so called—whether they inherit, or earn, or steal it. I think that Society has done nothing for us in this respect, or at least has undone what she has done. Cold and hunger seem more friendly to my nature than those methods which men have adopted and advise to ward them off.

The title *wise* is, for the most part, falsely applied. How can one be a wise man, if he does not know any better how to live than other men—if he is only more cunning and intellectually subtle? Does Wisdom work in a tread-mill? or does she teach how to succeed *by her example?* Is there any such thing as wisdom not applied to life? Is she merely the miller who grinds the finest logic? Is it pertinent to ask if Plato got his *living* in a better way or more successfully than his contemporaries—or did he succumb to the difficulties of life like other men? Did he seem to prevail over some of them merely by indifference, or by assuming grand airs? or find it easier to live, because his aunt remembered him in her will? The ways in which most men get their living, that is, live, are mere makeshifts, and a shirking of the real business of life—chiefly because they do not know, but partly because they do not mean, any better.

The rush to California, for instance, and the attitude, not merely of merchants, but of philosophers and prophets, so called, in relation to it, reflect the greatest disgrace on mankind. That so many are ready to live by luck, and so get the means of commanding the labor of others less lucky, without contributing any value to society! And that is called enterprise! I know of no more startling development of the immorality of trade, and all the common modes of getting a living. The philosophy and poetry and religion of such a mankind are not worth the dust of a puffball. The hog that gets his living by rooting, stirring up the soil so, would be ashamed of such company. If I could command the wealth of all the worlds by lifting my finger, I would not pay *such* a price for it. Even Mahomet knew that God did not make this world in jest. It makes God to be a moneyed gentleman who scatters a handful of pennies in order to see mankind scramble for them. The world's raffle! A subsistence in the domains of Nature a thing to be raffled for! What a comment, what a satire, on our institutions! The conclusion will be, that mankind will hang itself upon a tree. And have all the precepts in all the Bibles taught men only this? and is the last and most admirable invention of the human race only an improved muck-rake? Is this the ground on which Orientals and Occidentals meet? Did God direct us so to get our living, digging where we never planted—and He would, perchance, reward us with lumps of gold?

God gave the righteous man a certificate entitling him to food and raiment, but the unrighteous man found a facsimile of the same in God's coffers, and appropriated it, and obtained food and raiment like the former. It is one of the most extensive systems of counterfeiting the world has seen. I did not know that mankind was suffering for want of gold. I have seen a little of it. I know that it is very malleable, but not so malleable as wit. A grain of gold will gild a great surface, but not so much as a grain of wisdom.

The gold-digger in the ravines of the mountains is as much a gambler as his fellow in the saloons of San Francisco. What difference does it make whether you shake dirt or shake dice? If you win, society is the loser. The gold-digger is the enemy of the honest laborer, whatever checks and compensations there may be. It is not enough to tell me that you worked hard to get your gold. So does the Devil work hard. The way of transgressors may be hard in many respects. The humblest observer who goes to the mines sees and says that gold-digging is of the character of a lottery; the gold thus obtained is not the same thing with the wages of honest toil. But, practically, he forgets what he has seen, for he has seen only the fact, not the principle, and goes into trade there, that is, buys a ticket in what commonly proves another lottery, where the fact is not so obvious.

After reading Howitt's account of the Australian gold-diggings one evening, I had in my mind's eye, all night, the numerous valleys, with their streams, all cut up with foul pits, from ten to one hundred feet deep, and half a dozen feet across, as close as they can be dug, and partly filled with water—the locality to which men furiously rush to probe for their fortunes—uncertain where they shall break ground—not knowing but the gold is under their camp itself—sometimes digging one hundred and sixty feet before they strike the vein, or then missing it by a foot—turned into demons, and regardless of each others' rights, in their thirst for riches—whole valleys, for thirty miles, suddenly honeycombed by the pits of the miners, so that even hundreds are drowned in them—standing in water, and covered with mud and clay, they work night and day, dying of exposure and disease. Having read this, and partly forgotten it, I was thinking, accidently, of my own unsatisfactory life, doing as others do; and with that vision of the diggings still before me, I asked why I might not be washing some gold daily, though it were only the finest particles—why I might not sink a shaft down to the gold within me, and work that mine. *There* is a Ballarat, a Bendigo for you—what though it were a sulky-gully? At rate, I might pursue some path, however solitary and narrow and crooked, in which I could walk with love and reverence. Wherever a man separates from the multitude, and goes his own way in this mood, there indeed is a fork in the road, though ordinary travelers may see only a gap in the paling. His solitary path across lots will turn out the *higher way* of the two.

Men rush to California and Australia as if the true gold were to be found in that direction; but that is to go to the very opposite extreme to where it lies. They go prospecting farther and farther away from the true lead, and are most unfortunate when they think themselves most successful. Is not our *native* soil auriferous? Does not a stream from the golden mountains flow through our native valley? and has not this for more than geologic ages been bringing down the shining particles and forming the nuggets for us? Yet, strange to tell, if a digger steal away, prospecting for this true gold, into the unexplored solitudes around us, there is no danger that any will dog his steps, and endeavor to supplant him. He may claim and undermine the whole valley even, both the cultivated and the uncultivated portions, his whole life long in peace, for no one will ever dispute his claim. They will not mind his cradles or his toms. He is not confined to a claim twelve feet square, as at Ballarat, but may mine anywhere, and wash the whole wide world in his tom.

Howitt says of the man who found the great nugget which weighed twenty-eight pounds, at the Bendigo diggings in Australia: "He soon began to drink; got a horse, and rode all about, generally at full gallop, and, when he met people, called out to inquire if they knew who he was, and then kindly informed them that he was 'the bloody wretch that had found the nugget.' At last he rode full speed against a tree, and nearly knocked his brains out." I think, however, there was no danger of that, for he had already knocked his brains out against the nugget. Howitt adds, "He is a hopelessly ruined man." But he is a type of the class. They are all fast men. Hear some of the names of the places where they dig: "Jackass Flat"— "Sheep's-Head Gully"—"Murderer's Bar," etc. Is there no satire in these names? Let them carry their ill-gotten wealth where they will, I am thinking it will still be "Jackass Flat," if not "Murderer's Bar," where they live.

The last resource of our energy has been the robbing of graveyards on the Isthmus of Darien, an enterprise which appears to be but in its infancy; for, according to late accounts, an act has passed its second reading in the legislature of New Granada, regulating this kind of mining; and a correspondent of the *Tribune* writes: "In the dry season, when the weather will permit of the country being properly prospected, no doubt other rich *guacas* [that is, graveyards] will be found." To emigrants he says: "Do not come before December; take the Isthmus route in preference to the Boca del Toro one; bring no useless baggage, and do not cumber yourself with a tent; but a good pair of blankets will be necessary; a pick, shovel, and axe of good material will be almost all that is required:" advice which might have been taken from the "Burker's Guide." And he concludes with this line in Italics and small capitals: "*If you are doing well at home,* STAY THERE." which may fairly be interpreted to mean, "If you are getting a good living by robbing graveyards at home, stay there."

But why go to California for a text? She is the child of New England, bred at her own school and church.

It is remarkable that among all the preachers there are so few moral teachers. The prophets are employed in excusing the ways of men. The most reverend seniors, the *illuminati* of the age, tell me, with a gracious, reminiscent smile, betwixt an aspiration and a shudder, not to be too tender about these things—to lump all that, that is, make a lump of gold of it. The highest advice I have heard on these subjects was groveling. The burden of it was—It is not worth your while to undertake to reform the world in this particular. Do not ask how your bread is buttered; it will make you sick, if you do—and the like. A man had better starve at once than lose his innocence in the process of getting his bread. If within the sophisticated man there is not an unsophisticated one, then he is but one of the devil's angels. As we grow old, we live more coarsely, we relax a little in our disciplines, and, to some extent, cease to obey our finest instincts. But we should be fastidious to the extreme of sanity, disregarding the gibes of those who are more unfortunate than ourselves.

In our science and philosophy, even, there is commonly no true and absolute account of things. The spirit of sect and bigotry has planted its hoof amid the stars. You have only to discuss the problem, whether the stars are inhabited or not, in order to discover it. Why must we daub the heavens as well as the earth? It was an unfortunate discovery that Dr. Kane was a Mason, and that Sir John Franklin was another. But it was a more cruel suggestion that possibly that was the reason why the former went in search of the latter. There is not a popular magazine in this country that would dare to print a child's thought on important subjects without comment. It must be submitted to the D.D.'s. I would it were the chickadee-dees.

You come from attending the funeral of mankind to attend to a natural phenomenon. A little thought is sexton to all the world.

I hardly know an *intellectual* man, even, who is so broad and truly liberal that you can think aloud in his society. Most with whom you endeavor to talk soon come to a stand against some institution in which they appear to hold stock—that is, some particular, not universal, way of viewing things. They will continually thrust their own low roof, with its narrow skylight, between you and the sky, when it is the unobstructed heavens you would view. Get out of the way with your cobwebs; wash your windows, I say! In some lyceums they tell me that they have voted to exclude the subject of religion. But how do I know what their religion is, and when I am near to or far from it? I have walked into such an arena and done my best to make a clean breast of what religion I have experienced, and the audience never suspected what I was about. The lecture was as harmless as moonshine to them. Whereas, if I had read to them the biography of the greatest scamps in history, they might have thought that I had written the lives of the deacons of their church. Ordinarily, the inquiry is, Where did you come from? or, Where are you going? That was a more pertinent question which I overheard one my auditors put to another once—"What does he lecture for?" It made me quake in my shoes.

To speak impartially, the best men that I know are not serene, a world in themselves. For the most part, they dwell in forms, and flatter and study effect only more finely than the rest. We select granite for the underpinning of our houses and barns; we build fences of stone: but we do not ourselves rest on an underpinning of granitic truth, the lowest primitive rock. Our sills are rotten. What stuff is the man made of who is not coexistent in our thought with the purest and subtilest truth? I often accuse my finest acquaintances of an immense frivolty; for, while there are manners and compliments we do not meet, we do not teach one another the lessons of honesty and sincerity that the brutes do, or of steadiness and solidity that the rocks do. The fault is commonly mutual, however; for we do not habitually demand any more of each other.

That excitement about Kossuth, consider how characteristic, but superficial, it was!—only another kind of politics or dancing. Men were making speeches to him all over the country, but each expressed only the thought, or the want of thought, of the multitude. No man stood on truth. They were merely banded together, as usual one leaning on another, and all together on nothing; as the Hindoos made the world rest on an elephant, the elephant on a tortoise, and the tortoise on a serpent, and had nothing to put under the serpent. For all fruit of that stir we have the Kossuth hat.

Just so hollow and ineffectual, for the most part, is our ordinary conversation. Surface meets surface. When our life ceases to be inward and private, conversation degenerates into mere gossip. We rarely meet a man who can tell us any news which he has not read in a newspaper, or been told by his neighbor; and, for the most part, the only difference between us and our fellow is that he has seen the newspaper, or been out to tea, and we have not. In proportion as our inward life fails, we go more constantly and desperately to the post office. You may depend on it, that the poor fellow who walks away with the greatest number of letters, proud of his extensive correspondence, has not heard from himself this long while.

I do not know but it is too much to read one newspaper a week. I have tried it recently, and for so long it seems to me that I have not dwelt in my native region. The sun, the clouds, the snow, the trees say not so much to me. You cannot serve two masters. It requires more than a day's devotion to know and to possess the wealth of a day.

We may well be ashamed to tell what things we have read or heard in our day. I do not know why my news should be so trivial—considering what one's dreams and expectations are, why the developments should be so paltry. The news we hear, for the most part, is not news to our genius. It is the stalest repetition. You are often tempted to ask why such stress is laid on a particular experience which you have had—that, after twenty-five years, you should meet Hobbins, Registrar of Deeds, again on the sidewalk. Have you not budged an inch, then? Such is the daily news. Its facts appear to float in the atmosphere, insignificant as the sporules of fungi, and impinge on some neglected *thallus*, or surface of our minds, which affords a basis for them, and hence a parasitic growth. We should wash ourselves clean of such news. Of what consequence, though our planet explode, if there is no character involved in the explosion? In health we have not the least curiosity about such events. We do not live for idle amusement. I would not run round a corner to see the world blow up.

All summer, and far into the autumn, perchance, you unconsciously went by the newspapers and the news, and now you find it was because the morning and the evening were full of news to you. Your walks were full of incidents. You attended, not to the affairs of Europe, but to your own affairs in Massachusetts fields. If you chance to live and move and have your being in that thin stratum in which the events that make the news transpire —thinner than the paper on which it is printed—then these things will fill the world for you: but if you soar above or dive below that plane, you cannot remember nor be reminded of them. Really to see the sun rise or go down every day, so to relate ourselves to a universal fact, would preserve us sane forever. Nations! What are nations? Tartars, and Huns, and Chinamen! Like insects they swarm. The historian strives in vain to make them memorable. It is for want of a man that there are so many men. It is individuals that populate the world. Any man thinking may say with the Spirit of Lodin—

> "I look down from my height on nations,
> And they become ashes before me—
> Calm is my dwelling in the clouds;
> Pleasant are the great fields of my rest."

Pray, let us live without being drawn by dogs, Esquimaux-fashion, tearing over hill and dale, and biting each other's ears.

Not without a slight shudder at the danger, I often perceive how near I had come to admitting into my mind the details of some trivial affair—the news of the street; and I am astonished to observe how willing men are to lumber their minds with such rubbish—to permit idle rumors and incidents of the most insignificant kind to intrude on ground which should be sacred to thought. Shall the mind be a public arena, where the affairs of the street and the gossip of the tea-table chiefly are discussed? Or shall it be a quarter of heaven itself— hypæthral temple, consecrated to the service of the gods? I find it so difficult to dispose of the few facts which to me are significant, that I hesitate to burden my attention with those which are insignificant, which only a divine mind could illustrate. Such is, for the most part, the news in newspapers and conversation. It is important to preserve the mind's chastity in this respect. Think of admitting the details of a single case of the criminal court into our thoughts, to stalk profanely through their very *sanctum sanctorum* for an hour, ay, for many hours! to make a very barroom of the mind's inmost apartment, as if for so long the dust of the street had occupied us—the very street itself, with all its travel, its bustle, and filth, had passed through our thoughts' shrine! Would it not be an intellectual and moral suicide? When I have been compelled to sit spectator and auditor in a court-room for some hours, and have seen my neighbors, who were not compelled, stealing in from time to time, and tiptoeing about with washed hands and faces, it has appeared to my mind's eye, that, when they took off their hats, their ears suddenly expanded into vast hoppers for sound, between which even their narrow heads were crowded. Like the vanes of windmills, they caught the broad but shallow stream of sound, which, after a few titilating gyrations in their coggy brains, passed out the other side. I wondered if, when they got home, they were as careful to wash their ears as before their hands and faces. It has seemed to me, at such a time, that the auditors and the witnesses, the jury and the counsel, the judge and the criminal at the bar—if I may presume him guilty before he is convicted—were all equally criminal, and a thunderbolt might be expected to descend and consume them all together.

By all kinds of traps and signboards, threatening the extreme penalty of the divine law, exclude such trespassers from the only ground which can be sacred to you! It is so hard to forget what it is worse than useless to remember! If I am to be a thoroughfare, I prefer that it be of the mountain brooks, the Parnassian streams, and not the town sewers. There is inspiration, that gossip which comes to the ear of the attentive mind from the courts of heaven. There is the profane and stale revelation of the barroom and the police court. The same ear is fitted to receive both communications. Only the character of the hearer determines to which it shall be open, and to which closed. I believe that the mind can be permanently profaned by the habit of attending to trivial things, so that all our thoughts shall be tinged with triviality. Our very intellect shall be macadamized, as it were—its foundation broken into fragments for the wheels of travel to roll over; and if you would know what will make the most durable pavement, surpassing rolled stones, spruce blocks, and asphaltum, you have only to look into some of our minds which have been subjected to this treatment so long.

If we have thus desecrated ourselves—as who has not—the remedy will be by wariness and devotion to reconsecrate ourselves, and make once more a fane of the mind. We should treat our minds, that is, ourselves, as innocent and ingenuous children, whose guardians we are, and be careful what objects and subjects we thrust on their attention. Read not the *Times*. Read the Eternities. Conventionalities are at length as bad as impurities. Even the facts of science may dust the mind by their dryness, unless they are in a sense effaced each morning, or rather rendered fertile by the dews of fresh and living truth. Knowledge does not come to us by details, but in flashes of light from heaven. Yes, every thought that passes through the mind helps to wear and tear it, and to deepen the ruts, which, as in the streets of Pompeii, evince how much it has been used. How many things there are concerning which we might well deliberate whether we had better know them—had better let their peddling-carts be driven, even at the slowest trot or walk, over that bridge of glorious span by which we trust to pass at last from the farthest brink of time to the nearest shore of eternity! Have we no culture, no refinement—but skill only to live coarsely and serve the Devil—to acquire a little worldly wealth, or fame, or liberty, and make a false show with it, as if we were all husk and shell, with no tender and living kernel to us? Shall our institutions be like those chestnut burs which contain abortive nuts, perfect only to prick the fingers?

America is said to be the arena on which the battle of freedom is to be fought; but surely it cannot be freedom in a merely political sense that is meant. Even if we grant

that the American has freed himself from a political tyrant,
he is still the slave of an economical and moral tyrant.
Now that the republic—the *res-publica*—has been settled,
it is time to look after the *res-private*—the private state—
to see, as the Roman senate charged its consuls, *"ne quid
res*-PRIVATA *detrimenti caperet,"* that the *private* state
receive no detriment.

Do we call this the land of the free? What is it to be
free from King George and continue the slaves of King
Prejudice? What is it to be born free and not to live free?
What is the value of any political freedom, but as a means
to moral freedom? Is it a freedom to be slaves, or a freedom to be free, of which we boast? We are a nation of
politicians, concerned about the outmost defenses only of
freedom. It is our children's children who may perchance
be really free. We tax ourselves unjustly. There is a part of
us which is not represented. It is taxation without representation. We quarter troops, we quarter fools and cattle
of all sorts upon ourselves. We quarter our gross bodies
on our poor souls, till the former eat up all the latter's substance.

With respect to a true culture and manhood, we are
essentially provincial still, not metropolitan—mere Jona-
thans. We are provincial, because we do not find at
home our standards; because we do not worship truth,
but the reflection of truth; because we are warped and
narrowed by an exclusive devotion to trade and commerce
and manufactures and agriculture and the like, which are
but means, and not the end.

So is the English Parliament provincial. Mere country
bumpkins, they betray themselves, when any more important question arises for them to settle, the Irish question, for instance—the English question why did I not
say? Their natures are subdued to what they work in.
Their "good breeding" respects only secondary objects.
The finest manners in the world are awkwardness and
fatuity when contrasted with a finer intelligence. They appear but as the fashions of past days—mere courtliness,
knee-buckles and small-clothes, out of date. It is the vice,
but not the excellence of manners, that they are con-

tinually being deserted by the character; they are cast-off clothes or shells, claiming the respect which belonged to the living creature. You are presented with the shells instead of the meat, and it is no excuse generally, that, in the case of some fishes, the shells are of more worth than the meat. The man who thrusts his manners upon me does as if he were to insist on introducing me to his cabinet of curiosities, when I wished to see himself. It was not in this sense that the poet Decker called Christ "the first true gentleman that ever breathed." I repeat that in this sense the most splendid court in Christendom is provincial, having authority to consult about Transalpine interests only, and not the affairs of Rome. A prætor or proconsul would suffice to settle the questions which absorb the attention of the English Parliament and the American Congress.

Government and legislation! these I thought were respectable professions. We have heard of heaven-born Numas, Lycurguses, and Solons, in the history of the world, whose *names* at least may stand for ideal legislators; but think of legislating to *regulate* the breeding of slaves, or the exportation of tobacco! What have divine legislators to do with the exportation or the importation of tobacco? What humane ones with the breeding of slaves? Suppose you were to submit the question to any son of God—and has He no children in the Nineteenth Century? Is it a family which is extinct—in what condition would you get it again? What shall a State like Virginia say for itself at the last day, in which these have been the principal, the staple productions? What ground is there for patriotism in such a State? I derive my facts from statistical tables which the States themselves have published.

A commerce that whitens every sea in quest of nuts and raisins, and makes slaves of its sailors for this purpose! I saw, the other day, a vessel which had been wrecked, and many lives lost, and her cargo of rags, juniper berries, and bitter almonds were strewn along the shore. It seemed hardly worth the while to tempt the dangers of the sea between Leghorn and New York for the sake of a cargo of juniper berries and bitter almonds. America sending to the Old World for her bitters! Is not the sea-brine, is not shipwreck, bitter enough to make the cup of life go down here? Yet such, to a great extent, is our boasted commerce; and there are those who style themselves statesmen and philosophers who are so blind as to think that progress and civilization depend on precisely this kind of interchange and activity—the activity of flies about a molasses-hogshead. Very well, observes one, if men were oysters. And very well, answer I, if men were mosquitoes.

Lieutenant Herndon, whom our government sent to explore the Amazon, and, it is said, to extend the area of slavery, observed that there was wanting there "an industrious and active population, who know what the comforts of life are, and who have artificial wants to draw out the great resources of the country." But what are the "artificial wants" to be encouraged? Not the love of luxuries, like the tobacco and slaves of, I believe, his native Virginia, nor the ice and granite and other material wealth of our native New England; nor are "the great resources of a country" that fertility or barrenness of soil which produces these. The chief want, in every State that I have been into, was a high and earnest purpose of its inhabitants. This alone draws out "the great resources" of Nature, and at last taxes her beyond her resources; for man naturally dies out of her. When we want culture more than potatoes, and illumination more than sugar-plums, then the great resources of a world are taxed and drawn out, and the result, or staple production, is, not slaves, nor operatives, but men—those rare fruits called heroes, saints, poets, philosophers, and redeemers.

In short, as a snow-drift is formed where there is a lull in the wind, so, one would say, where there is a lull of truth, an institution springs up. But the truth blows right on over it, nevertheless, and at length blows it down.

What is called politics is comparatively something so superficial and inhuman, that practically I have never fairly recognized that it concerns me at all. The newspapers, I perceive, devote some of their columns specially to politics or government without charge; and this, one would say, is all that saves it; but as I love literature and to some extent the truth also, I never read those columns at any rate. I do not wish to blunt my sense of right so much. I have not got to answer for having read a single President's Message. A strange age of the world this, when empires, kingdoms, and republics come a-begging to a private man's door, and utter their complaints at his elbow! I cannot take up a newspaper but I find that some wretched government or other, hard pushed and on its last legs, is interceding with me, the reader, to vote for it—more importunate than an Italian beggar; and if I have a mind to look at its certificate, made, perchance, by some benevolent merchant's clerk, or the skipper that brought it over, for it cannot speak a word of English itself, I shall probably read of the eruption of some Vesuvius, or the overflowing of some Po, true or forged, which brought it into this condition. I do not hesitate, in such a case, to suggest work, or the almshouse; or why not keep its castle in silence, as I do commonly? The poor President, what with preserving his popularity and doing his duty, is completely bewildered. The newspapers are the ruling power. Any other government is reduced to a few marines at Fort Independence. If a man neglects to read the *Daily Times,* government will go down on its knees to him, for this is the only treason in these days.

Those things which now most engage the attention of men, as politics and the daily routine, are, it is true, vital functions of human society, but should be unconsciously performed, like the corresponding functions of the physical body. They are *infra*-human, a kind of vegetation. I sometimes awake to a half-consciousness of them going on about me, as a man may become conscious of some of the processes of digestion in a morbid state, and so have the dyspepsia, as it is called. It is as if a thinker submitted himself to be rasped by the great gizzard of creation. Politics is, as it were, the gizzard of society, full of grit and gravel, and the two political parties are its two opposite halves—sometimes split into quarters, it may be, which grind on each other. Not only individuals, but states, have thus a confirmed dyspepsia, which expresses itself, you can imagine by what sort of eloquence. Thus our life is not altogether a forgetting, but also, alas! to a great extent, a remembering, of that which we should never have been conscious of, certainly not in our waking hours. Why should we not meet, not always as dyspeptics, to tell our bad dreams, but sometimes as *eu*peptics, to congratulate each other on the ever-glorious morning? I do not make an exorbitant demand, surely.

3. MARGARET FULLER, 1810–1850

[After she left America, once she became a partisan of Mazzini's revolution in Rome, Margaret Fuller qualified as a "liberal" in the Continental sense of the term. We may doubt that the other Transcendentalists, though everywhere the champions of freedom, ever quite understood, or even were prepared intellectually to cope with, the European revolutions of 1848. They had no clues, out of their American experience, for comprehending what was meant by fighting Metternich, nor could they even begin to imagine the wiles of a Louis Napoleon. Margaret learned the bitter lesson of Europe: she would indeed have had her work cut out for her trying to explain it in public lectures to Americans of 1850.

Yet, though she came from the intensely provincial school of New England, her career in Rome should not be surprising. "Ardent and uplifted" the eager band might appear to the next generation of sophisticates, and in that perspective Margaret Fuller's voice sound less authentic than that of the mocking Caroline Sturgis; yet even in that primitive context, and with so little to rebel against, Transcendentalism *was* a revolutionary creed. Before she went to Europe, before she met George Sand, Margaret Fuller became a major spokesman for the century's liberality by publishing, in 1845, *Woman in the Nineteenth Century.*

She had put the substance of her thesis in an article for *The Dial* of July, 1843 (to which she refers at the beginning of this extract), then called "The Great Lawsuit."

The book is somewhat more dithyrambic than the article; I quote only its concluding pages. She was not one to submit herself, any more than Thoreau would yield himself, to logical progression.

It is lamentable that in subsequent conventions of feminists, Margaret Fuller became stereotyped as a pioneer of "votes for women." The vote was incidental to her grand design. Along with her initial *cri du coeur* in *The Dial* and throughout the composition of this volume, she was also the critic who did the piece on Goethe, who was proving her mettle by her work on the *Tribune,* and who always, despite her emotionalism and her unrestrained rhetoric, could see that the cause of "women's rights" was only a subordinate part of the most comprehensive program of nineteenth-century liberation. She was a great radical, and so we should remember her.]

WOMAN IN THE NINETEENTH CENTURY

In the earlier tract I was told I did not make my meaning sufficiently clear. In this I have consequently tried to illustrate it in various ways, and may have been guilty of much repetition. Yet, as I am anxious to leave no room for doubt, I shall venture to retrace, once more, the scope of my design in points, as was done in old-fashioned sermons.

Man is a being of two-fold relations, to nature beneath, and intelligences above him. The earth is his school, if not his birth-place; God his object; life and thought his means of interpreting nature, and aspiring to God.

Only a fraction of this purpose is accomplished in the life of any one man. Its entire accomplishment is to be hoped only from the sum of the lives of men, or Man considered as a whole.

As this whole has one soul and one body, any injury or obstruction to a part, or to the meanest member, affects the whole. Man can never be perfectly happy or virtuous, till all men are so.

To address Man wisely, you must not forget that his

life is partly animal, subject to the same laws with Nature.

But you cannot address him wisely unless you consider him still more as soul, and appreciate the conditions and destiny of soul.

The growth of Man is two-fold, masculine and feminine.

So far as these two methods can be distinguished, they are so as:

Energy and Harmony;

Power and Beauty;

Intellect and Love;

or by some such rude classification; for we have not language primitive and pure enough to express such ideas with precision.

Those two sides are supposed to be expressed in Man and Woman, that is, as the more and the less, for the faculties have not been given pure to either, but only in preponderance. There are also exceptions in great number, such as men of far more beauty than power, and the reverse. But, as a general rule, it seems to have been the intention to give a preponderance on the one side, that is called masculine, and on the other, one that is called feminine.

There cannot be a doubt that, if these two developments were in perfect harmony, they would correspond to and fulfil one another, like hemispheres, or the tenor and bass in music.

But there is no perfect harmony in human nature; and the two parts answer one another only now and then; or, if there be a persistent consonance, it can only be traced at long intervals, instead of discoursing an obvious melody.

What is the cause of this?

Man, in the order of time, was developed first; as energy comes before harmony; power before beauty.

Woman was therefore under his care as an elder. He might have been her guardian and teacher.

But, as human nature goes not straight forward, but by excessive action and then reäction in an undulated course, he misunderstood and abused his advantages, and became her temporal master instead of her spiritual sire.

On himself came the punishment. He educated Woman more as a servant than a daughter, and found himself a king without a queen.

The children of this unequal union showed unequal natures, and more and more, men seemed sons of the handmaid, rather than princess.

At last, there were so many Ishmælites that the rest grew frightened and indignant. They laid the blame on Hagar, and drove her forth into the wilderness.

But there were none the fewer Ishmælites for that.

At last men became a little wiser, and saw that the infant Moses was, in every case, saved by the pure instincts of Woman's breast. For, as too much adversity is better for the moral nature than too much prosperity, Woman, in this respect, dwindled less than Man, though in other respects still a child in leading-strings.

So Man did her more and more justice, and grew more and more kind.

But yet—his habits and his will corrupted by the past—he did not clearly see that Woman was half himself; that her interests were identical with his; and that, by the law of their common being, he could never reach his true proportions while she remained in any wise shorn of hers.

And so it has gone on to our day; both ideas developing, but more slowly than they would under a clearer recognition of truth and justice, which would have permitted the sexes their due influence on one another, and mutual improvement from more dignified relations.

Wherever there was pure love, the natural influences were, for the time, restored.

Wherever the poet or artist gave free course to his genius, he saw the truth, and expressed it in worthy forms, for these men especially share and need the feminine principle. The divine birds need to be brooded into life and song by mothers.

Wherever religion (I mean the thirst for truth and good, not the love of sect and dogma) had its course, the original design was apprehended in its simplicity, and the dove presaged sweetly from Dodona's oak.

I have aimed to show that no age was left entirely

without a witness of the equality of the sexes in function, duty and hope.

Also that, when there was unwillingness or ignorance, which prevented this being acted upon, women had not the less power for their want of light and noble freedom. But it was power which hurt alike them and those against whom they made use of the arms of the servile—cunning, blandishment, and unreasonable emotion.

That now the time has come when a clearer vision and better action are possible—when Man and Woman may regard one another as brother and sister, the pillars of one porch, the priests of one worship.

I have believed and intimated that this hope would receive an ampler fruition, than ever before, in our own land.

And it will do so if this land carry out the principles from which sprang our national life.

I believe that, at present, women are the best helpers of one another.

Let them think; let them act; till they know what they need.

We ask of men to remove arbitrary barriers. Some would like to do more. But I believe it needs that Woman show herself in her native dignity, to teach them how to aid her; their minds are so encumbered by tradition.

When Lord Edward Fitzgerald travelled with the Indians, his manly heart obliged him at once to take the packs from the squaws and carry them. But we do not read that the red men followed his example, though they are ready enough to carry the pack of the white woman, because she seems to them a superior being.

Let Woman appear in the mild majesty of Ceres, and rudest churls will be willing to learn from her.

You ask, what use will she make of liberty, when she has so long been sustained and restrained?

I answer: in the first place, this will not be suddenly given. I read yesterday a debate of this year on the subject of enlarging women's rights over property. It was a leaf from the class-book that is preparing for the needed instruction. The men learned visibly as they spoke. The champions of Woman saw the fallacy of arguments on the opposite side, and were startled by their own convictions. With their wives at home, and the readers of the paper, it was the same. And so the stream flows on; thought urging action, and action leading to the evolution of still better thought.

But, were this freedom to come suddenly, I have no fear of the consequences. Individuals might commit excesses, but there is not only in the sex a reverence for decorums and limits inherited and enhanced from generation to generation, which many years of other life could not efface, but a native love, in Woman as Woman, of proportion, of "the simple art of not too much"—a Greek moderation, which would create immediately a restraining party, the natural legislators and instructors of the rest, and would gradually establish such rules as are needed to guard, without impeding, life.

The Graces would lead the choral dance, and teach the rest to regulate their steps to the measure of beauty.

But if you ask me what offices they may fill, I reply—any. I do not care what case you put; let them be sea-captains, if you will. I do not doubt there are women well fitted for such an office, and, if so, I should be as glad to see them in it, as to welcome the maid of Saragossa, or the maid of Missolonghi, or the Suliote heroine, or Emily Plater.

I think women need, especially at this juncture, a much greater range of occupation than they have, to rouse their latent powers. A party of travellers lately visited a lonely hut on a mountain. There they found an old woman, who told them she and her husband had lived there forty years. "Why," they said, "did you choose so barren a spot?" She "did not know; *it was the man's notion.*"

And, during forty years, she had been content to act, without knowing why, upon "the man's notion." I would not have it so.

In families that I know, some little girls like to saw wood, others to use carpenters' tools. Where these tastes are indulged, cheerfulness and good-humor are promoted. Where they are forbidden, because "such things are not proper for girls," they grow sullen and mischievous.

Fourier had observed these wants of women, as no one can fail to do who watches the desires of little girls, or knows the ennui that haunts grown women, except where they make to themselves a serene little world by art of some kind. He, therefore, in proposing a great variety of employments, in manufactures or the care of plants and animals, allows for one-third of women as likely to have a taste for masculine pursuits, one third of men for feminine.

Who does not observe the immediate glow and serenity that is diffused over the life of women, before restless or fretful, by engaging in gardening, building, or the lowest department of art? Here is something that is not routine, something that draws forth life towards the infinite.

I have no doubt, however, that a large proportion of women would give themselves to the same employments as now, because there are circumstances that must lead them. Mothers will delight to make the nest soft and warm. Nature would take care of that; no need to clip the wings of any bird that wants to soar and sing, or finds in itself the strength of pinion for a migratory flight unusual to its kind. The difference would be that *all* need not be constrained to employments for which *some* are unfit.

I have urged upon the sex self-subsistence in its two forms of self-reliance and self-impulse, because I believe them to be the needed means of the present juncture.

I have urged on Woman independence of Man, not that I do not think the sexes mutually needed by one another, but because in Woman this fact has led to an excessive devotion, which has cooled love, degraded marriage, and prevented either sex from being what it should be to itself or the other.

I wish Woman to live, *first* for God's sake. Then she will not make an imperfect man her god, and thus sink to idolatry. Then she will not take what is not fit for her from a sense of weakness and poverty. Then, if she finds what she needs in Man embodied, she will know how to love, and be worthy of being loved.

By being more a soul, she will not be less Woman, for nature is perfected through spirit.

Now there is no woman, only an overgrown child.

That her hand may be given with dignity, she must be able to stand alone. I wish to see men and women capable of such relations as are depicted by Landor in his Pericles and Aspasia, where grace is the natural garb of strength, and the affections are calm, because deep. The softness is that of a firm tissue, as when

> "The gods approve
> The depth, but not the tumult of the soul,
> A fervent, not ungovernable love."

A profound thinker has said, "No married woman can represent the female world, for she belongs to her husband. The idea of Woman must be represented by a virgin."

But that is the very fault of marriage, and of the present relation between the sexes, that the woman *does* belong to the man, instead of forming a whole with him. Were it otherwise, there would be no such limitation to the thought.

Woman, self-centered, would never be absorbed by any relation; it would be only an experience to her as to man. It is a vulgar error that love, *a* love, to Woman is her whole existence; she also is born for Truth and Love in their universal energy. Would she but assume her inheritance, Mary would not be the only virgin mother. Not Manzoni alone would celebrate in his wife the virgin mind with the maternal wisdom and conjugal affections. The soul is ever young, ever virgin.

And will not she soon appear—the woman who shall vindicate their birthright for all women; who shall teach them what to claim, and how to use what they obtain? Shall not her name be for her era Victoria, for her country and life Virginia? Yet predictions are rash; she herself must teach us to give her the fitting name.

An idea not unknown to ancient times has of late been revived, that, in the metamorphoses of life, the soul assumes the form, first of Man, then of Woman, and takes the chances, and reaps the benefits of either lot. Why then, say some, lay such emphasis on the rights or needs of Woman? What she wins not as Woman will come to her as Man.

That makes no difference. It is not Woman, but the law of right, the law of growth, that speaks in us, and demands the perfection of each being in its kind—apple as apple, Woman as Woman. Without adopting your theory, I know that I, a daughter, live through the life of Man; but what concerns me now is, that my life be a beautiful, powerful, in a word, a complete life in its kind. Had I but one more moment to live I must wish the same.

Suppose, at the end of your cycle, your great world-year, all will be completed, whether I exert myself or not (and the supposition is *false*—but suppose it true), am I to be indifferent about it? Not so! I must beat my own pulse true in the heart of the world; for *that* is virtue, excellence, health.

Thou, Lord of Day! didst leave us to-night so calmly glorious, not dismayed that cold winter is coming, not postponing thy beneficence to the fruitful summer! Thou didst smile on thy day's work when it was done, and adorn thy down-going as thy up-rising, for thou art loyal, and it is thy nature to give life, if thou canst, and shine at all events!

I stand in the sunny noon of life. Objects no longer glitter in the dews of morning, neither are yet softened by the shadows of evening. Every spot is seen, every chasm revealed. Climbing the dusty hill, some fair effigies that once stood for symbols of human destiny have been broken; those I still have with me show defects in this broad light. Yet enough is left, even by experience, to point distinctly to the glories of that destiny; faint, but not to be mistaken streaks of the future day. I can say with the bard.

"Though many have suffered shipwreck, still beat noble hearts."

Always the soul says to us all, cherish your best hopes as a faith, and abide by them in action. Such shall be the effectual fervent means to their fulfilment:

> For the Power to whom we bow
> Has given its pledge that, if not now,
> They of pure and steadfast mind,
> By faith exalted, truth refined,
> *Shall* hear all music loud and clear,
> Whose first notes they ventured here.
> Then fear not thou to wind the horn,
> Though elf and gnome thy courage scorn;
> Ask for the castle's King and Queen;
> Though rabble rout may rush between,
> Beat thee senseless to the ground,
> In the dark beset thee round;
> Persist to ask, and it will come;
> Seek not for rest in humbler home;
> So shalt thou see, what few have seen,
> The palace home of King and Queen.

4. ORESTES AUGUSTUS BROWNSON, 1803–1876

[Surely in "Aristocracy," and somewhat in the "Historic Notes," Emerson hints that the metaphysical postulates of Transcendentalism could legitimately lead, at least in realm of social theory, not so much toward anarchic individualism as to conservative submission to the totality of things. While he strove never to "take sides," still when the challenge came from George Ripley in the form of an invitation to join Brook Farm, Emerson proved incapable of merging his personal independence in a socialistic fraternity. We are not sure that he, astute observer of his century though he was, ever understood that there *was* a logic which moved from Kant's categories through Hegel's dialectics to *The Communist Manifesto* of Marx and Engels in 1848; yet there is evidence, in the *Journal* and many of the essays, that he did appreciate how the basic precepts had in fact been developed by Wordsworth and Coleridge (in their later period) into a High-Church Toryism, or how on the Continent, Chateaubriand enlisted them into the service of a "romantic Catholicism." Emerson mistrusted these simplifications as scrupulously as he came, gradually, to distrust Thoreau's doctrinaire intransigence, but then these skepticisms only prove the largeness of the comprehension into which, in *Nature* of 1836, he strove to incorporate and reconcile the contradictory tendencies.

For later American students, the vehemence of the contradiction has been softened simply because they do not read Orestes Brownson. In 1836, no member of the band had been more "radical" nor, as we have heard him say, more aware of the libertarian opportunities of their situation. He staked his faith and hope on the Democratic Party's campaign in 1840; in an effort to help, he printed his notorious essay, "The Laboring Classes," which the Whigs gleefully reprinted in order to show that the philosophers of Democracy were reckless *sans-culottes*. Brownson was terribly beaten when the Whigs, electioneering on the stupid slogan of "Tippecanoe and Tyler too," won the mob by displaying the factitious symbols of log cabin and hard cider.

In the depths of this spiritual despair, Brownson discovered in the theories he had taken from Dr. Channing or from Emerson a clear indication that eventually the liberal mentality would require some authority strong enough to check or to rule the vulgar surge of the commonality—who were bound, on the purest of Transcendental principles, to pervert the concept of democracy into a rule of vulgarity.

In 1843, he tried to join forces with what he still hoped would prove the bastion of Jacksonian Democracy, with John Louis O'Sullivan's *Democratic Review*. Merging his own *Quarterly* with this journal, he contributed to it a series of articles which progressively alienated O'Sullivan's subscribers, until at the end of the year O'Sullivan announced a termination of the agreement and then strove in vain to salvage his magazine from the terrible doubts Brownson had sown broadcast by thus misusing it.

Part-way into his blatent series, Brownson wrote for the April number this essay (I give it in extracts: he was terribly prolix!). To this article O'Sullivan was obliged to append a note, disclaiming it as in any sense the official view of the Democratic Party. Yes, all Democrats would admit that 1840 was defeat, still the American people would return to their Jacksonian allegiance. Thus O'Sullivan prophesied: in 1844 Brownson announced his conversion to the Catholic Church. Thereafter his Transcendental associates entered a spontaneous and tacit conspiracy to forget him, to pretend he never had existed.

"Democracy and Liberty" (what I can extract from it) was a next-to-the-last stage on Brownson's pilgrimage. Since it does come just before his turning to Rome, it may conveniently represent to us the most effectual counter-statement composed in America—the nearest that any American could come to Chateaubriand—against the liberalism of Thoreau or Margaret Fuller. Amusingly enough, in his career as a Catholic Brownson proved every bit as recalcitrant, as violently self-opinionated, as ever Thoreau was in worship of "wild" independence.]

DEMOCRACY AND LIBERTY

Mentioning this 1840, we must say that it marks an epoch in *our*—we speak personally, not for *The Democratic Review*—political and social doctrines. The famous election of that year wrought a much greater revolution in us than in the Government; and we confess, here on the threshold, that since then we—that is the writer of this—have pretty much ceased to speak of, or to confide in, the "Intelligence of the people." ... They who had devoted their lives to the cause of their country, of truth, justice, liberty, humanity, were looked upon as enemies of the people, and were unable to make themselves heard amid the maddened and maddening hurrahs of the drunken mob that went for "Tippecanoe, and Tyler Too." ... We confess that we could hardly forbear exclaiming, in vexation and contempt, "Well, after all, nature will out; the poor devils, if we but let them alone, will make cattle of themselves, and why should we waste our time and substance in trying to hinder them from making themselves cattle?" ...

The great end with all men in their religious, their political, and their individual actions, is FREEDOM. The perfection of our nature is in being able "to look into the perfect law of Liberty," for Liberty is only another name for power. The measure of my ability is the exact measure of my freedom. The glory of humanity is in proportion to its freedom. Hence, humanity always applauds him who labors in right down earnest to advance the cause of freedom. There is something intoxicating to every young and enthusiastic heart in this applause—always something intoxicating, too, in standing up for freedom, in opposing authority, in warring against fixed order, in throwing off the restraints of old and rigid customs, and enabling the soul and body to develop themselves freely and in the natural proportions. Liberty is a soul-stirring word. It kindles all that is noble, generous and heroic within us. Whoso speaks out for it can always be eloquent, and always sure of his audience. One loves so to speak if he be of a warm and generous temper, and we all love him who dares so to speak. . . .

We mean not here to say that we can have too much Liberty, or that there is danger that any portion of our fellow citizens will become too much in earnest for the advancement and security of Liberty. What we fear is, on the one hand, the misinterpretation of Liberty; and, on the other, the adoption of wrong or inadequate measures to establish or guaranty it. We fear that a large portion of the younger members of the Democratic party do misinterpret Liberty. If they analyse their own minds, they will find that they are yet virtually understanding Liberty as we did when the great work to be done was to free the mass of the people from the dominion of kings and nobilities. They will find, we fear, that they have not thought, that in order to secure freedom anything more was necessary, than to establish universal suffrage and eligibility, and to leave the people free to follow their own will, uncontrolled, unchecked. Hence, Liberty with them is merely *political*. Where all are free to vote and to be voted for, there is all the freedom they contemplate.

Perhaps this is stated too positively. Perhaps it would

be truer to say, that they do not see that anything more is necessary, in order to render every man practically free, than the establishment of a perfectly democratic government. Where all the people take part in the government, are equally possessed of the right of suffrage and that of eligibility, and where the people are free to take any direction, at any time, that the majority may determine, they suppose that there perfect freedom is as a matter of course. But this we have seen is not the fact, and cannot be the fact till the virtue and intelligence of the people are perfect, instead of being, as they now are, altogether imperfect, and, in reference to what they should be, in order to render certain the end contemplated, as good as no virtue and intelligence at all. But ignorant of this fact, confiding in the virtue and intelligence of the people, feeling that all the obstacles Liberty encounters are owing to the fact that the will of the people is not clearly and distinctly expressed, they labor to remove whatever tends in their judgment to restrain the action of the people, or the authoritative expression of the will of the majority. But when they have removed all these restraints, broken down all barriers, and obtained an open field and fair play for the will of the people, what is there to guaranty us the enjoyment of Liberty? . . .

We solemnly protest against construing one word we have said into hostility to the largest freedom for all men; but we put it to our young friends, in sober earnest too, whether with them freedom is something positive; or whether they are in the habit of regarding it as merely negative? Do they not look upon liberty merely as freedom from certain restraints or obstacles, rather than as positive ability possessed by those who are free? They assume that we have the ability, the power, both individually and collectively—when once the external restraints are taken off—to be and to do all that is requisite for our highest individual and social weal. Is this assumption warrantable? Is man individually or socially sufficient for himself? Should not our politics, as well as our religion, teach us that it is not in man that walketh to direct his steps, and that he can work out his own salvation, only as a higher power, through grace, works in him to will and to do? . . .

In all their speculations, they who differ from us, overlook the important fact that *government is needed for the people as the State, as well as for the people as individuals.* They assume, consciously or unconsciously, that the people, as the body politic, need no governing, and that, so viewed, they have in themselves a sort of inherent wisdom and virtue, which will lead them always to will and ordain what is wise and just, and only what is wise and just. They therefore seek government, not for the people as the body politic, but for the people as individuals. That is to say, they seek not to restrain the power of the sovereign, but are willing to leave it absolute. Hence they proclaim the absolute sovereignty of the people, never ceasing to repeat, in season and out of season, that all legitimate power emanates from the people, and that the chief glory of the statesman is to find out and conform to the will of the people. We do not err in declaring that this is that theory of Democracy which is becoming the dominant theory of all parties in the country. But, when we have reduced this theory to practice, when we have made the people supreme in the sense, and to the extent, here implied, where is the practical guaranty for freedom? On what can we rely to protect our rights as men? Nay, what are we all in this case, as individuals, but the veriest slaves of the body politic? We have talked of certain inalienable rights, that is, rights which we possess by virtue of the fact that we are men, which we cannot ourselves surrender up, and which cannot be taken from us; but what is the use of talking about rights when we have no *power* to maintain them? My rights are worth nothing beyond my might to assert and maintain them against whosoever or whatsoever would usurp them. . . .

The ends the people seek to gain are, we willingly admit, for the most part just and desirable; but the justice and desirableness of the end, almost always blind them to the true character and tendency of the means by which they seek to gain it. They become intent on the end, so intent as to be worked up to a passion for it—for the people never act but in a passion—and then in going to it, they break down everything which obstructs or hinders their progress. Now, what they break down, though in the way of gaining that particular end, may after all be our only guaranty of other ends altogether more valuable. Here is the danger. What more desirable than personal freedom? What more noble than to strike off the fetters of the slave? Aye, but if in striking off his fetters, you trample on the constitution and law, which are your only guaranty of freedom for those who are now free, and also for those you propose to make free, what do you gain to freedom? Great wrong may be done in seeking even a good end, if we look not well to the means we adopt. Philanthropy itself not unfrequently is so intent on the end, that in going to it, it tramples down more rights than it vindicates by success. We own, therefore, that the older we grow, and the longer we study in that school, the only one in which fools will learn, the more danger do we see in popular passions, and the less is our confidence in the wisdom and virtue of the people.

"But what is our resource against all these evils? What remedy do you propose?" These are fair questions, but we do not propose to answer them now. We may hereafter undertake to do it, and what we shall have to say will be arranged under the heads of the Constitution, the Church, and Individual Statesmen. Without an efficient Constitution, which is not only an instrument through which the people govern, but which is a power that governs them, by effectually confining their action to certain specific subjects, there is and can be no good government, no individual liberty. Without the influence of wise and patriotic statesmen, whose importance, in our adulation of the people as a mass, we have underrated, and without the Christian Church exerting the hallowed and hallowing influences of Christianity upon the people both as individuals and as the body politic, we see little hope, even with the best constitution, of securing the blessings of freedom and good government. But these are matters into the discussion of which we cannot now enter. Our purpose in this Article has been to draw the attention of our political friends to certain heresies of doctrine which are springing up amongst us, and enlisting quite too much sympathy, and which we believe pregnant with mischief.

Democracy, in our judgment, has been wrongly defined to be a *form* of government; it should be understood of the *end*, rather than of the *means*, and be regarded as a principle rather than a form. The end we are to aim at, is the Freedom and progress of all men, especially of the poorest and most numerous class. He is a democrat who goes for the highest moral, intellectual, and physical elevation of the great mass of the people, especially of the laboring population, in distinction from a special devotion to the interests and pleasures of the wealthier, more refined, or more distinguished few. But the means by which this elevation is to be obtained, are not necessarily the institution of the purely democratic form of government. Here has been our mistake. We have been quite too ready to conclude that if we only once succeed in establishing Democracy—universal suffrage and eligibility, without constitutional restraints on the power of the people—as a form of government, the end will follow as a matter of course. The considerations we have adduced, we think prove to the contrary.

In coming to this conclusion, it will be seen that we differ from our friends not in regard to the end, but in regard to the means. We believe, and this is the point on which we insist, that the end, freedom and progress, will not be secured by this loose radicalism with regard to popular sovereignty, and these demagogical boasts of the virtue and intelligence of the people, which have begun to be so fashionable. They who are seeking to advance the cause of humanity by warring against all existing institutions, religious, civil, or political, do seem to us to be warring against the very end they wish to gain.

It has been said, that mankind are always divided into two parties, one of which may be called the Stationary Party, the other the Movement Party, or Party of Progress. Perhaps it is so; if so, all of us who have any just conceptions of our manhood, and of our duty to our fellowmen, must arrange ourselves on the side of the Movement. But the Movement itself is divided into two sections—one the radical section, seeking progress by destruction; the other the conservative section, seeking progress through and in obedience to existing institutions. Without asking whether the rule applies beyond our own country, we contend that the conservative section is the only one that a wise man can call his own. In youth we feel differently. We find evil around us; we are in a dungeon; loaded all over with chains; we cannot make a single free movement; and we utter one long, loud, indignant protest against whatever is. We feel then that we can advance religion only by destroying the Church; learning only by breaking down the universities; and freedom only by abolishing the State. Well, this is one method of progress; but we ask, has it ever been known to be successful? Suppose that we succeed in demolishing the old edifice, in sweeping away all that the human race has been accumulating for the last six thousand years, what have we gained? Why, we are back where we were six thousand years ago; and without any assurance that the human race will not re-assume its old course and rebuild what we have destroyed.

As we grow older, sadder, and wiser, and pass from Idealists to Realists, we change all this, and learn that the only true way of carrying the race forward is through its existing institutions. We plant ourselves, if on the sad, still on the firm reality of things, and content ourselves with gaining what can be gained with the means existing institutions furnish. We seek to advance religion through and in obedience to the Church; law and social well-being through and in obedience to the State. Let it not be said that in adopting this last course, we change sides, leave the Movement, and go over to the Stationary Party. No such thing. We do not thus in age forget the dreams of our youth. It is because we remember those dreams, because young enthusiasm has become firm and settled principle, and youthful hopes positive convictions, and because we would realize what we dared dream, when we first looked forth on the face of humanity, that we cease to exclaim "Liberty *against* Order," and substitute the practical formula, "LIBERTY ONLY IN AND THROUGH ORDER." The love of liberty loses none of its intensity. In the true manly heart it burns deeper and clearer with age, but it burns to enlighten and to warm, not to consume.

Here is the practical lesson we have sought to unfold. While we accept the end our democratic friends seek, while we feel our lot is bound up with theirs, we have wished to impress upon their minds, that we are to gain that end only through fixed and established order; not against authority, but by and in obedience to authority, and an authority competent to ordain and to guaranty it. Liberty without the guaranties of Authority, would be the worst of tyrannies.

CHAPTER SEVEN

FUTURE REFERENCE

1. THEODORE PARKER, 1810–1860

[Though conceiving himself primarily a minister, and so an inheritor of the mantle of the Puritan prophets, Theodore Parker also considered that in his century the pulpit had a mission to discuss everything of national or cultural concern. Furthermore, he was incessantly invited, besought, to lecture up and down the land, in every "Lyceum." He travelled as extensively as did Emerson; second only to Emerson, he was a voice speaking culture, philosophy, wonderment, to the rustic American people.

The nature of his audience must be remembered by one who today reads (even in my necessarily abbreviated version) the remarkable address he gave here and there throughout 1848, the year in which General Zachary Taylor was being elected by the Whigs, in which the Democrats were split over the Free Soil issue, and the terrible Civil War seemed about to flare up. It did not in 1848, though it did thirteen years later; from another speech of Parker's Lincoln is reputed to have learned the phrase "of the people, by the people, for the people." We do not know whether Lincoln heard this one; it was printed in final form—that stage was hard for Parker to achieve—in *Speeches, Addresses, and Occasional Sermons,* in 1852.

Parker was one of very few in his day who could perceive that Nathaniel Bowditch, amateur mathematician and geometer of Salem (1773–1838), who while working as president of an insurance company translated Laplace, was truly a Genius. Bowditch had the satisfaction of refusing an invitation to become Professor of Mathematics at Harvard.

By temperament, Theodore Parker was a rationalist who, one imagines, might have been more at home in the eighteenth century than in the post-Kantian nineteenth. Still, metaphysics made little difference to him: he would speak up, on any basis, for every form of freedom. Here he makes himself spokesman for the "philosophical party" in politics, which has equal scorn for both the Whig and Democratic. The "great politician" ridiculed on pp. 356-357 is Daniel Webster, whom Parker despised; the "President" is General Taylor, elected in 1848 on the announced platform that he knew nothing and took no positions. Parker's reading of the situation of American culture in 1848, his sense for the vigor of newspapers and magazines, his estimate of Bryant (pp. 361-362) and of Emerson (pp. 362-363)—all these passages and a hundred others make this one of the clairvoyant utterances in American literature. Most amusing, perhaps, is the slur, on p. 363, upon the "American-mad" nationalists, from whom Herman Melville was in 1848 learning his lessons; yet oddly enough, at the end of his discourse, Theodore Parker finds himself sounding the chant of Cornelius Mathews. But with a difference: "Young as we are," he says of his America, we are also "wicked." The most sanguine, the most resolutely optimistic of the Trancendentalists, Parker more than any of the others possessed accurate statistics about the violence and corruption of American society.]

THE POLITICAL DESTINATION OF AMERICA AND THE SIGNS OF THE TIMES

Every nation has a peculiar character, in which it differs from all others that have been, that are, and possibly from all that are to come; for it does not yet appear that the Divine Father of the nations ever repeats himself and creates either two nations or two men exactly alike. However, as nations, like men, agree in more things than they differ, and in obvious things too, the special peculiarity of any one tribe does not always appear at first sight. But if we look through the history of some nation which has passed off from the stage of action, we find certain prevailing traits which continually reappear in the language and laws thereof; in its arts, literature, manners, modes of religion—in short, in the whole life of the people. . . .

Now this idiosyncrasy of a nation is a sacred gift; like the genius of a Burns, a Thorwaldsen, a Franklin, or a Bowditch, it is given for some divine purpose, to be sacredly cherished and patiently unfolded. The cause of the peculiarities of a nation or an individual man we cannot fully determine as yet, and so we refer it to the chain of causes which we call Providence. But the national persistency in a common type is easily explained. The qualities of father and mother are commonly transmitted to their children, but not always, for peculiarities may lie latent in a family for generations, and reappear in the genius or the folly of a child—often in the complexion and features: and besides, father and mother are often no match. But such exceptions are rare, and the qualities of a race are always thus reproduced, the deficiency of one man getting counterbalanced by the redundancy of the next: the marriages of a whole tribe are not far from normal. . . .

The most marked characteristic of the American nation is Love of Freedom; of man's natural rights. This is so plain to a student of American history, or of American politics, that the point requires no arguing. We have a genius for liberty: the American idea is freedom, natural rights. Accordingly, the work providentially laid out for us to do seems this—to organize the rights of man. This is a problem hitherto unattempted on a national scale, in human history. Often enough attempts have been made to organize the powers of priests, kings, nobles, in a theocracy, monarchy, oligarchy, powers which had no foundation in human duties or human rights, but solely in the selfishness of strong men. Often enough have the mights of men been organized, but not the rights of man. Surely there has never been an attempt made on a national scale to organize the rights of man as man; rights resting on the nature of things; rights derived from no conventional compact of men with men; not inherited from past generations, nor received from parliaments and kings, nor secured by their parchments; but rights that are derived straightway from God, the Author of Duty and the Source of Right, and which are secured in the great charter of our being.

At first view it will be said, the peculiar genius of America is not such, nor such her fundamental idea, nor that her destined work. It is true that much of the national conduct seems exceptional when measured by that standard, and the nation's course as crooked as the Rio Grande; it is true that America sometimes seems to spurn liberty, and sells the freedom of three million men for less than three million annual bales of cotton; true, she often tramples, knowingly, consciously tramples, on the most unquestionable and sacred rights. Yet, when one looks through the whole character and history of America, spite of the exceptions, nothing comes out with such relief as this love of freedom, this idea of liberty, this attempt to organize right. There are numerous subordinate qualities which conflict with the nation's idea and work, coming from our circumstances, not our soul, as well as many others which help the nation perform her providential work. They are signs of the times, and it is important to look carefully among the most prominent of them, where, indeed, one finds striking contradictions.

The first is an impatience of authority. Every thing must render its reason, and show cause for its being. We will not be commanded, at least only by such as we choose to obey. Does some one say, "Thou shalt," or "Thou shalt not," we ask, "Who are you?" Hence comes a seeming irreverence. The shovel hat, the symbol of authority, which awed our fathers, is not respected unless it covers a man, and then it is the man we honor, and no longer the shovel hat. "I will complain of you to the government!" said a Prussian nobleman to a Yankee stage-driver, who uncivilly threw the nobleman's trunk to the top of the coach. "Tell the government to go to the devil!" was the symbolical reply.

Old precedents will not suffice us, for we want something anterior to all precedents; we go beyond what is written, asking the cause of the precedent and the reason of the writing. "Our fathers did so," says some one. "What of that?" say we. "Our fathers—they were giants, were they? Not at all, only great boys, and we are not only taller than they, but mounted on their shoulders to boot, and see twice as far. My dear wise man, or wiseacre, it is we that are the ancients, and have forgotten more than all our fathers knew. We will take their wisdom joyfully, and thank God for it, but not their authority, we know better; and of their nonsense not a word. It was very well that they lived, and it is very well that they are dead. Let them keep decently buried, for respectable dead men never walk." . . .

Such is our dread of authority, that we like not old things; hence we are always a-changing. Our house must be new, and our book, and even our church. So we choose a material that soon wears out, though it often outlasts our patience. The wooden house is an apt emblem of this sign of the times. But this love of change appears not less in important matters. We think "Of old things all are over old, of new things none are new enough." So the age asks of all institutions their right to be: What right has the government to existence? . . .

Then there is a philosophical tendency, distinctly visible; a groping after ultimate facts, first principles, and universal ideas. We wish to know first the fact, next the law of that fact, and then the reason of the law. A sign of this tendency is noticeable in the titles of books; we have no longer "treatises" on the eye, the ear, sleep, and so forth, but in their place we find works professing to treat of the "philosophy" of vision, of sound, of sleep. Even in the pulpits, men speak about the "philosophy" of religion; we have philosophical lectures, delivered to men of little culture, which would have amazed our grandfathers, who thought a shoemaker should never go beyond his last, even to seek for the philosophy of shoes. "What a pity," said a grave Scotchman, in the beginning of this century, "to teach the beautiful science of geometry to weavers and cobblers." Here nothing is too good or high for any one tall and good enough to get hold of it. What audiences attend the Lowell lectures in Boston—two or three thousand men, listening to twelve lectures on the philosophy of fish! It would not bring a dollar or a vote, only thoughts to their minds! Young ladies are well versed in the philosophy of the affections, and understand the theory of attraction, while their grandmothers, good easy souls, were satisfied with the possession of the fact. The circumstance, that philosophical lectures get delivered by men like Walker, Agassiz, Emerson, and their coadjutors, men who do not spare abstruseness, get listened to, and even understood, in town and village, by large crowds of men, of only the most common culture; this indicates a philosophical tendency, unknown in any other land or age. Our circle of professed scholars, men of culture and learning, is a very small one, while our circle of thinking men is disproportionately large. The best thought of France and Germany finds a readier welcome here than in our parent land: nay, the newest and best thought of England, finds its earliest and warmest welcome in America. It was a little remarkable, that Bacon and Newton should be reprinted here, and Laplace should have found his translator and expositor coming out of an insurance office in Salem! Men of no great pretensions object to an accomplished and eloquent politician: "That is all very well; he made us cry and laugh, but the discourse was not philosophical; he never tells us the reason of the thing; he seems not only not to know it, but not to know that there *is* a reason for the thing, and if not, what is the use of this bobbing on the surface?" Young maidens complain of the minister, that he has no philosophy in his sermons, nothing but precepts, which they could read in the Bible, as well as he, perhaps in heathen Seneca. He does not feed their souls.

One finds this tendency where it is least expected: there is a philosophical party in politics, a very small party it may be, but an actual one. They aim to get at everlasting ideas and universal laws, not made by man, but by God, and for man, who only finds them; and from them they aim to deduce all particular enactments, so that each statute in the code shall represent a fact in the universe; a point of thought in God; so, indeed, that legislation shall be divine in the same sense that a true system of astronomy is divine—or the Christian religion—the law corresponding to a fact. Men of this party, in New England, have more ideas than precedents, are spontaneous more than logical; have intuitions, rather than intellectual convictions, arrived at by the process of reasoning. They think it is not philosophical to take a young scoundrel and shut him up with a party of old ones, for his amendment; not philosophical to leave children with no culture, intellectual, moral, or religious, exposed to the temptations of a high and corrupt civilization, and then, when they go astray—as such barbarians must, in such temptations—to hang them by the neck for the example's sake. They doubt if war is a more philosophical mode of getting justice between two nations, than blows to settle a quarrel between two men. In either case, they do not see how it follows, that he who can strike the hardest blow is always in the right. In short, they think that judicial murder, which is hanging, and national murder, which is war, are not more philosophical than homicide, which one man commits on his own private account. . . .

True, there are antagonistic tendencies, for, soon as one pole is developed, the other appears; objections are made to philosophy, the old cry is raised—"Infidelity," "Denial," "Free-thinking." It is said that philosophy will corrupt the young men, will spoil the old ones, and deceive the very elect. "Authority and tradition," say some, "are all we need consult; reason must be put down, or she will soon ask terrible questions." There is good cause for these men warring against reason and philosophy: it is purely in self-defence. But this counsel and that cry come from those quarters where the men of past ages have their place, where the forgotten is re-collected, the obsolete preserved, and the useless held in esteem. The counsel is not dangerous; the bird of night, who overstays his hour, is only troublesome to himself, and was never known to hurt a dovelet or a mouseling after sunrise. In the night only is the owl destructive. Some of those who thus cry out against this tendency, are excellent men in their way, and highly useful, valuable as conveyancers of opinions. So long as there are men who take opinions as real estate, "to have and to hold for themselves and their heirs for ever," why should there not be such conveyancers of opinions, as well as of land? And as it is not the duty of the latter functionary to ascertain the quality or the value of the land, but only its metes and bounds, its appurtenances and the title thereto; to see if the grantor is regularly seized and possessed thereof, and has good right to convey and devise the same, and to make sure that the whole conveyance is regularly made out—so is it with these conveyancers of opinion; so should it be, and they are valuable men. It is a good thing to know that we hold under Scotus, and Ramus, and Albertus Magnus, who were regularly seized of this or that opinion. It gives an absurdity the dignity of a relic. Sometimes these worthies, who thus oppose reason and her kin, seem to have a good deal in them, and, when one examines, he finds more than he looked for. They are like a nest of boxes from Hingham or Nuremburg, you open one, and behold another; that, and lo! a third. So you go on opening and opening, and finding and finding, till at last you come to the heart of the matter, and then you find a box that is very little, and entirely empty.

Yet, with all this tendency—and it is now so strong that it cannot be put down, nor even howled down, much as it may be howled over there is a lamentable want of first principles, well known and established; we have rejected the authority of tradition, but not yet accepted the authority of truth and justice. We will not be treated as striplings, and are not old enough to go alone as men. Accordingly, nothing seems fixed. There is a perpetual see-sawing of opposite principles. Somebody said ministers ought to be ordained on horseback, because they are to remain so short a time in one place. It would be as emblematic to inaugurate American politicians, by swearing them on a weathercock. The great men of the land have as many turns in their course as the Euripus or the Missouri. Even the facts given in the spiritual nature of man are called in question. An eminent Unitarian divine regards the existence of God as a matter of opinion, thinks it cannot be demonstrated, and publicly declares that it is "not a certainty." Some American Protestants no longer take the Bible as the standard of ultimate appeal, yet venture not to set up in that place reason, conscience, the soul getting help of God; others, who affect to accept the Scripture as the last authority, yet, when questioned as to their belief in the miraculous and divine birth of Jesus of Nazareth, are unable to say yes or no, not having made up their minds. . . .

In this lack of first principles, it is not settled in the popular consciousness, that there is such a thing as an absolute right, a great law of God, which we are to keep, come what will come. So that the nation is not upright, but goes stooping. Hence, in private affairs, law takes the place of conscience, and, in public, might of right. So the bankrupt pays his shilling in the pound, and gets his discharge, but afterwards, becoming rich, does not think of paying the other nineteen shillings. He will tell you the law is his conscience; if that be satisfied, so is he. But you will yet find him letting money at one or two per cent a month, contrary to law; and then he will tell you that paying a debt is a matter of law, while letting money is only a matter of conscience. So he rides either indifferently—now the public hack, and now his own private nag, according as it serves his turn. . . .

It is a great mischief that comes from lacking first principles, and the worst part of it comes from lacking first principles in morals. Thereby our eyes are holden so that we see not the great social evils all about us. We attempt to justify slavery, even to do it in the name of Jesus Christ. The Whig Party of the North loves slavery; the Democratic Party does not even seek to conceal its affection therefore. A great politician declares the Mexican War wicked, and then urges men to go and fight it; he thinks a famous general not fit to be nominated for President, but then invites men to elect him. Politics are national morals, the morals of Thomas and Jeremiah, multiplied by millions. But it is not decided yet that honesty is the best policy for a politician; it is thought that the best policy is honesty, at least as near it as the times will allow. Many politicians seem undecided how to turn, and so sit on the fence between honesty and dishonesty. Mr. Facing-both-ways is a popular politician in America just now, sitting on the fence between honesty and dishonesty, and, like the blank leaf between the Old and New Testaments, belonging to neither dispensation. It is a little amusing to a trifler to hear a man's fitness for the Presidency defended on the ground that he has no definite convictions or ideas! . . .

Since the nation loves freedom above all things, the name democracy is a favorite name. No party could live a twelvemonth that should declare itself anti-democratic. Saint and sinner, statesman and politician, alike love the name. So it comes to pass that there are two things which bear that name; each has its type and its motto. The motto of one is, "You are as good as I, and let us help one another." That represents the democracy of the Declaration of Independence, and of the New Testament; its type is a free school, where children of all ranks meet under the guidance of intelligent and Christian men, to be educated in mind, and heart, and soul. The other has for its motto, "I am as good as you, so get out of my way." Its type is the barroom of a tavern—dirty, offensive, stained with tobacco, and full of drunken, noisy, quarrelsome "rowdies," just returned from the Mexican War, and ready for a "buffalo hunt," for privateering, or to go and plunder any one who is better off than themselves, especially if also better. That is not exactly the democracy of the Declaration, or of the New Testament; but of—no matter whom.

Then, again, there is a great intensity of life and purpose. This displays itself in our actions and speeches; in our speculations; in the "revivals" of the more serious sects; in the excitements of trade, in the general character of the people. All that we do we overdo. It appears in our hopefulness; we are the most aspiring of nations. Not content with half the continent, we wish the other half. We have this characteristic of genius: we are dissatisfied with all that we have done. Somebody once said we were too vain to be proud. It is not wholly so; the national ideal is so far above us that any achievement seems little and low. The American soul passes away from its work soon as it is finished. So the soul of each great artist refuses to dwell in his finished work, for that seems little to his dream. Our fathers deemed the Revolution a great work; it was once thought a surprising thing to found that little colony on the shores of New England; but young America looks to other revolutions, and thinks she has many a Plymouth colony in her bosom. If other nations wonder at our achievements, we are a disappointment to ourselves, and wonder we have not done more. Our national idea out-travels our experience, and all experience. We began our national career by setting all history at defiance—for that said, "A republic on a large scale cannot exist." Our progress since has shown that we were right in refusing to be limited by the past. The political ideas of the nation are transcendant, not empirical. Human history could not justify the Declaration of Independence and its large statements of the new idea: the nation went behind human history and appealed to human nature. . . .

If this intensity of life and hope have its good side, it has also its evil; with much of the excellence of youth we have its faults—rashness, haste, superficiality. Our work is seldom well done. In English manufactures there is a certain solid honesty of performance; in the French a certain air of elegance and refinement: one misses both these in American works. It is said America invents the most machines, but England builds them best. We lack the phlegmatic patience of older nations. We are always in a hurry, morning, noon and night. We are impatient of the process, but greedy of the result; so we make short experiments but long reports, and talk much though we say little. We forget that a sober method is a short way of coming to the end, and that he who, before he sets out, ascertains where he is going and the way thither, ends his journey more prosperously than one who settles these matters by the way. Quickness is a great desideratum with us. It is said an American ship is known far off at sea by the quantity of canvas she carries. Rough and ready is a popular attribute. Quick and off would be a symbolic motto for the nation at this day, representing one phase of our character. We are sudden in deliberation; the "one-hour rule" works well in Congress. A committee of the British Parliament spends twice or thrice our time in collecting facts, understanding and making them intelligible, but less than our time in speech-making after the report; speeches there commonly being for the purpose of facilitating the business, while here one sometimes is half ready to think, notwithstanding our earnestness, that the business is to facilitate the speaking. A State revises her statute with a rapidity that astonishes a European. Yet each revision brings some amendment, and what is found good in the constitution or laws of one State gets speedily imitated by the rest; each new State of the North becoming more democratic than its predecessor.

We are so intent on our purpose that we have no time for amusement. We have but one or two festivals in the year, and even then we are serious and reformatory. Jonathan thinks it a very solemn thing to be merry. A Frenchman said we have but two amusements in America —theology for the women and politics for the men; preaching and voting. If this be true, it may help to explain the fact that most men take their theology from their wives, and women politics from their husbands. No nation ever tried the experiment of such abstinence from amusement. We have no time for sport, and so lose much of the poetry of life. All work and no play does not always make a dull boy, but it commonly makes a hard man.

We rush from school into business early; we hurry while in business; we aim to be rich quickly, making a fortune at a stroke, making or losing it twice or thrice in a lifetime. "Soft and fair, goes safe and far," is no proverb to our taste. We are the most restless of people. How we crowd into cars and steamboats; a locomotive would well typify our fuming, fizzing spirit. In our large towns life seems to be only a scamper. Not satisfied with bustling about all day, when night comes we cannot sit still, but alone of all nations have added rockers to our chairs. . . .

In education the aim is not to get the most we can, but the least we can get along with. A ship with over-much canvass and over-little ballast were no bad emblem of many amongst us. In no country is it so easy to get a reputation for learning—accumulated thought, because so few devote themselves to that accumulation. In this respect our standard is low. So a man of one attainment is sure to be honored, but a man of many and varied abilities is in danger of being undervalued. A Spurzheim would be warmly welcomed, while a Humboldt would be suspected of superficiality, as we have not the standard to judge him by. Yet in no country in the world is it so difficult to get a reputation for eloquence, as many speak and that well. It is surprising with what natural strength and beauty the young American addresses himself to speak. Some hatter's apprentice, or shoemaker's journeyman, at a temperance or anti-slavery meeting, will speak words like the blows of an axe, that cut clean and deep. The country swarms with orators, more abundantly where education is least esteemed—in the West or South. . . .

One is amazed at the amount of ready skill and general ability which he finds in all the North, where each man has a little culture, takes his newspaper, manages his own business, and talks with some intelligence of many things —especially of politics and theology. In respect to this general intellectual ability and power of self-help, the mass of people seem far in advance of any other nation. But at the same time our scholars, who always represent the nation's higher modes of consciousness, will not bear comparison with the scholars of England, France, and Germany, men thoroughly furnished for their work. This is a great reproach and mischief to us, for we need most accomplished leaders, who by their thought can direct this national intensity of life. Our literature does not furnish them; we have no great men there; Irving, Channing, Cooper, are not names to conjure with in literature. One reads thick volumes devoted to the poets of America, or her prose writers, and finds many names which he wonders he never heard of before, but when he turns over their works, he finds consolation and recovers his composure.

American literature may be divided into two departments: the permanent literature, which gets printed in books, that sometimes reach more than one edition; and the evanescent literature, which appears only in the form of speeches, pamphlets, reviews, newspaper articles, and the like extempore productions. Now our permanent literature, as a general thing, is superficial, tame and weak; it is not American; it has not our ideas, our contempt of authority, our philosophical turn, nor even our uncertainty as to first principles, still less our national intensity, our hope, and fresh intuitive perceptions of truth. It is a miserable imitation. Love of freedom is not there. The real national literature is found almost wholly in speeches, pamphlets, and newspapers. The latter are pretty thoroughly American; mirrors in which we see no very flattering likeness of our morals or our manners. Yet the picture is true: that vulgarity, that rant, that bragging violence, that recklessness of truth and justice, that disregard of right and duty are a part of the nation's every-day life. Our newspapers are low and "wicked to a fault"; only in this weakness are they un-American. Yet they exhibit, and abundantly, the four qualities we have mentioned as belonging to the signs of our times. As a general rule, our orators are also American, with our good and ill. Now and then one rises who has studied Demosthenes in Leland or Francis, and got a second-hand acquaintance with old models: a man who uses literary common-places, and thinks himself original and classic because he can quote a line or so of Horace, in a Western House of Representatives, without getting so many words wrong as his reporter; but such men are rare, and after making due abatement for them, our orators all over the land are pretty thoroughly American, a little turgid, hot, sometimes brilliant, hopeful, intuitive, abounding in half truths, full of great ideas; often inconsequent; sometimes coarse; patriotic, vain, self-confident, rash, strong, and young-mannish. Of course the most of our speeches are vulgar, ranting, and worthless but we have produced some magnificent specimens of oratory, which are fresh, original, American, and brand new.

The more studied, polished, and elegant literature is not so; that is mainly an imitation. It seems not a thing of native growth. Sometimes, as in Channing, the thought and the hope are American, but the form and the coloring old and foreign. We dare not be original; our American pine must be cut to the trim pattern of the English yew, though the pine bleed at every clip. This poet tunes his lyre at the harp of Goethe, Milton, Pope, or Tennyson. His songs might better be sung on the Rhine than the Kennebec. They are not American in form and feeling; they have not the breath of our air; the smell of our ground is not in them. Hence our poet seems cold and poor. He loves the old mythology; talks about Pluto—the Greek devil, the fates and furies—witches of old times in Greece, but would blush to use our mythology, or breathe the name in verse of our devil, or our own witches, lest he should be thought to believe what he wrote. The mothers and sisters, who with many a pinch and pain sent the hopeful boy to college, must turn over the classical dictionary before they can find out what the youth would be at in his rhymes. Our poet is not deep enough to see that Aphrodite came from the ordinary waters, that Homer only hitched into rhythm and furnished the accomplishment of verse to street-talk, nursery tales, and old men's gossip in Ionian towns; he thinks what is common is unclean. So he sings of Corinth and Athens, which he never saw, but has not a word to say of Boston, and Fall River, and Baltimore, and New York, which are just as meet for song. He raves of Thermopylae and Marathon, with never a word for Lexington and Bunker-hill, for Cowpens, and Lundy's Lane, and Bemis's Heights. He loves to tell of the Ilyssus, of "smooth sliding Mincius, crowned with vocal reeds," yet sings not of the Petapsco, the Susquehanna, the Aroostook, and the Willimantick. He prates of the narcissus and the daisy, never of American dandelions and blue-eyed grass; he dwells on the lark and nightingale, but has not a thought for the brown thrasher and the bobolink, who every morning in June rain down such showers of melody on his affected head. What a lesson Burns teaches us, addressing his "rough bur-thistle." his daisy, "wee crimson tippit thing," and finding marvellous poetry in the mouse whose nest his plough turned over! Nay, how beautifully has even our sweet poet sung of our own Green River, our waterfowl, of the blue and fringed gentian, the glory of autumnal days.

Hitherto, spite of the great reading public, we have no permanent literature which corresponds to the American idea. Perhaps it is not time for that; it must be organized in deeds before it becomes classic in words; but as yet we have no such literature which reflects even the surface of American life, certainly nothing which portrays our intensity of life, our hope, or even our daily doings and drivings, as the Odyssey paints old Greek life, or Don Quixote and Gil Blas portray Spanish life. Literary men are commonly timid; ours know they are but poorly fledged as yet, so dare not fly away from the parent tree, but hop timidly from branch to branch. Our writers love to creep about in the shadow of some old renown, not venturing to soar away into the unwinged air, to sing of things here and now making our life classic. So, without the grace of high culture and the energy of American thought, they become weak, cold, and poor; are "curious, not knowing, not exact, but nice." Too fastidious to be wise, too unlettered to be elegant, too critical to create, they prefer a dull saying that is old to a novel form of speech, or a natural expression of a new truth. In a single American work—and a famous one, too—there are over sixty similes, not one original, and all poor. A few men, conscious of this defect, this sin against the Holy Spirit of Literature, go to the opposite extreme, and are American-mad; they wilfully talk rude, write in-numerous verse, and play their harps all jangling out of tune. A yet fewer few are American without madness. One such must not here be passed by, alike philosopher and bard, in whose writings "ancient wisdom shines with new-born beauty," and who has enriched a genius thoroughly American in the best sense, with a cosmopolitan culture and literary skill, which were wonderful in any land. . . .

In these secondary qualities of the people which mark the special signs of the times, there are many contradictions, quality contending with quality; all by no means balanced into harmonious relations. Here are great faults not less than great virtues. Can the national faults be corrected? Most certainly; they are but accidental, coming from our circumstances, our history, our position as a people—heterogeneous, new, and placed on a new and untamed continent. They come not from the nation's soul; they do not belong to our fundamental idea, but are hostile to it. One day our impatience of authority, our philosophical tendency, will lead us to a right method, that to fixed principles, and then we shall have a continuity of national action. Considering the pains taken by the fathers of the better portion of America to promote religion here, remembering how dear is Christianity to the heart of all, conservative and radical—though men often name as Christian what is not—and seeing how truth and right are sure to win at last—it becomes pretty plain that we shall arrive at true principles, laws of the universe, ideas of God; then we shall be in unison also with it and Him. When that great defect—lack of first principles— is corrected, our intensity of life, with the hope and confidence it inspires, will do a great work for us. We have already secured an abundance of material comforts hitherto unknown; no land was ever so full of corn and cattle, clothing, comfortable houses, and all things needed for the flesh. The desires of those things, even the excessive desire thereof, performs an important part in the divine economy of the human race; nowhere is its good effect more conspicuous than in America, where in two generations the wild Irishman becomes a decent citizen, orderly, temperate, and intelligent. This done or even a-doing, as it is now, we shall go forth to realize our great national idea, and accomplish the great work of organizing into institutions the unalienable rights of man. The great obstacle in the way of that is African slavery—the great

exception in the nation's history; the national sin. When
that is removed, as soon it must be, lesser but kindred
evils will easily be done away; the truth which the land-
reformers, which the associationists, the free-traders, and
others, have seen, dimly or clearly, can readily be carried
out. But while this monster vice continues, there is little
hope of any great and permanent national reform. The
positive things which we chiefly need for this work, are
first, education, next, education, and then education, a
vigorous development of the mind, conscience, affections,
religious power of the whole nation. . . .

The organization of human rights, the performance of
human duties, is an unlimited work. If there shall ever
be a time when it is all done, then the race will have
finished its course. Shall the American nation go on in this
work, or pause, turn off, fall, and perish? To me it seems
almost treason to doubt that a glorious future awaits us.
Young as we are, and wicked, we have yet done something which the world will not let perish. One day we shall
attend more emphatically to the rights of the hand, and
organize labor and skill; then to the rights of the head,
looking after education, science, literature, and art; and
again to the rights of the heart, building up the State
with its laws, society with its families, the church with
its goodness and piety. One day we shall see that it is a
shame, and a loss, and a wrong, to have a criminal, or an
ignorant man, or a pauper, or an idler, in the land; that
the jail, and the gallows, and the almshouse are a reproach
which need not be. Out of new sentiments and ideas, not
seen as yet, new forms of society will come, free from
the antagonism of races, classes, men—representing the
American idea in its length, breadth, depth, and height, its
beauty and its truth, and then the old civilization of our
time shall seem barbarous and even savage. There will be
an American art commensurate with our idea and akin to
this great continent; not an imitation, but a fresh, new
growth. An American literature also must come with democratic freedom, democratic thought, democratic power—
for we are not always to be pensioners of other lands,
doing nothing but import and quote; a literature with all

of German philosophic depth, with English solid sense, with French vivacity and wit, Italian fire of sentiment and soul, with all of Grecian elegance of form, and more than Hebrew piety and faith in God. We must not look for the maiden's ringlets on the baby's brow; we are yet but a girl; the nameless grace of maturity, and womanhood's majestic charm, are still to come. At length we must have a system of education, which shall uplift the humblest, rudest, worst born child in all the land; which shall bring forth and bring up noble men.

An American State is a thing that must also be; a State of free men who give over brawling, resting on industry, justice, love, not on war, cunning, and violence—a State where liberty, equality, and fraternity are deeds as well as words. In its time the American Church must also appear, with liberty, holiness, and love for its watchwords, cultivating reason, conscience, affection, faith, and leading the world's way in justice, peace, and love. The Roman Church has been all men know what and how; the American Church, with freedom for the mind, freedom for the heart, freedom for the soul, is yet to be, sundering no chord of the human harp, but tuning all to harmony. This also must come; but hitherto no one has risen with genius fit to plan its holy walls, conceive its columns, project its towers, or lay its corner-stone. Is it too much to hope all this? Look at the arena before us—look at our past history. Hark! there is the sound of many million men, the trampling of their freeborn feet, the murmuring of their voice; a nation born of this land that God reserved so long a virgin earth, in a high day married to the human race—rising, and swelling, and rolling on, strong and certain as the Atlantic tide; they come numerous as ocean waves when east winds blow, their destination commensurate with the continent, with ideas vast as the Mississippi, strong as the Alleghenies, and awful as Niagara; they come murmuring little of the past, but, moving in the brightness of their great idea, and casting its light far on to other lands and distant days—come to the world's great work, to organize the rights of man.

2. RALPH WALDO EMERSON, 1803–1882

[While Parker was lamenting the deficiencies of American literature, its inabiliity to match the grandeur of the scenery, while Thoreau was privately calling for more wildness, Walter Whitman, journalist and Democratic editor, entered into a period, still mysterious, of intense inner excitement. He emerged from it as Walt Whitman, author of a privately printed book, *Leaves of Grass*, in 1855. It attracted little attention, but Emerson realized that in it the Transcendental aspiration was indeed being carried a long way forward. On July 21 Emerson wrote this letter to Whitman. In later years Emerson checked his enthusiasm, argued against Whitman's frankness in the "Children of Adam" poems, and never quite became the champion he almost nominated himself to be by this welcome. Still, the important point is that upon receiving the first copy of *Leaves of Grass* Emerson was capable of the shock of recognizing that this strange New Yorker did represent the future of what he and his colleagues had striven to realize in New England; Emerson had the courage and the grace thus to salute what he recognized as surpassing himself.]

LETTER TO MR. WALTER WHITMAN

Concord, Massachusetts, 21 July, 1855

Dear Sir—I am not blind to the worth of the wonderful gift of *Leaves of Grass*. I find it the most extraordinary piece of wit and wisdom that America has yet contributed. I am very happy in reading it, as great power makes us happy. It meets the demand I am always making of what seemed the sterile and stingy Nature, as if too much handiwork, or too much lymph in the temperament, were making our Western wits fat and mean.

I give you joy of your free and brave thought. I have

great joy in it. I find incomparable things said incomparably well, as they must be. I find the courage of treatment which so delights us, and which large perception only can inspire.

I greet you at the beginning of a great career, which yet must have had a long foreground somewhere, for such a start. I rubbed my eyes a little, to see if this sunbeam were no illusion; but the solid sense of the book is a sober certainty. It has the best merits, namely of fortifying and encouraging.

I did not know until I last night saw the book advertised in a newspaper that I could trust the name as real and available for a post-office. I wish to see my benefactor, and have felt much like striking my tasks and visiting New York to pay you my respects.

R. W. Emerson

3.   HENRY DAVID THOREAU, 1817–1862

[Charles Eliot Norton, aged twenty-eight, son of Emerson's pontifical opponent, Andrews Norton, wrote for *Putnam's Monthly* of September, 1855, one of the few reviews that took *Leaves of Grass* seriously. The book, he said, was a "compound of the New England transcendentalist and New York rowdy." So, with Norton and Emerson calling attention to the unpredictable fulfillment that New England had found in New York, other Transcendentalists were moved to investigate the mystery.

Bronson Alcott first found him out in Brooklyn, then led Henry Thoreau to the cottage in November, 1856. Alcott's account has an amusing description of the two staring at each other like two wary animals. They were such uncompromising rivals "in smelling out 'all Nature,'" Alcott put it, that they never could become friends. But once back in Concord, Thoreau wrote on December 7, 1856, to Harrison Blake this frank appraisal both of Whitman and of himself. It ends with Thoreau's prophecy of the literary future for Transcendentalism in America.]

MEETING WHITMAN

December 7 [1856].

That Walt Whitman, of whom I wrote to you, is the most interesting fact to me at present. I have just read his second edition (which he gave me), and it has done me more good than any reading for a long time. Perhaps I remember best the poem of Walt Whitman, an American, and the Sun-Down Poem. There are two or three pieces in the book which are disagreeable, to say the least; simply sensual. He does not celebrate love at all. It is as if the beasts spoke. I think that men have not been ashamed of themselves without reason. No doubt there have always been dens where such deeds were unblushingly recited, and it is no merit to compete with their inhabitants. But even on this side he has spoken more truth than any American or modern that I know. I have found his poem exhilarating, encouraging. As for its sensuality—and it may turn out to be less sensual than it appears—I do not so much wish that those parts were not written, as that men and women were so pure that they could read them without harm, that is, without understanding them. One woman told me that no woman could read it—as if a man could read what a woman could not. Of course Walt Whitman can communicate to us no experience, and if we are shocked, whose experience is it that we are reminded of?

On the whole, it sounds to me very brave and American, after whatever deductions. I do not believe that all the sermons, so called, that have been preached in this land put together are equal to it for preaching.

We ought to rejoice greatly in him. He occasionally suggests something a little more than human. You can't confound him with the other inhabitants of Brooklyn or New York. How they must shudder when they read him! He is awfully good.

To be sure I sometimes feel a little imposed on. By his heartiness and broad generalities he puts me into a liberal frame of mind prepared to see wonders—as it were, sets me upon a hill or in the midst of a plain—stirs me well up, and then—throws in a thousand of brick. Though rude, and sometimes ineffectual, it is a great primitive poem— an alarum or trumpet-note ringing through the American camp. Wonderfully like the Orientals, too, considering that when I asked him if he had read them, he answered, "No: tell me about them."

I did not get far in conversation with him—two more being present—and among the few things which I chanced to say, I remember that one was, in answer to him as representing America, that I did not think much of America or of politics, and so on, which may have been somewhat of a damper to him.

Since I have seen him, I find that I am not disturbed by any brag or egoism in his book. He may turn out the least of a braggart of all, having a better right to be confident.

He is a great fellow.

4. RALPH WALDO EMERSON, 1803–1882

[On May 6, 1862, Henry Thoreau died, only forty-four years of age, his rugged health ruined by long exposure to wind and weather, worn out by the consuming ferocity of his quest. A funeral service was held in the First Church, attended by a small company to whom Emerson made an address. After revising and probably enlarging it, Emerson printed his talk in the *Atlantic Monthly* for August.

In the opinion of the world, in so far as it paid any attention at all, this was taken to mean that the memory of Emerson's cranky and idle imitator was decently interred and that the future would forget him. He had published only two books, both abysmal failures as concerned sales, and his reputation was that of a misfit who had compensated for his inferiority by a cultivated insolence. It was known in Concord that in his last years he had proven an ingrate for all that Emerson had done for him; Emerson was thought to be displaying the utmost of nobility and forgiveness by overlooking Thoreau's shabby behavior and saying something nice about him at the funeral.

By all his lights, Emerson was indeed generous; but how could he or any of his contemporaries have dreamed that in that future in which Emerson did foresee Whitman looming as an important writer, the stature of Henry Thoreau would steadily grow, that in the middle of the next century there would be almost unanimous agreement that he is the supreme artist to come out of the Transcendental ferment, and that as a writer he stands above the pale wraith of Emerson.]

THOREAU

No truer American existed than Thoreau. His preference of his country and condition was genuine, and his aversation from English and European manners and tastes almost reached contempt. He listened impatiently to news or *bonmots* gleaned from London circles; and though he tried to be civil, these anecdotes fatigued him. The men were all imitating each other, and on a small mould. Why can they not live as far apart as possible, and each be a man by himself? What he sought was the most energetic nature; and he wished to go to Oregon, not to London. "In every part of Great Britain," he wrote in his diary, "are discovered traces of the Romans, their funereal urns, their camps, their roads, their dwellings. But New England, at least, is not based on any Roman ruins. We have not to lay the foundations of our houses on the ashes of a former civilization."

But idealist as he was, standing for abolition of slavery, abolition of tariffs, almost for abolition of government, it is needless to say he found himself not only unrepresented in actual politics, but almost equally opposed to every class of reformers. Yet he paid the tribute of his uniform respect to the Anti-Slavery party. One man, whose personal acquaintance he had formed, he honored with exceptional regard. Before the first friendly word had been spoken for Captain John Brown, he sent notices to most houses in Concord that he would speak in a public hall on the condition and character of John Brown, on Sunday evening, and invited all people to come. The Republican Committee, the Abolitionist Committee, sent him word that it was premature and not advisable. He replied—"I did not send to you for advice, but to announce that I am to speak." The hall was filled at an early hour by people of all parties, and his earnest eulogy of the hero was heard by all respectfully, by many with a sympathy that surprised themselves. . . .

It was a pleasure and a privilege to walk with him. He knew the country like a fox or a bird, and passed through it as freely by paths of his own. He knew every track in the snow or on the ground, and what creature had taken this path before him. One must submit abjectly to such a guide, and the reward was great. Under his arm he carried an old music-book to press plants; in his pocket, his diary and pencil, a spy-glass for birds, microscope, jack-knife and twine. He wore a straw hat, stout shoes, strong gray trousers, to brave scrub-oaks and smilax, and to climb a tree for a hawk's or a squirrel's nest. He waded into the pool for the waterplants, and his strong legs were no insignificant part of his armor. On the day I speak of he looked for the Menyanthes, detected it across the wide pool, and, on examination of the florets, decided that it had been in flower five days. He drew out of his breast-pocket his diary, and read the names of all the plants that should bloom on this day, whereof he kept account as a banker when his notes fall due. The Cypripedium not due till to-morrow. He thought that, if waked up from a trance, in this swamp, he could tell by the plants what time of the year it was within two days. The redstart was flying about, and presently the fine grosbeaks, whose brilliant scarlet "makes the rash gazer wipe his eye," and whose fine clear note Thoreau compared to that of a tanager which has got rid of its hoarseness. Presently he heard a note which he called that of the night-warbler, a bird he had never identified, had been in search of twelve years, which always, when he saw it, was in the act of diving down into a tree or bush, and which it was vain to seek; the only bird which sings indifferently by night and by day. I told him he must beware of finding and booking it, lest life should have nothing more to show him. He said, "What you seek in vain for, half your life, one day you come full upon, all the family at dinner. You seek it like a dream, and as soon as you find it you become its prey."

His interest in the flower or the bird lay very deep in his mind, was connected with Nature—and the meaning of Nature was never attempted to be defined by him. He would not offer a memoir of his observations to the Natural History Society. "Why should I? To detach the description from its connections in my mind would make it no longer true or valuable to me: and they do not wish what belongs to it." His power of observation seemed to indicate additional senses. He saw as with microscope, heard as with ear-trumpet, and his memory was a photographic register of all he saw and heard. And yet none knew better than he that it is not the fact that imports, but the impression or effect of the fact on your mind. Every fact lay in glory in his mind, a type of the order and beauty of the whole. . . .

Thoreau was sincerity itself, and might fortify the convictions of prophets in the ethical laws by his holy living. It was an affirmative experience which refused to be set aside. A truth-speaker he, capable of the most deep and strict conversation; a physician to the wounds of any soul; a friend, knowing not only the secret of friendship, but almost worshipped by those few persons who resorted to him as their confessor and prophet, and knew the deep value of his mind and great heart. He thought that without religion or devotion of some kind nothing great was ever accomplished: and he thought that the bigoted sectarian had better bear this in mind.

His virtues, of course, sometimes ran into extremes. It was easy to trace to the inexorable demand on all for exact truth that austerity which made this willing hermit more solitary even than he wished. Himself of a perfect probity, he required not less of others. He had a disgust at crime, and no worldly success would cover it. He detected paltering as readily in dignified and prosperous persons as in beggars, and with equal scorn. Such dangerous frankness was in his dealing that his admirers called him "that terrible Thoreau," as if he spoke when silent, and was still present when he had departed. I think the severity of his ideal interfered to deprive him of a healthy sufficiency of human society.

The habit of a realist to find things the reverse of their appearance inclined him to put every statement in a paradox. A certain habit of antagonism defaced his earlier writings—a trick of rhetoric not quite outgrown in his later, of substituting for the obvious word and thought its diametrical opposite. He praised wild mountains and winter forests for their domestic air, in snow and ice he would find sultriness, and commended the wilderness for resembling Rome and Paris. "It was so dry, that you might call it wet."

The tendency to magnify the moment, to read all the laws of Nature in the one object or one combination under your eye, is of course comic to those who do not share the philosopher's perception of identity. To him there was no such thing as size. The pond was a small ocean; the Atlantic, a large Walden Pond. He referred every minute fact to cosmical laws. Though he meant to be just, he seemed haunted by a certain chronic assumption that the science of the day pretended completeness, and he had just found out that the *savans* had neglected to discriminate a particular botanical variety, had failed to describe the seeds or count the sepals. "That is to say," we replied, "the blockheads were not born in Concord; but who said they were? It was their unspeakable misfortune to be born in London, or Paris, or Rome; but, poor fellows, they did what they could, considering that they never saw Bateman's Pond, or Nine-Acre Corner, or Becky Stow's Swamp; besides, what were you sent into the world for, but to add this observation?"

Had his genius been only contemplative, he had been fitted to his life, but with his energy and practical ability he seemed born for great enterprise and for command; and I so much regret the loss of his rare powers of action, that I cannot help counting it a fault in him that he had no ambition. Wanting this, instead of engineering for all America, he was the captain of a huckleberry-party. Pounding beans is good to the end of pounding empires one of these days; but if, at the end of years, it is still only beans!

But these foibles, real or apparent, were fast vanishing in the incessant growth of a spirit so robust and wise, and which effaced its defeats with new triumphs. His study of Nature was a perpetual ornament to him, and inspired his friends with curiosity to see the world through his eyes, and to hear his adventures. They possessed every kind of interest.

He had many elegancies of his own, whilst he scoffed at conventional elegance. Thus, he could not bear to hear the sound of his own steps, the grit of gravel; and therefore never willingly walked in the road, but in the grass, on mountains and in woods. His senses were acute, and he remarked that by night every dwelling-house gives out bad air, like a slaughter-house. He liked the pure fragrance of melilot. He honored certain plants with special regard, and, over all, the pond-lily—then, the gentian, and the *Mikania scandens*, and "life-everlasting," and a bass-tree which he visited every year when it bloomed, in the middle of July. He thought the scent a more oracular inquisition than the sight—more oracular and trustworthy. The scent, of course, reveals what is concealed from the other senses. By it he detected earthiness. He delighted in echoes, and said they were almost the only kind of kindred voices that he heard. He loved Nature so well, was so happy in her solitude, that he became very jealous of cities and the sad work which their refinements and artifices made with man and his dwelling. The axe was always destroying his forest. "Thank God," he said, "they cannot cut down the clouds!" "All kinds of figures are drawn on the blue ground with this fibrous white paint." . . .

There is a flower known to botanists, one of the same genus with our summer plant called "Life-Everlasting," a

Gnaphalium like that, which grows on the most inaccessible cliffs of the Tyrolese mountains, where the chamois dare hardly venture, and which the hunter, tempted by its beauty, and by his love (for it is immensely valued by the Swiss maidens), climbs the cliffs to gather, and is sometimes found dead at the foot, with the flower in his hand. It is called by botanists the *Gnaphalium leontopodium,* but by the Swiss *Edelweisse,* which signifies *Noble Purity.* Thoreau seemed to me living in the hope to gather this plant, which belonged to him of right. The scale on which his studies proceeded was so large as to require longevity, and we were the less prepared for his sudden disappearance. The country knows not yet, or in the least part, how great a son it has lost. It seems an injury that he should leave in the midst his broken task which none else can finish, a kind of indignity to so noble a soul that he should depart out of Nature before yet he has been really shown to his peers for what he is. But he, at least, is content. His soul was made for the noblest society; he had in a short life exhausted the capabilities of this world; wherever there is knowledge, wherever there is virtue, wherever there is beauty, he will find a home.

BIBLIOGRAPHY

Those who participated in the "Movement" and who lived long enough to write reminiscences were conscious in their old age that they had taken part in something vaguely glorious, and so spent their elderly energies in trying to say what it had been. Younger admirers, in the late nineteenth century, envied the older generation's experience, and tried to say what it was they had missed. In recent years, with the surge of professional eagerness to build up an "American Past," the Transcendentalists have been bewritten to an extent that more than compensates for the little attention that was paid to them in their lifetime by the vast majority of Americans. Therefore the bibliography is large—one might almost say too large, even though scholars, in their inexhaustable determination to tell everything over again, seem resolved to augment it year by year.

The ordinary reader has and should have no interest in keeping up with this output. I give only the titles of most general or literary value.

GENERAL

Boas, George, editor, *Romanticism in America* (1940).

Brooks, Van Wyck, *The Flowering of New England, 1815-1865.* (Revised edition, 1941).

Frothingham, Octavius B., *Transcendentalism in New England: A History* (1876).

Goddard, Harold C., *Studies in New England Transcendentalism* (1908).

Matthiessen, F. O., *American Renaissance* (1941).

Miller, Perry, *The Transcendentalists* (1950).

Mumford, Lewis, *The Golden Day* (1926).

Parrington, Vernon L., *Main Currents in American Thought* (1927). (Volume II: *The Romantic Revolution in America.*)

Schneider, Herbert W., *A History of American Philosophy* (1946).

AMOS BRONSON ALCOTT

Shepard, Odell, editor, *The Journals of Bronson Alcott* (1938).

Shepard, Odell, *Pedlar's Progress: The Life of Bronson Alcott* (1937).

ORESTES A. BROWNSON

Maynard, Theodore, *Orestes Brownson: Yankee, Radical, Catholic* (1943).

Schlesinger, Arthur M., Jr., *Orestes A. Brownson* (1939).

CHRISTOPHER PEARSE CRANCH

Miller, F. DeWolfe, *Christopher Pearse Cranch and His Caricatures of New England Transcendentalism* (1951).

Scott, Leonora Cranch, *The Life and Letters of Christopher Pearse Cranch* (1917).

RALPH WALDO EMERSON

Cameron, Kenneth W., *Emerson the Essayist* (1945).

Carpenter, Frederic Ives, *Emerson Handbook* (1953). (Contains a survey of all the scholarship and a complete bibliography up to the date of publication.)

Hopkins, Vivian C., *Spires of Form: A Study of Emerson's Æsthetic Theory* (1951).

Miller, Perry, "From Edwards to Emerson," in *Errand Into The Wilderness* (1956).

Paul, Sherman, *Emerson's Angle of Vision: Man and Nature in American Experience* (1952).

Rusk, Ralph L., *The Life of Ralph Waldo Emerson* (1949).

Whicher, Stephen E., *Freedom and Fate: An Inner Life of Ralph Waldo Emerson* (1953).

MARGARET FULLER

Anthony, Katherine, *Margaret Fuller: A Psychological Biography* (1920).

Higginson, Thomas W., *Margaret Fuller Ossoli* (1884).

Wade, Mason, *Margaret Fuller: Whetstone of Genius* (1940).

THEODORE PARKER

Chadwick, John W., *Theodore Parker, Preacher and Reformer* (1900).

Commager, Henry Steele, *Theodore Parker* (1936).

Frothingham, Octavius B., *Theodore Parker* (1874).

Weiss, John, *Life and Correspondence of Theodore Parker* (1864).

HENRY DAVID THOREAU

Canby, Henry Seidel, *Thoreau* (1939).

Channing, William Ellery, *Thoreau, the Poet-Naturalist* (1873). (New edition, enlarged, 1902).

Harding, Walter, *Thoreau: A Century of Criticism* (1954).

Krutch, Joseph Wood, *Henry David Thoreau* (1948).

Sanborn, Frank B., *Henry D. Thoreau* (1886).

JONES VERY

Baker, Carlos, "Emerson and Jones Very," *The New England Quarterly* VII (1934), 90-99.

Bartlett, William Irving, *Jones Very, Emerson's "Brave Saint"* (1942).

Winters, Yvor, *Maule's Curse* (1938).

INDEX

L